RUN ON YOUR NEW LEGS 2

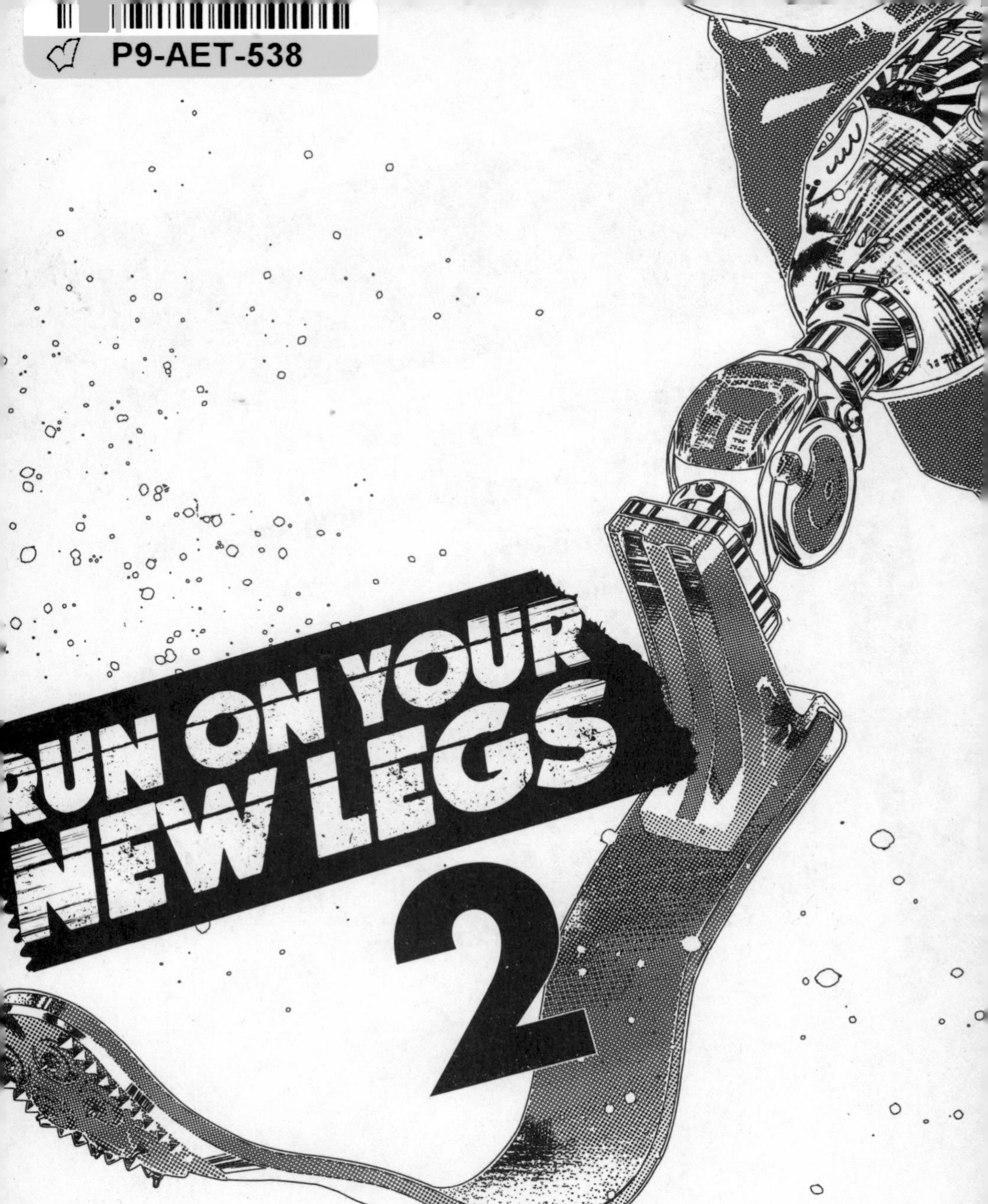

WATARU MIDORI

TABLE OF CONTENTS

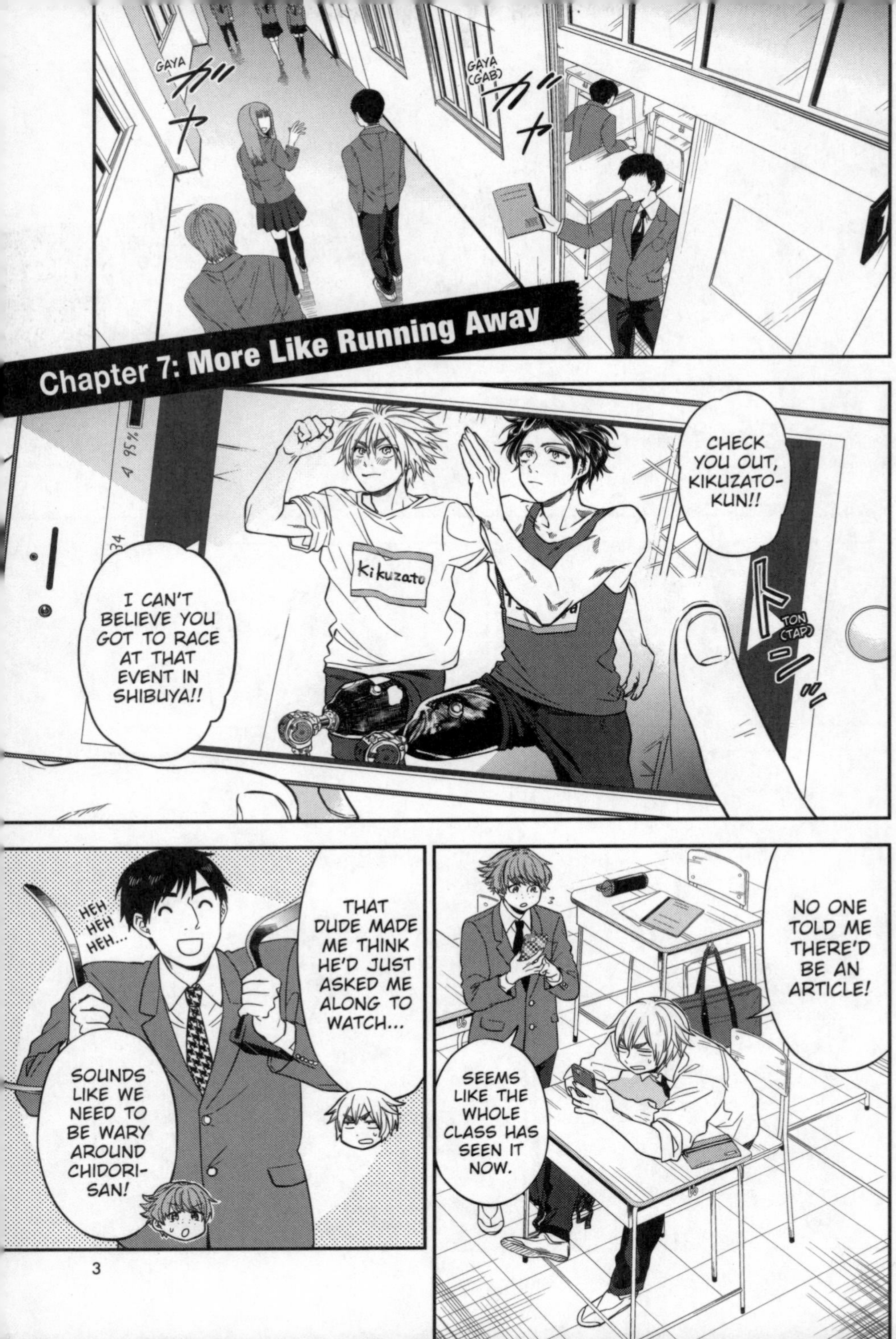
GAYA (GAB)
GAYA
Chapter 7: More Like Running Away
CHECK YOU OUT, KIKUZATO-KUN!!
Kikuzato
TON (TAP)
I CAN'T BELIEVE YOU GOT TO RACE AT THAT EVENT IN SHIBUYA!!
NO ONE TOLD ME THERE'D BE AN ARTICLE!
SEEMS LIKE THE WHOLE CLASS HAS SEEN IT NOW.
THAT DUDE MADE ME THINK HE'D JUST ASKED ME ALONG TO WATCH...
HEH HEH HEH...
SOUNDS LIKE WE NEED TO BE WARY AROUND CHIDORI-SAN!

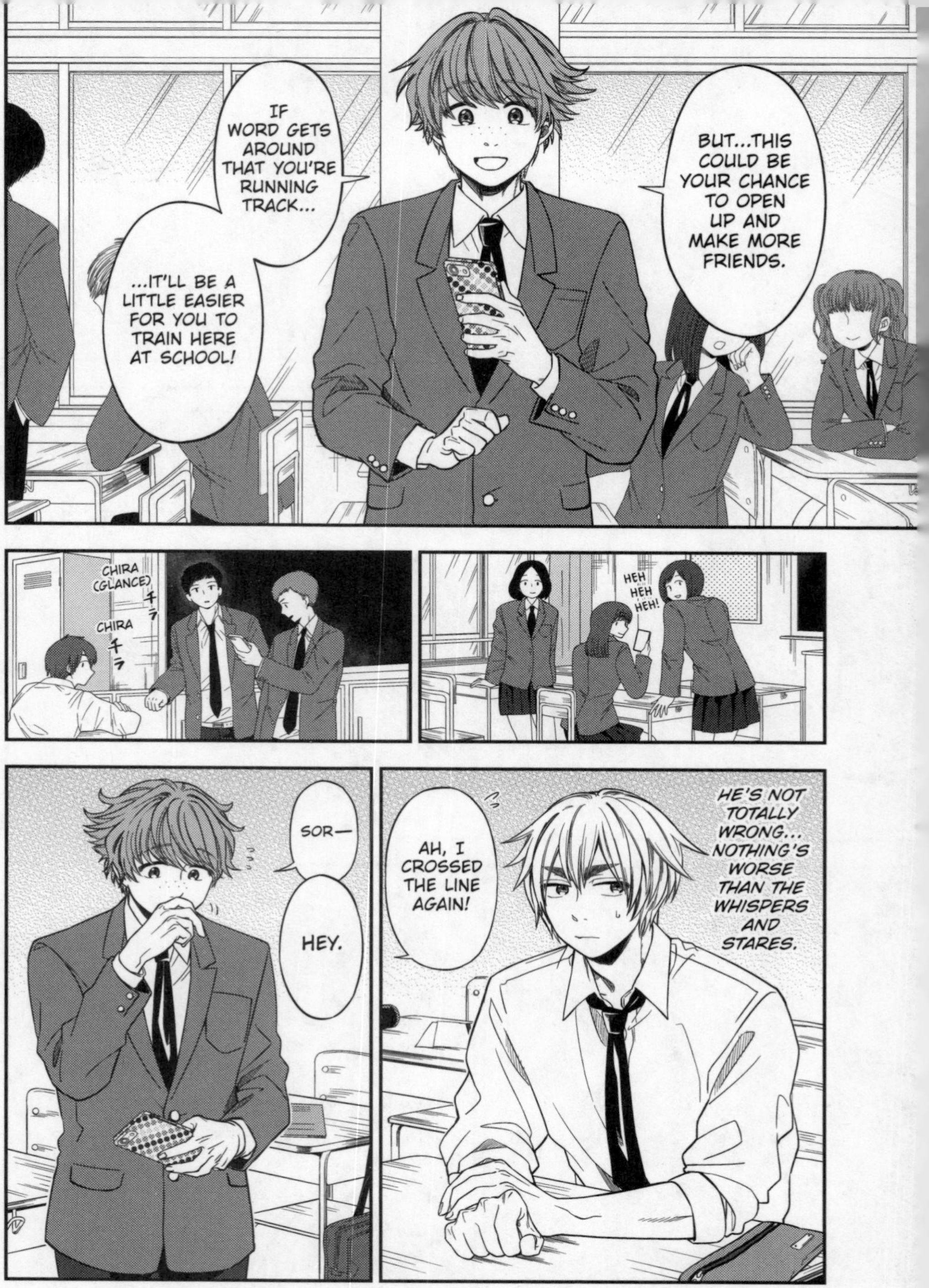
IF WORD GETS AROUND THAT YOU'RE RUNNING TRACK...
...IT'LL BE A LITTLE EASIER FOR YOU TO TRAIN HERE AT SCHOOL!
BUT...THIS COULD BE YOUR CHANCE TO OPEN UP AND MAKE MORE FRIENDS.
HEH HEH HEH!
CHIRA (GLANCE)
チラ
CHIRA
チラ
HE'S NOT TOTALLY WRONG... NOTHING'S WORSE THAN THE WHISPERS AND STARES.
AH, I CROSSED THE LINE AGAIN!
SOR—
HEY.

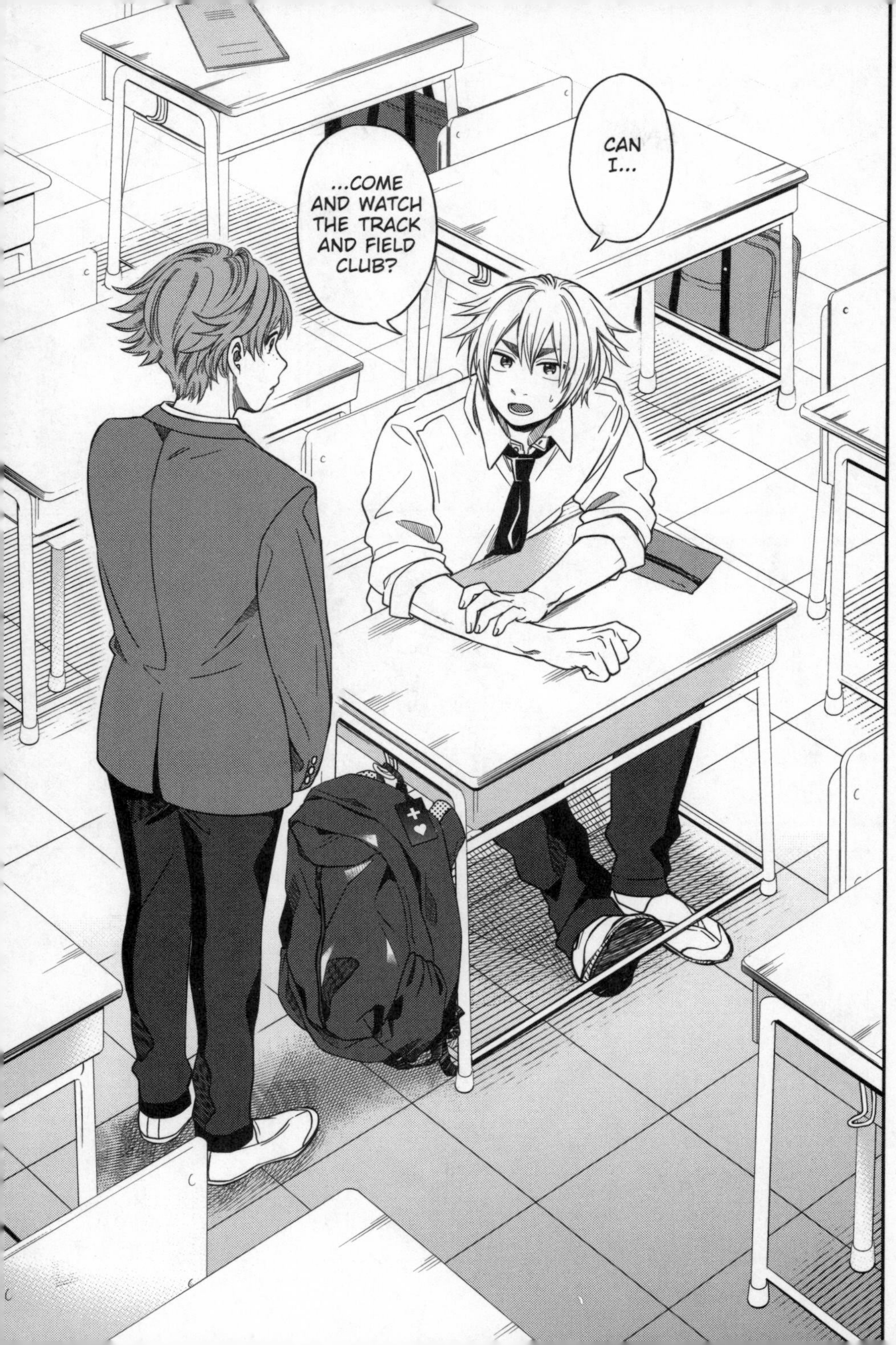
CAN I...
...COME AND WATCH THE TRACK AND FIELD CLUB?

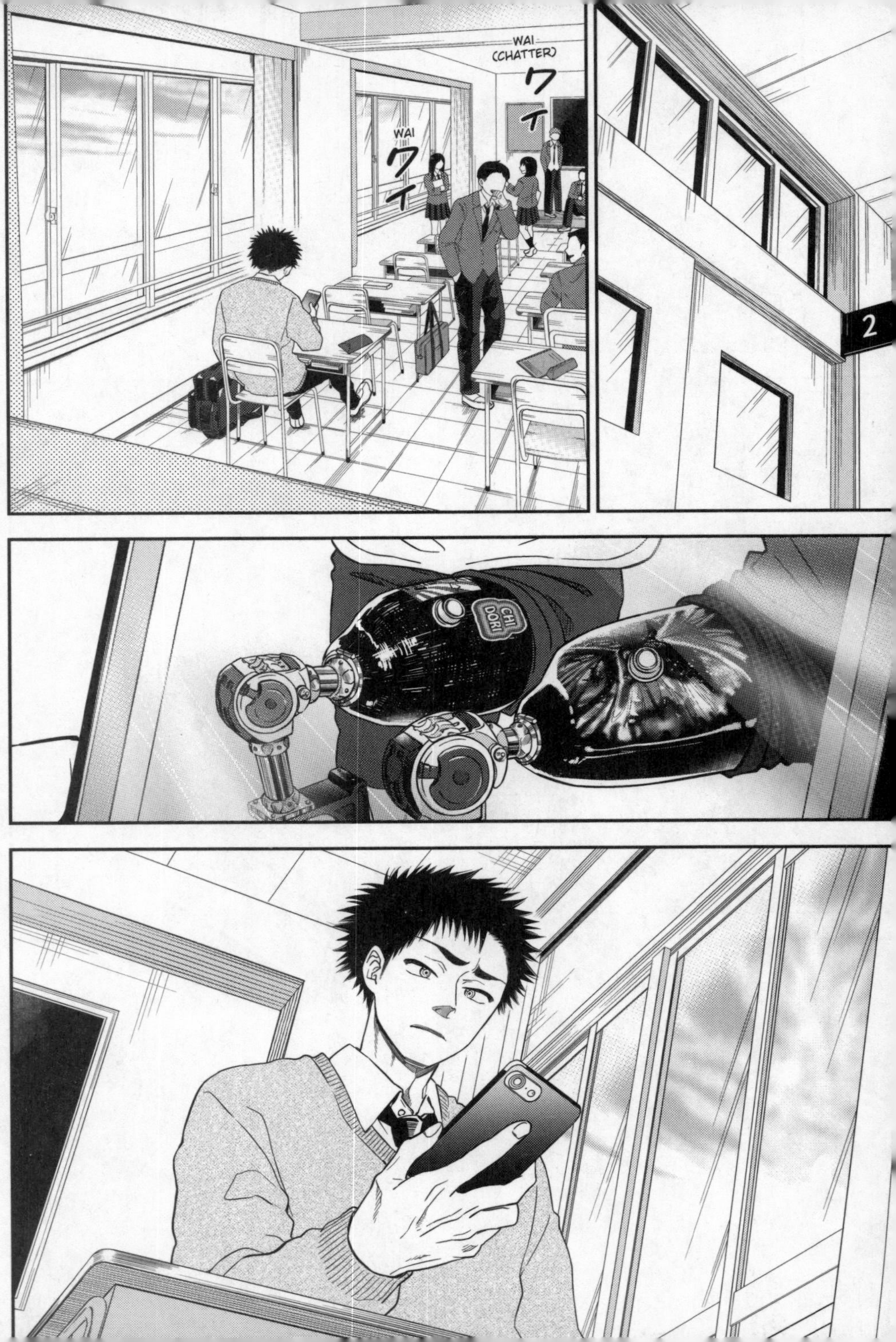
2
ワイ
WAI (CHATTER)
ワイ
WAI
CHI DORI

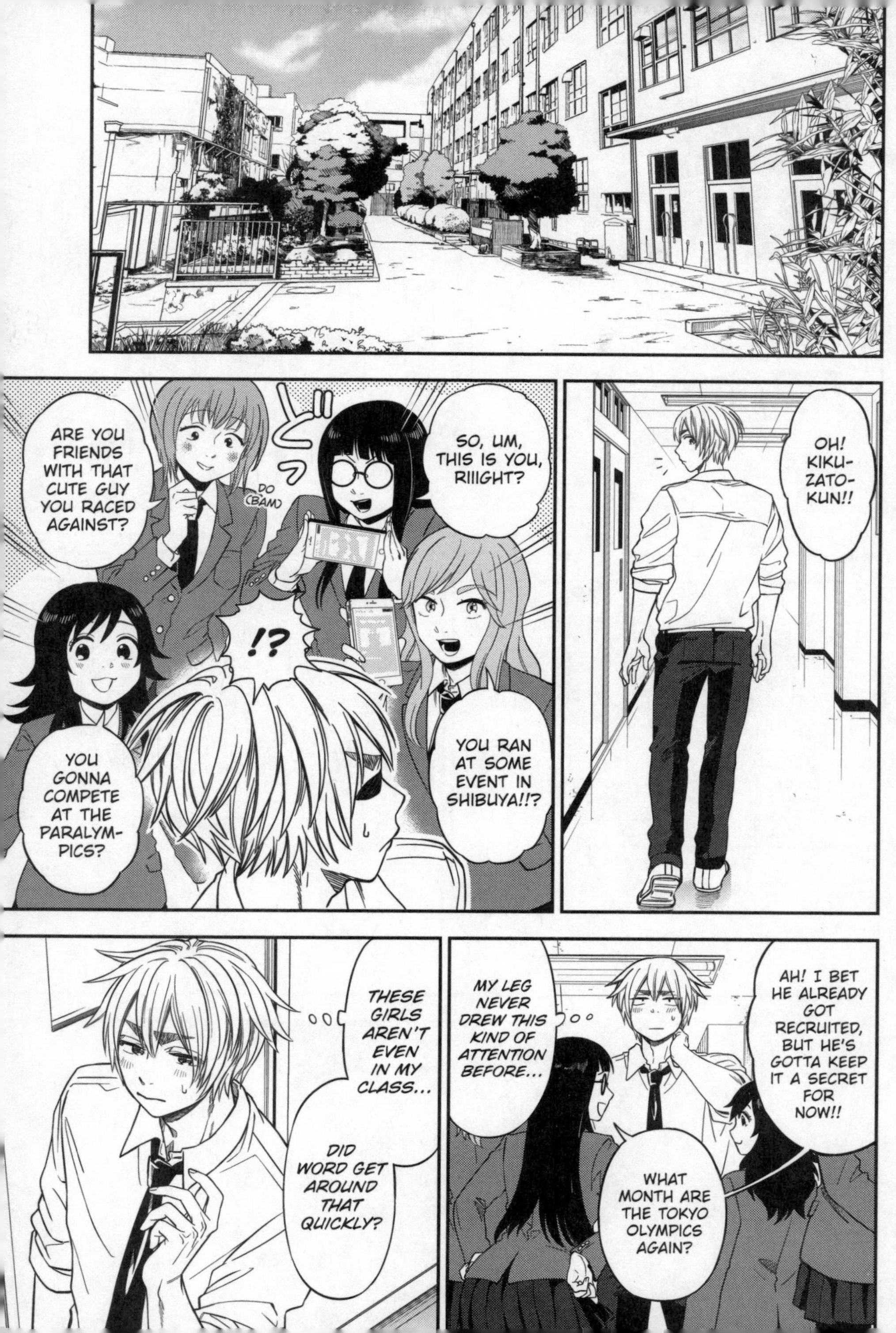
OH! KIKU-ZATO-KUN!!
SO, UM, THIS IS YOU, RIIIGHT?
DO (BAM)
ARE YOU FRIENDS WITH THAT CUTE GUY YOU RACED AGAINST?
!?
YOU RAN AT SOME EVENT IN SHIBUYA!!?
YOU GONNA COMPETE AT THE PARALYMPICS?
AH! I BET HE ALREADY GOT RECRUITED, BUT HE'S GOTTA KEEP IT A SECRET FOR NOW!!
MY LEG NEVER DREW THIS KIND OF ATTENTION BEFORE...
WHAT MONTH ARE THE TOKYO OLYMPICS AGAIN?
THESE GIRLS AREN'T EVEN IN MY CLASS...
DID WORD GET AROUND THAT QUICKLY?

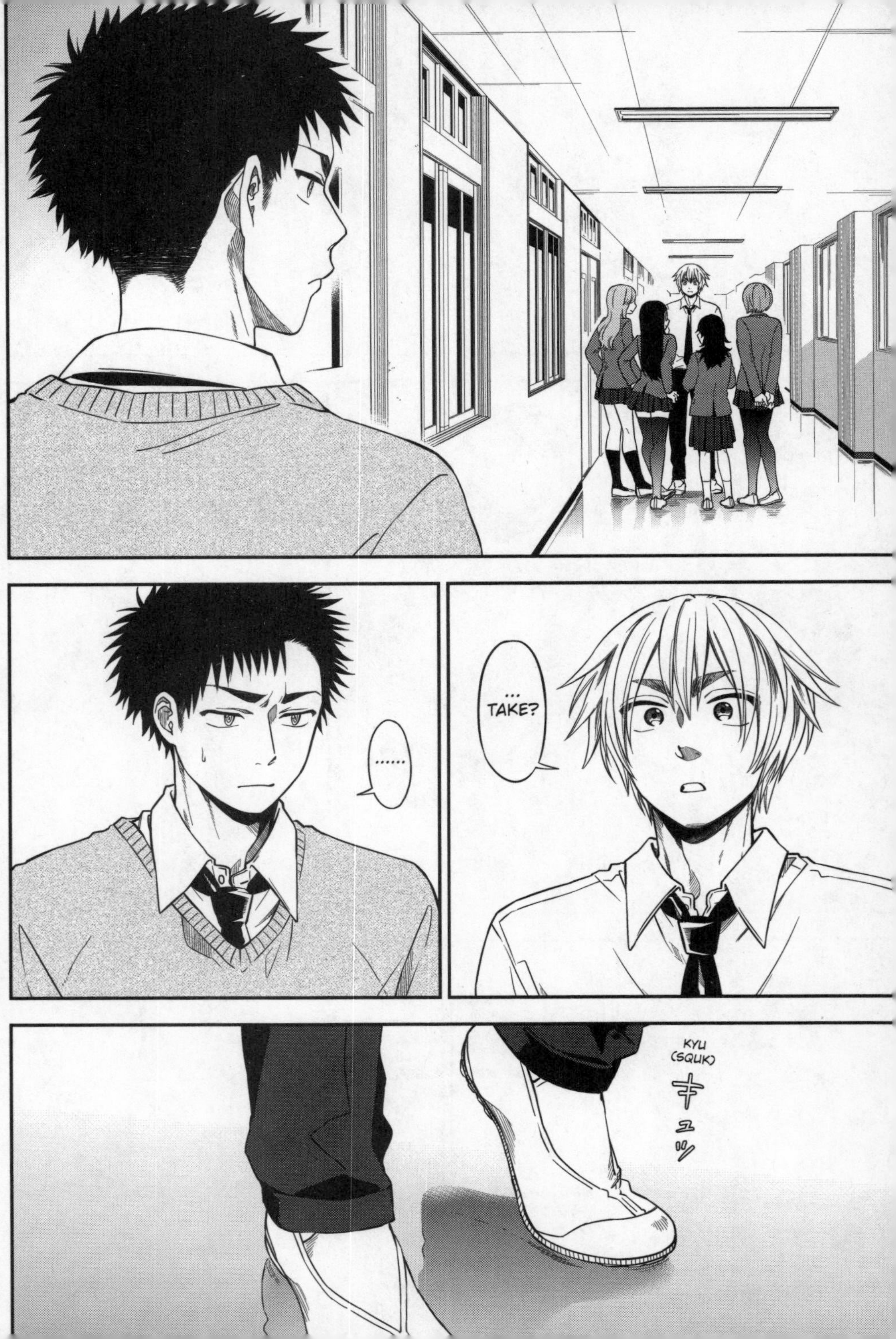
...
TAKE?
......
KYU (SQUK)
キュッ

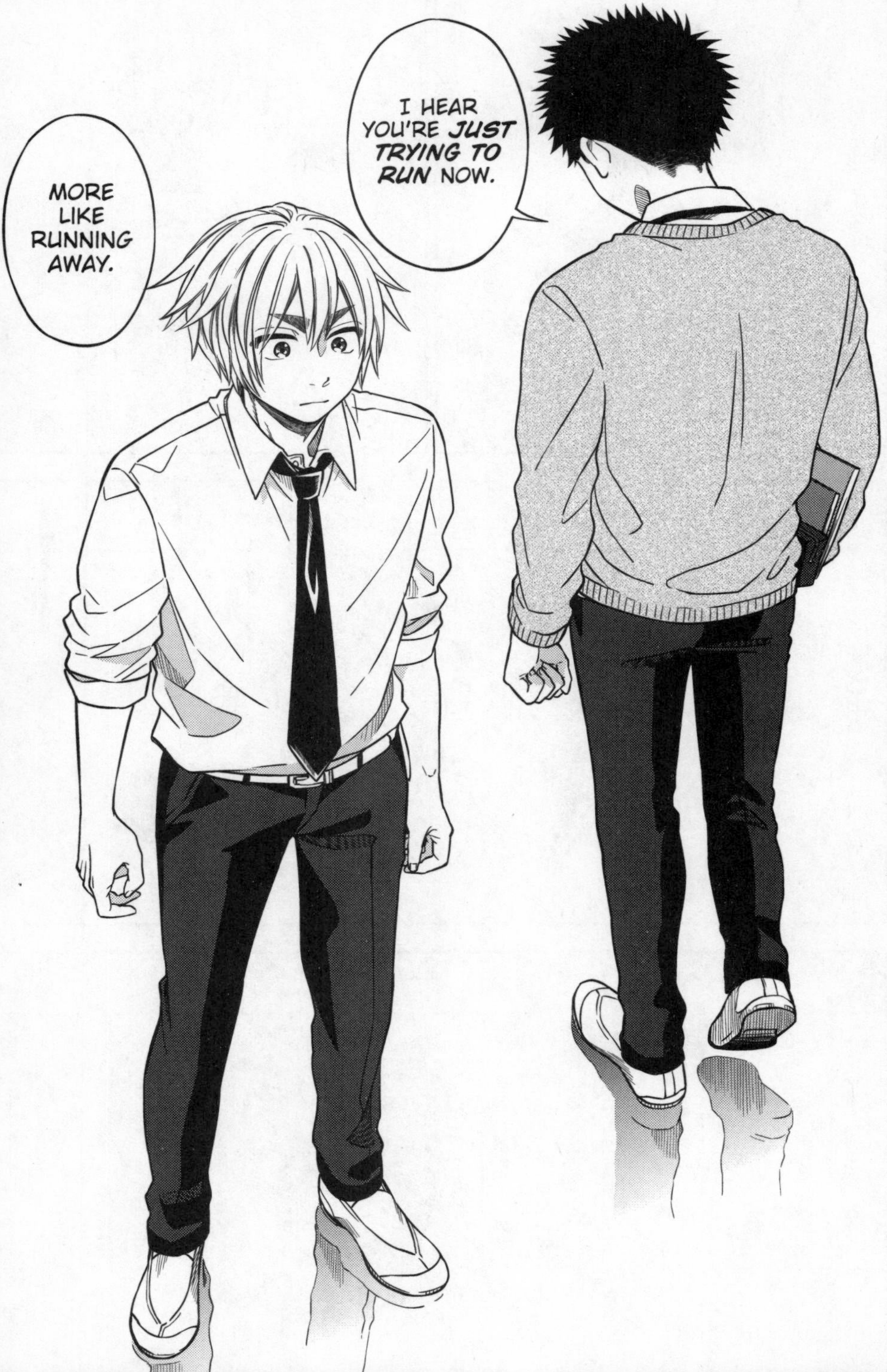
I HEAR YOU'RE JUST TRYING TO RUN NOW.
MORE LIKE RUNNING AWAY.

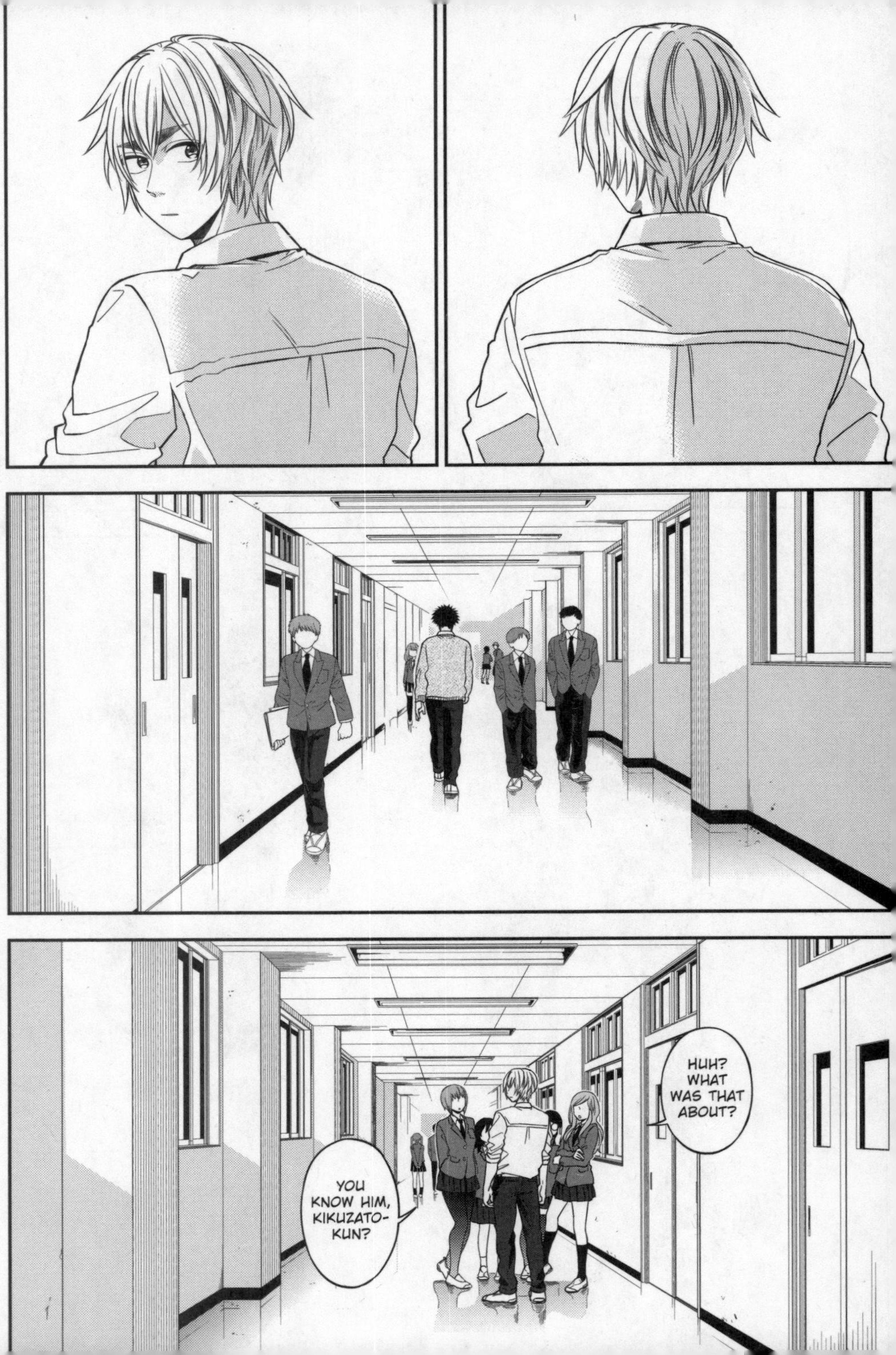
HUH? WHAT WAS THAT ABOUT?
YOU KNOW HIM, KIKUZATO-KUN?

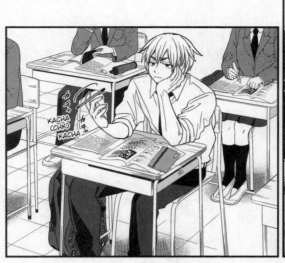

KACHA (CHK) KACHA
I HEAR YOU'RE JUST TRYING TO RUN NOW. MORE LIKE RUNNING AWAY.
WE HAVEN'T TALKED IN FOREVER, AND HE OPENS WITH THAT!?
KATSUN (TAP)
SINCE I CAN'T PLAY SOCCER WITH TAKE ANYMORE, I CAN'T KEEP MY PROMISE FROM BACK THEN.
YUSA (SWAY)
BUT...
GATA (KLATTER)
GATA

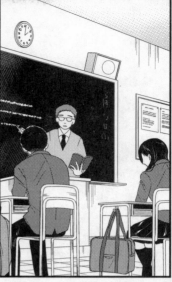

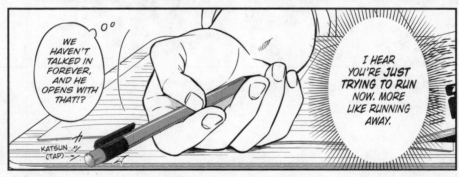

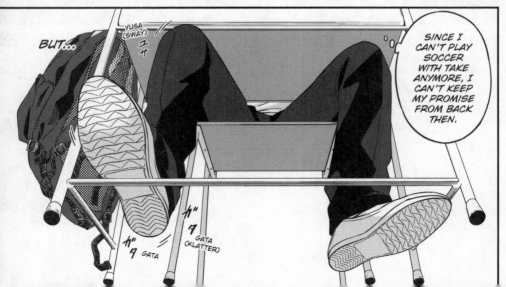

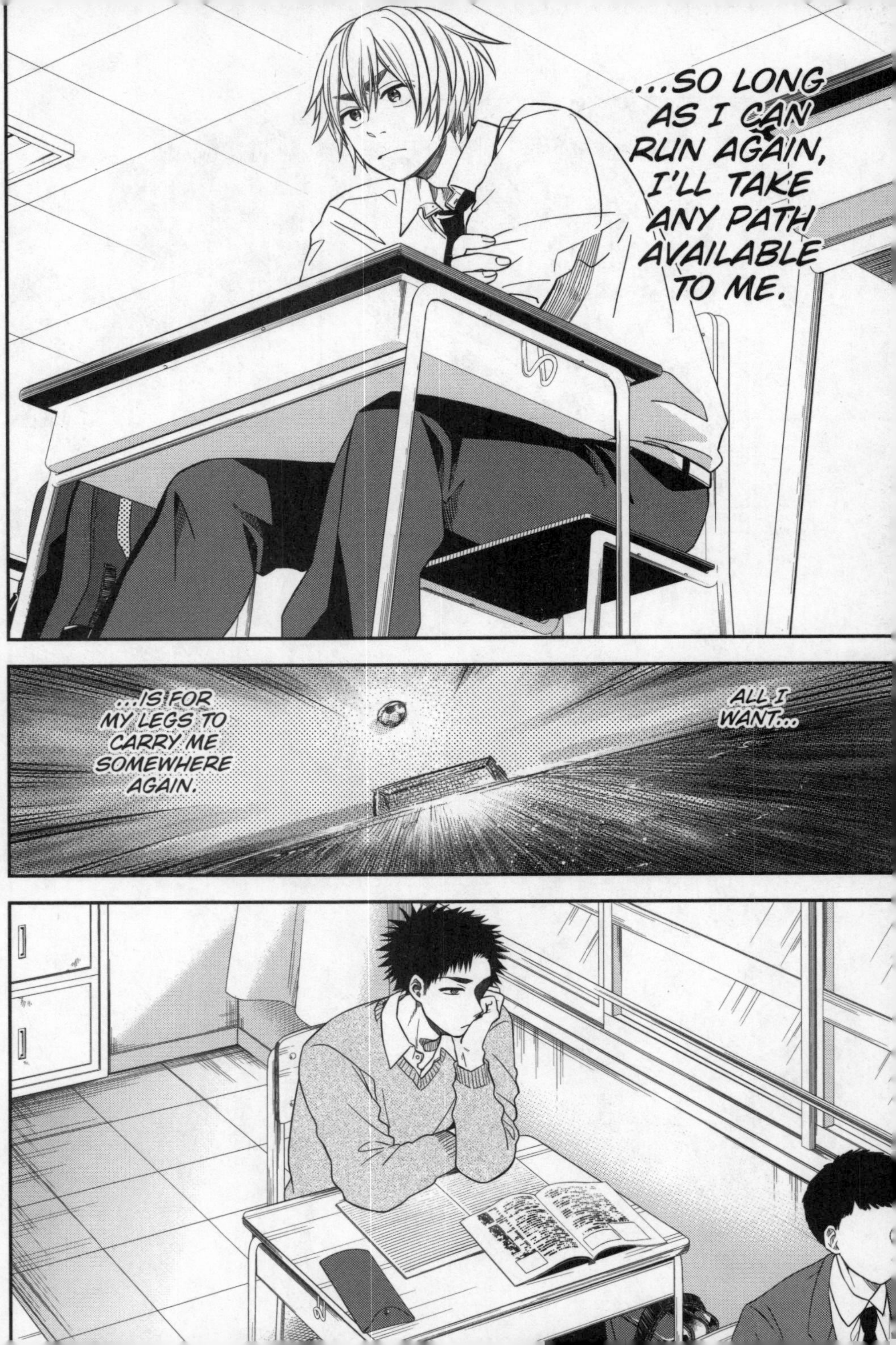
...SO LONG AS I CAN RUN AGAIN, I'LL TAKE ANY PATH AVAILABLE TO ME.
ALL I WANT...
...IS FOR MY LEGS TO CARRY ME SOMEWHERE AGAIN.

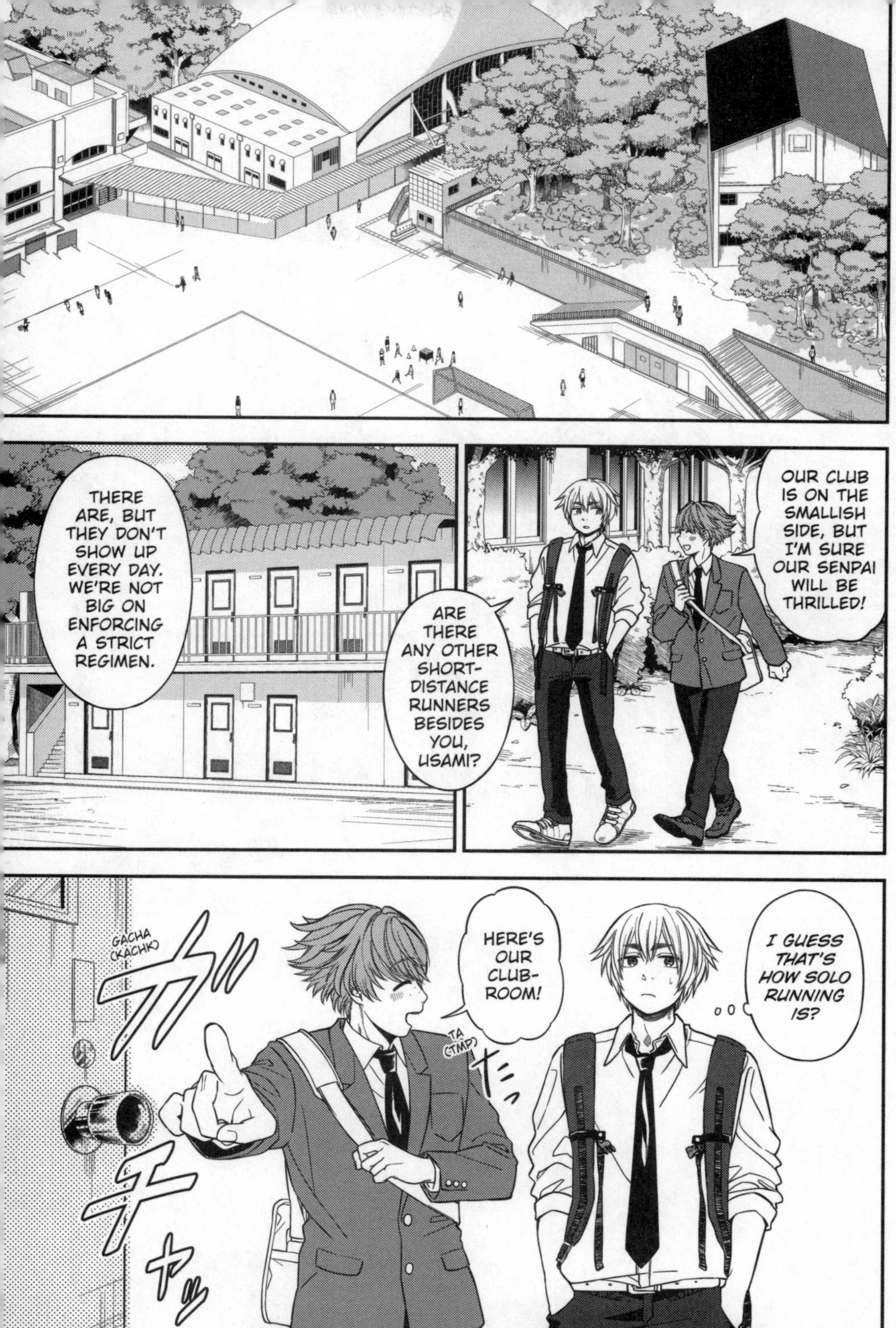
OUR CLUB IS ON THE SMALLISH SIDE, BUT I'M SURE OUR SENPAI WILL BE THRILLED!
ARE THERE ANY OTHER SHORT-DISTANCE RUNNERS BESIDES YOU, USAMI?
THERE ARE, BUT THEY DON'T SHOW UP EVERY DAY. WE'RE NOT BIG ON ENFORCING A STRICT REGIMEN.
I GUESS THAT'S HOW SOLO RUNNING IS?
HERE'S OUR CLUB-ROOM!
TA (TMP)
GACHA (KACHK)

WHOA!

YAMAGAMINE
00

ZA
(FWAH)

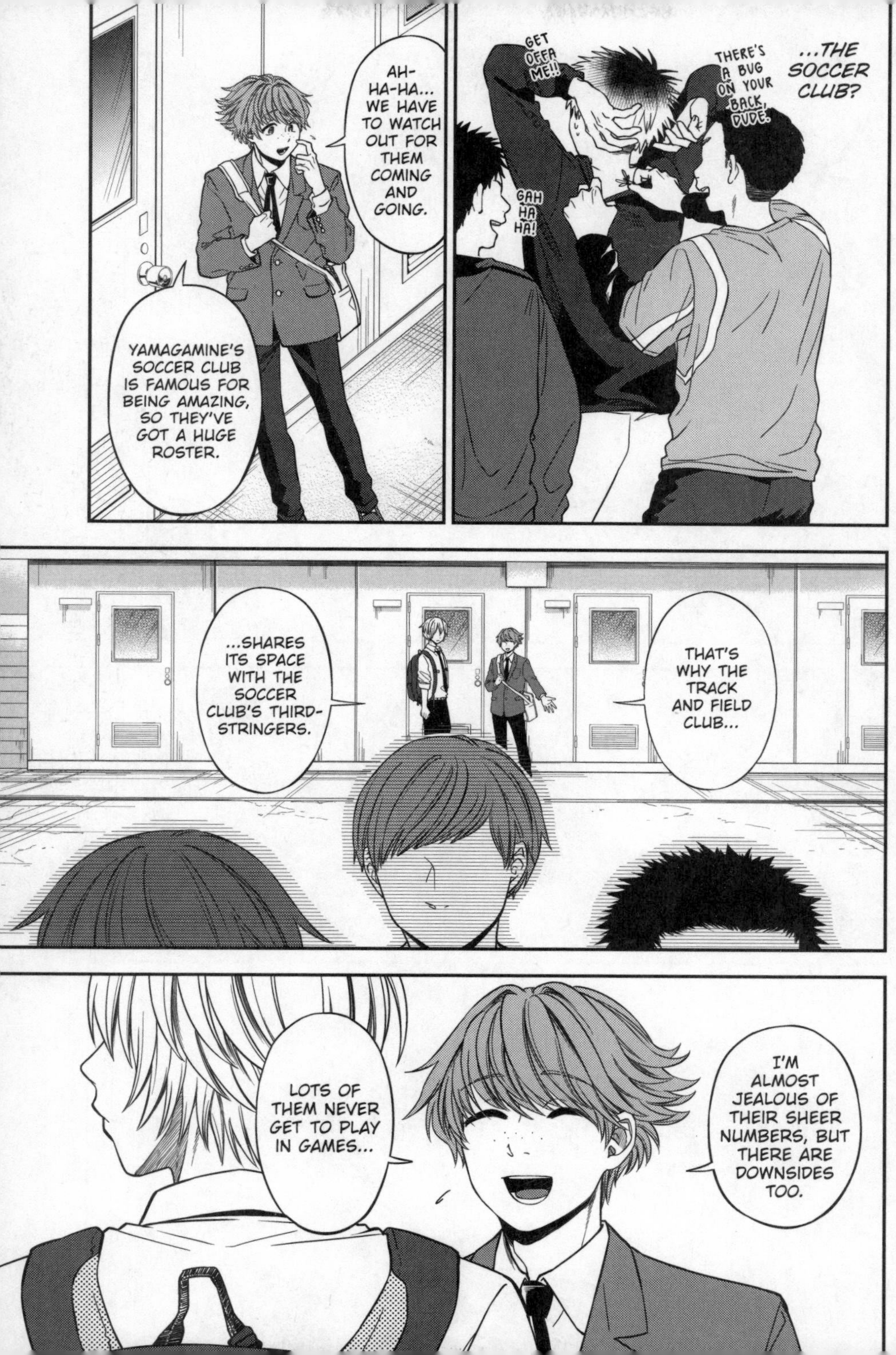
...THE SOCCER CLUB?
THERE'S A BUG ON YOUR BACK, DUDE.
GET OFFA ME!!
GAH HA HA!
AH-HA-HA... WE HAVE TO WATCH OUT FOR THEM COMING AND GOING.
YAMAGAMINE'S SOCCER CLUB IS FAMOUS FOR BEING AMAZING, SO THEY'VE GOT A HUGE ROSTER.
THAT'S WHY THE TRACK AND FIELD CLUB...
...SHARES ITS SPACE WITH THE SOCCER CLUB'S THIRD-STRINGERS.
I'M ALMOST JEALOUS OF THEIR SHEER NUMBERS, BUT THERE ARE DOWNSIDES TOO.
LOTS OF THEM NEVER GET TO PLAY IN GAMES...

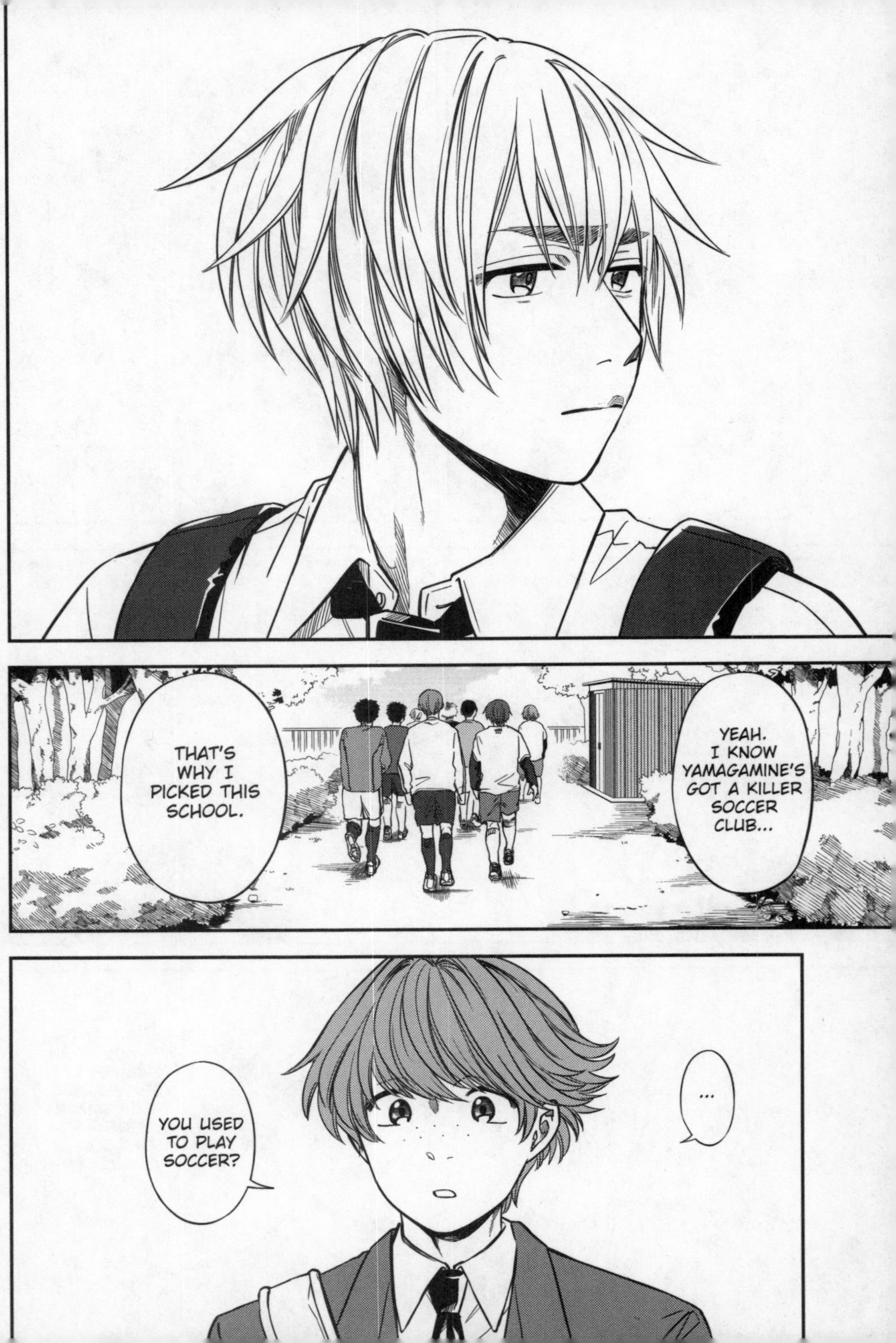
YEAH. I KNOW YAMAGAMINE'S GOT A KILLER SOCCER CLUB...
THAT'S WHY I PICKED THIS SCHOOL.
...
YOU USED TO PLAY SOCCER?

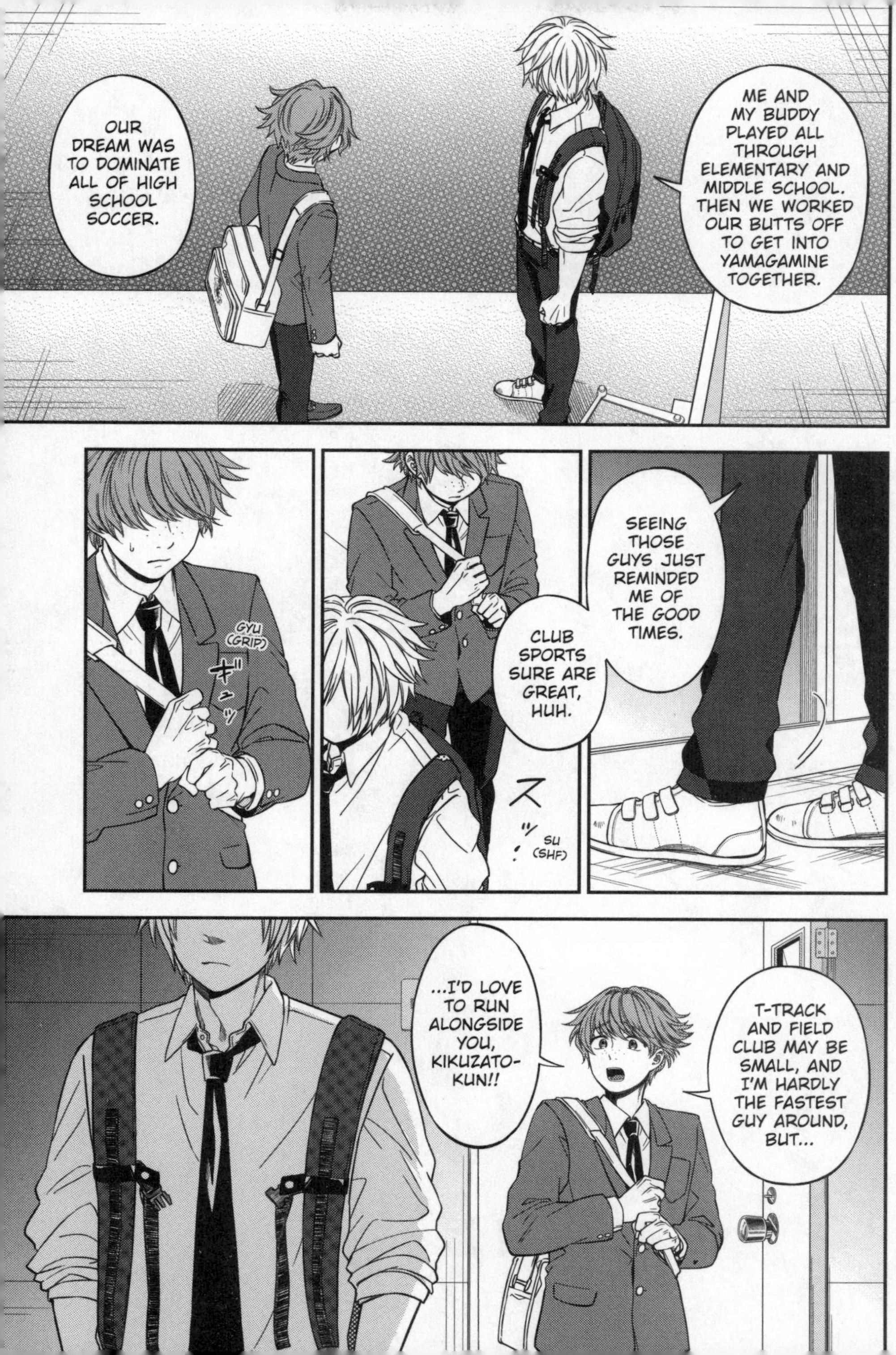
ME AND MY BUDDY PLAYED ALL THROUGH ELEMENTARY AND MIDDLE SCHOOL. THEN WE WORKED OUR BUTTS OFF TO GET INTO YAMAGAMINE TOGETHER.
OUR DREAM WAS TO DOMINATE ALL OF HIGH SCHOOL SOCCER.
SEEING THOSE GUYS JUST REMINDED ME OF THE GOOD TIMES.
CLUB SPORTS SURE ARE GREAT, HUH.
スッ
SU (SHF)
ギュッ
GYU (GRIP)
T-TRACK AND FIELD CLUB MAY BE SMALL, AND I'M HARDLY THE FASTEST GUY AROUND, BUT...
...I'D LOVE TO RUN ALONGSIDE YOU, KIKUZATO-KUN!!

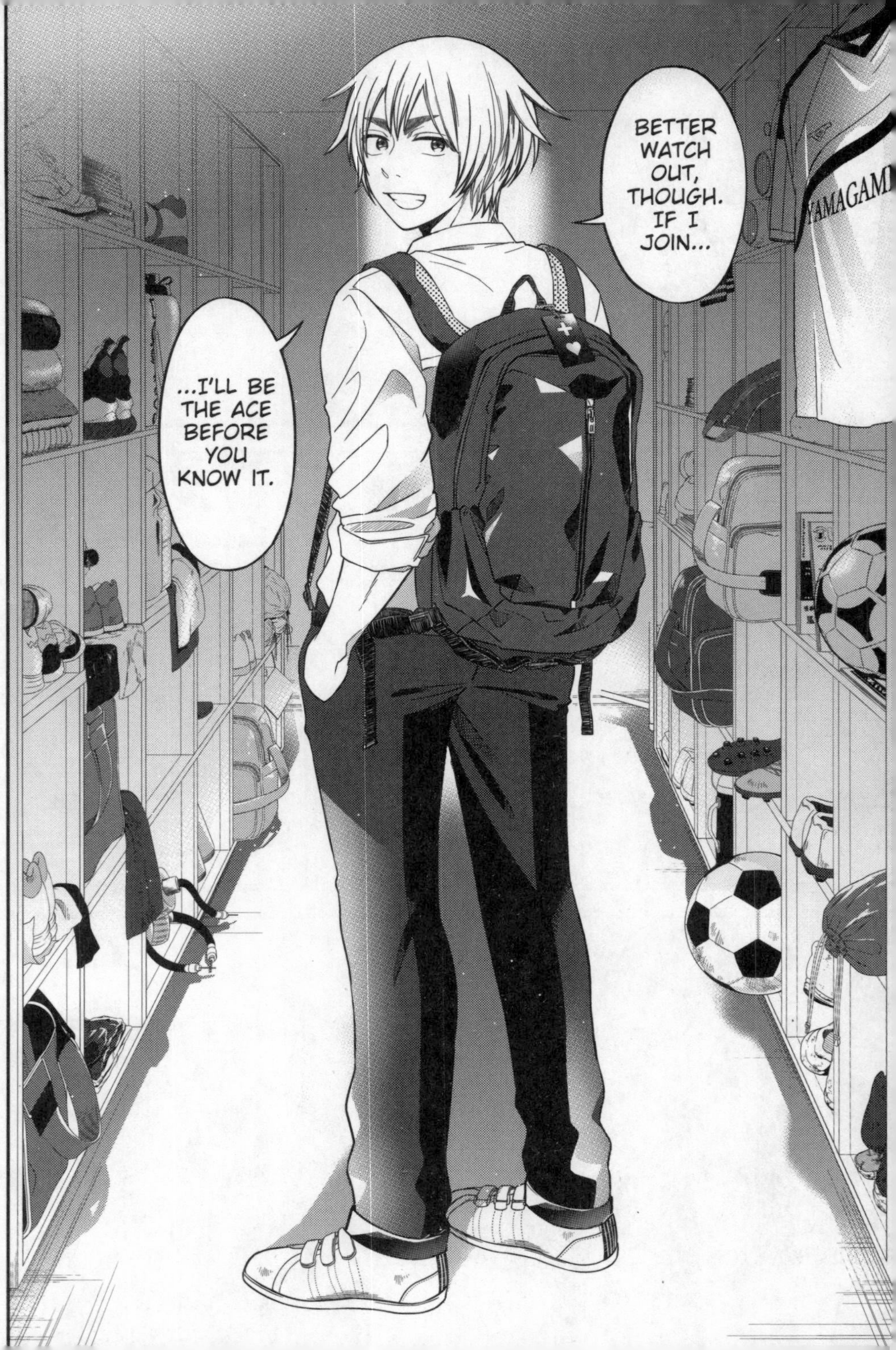
BETTER WATCH OUT, THOUGH. IF I JOIN...
...I'LL BE THE ACE BEFORE YOU KNOW IT.

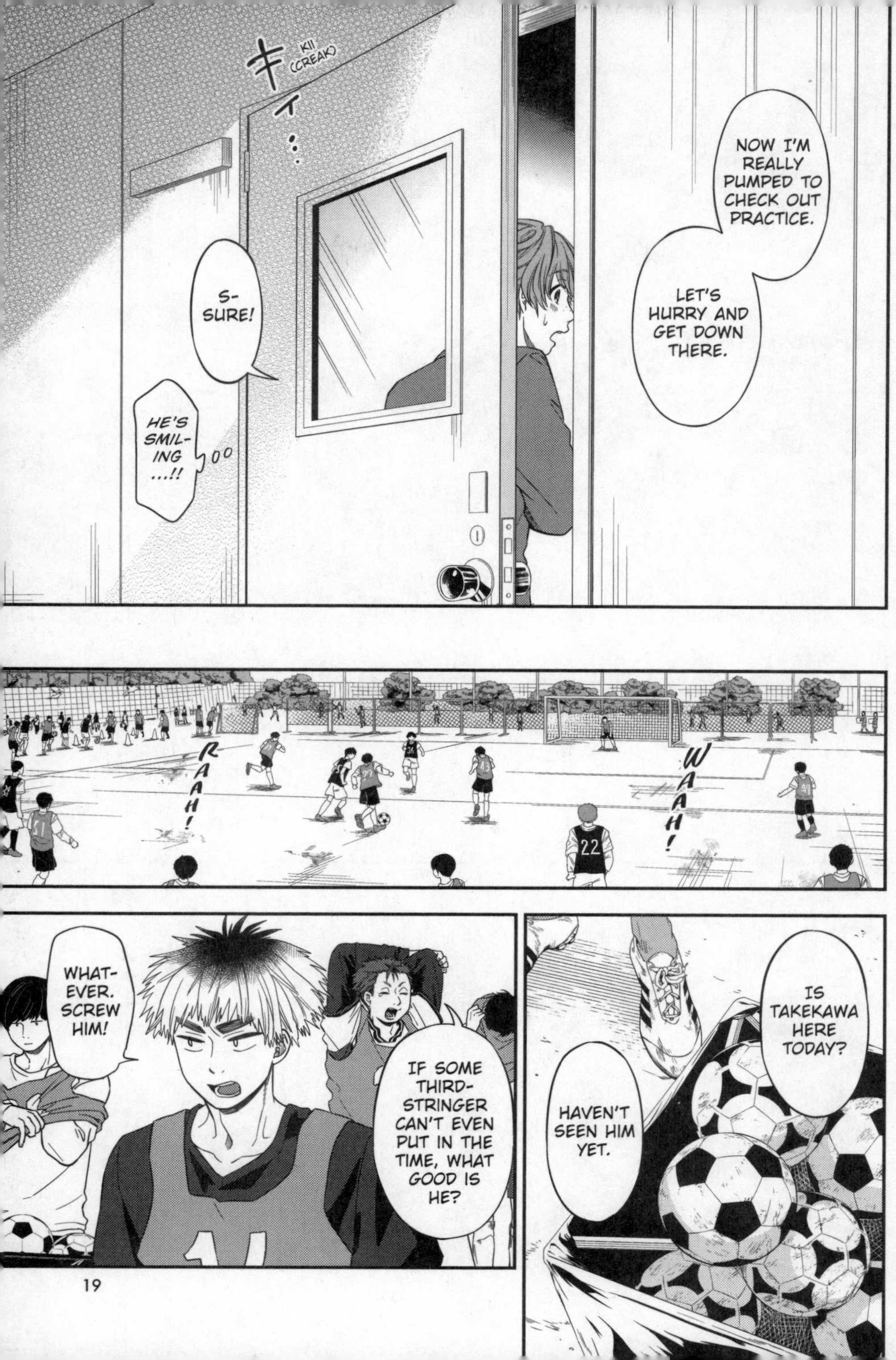
NOW I'M REALLY PUMPED TO CHECK OUT PRACTICE.
LET'S HURRY AND GET DOWN THERE.
KII (CREAK)
S-SURE!
HE'S SMILING...!!
WAAH!
RAAH!
IS TAKEKAWA HERE TODAY?
HAVEN'T SEEN HIM YET.
IF SOME THIRD-STRINGER CAN'T EVEN PUT IN THE TIME, WHAT GOOD IS HE?
WHATEVER. SCREW HIM!

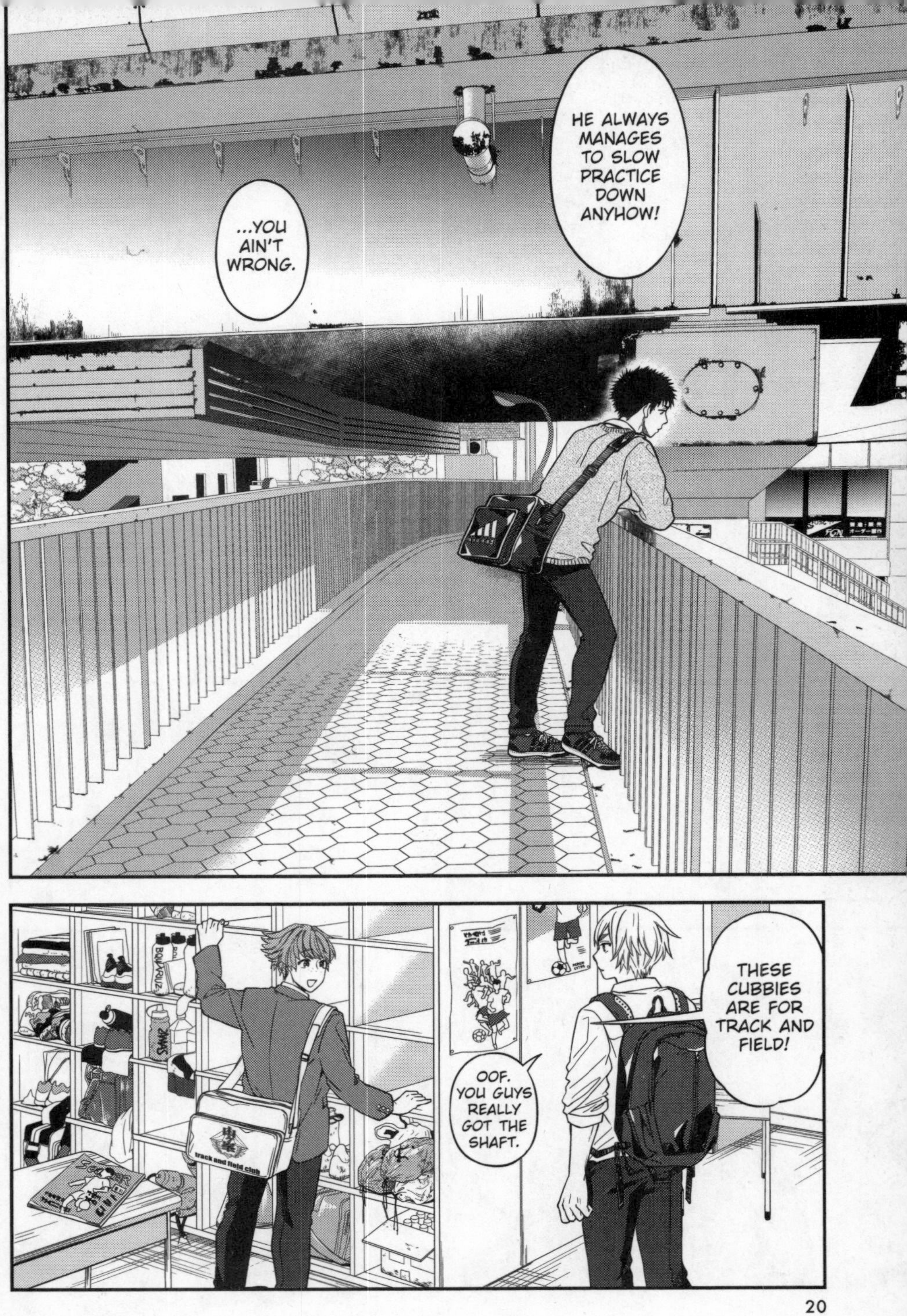
HE ALWAYS MANAGES TO SLOW PRACTICE DOWN ANYHOW!
...YOU AIN'T WRONG.
THESE CUBBIES ARE FOR TRACK AND FIELD!
OOF. YOU GUYS REALLY GOT THE SHAFT.
track and field club

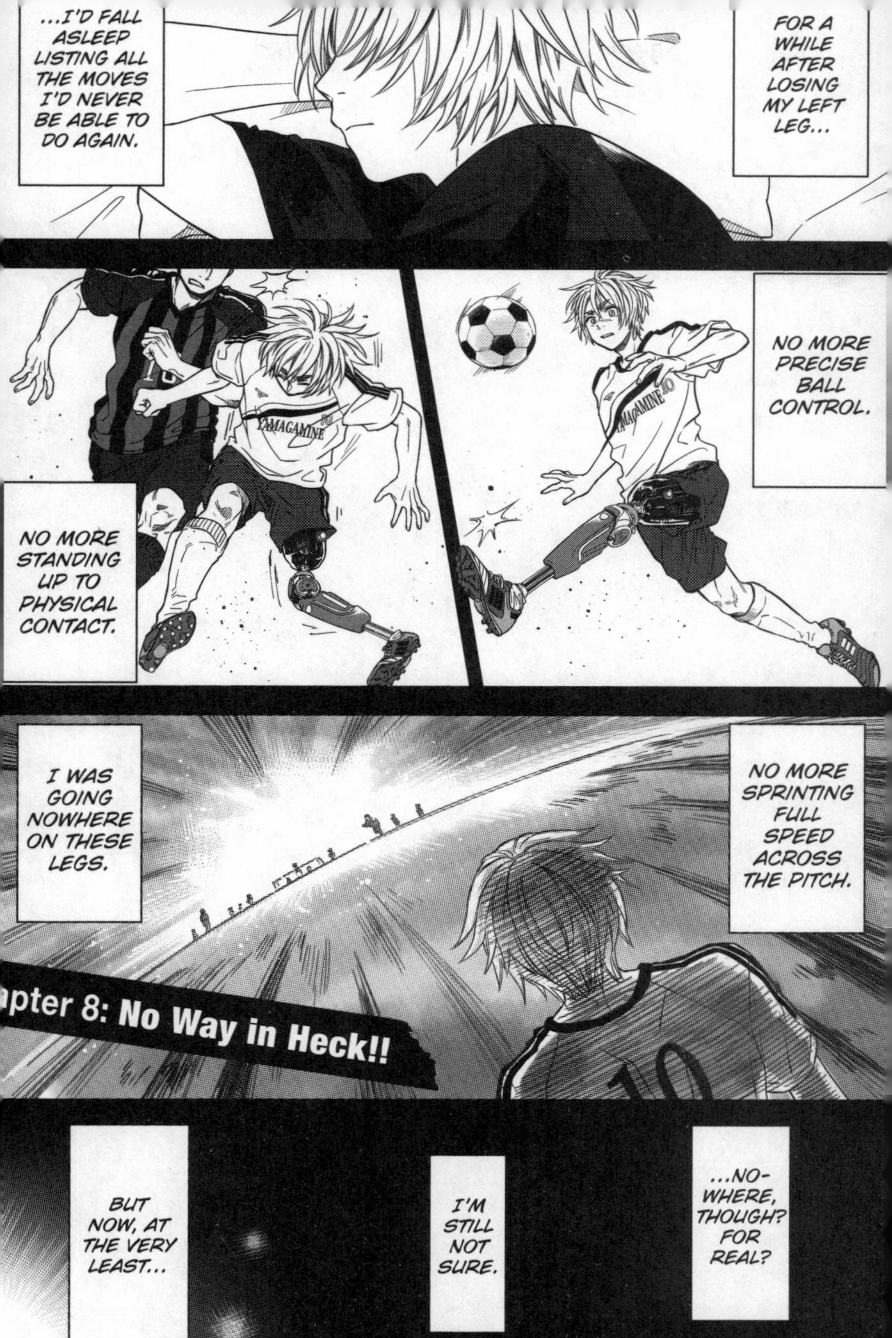
FOR A WHILE AFTER LOSING MY LEFT LEG...
...I'D FALL ASLEEP LISTING ALL THE MOVES I'D NEVER BE ABLE TO DO AGAIN.
NO MORE PRECISE BALL CONTROL.
YAMAGAMINE 10
YAMAGAMINE 10
NO MORE STANDING UP TO PHYSICAL CONTACT.
NO MORE SPRINTING FULL SPEED ACROSS THE PITCH.
I WAS GOING NOWHERE ON THESE LEGS.
pter 8: No Way in Heck!!
...NO-WHERE, THOUGH? FOR REAL?
I'M STILL NOT SURE.
BUT NOW, AT THE VERY LEAST...

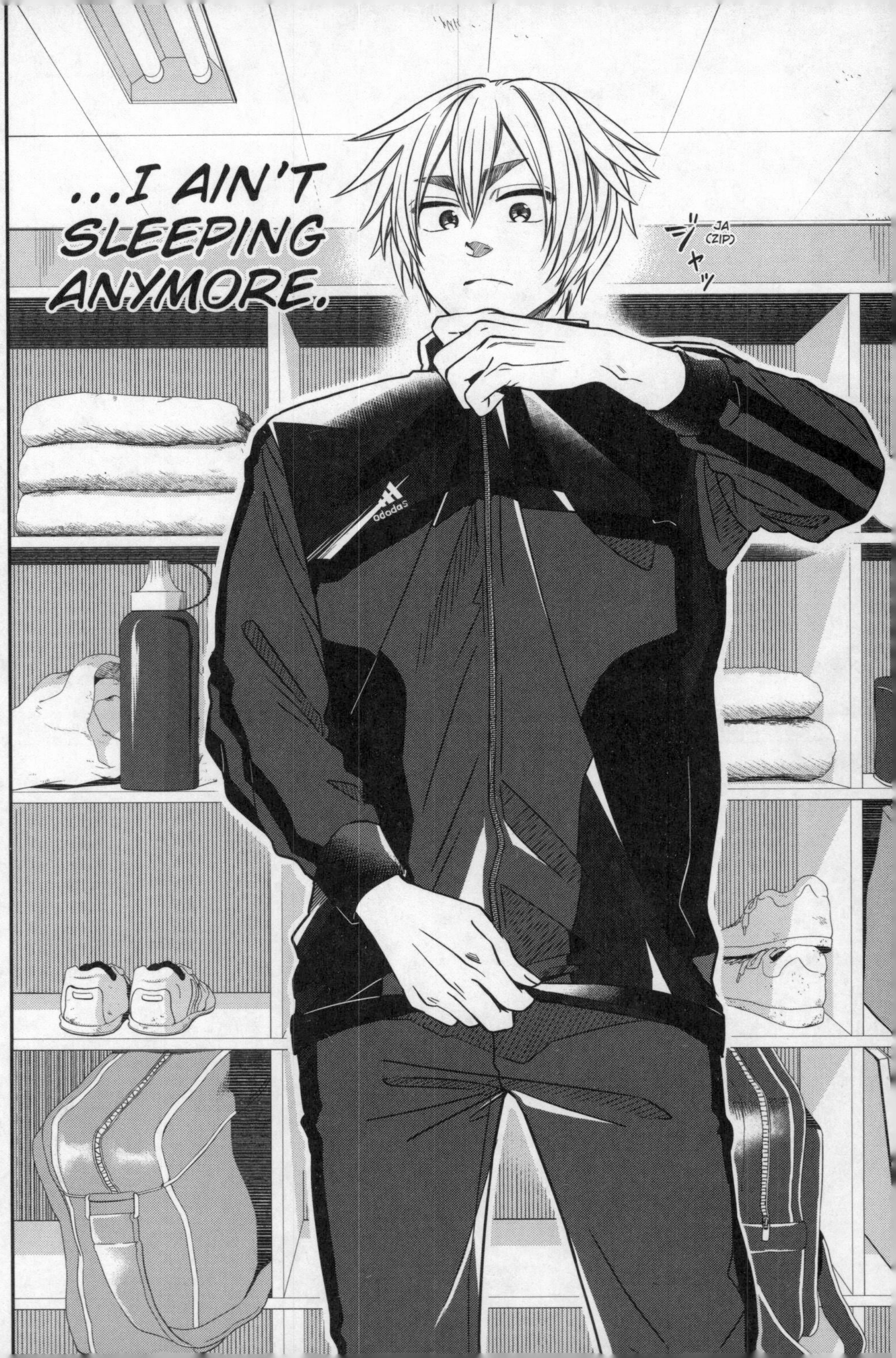
...I AIN'T SLEEPING ANYMORE.
ジャッ
JA (ZIP)
ododaS

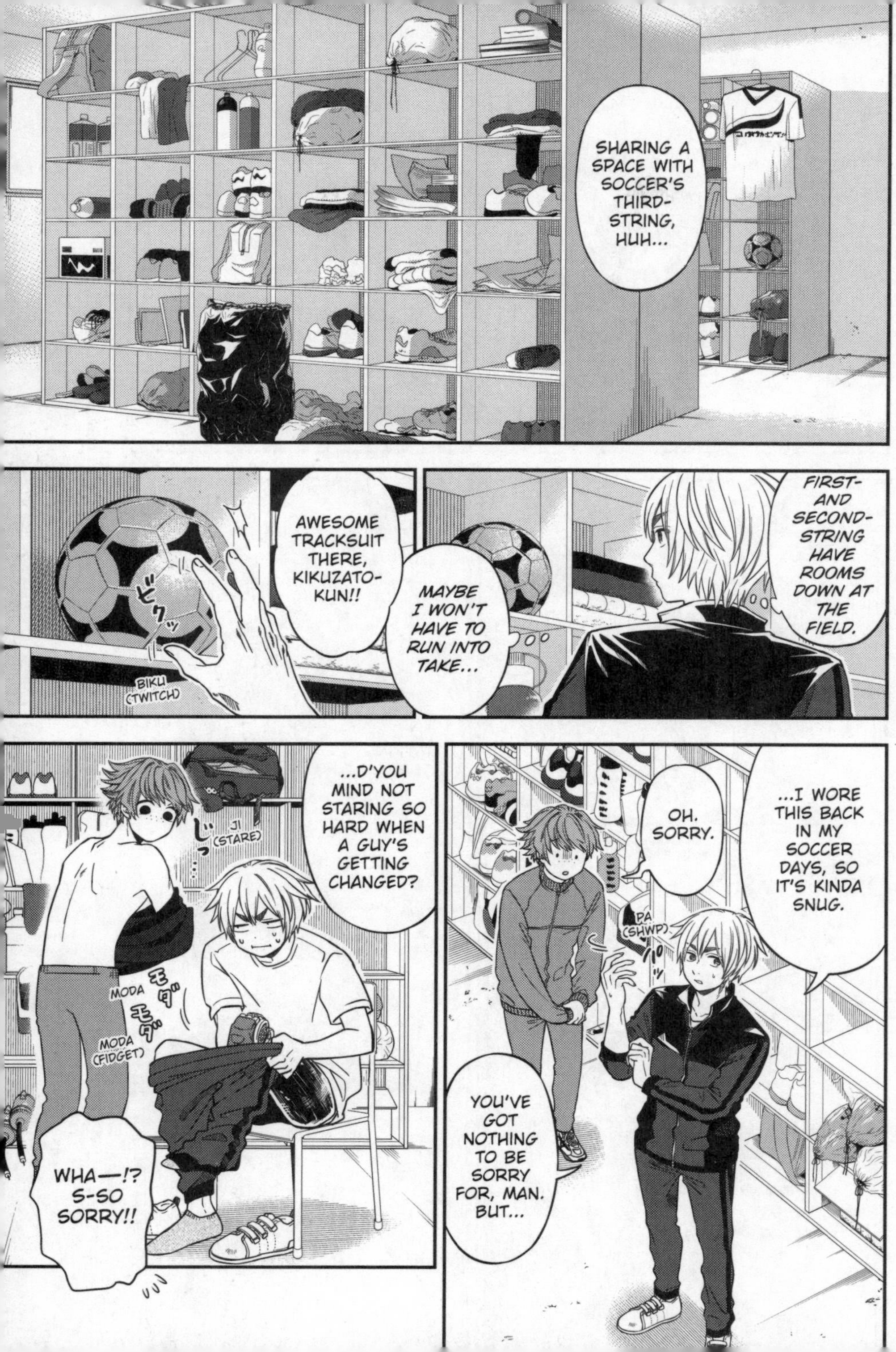
SHARING A SPACE WITH SOCCER'S THIRD-STRING, HUH...
FIRST- AND SECOND-STRING HAVE ROOMS DOWN AT THE FIELD.
MAYBE I WON'T HAVE TO RUN INTO TAKE...
AWESOME TRACKSUIT THERE, KIKUZATO-KUN!!
BIKU (TWITCH)
...I WORE THIS BACK IN MY SOCCER DAYS, SO IT'S KINDA SNUG.
OH. SORRY.
PA (SHWP)
YOU'VE GOT NOTHING TO BE SORRY FOR, MAN. BUT...
...D'YOU MIND NOT STARING SO HARD WHEN A GUY'S GETTING CHANGED?
JI (STARE)
MODA
MODA (FIDGET)
WHA—!? S-SO SORRY!!

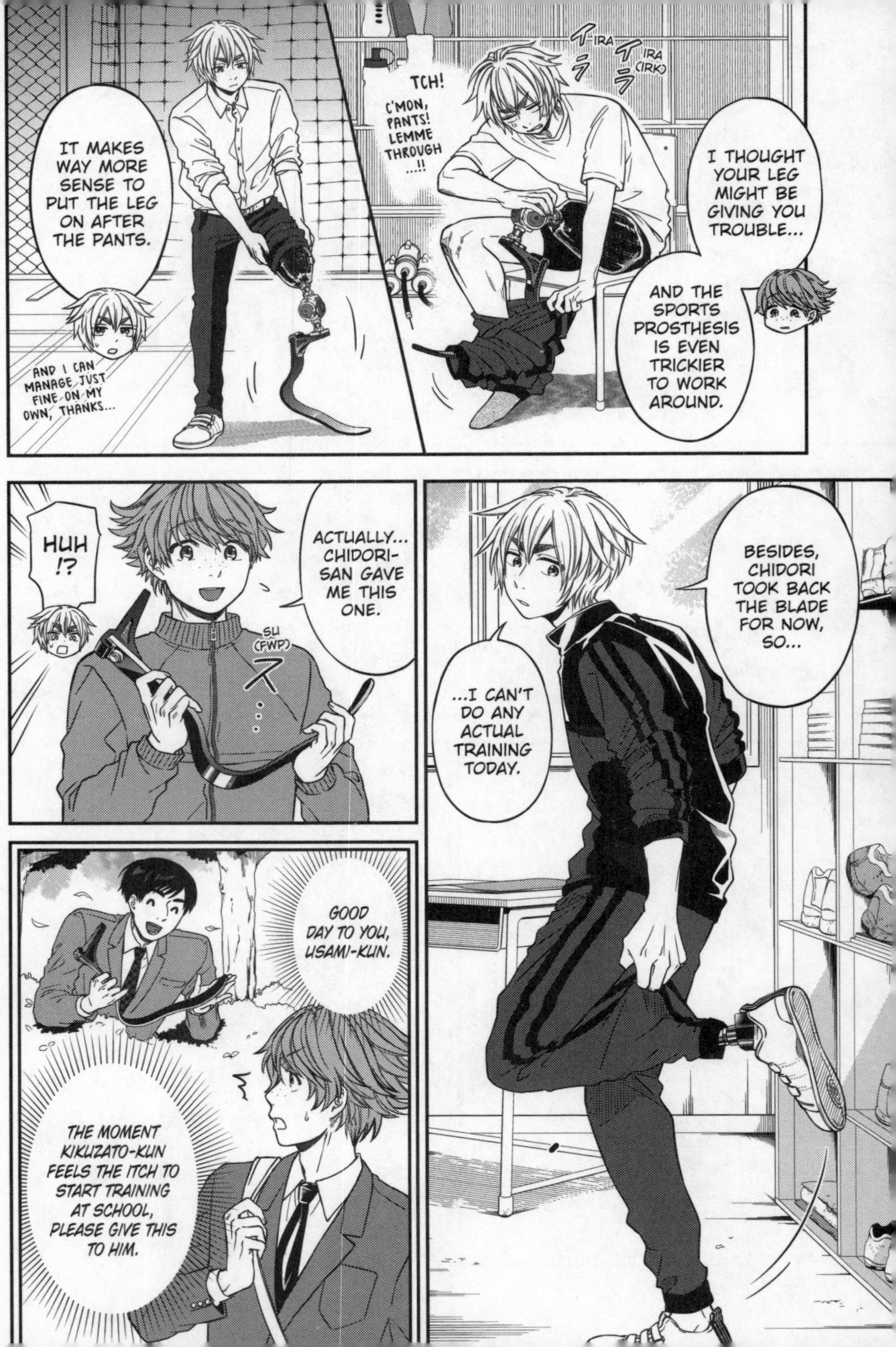
IRA IRA (IRK)
I THOUGHT YOUR LEG MIGHT BE GIVING YOU TROUBLE...
TCH!
C'MON, PANTS! LEMME THROUGH ...!!
AND THE SPORTS PROSTHESIS IS EVEN TRICKIER TO WORK AROUND.
IT MAKES WAY MORE SENSE TO PUT THE LEG ON AFTER THE PANTS.
AND I CAN MANAGE JUST FINE ON MY OWN, THANKS...
BESIDES, CHIDORI TOOK BACK THE BLADE FOR NOW, SO...
...I CAN'T DO ANY ACTUAL TRAINING TODAY.
ACTUALLY... CHIDORI-SAN GAVE ME THIS ONE.
HUH!?
SU (FWP)
GOOD DAY TO YOU, USAMI-KUN.
THE MOMENT KIKUZATO-KUN FEELS THE ITCH TO START TRAINING AT SCHOOL, PLEASE GIVE THIS TO HIM.

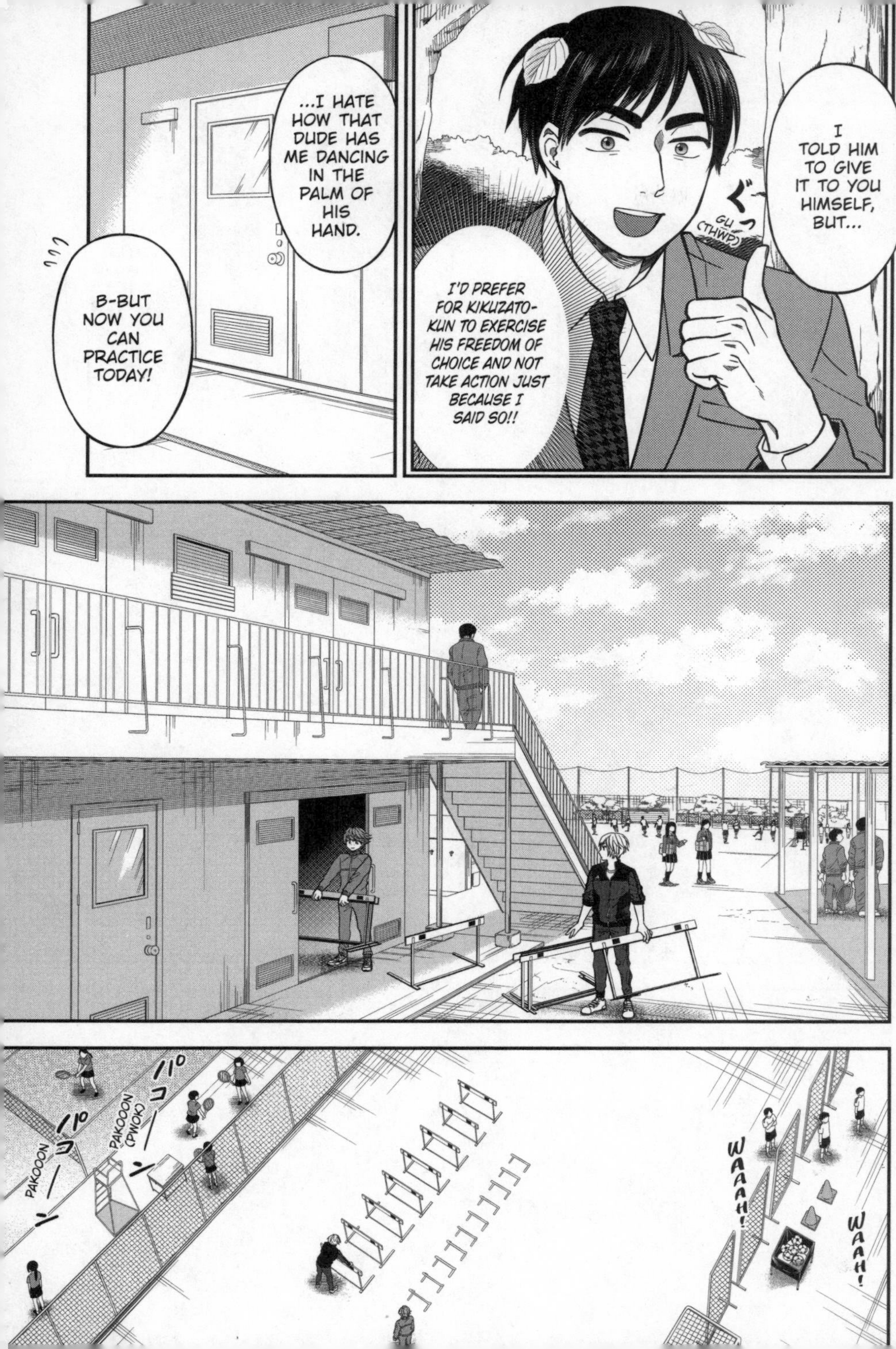
I TOLD HIM TO GIVE IT TO YOU HIMSELF, BUT...
ぐっ GU (THWP)
I'D PREFER FOR KIKUZATO-KUN TO EXERCISE HIS FREEDOM OF CHOICE AND NOT TAKE ACTION JUST BECAUSE I SAID SO!!
...I HATE HOW THAT DUDE HAS ME DANCING IN THE PALM OF HIS HAND.
B-BUT NOW YOU CAN PRACTICE TODAY!
WAAAH!
WAAAH!
WAAAH!
PAKOOON (PWOK)
PAKOOON

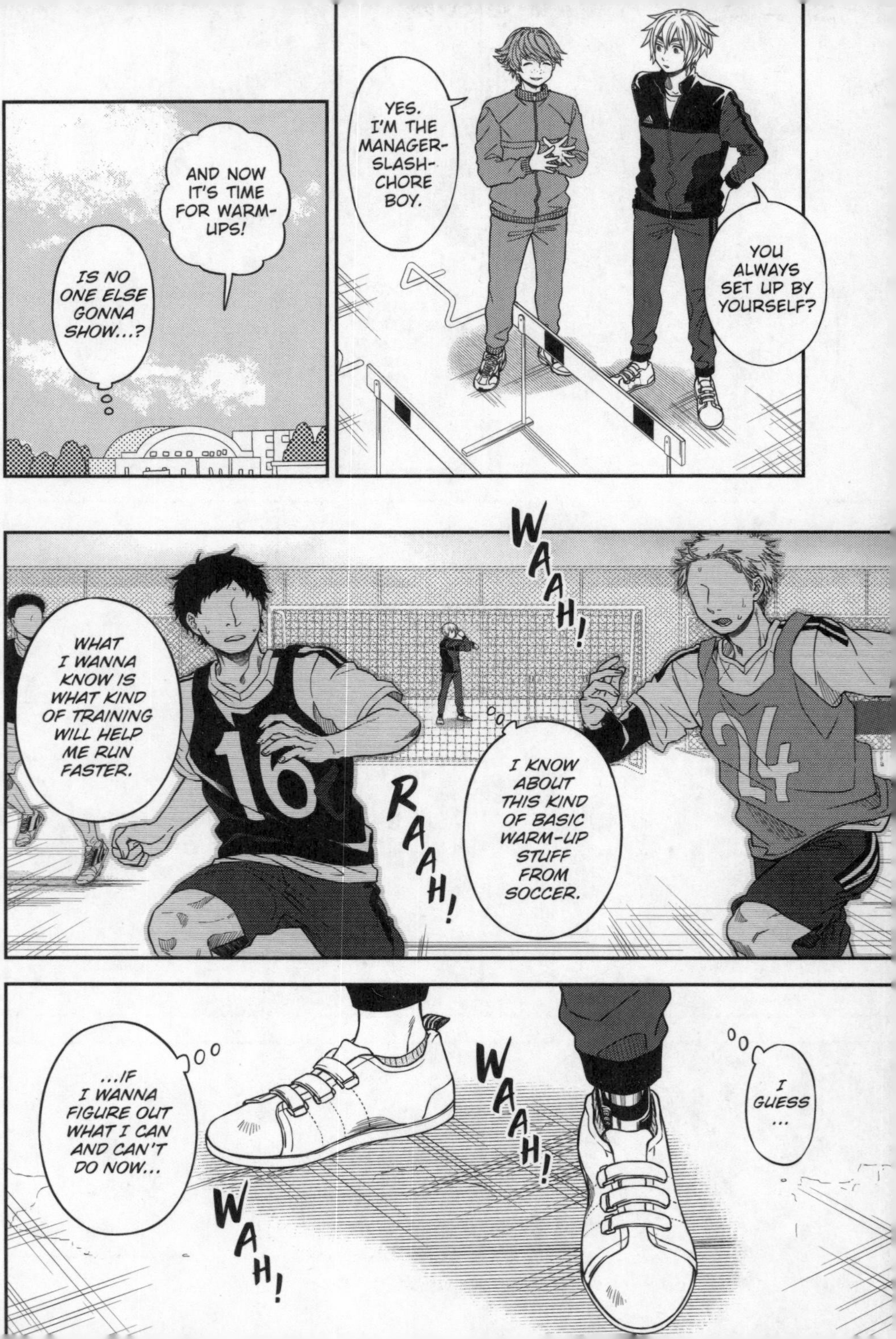
YOU ALWAYS SET UP BY YOURSELF?
YES. I'M THE MANAGER-SLASH-CHORE BOY.
AND NOW IT'S TIME FOR WARM-UPS!
IS NO ONE ELSE GONNA SHOW...?
WAAH!
I KNOW ABOUT THIS KIND OF BASIC WARM-UP STUFF FROM SOCCER.
RAAH!
WHAT I WANNA KNOW IS WHAT KIND OF TRAINING WILL HELP ME RUN FASTER.
I GUESS...
WAAH!
...IF I WANNA FIGURE OUT WHAT I CAN AND CAN'T DO NOW...
WAH!

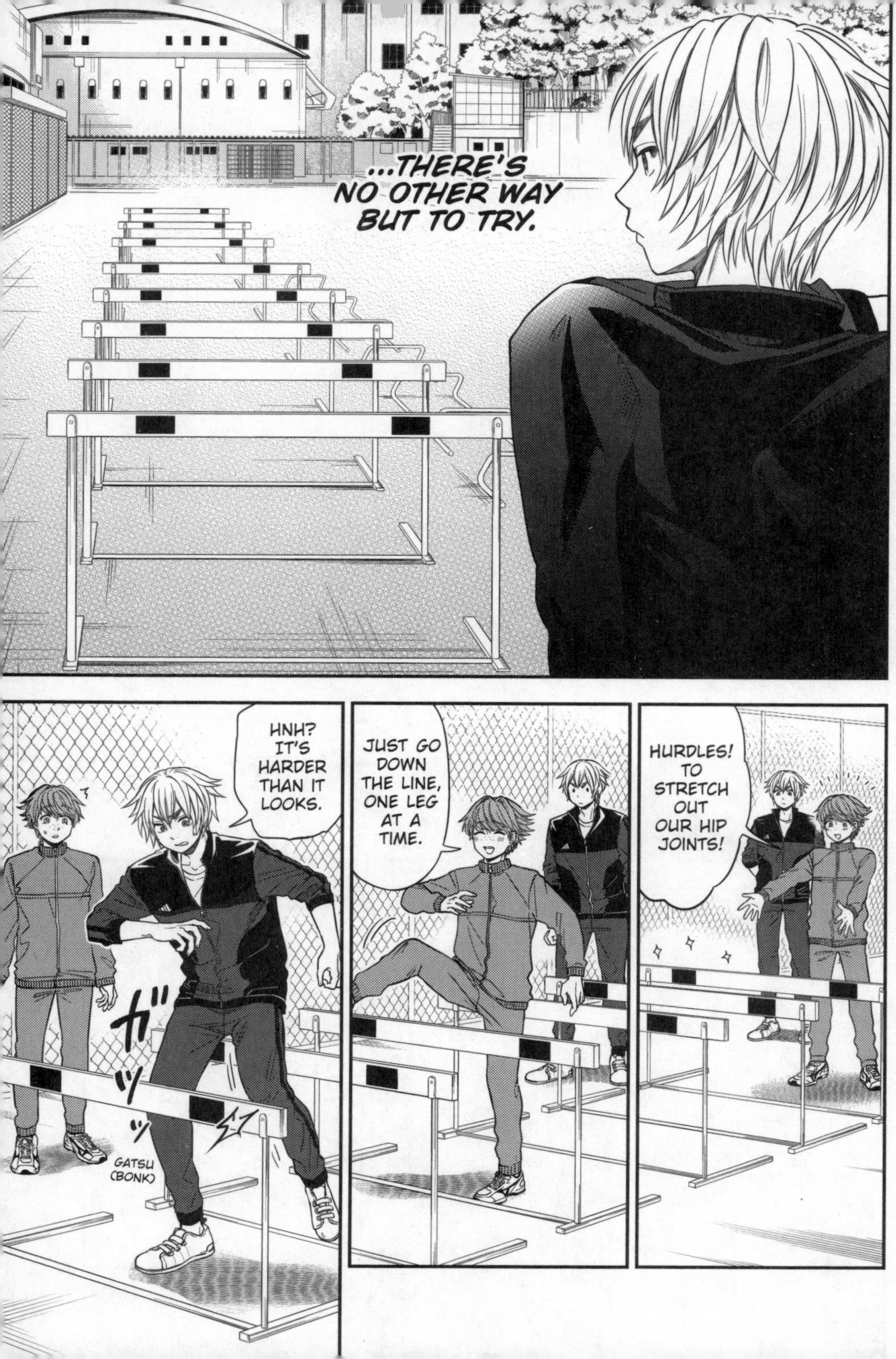
...THERE'S NO OTHER WAY BUT TO TRY.
HURDLES! TO STRETCH OUT OUR HIP JOINTS!
JUST GO DOWN THE LINE, ONE LEG AT A TIME.
HNH? IT'S HARDER THAN IT LOOKS.
ガッ
GATSU (BONK)

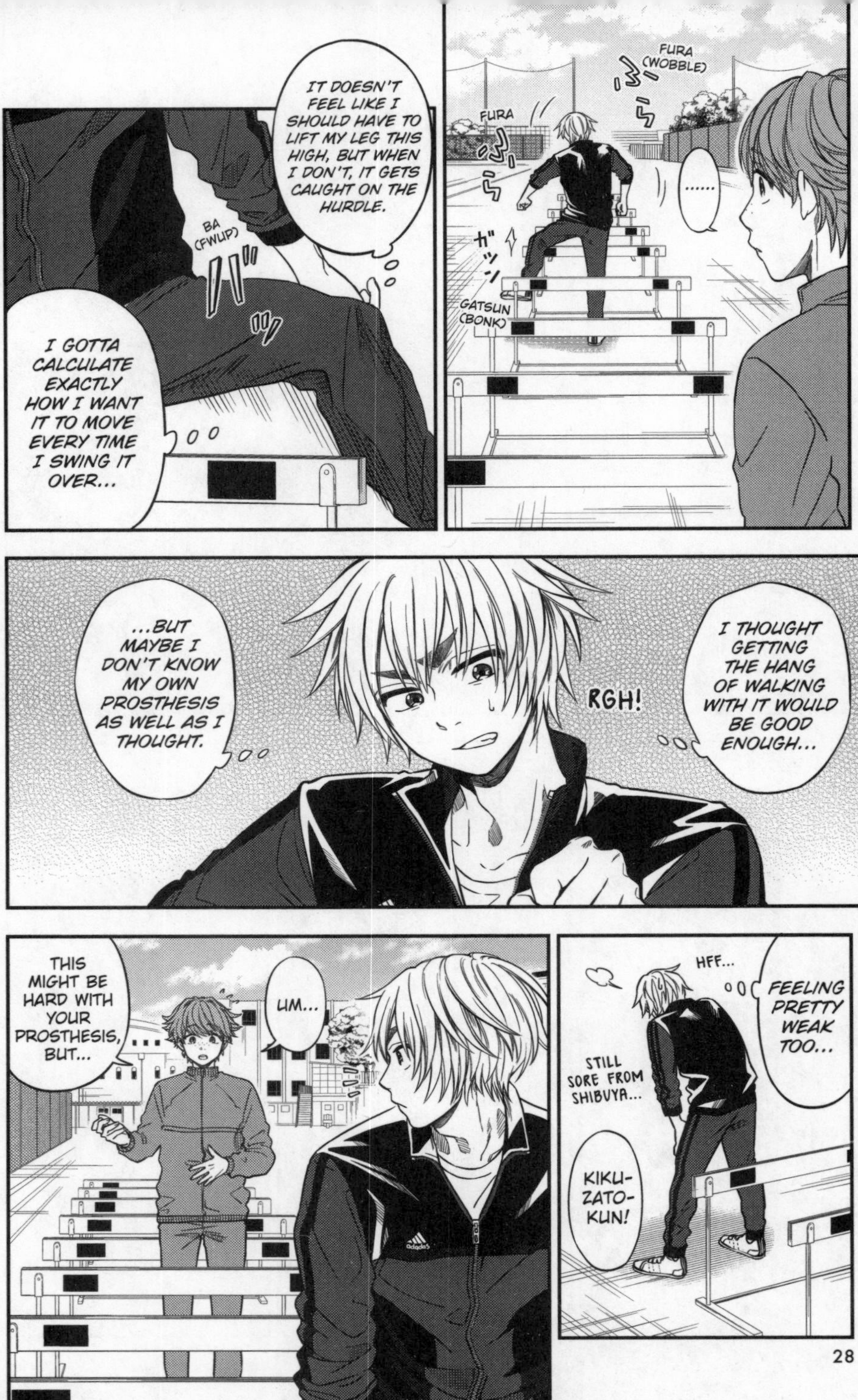
FURA (WOBBLE)
FURA
......
ガッ
GATSUN (BONK)
IT DOESN'T FEEL LIKE I SHOULD HAVE TO LIFT MY LEG THIS HIGH, BUT WHEN I DON'T, IT GETS CAUGHT ON THE HURDLE.
BA (FWUP)
I GOTTA CALCULATE EXACTLY HOW I WANT IT TO MOVE EVERY TIME I SWING IT OVER...
I THOUGHT GETTING THE HANG OF WALKING WITH IT WOULD BE GOOD ENOUGH...
RGH!
...BUT MAYBE I DON'T KNOW MY OWN PROSTHESIS AS WELL AS I THOUGHT.
HFF...
FEELING PRETTY WEAK TOO...
STILL SORE FROM SHIBUYA...
KIKUZATO-KUN!
UM...
THIS MIGHT BE HARD WITH YOUR PROSTHESIS, BUT...

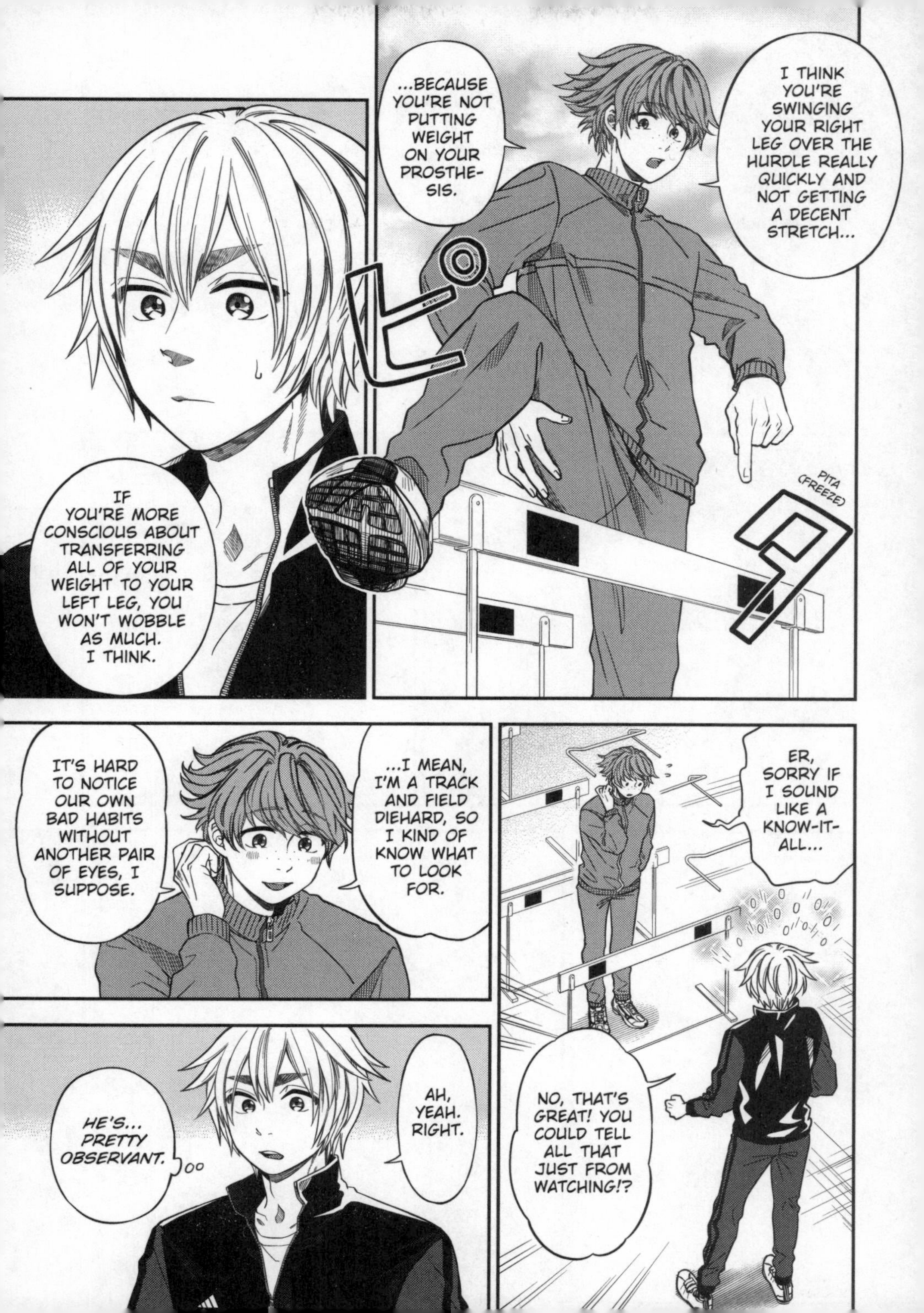
I THINK YOU'RE SWINGING YOUR RIGHT LEG OVER THE HURDLE REALLY QUICKLY AND NOT GETTING A DECENT STRETCH...
...BECAUSE YOU'RE NOT PUTTING WEIGHT ON YOUR PROSTHE-SIS.
PITA (FREEZE)
IF YOU'RE MORE CONSCIOUS ABOUT TRANSFERRING ALL OF YOUR WEIGHT TO YOUR LEFT LEG, YOU WON'T WOBBLE AS MUCH. I THINK.
ER, SORRY IF I SOUND LIKE A KNOW-IT-ALL...
NO, THAT'S GREAT! YOU COULD TELL ALL THAT JUST FROM WATCHING!?
...I MEAN, I'M A TRACK AND FIELD DIEHARD, SO I KIND OF KNOW WHAT TO LOOK FOR.
IT'S HARD TO NOTICE OUR OWN BAD HABITS WITHOUT ANOTHER PAIR OF EYES, I SUPPOSE.
AH, YEAH. RIGHT.
HE'S... PRETTY OBSERVANT.

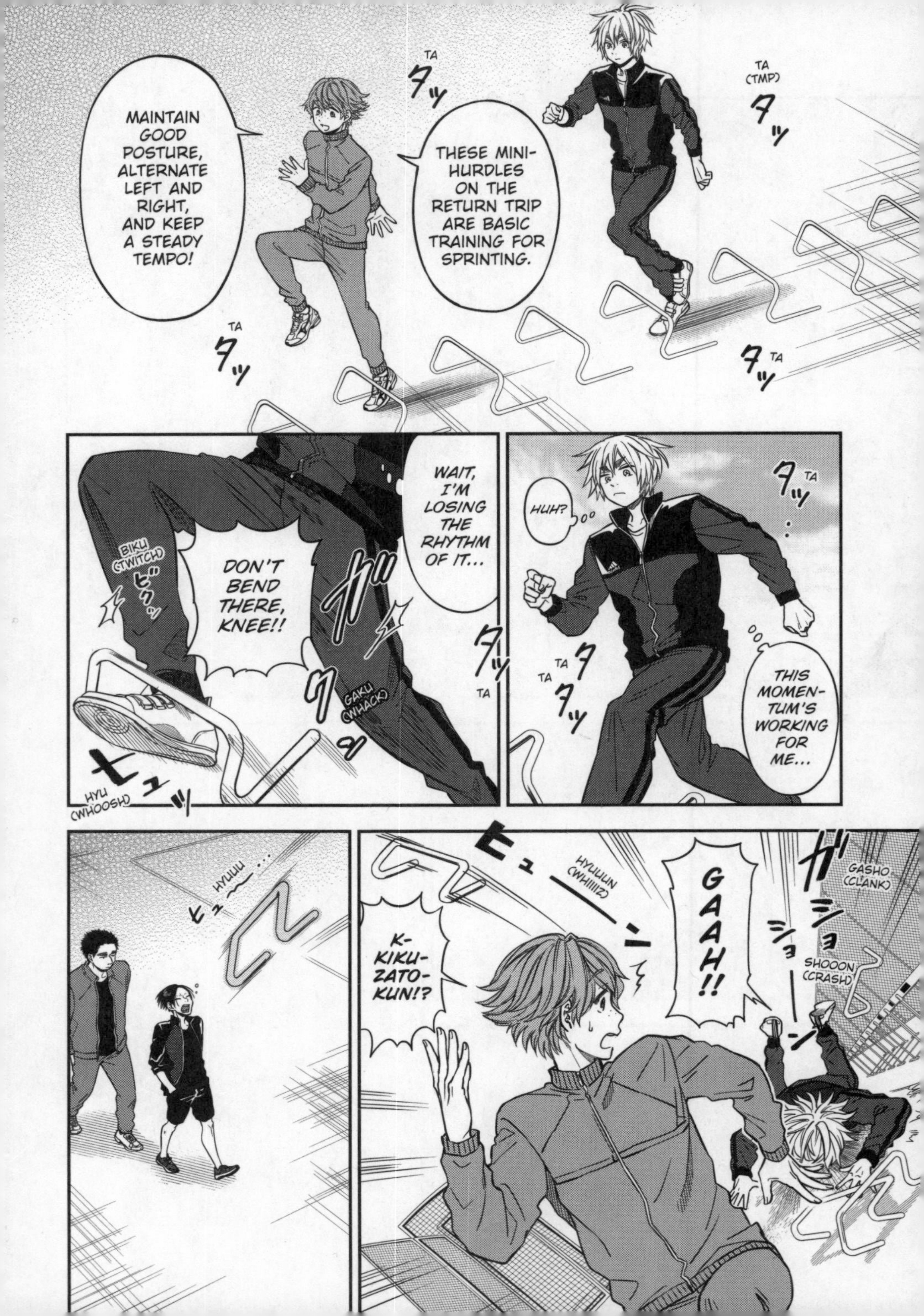
TA (TMP)
タッ
THESE MINI-HURDLES ON THE RETURN TRIP ARE BASIC TRAINING FOR SPRINTING.
TA
タッ
MAINTAIN GOOD POSTURE, ALTERNATE LEFT AND RIGHT, AND KEEP A STEADY TEMPO!
TA
タッ
TA
タッ
TA
タッ
HUH?
THIS MOMENTUM'S WORKING FOR ME...
TA TA
タタッ
WAIT, I'M LOSING THE RHYTHM OF IT...
DON'T BEND THERE, KNEE!!
BIKU (TWITCH)
GAKU (WHACK)
TA
タッ
HYU (WHOOSH)
GASHO (CLANK)
SHOOON (CRASH)
GAAAH!!
HYUUUN (WHIIIZ)
K-KIKUZATO-KUN!?
HYUUU...

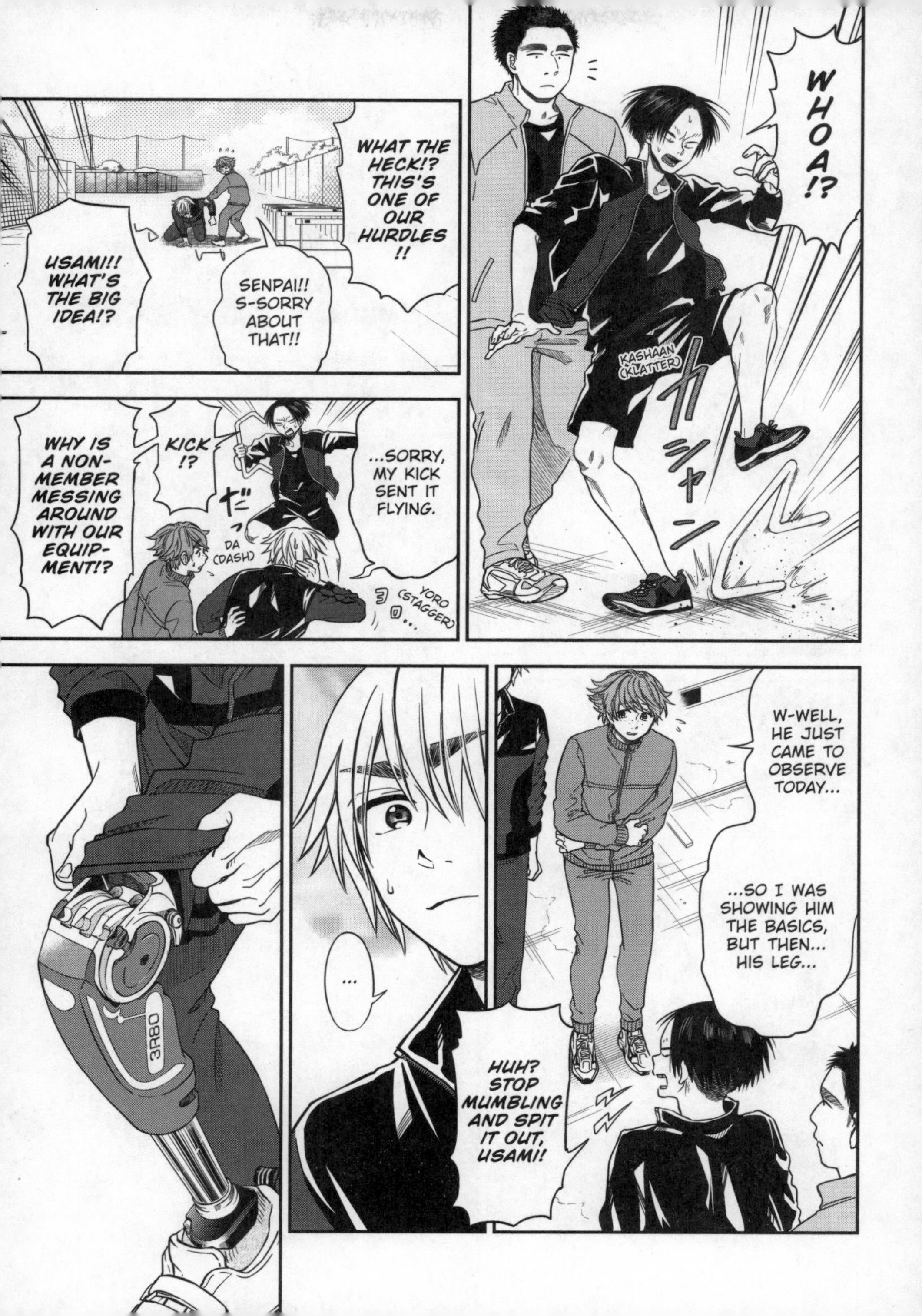
WHOA!?
KASHAAN (KLATTER)
WHAT THE HECK!? THIS'S ONE OF OUR HURDLES!!
SENPAI!! S-SORRY ABOUT THAT!!
USAMI!! WHAT'S THE BIG IDEA!?
...SORRY, MY KICK SENT IT FLYING.
KICK!?
WHY IS A NON-MEMBER MESSING AROUND WITH OUR EQUIPMENT!?
DA (DASH)
YORO (STAGGER)
W-WELL, HE JUST CAME TO OBSERVE TODAY...
...SO I WAS SHOWING HIM THE BASICS, BUT THEN... HIS LEG...
HUH? STOP MUMBLING AND SPIT IT OUT, USAMI!
...
3R80

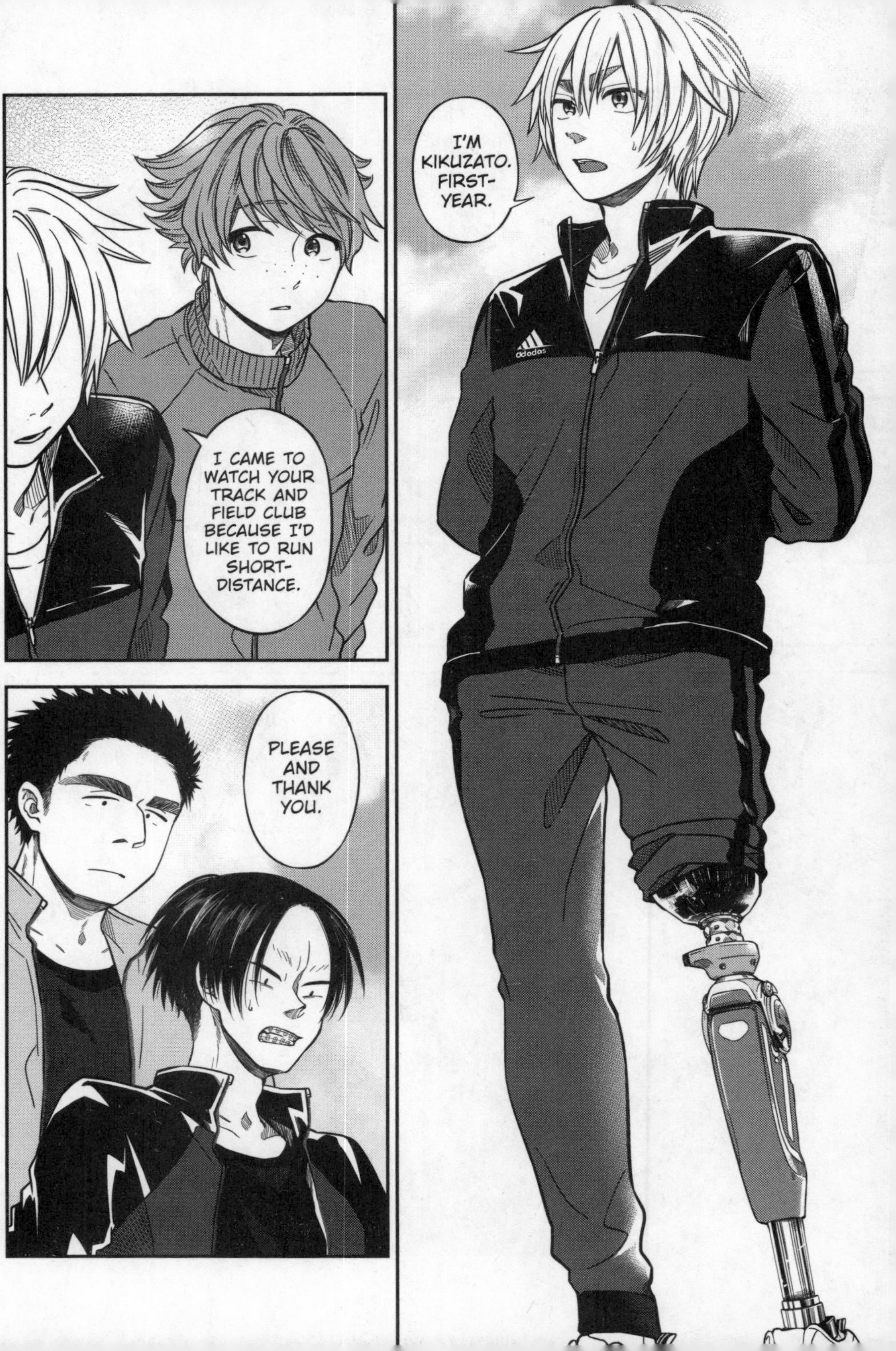
I'M KIKUZATO. FIRST-YEAR.
I CAME TO WATCH YOUR TRACK AND FIELD CLUB BECAUSE I'D LIKE TO RUN SHORT-DISTANCE.
PLEASE AND THANK YOU.

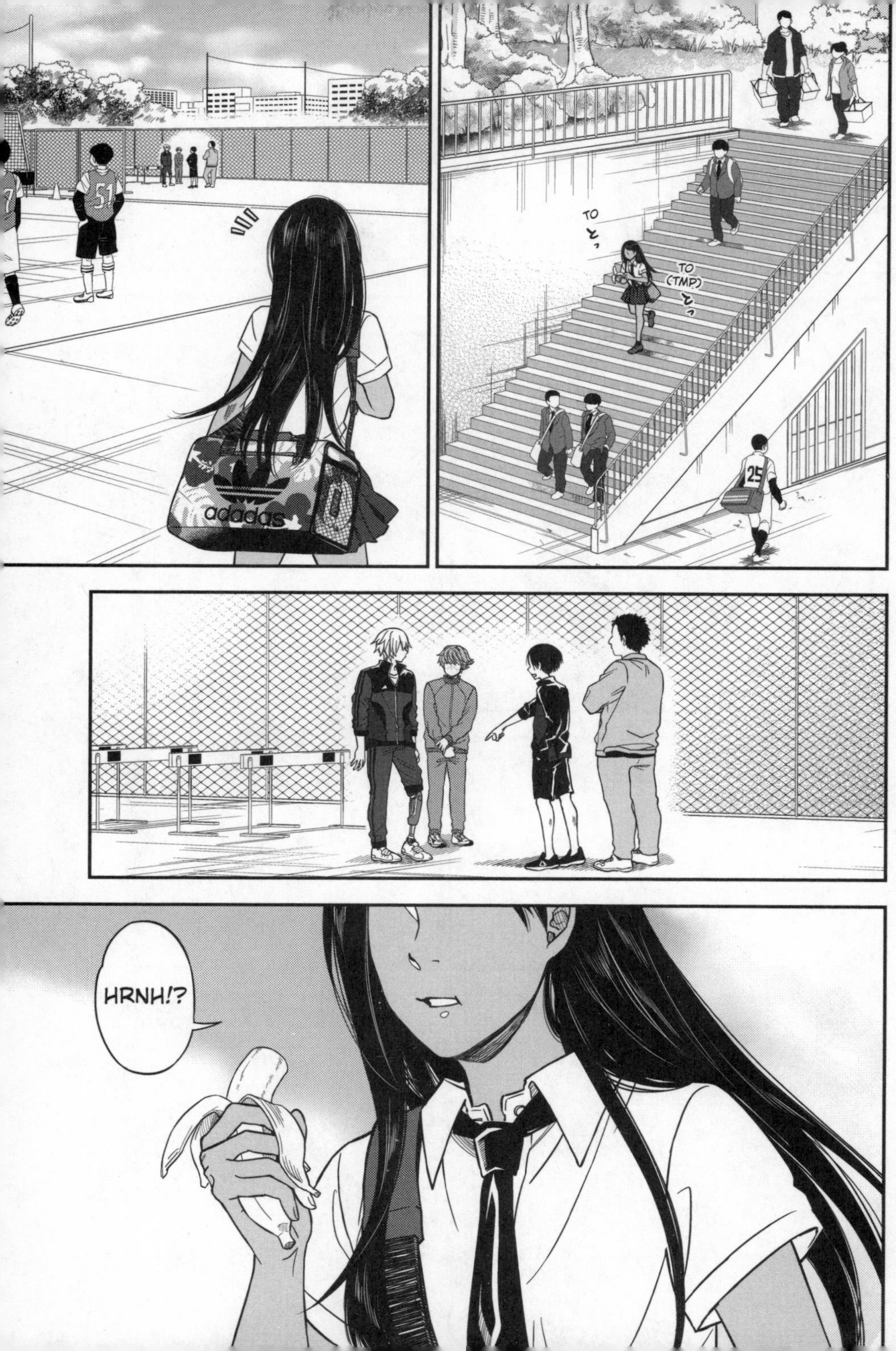
TO
と
TO (TMP)
と
adadas
HRNH!?

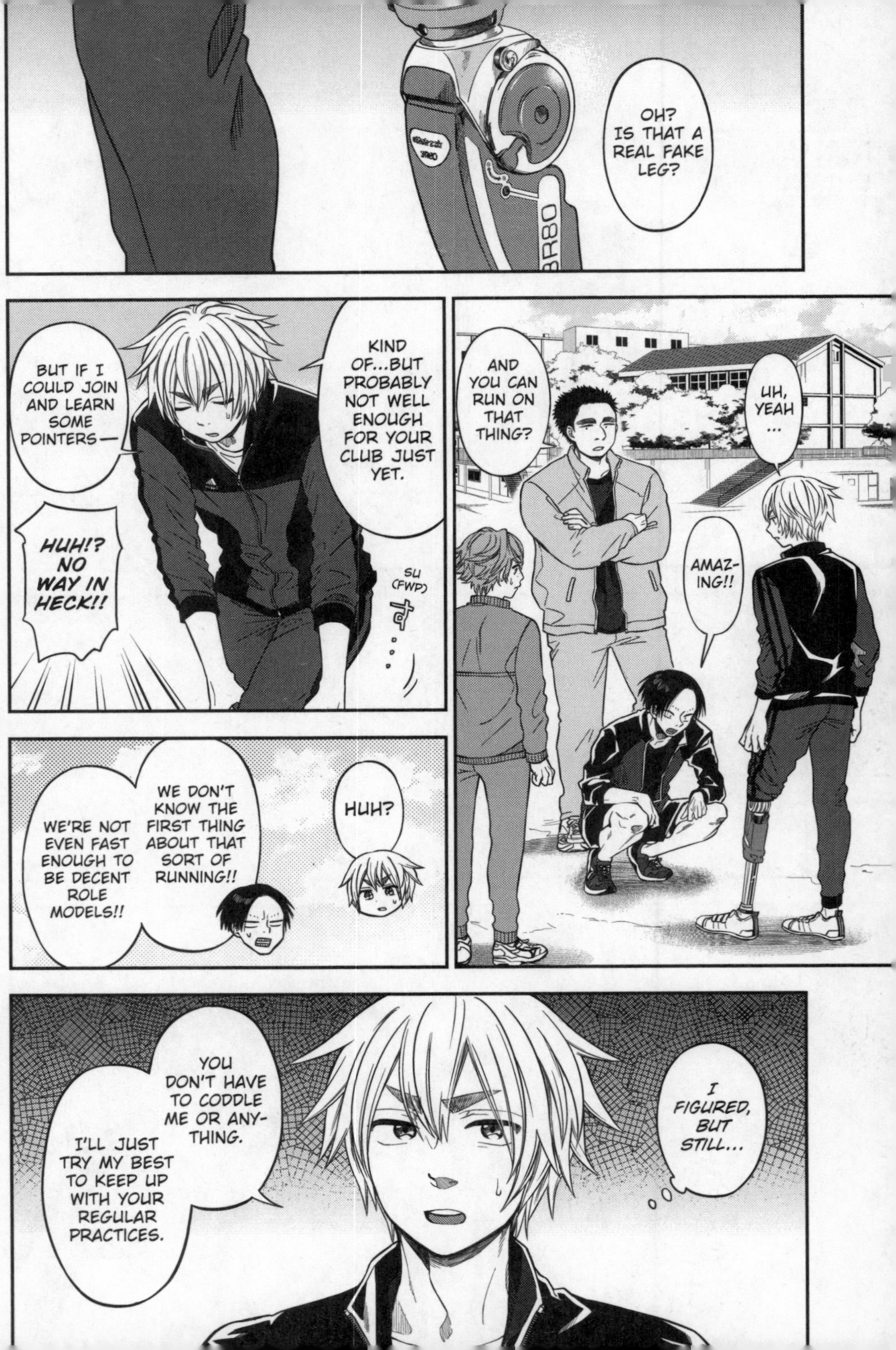
OH? IS THAT A REAL FAKE LEG?
AND YOU CAN RUN ON THAT THING?
UH, YEAH...
AMAZ-ING!!
KIND OF...BUT PROBABLY NOT WELL ENOUGH FOR YOUR CLUB JUST YET.
SU (FWP) す...
BUT IF I COULD JOIN AND LEARN SOME POINTERS—
HUH!? NO WAY IN HECK!!
HUH?
WE DON'T KNOW THE FIRST THING ABOUT THAT SORT OF RUNNING!!
WE'RE NOT EVEN FAST ENOUGH TO BE DECENT ROLE MODELS!!
I FIGURED, BUT STILL...
YOU DON'T HAVE TO CODDLE ME OR ANY-THING.
I'LL JUST TRY MY BEST TO KEEP UP WITH YOUR REGULAR PRACTICES.

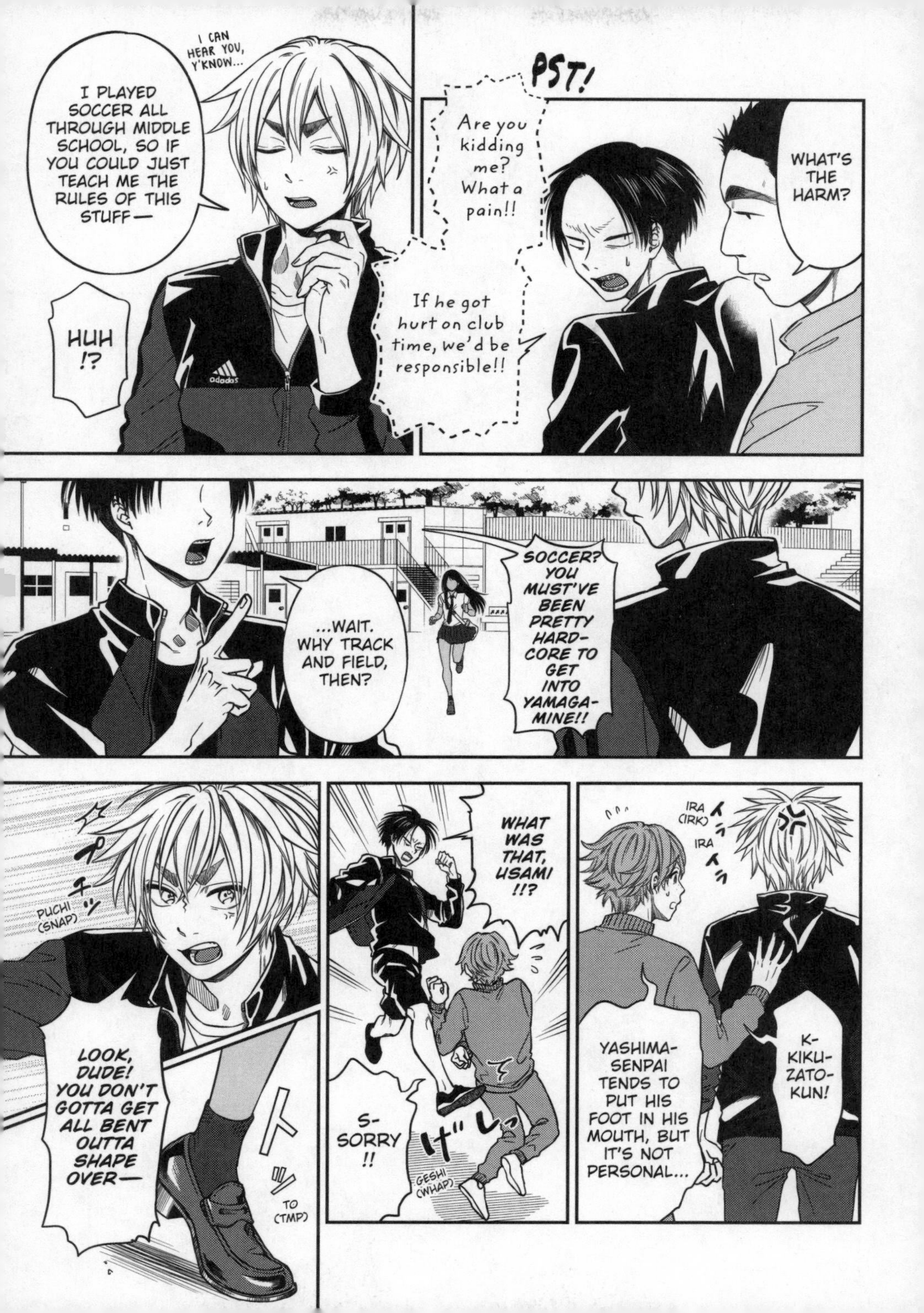
PST!
WHAT'S THE HARM?
Are you kidding me? What a pain!!
If he got hurt on club time, we'd be responsible!!
I CAN HEAR YOU, Y'KNOW...
I PLAYED SOCCER ALL THROUGH MIDDLE SCHOOL, SO IF YOU COULD JUST TEACH ME THE RULES OF THIS STUFF—
HUH!?
SOCCER? YOU MUST'VE BEEN PRETTY HARD-CORE TO GET INTO YAMAGA-MINE!!
...WAIT. WHY TRACK AND FIELD, THEN?
IRA (IRK)
IRA
K-KIKU-ZATO-KUN!
YASHIMA-SENPAI TENDS TO PUT HIS FOOT IN HIS MOUTH, BUT IT'S NOT PERSONAL...
WHAT WAS THAT, USAMI!!?
S-SORRY!!
GESHI (WHAP)
PUCHI (SNAP)
LOOK, DUDE! YOU DON'T GOTTA GET ALL BENT OUTTA SHAPE OVER—
TO (TMP)

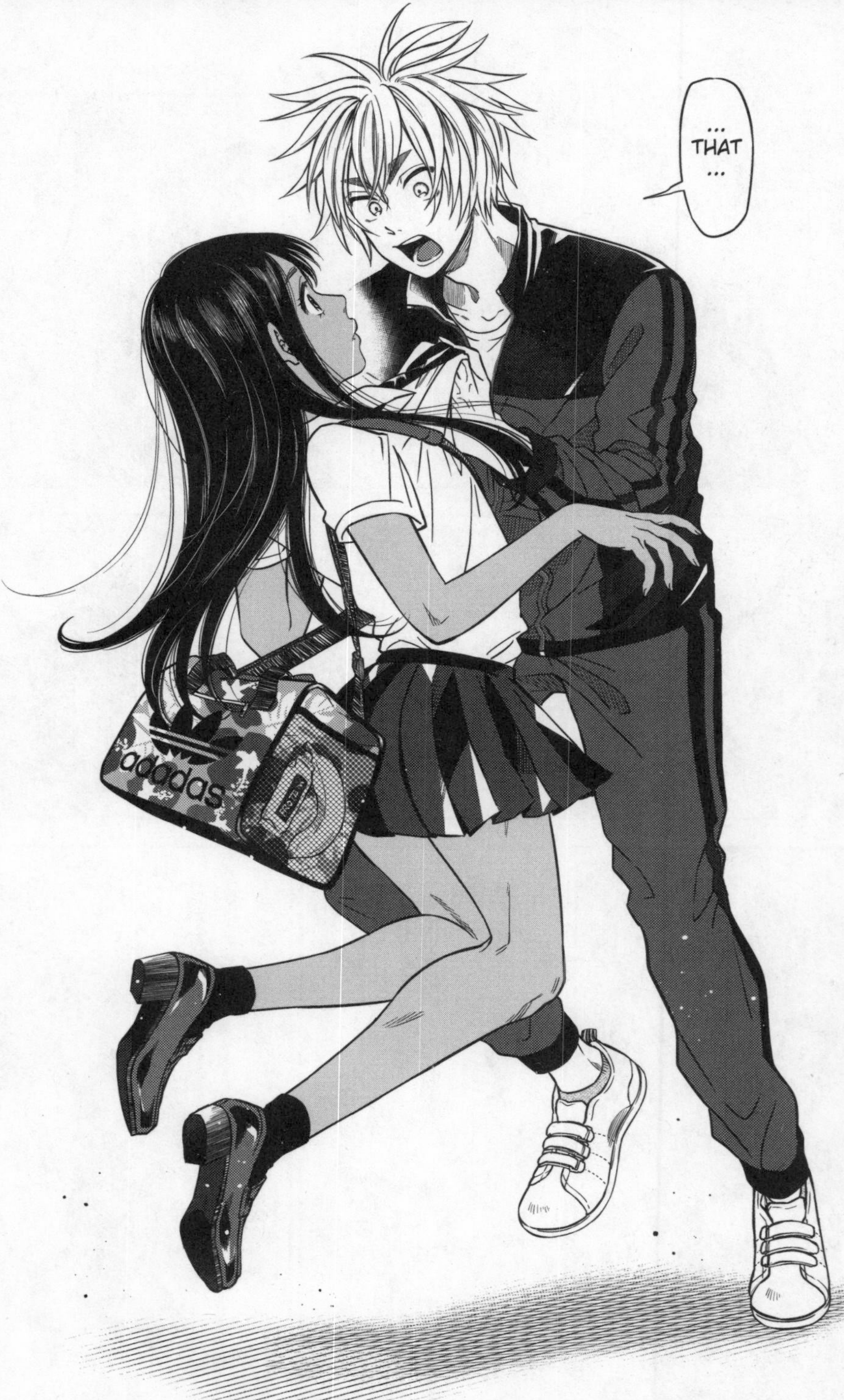
...THAT...

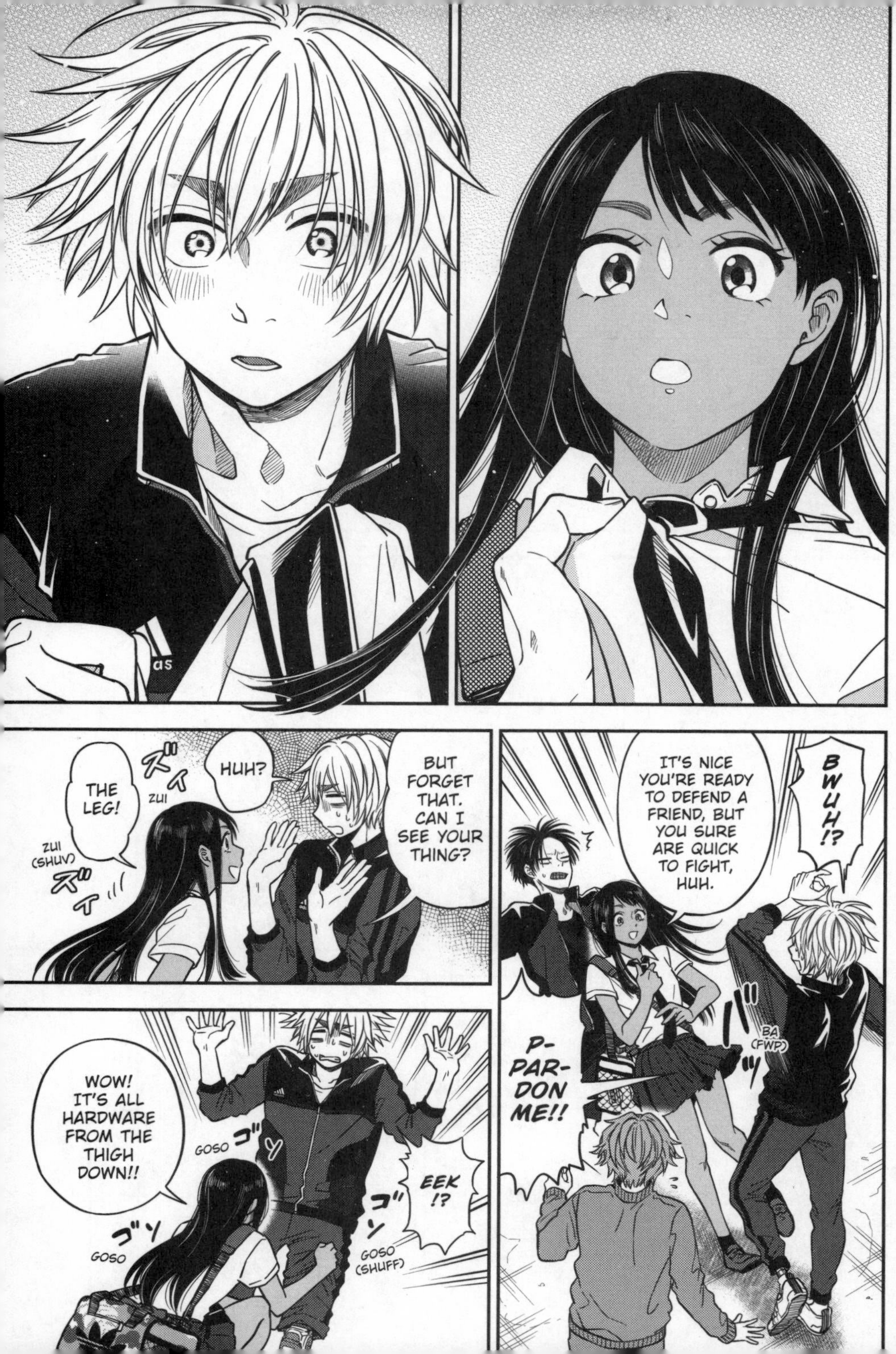
BWUH!?
IT'S NICE YOU'RE READY TO DEFEND A FRIEND, BUT YOU SURE ARE QUICK TO FIGHT, HUH.
BA (FWP)
P-PARDON ME!!
BUT FORGET THAT. CAN I SEE YOUR THING?
HUH?
ZUI
THE LEG!
ZUI (SHUV)
EEK!?
GOSO (SHUFF)
WOW! IT'S ALL HARDWARE FROM THE THIGH DOWN!!
GOSO
GOSO

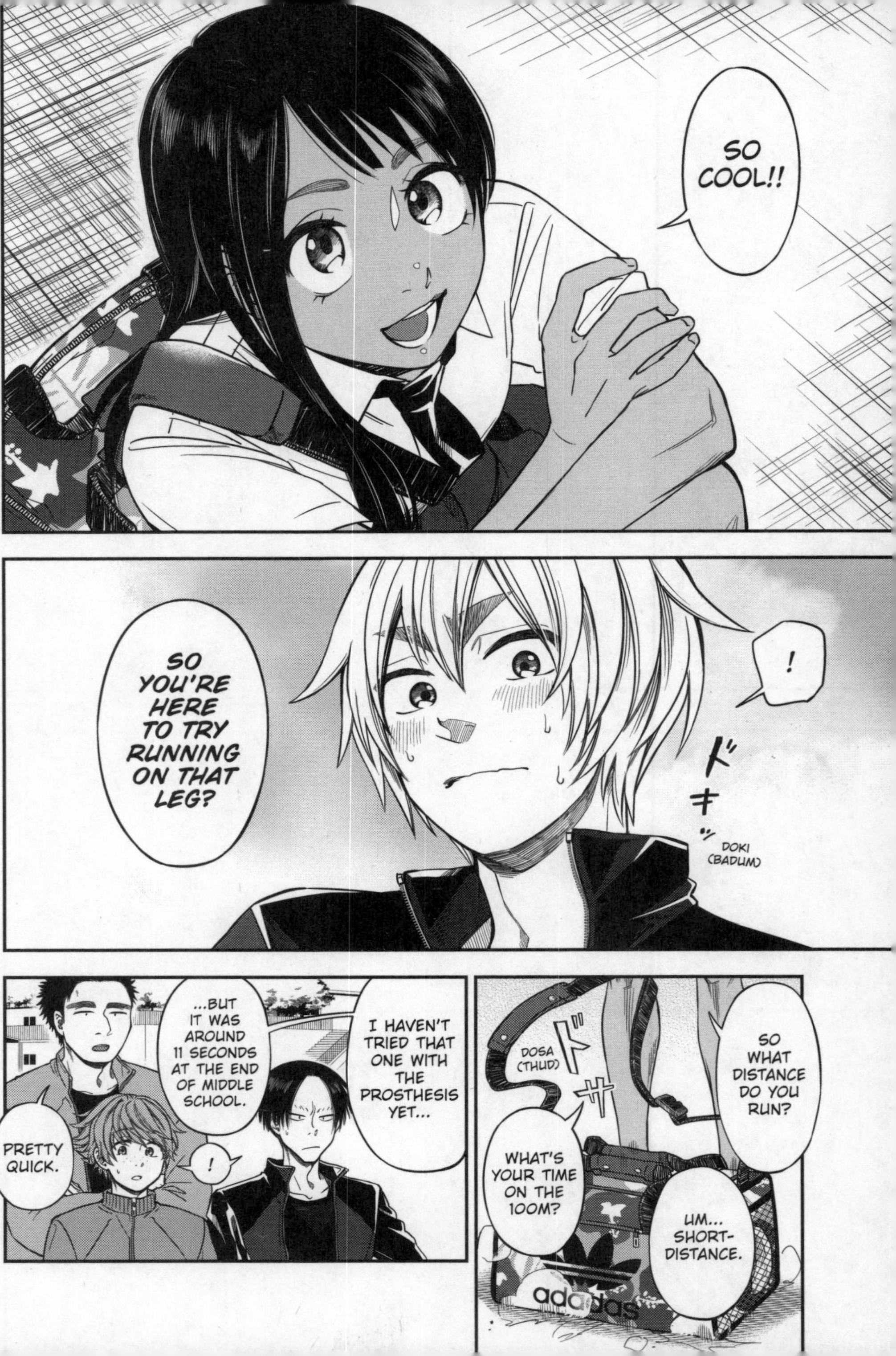
SO COOL!!
SO YOU'RE HERE TO TRY RUNNING ON THAT LEG?
!
ドキッ
DOKI (BADUM)
SO WHAT DISTANCE DO YOU RUN?
ドサ
DOSA (THUD)
UM... SHORT-DISTANCE.
WHAT'S YOUR TIME ON THE 100M?
I HAVEN'T TRIED THAT ONE WITH THE PROSTHESIS YET...
...BUT IT WAS AROUND 11 SECONDS AT THE END OF MIDDLE SCHOOL.
!
PRETTY QUICK.

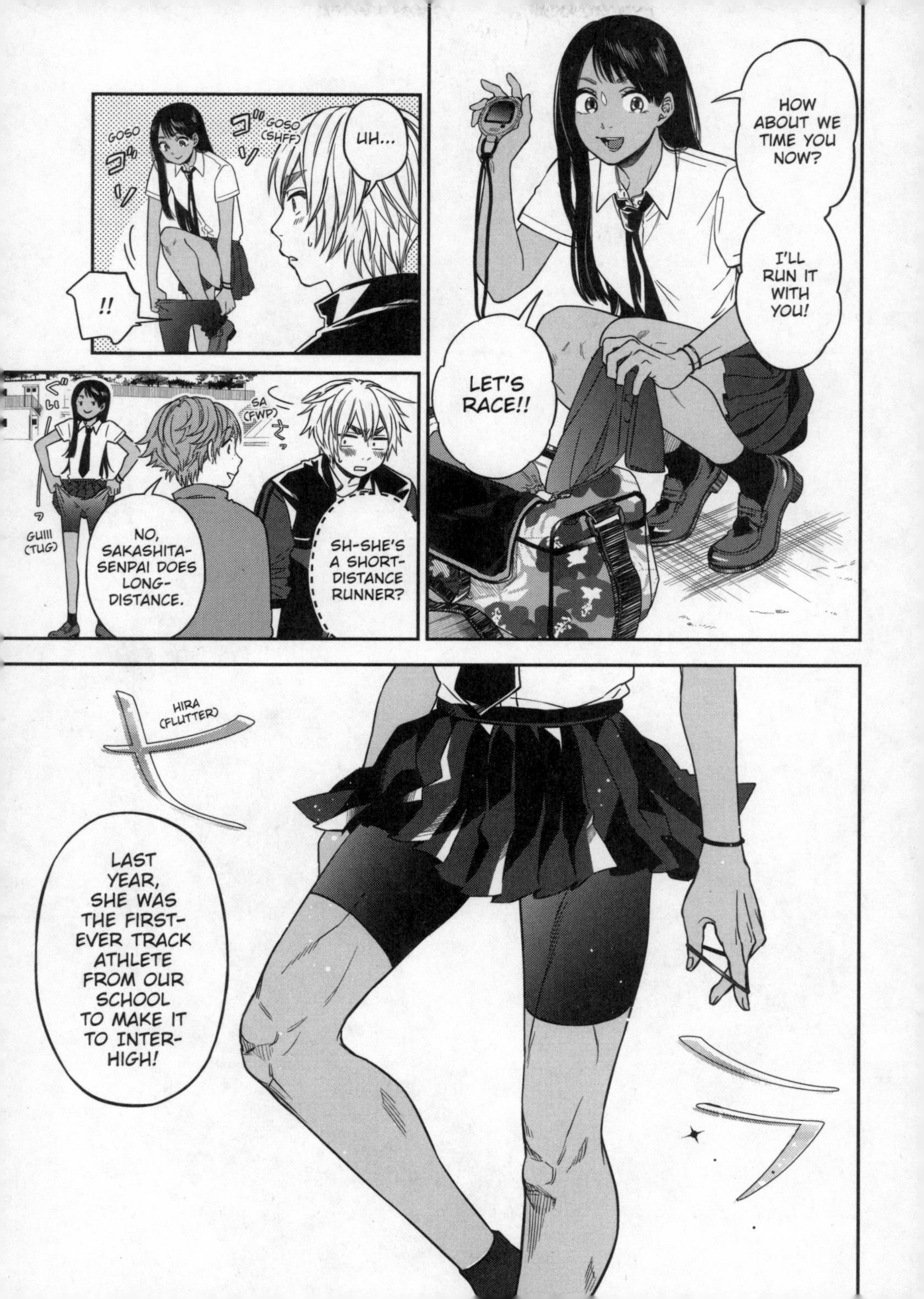
HOW ABOUT WE TIME YOU NOW?
I'LL RUN IT WITH YOU!
LET'S RACE!!
GOSO (SHFF)
GOSO
UH...
!!
SA (FWP)
SH-SHE'S A SHORT-DISTANCE RUNNER?
NO, SAKASHITA-SENPAI DOES LONG-DISTANCE.
GUIII (TUG)
HIRA (FLUTTER)
LAST YEAR, SHE WAS THE FIRST-EVER TRACK ATHLETE FROM OUR SCHOOL TO MAKE IT TO INTER-HIGH!

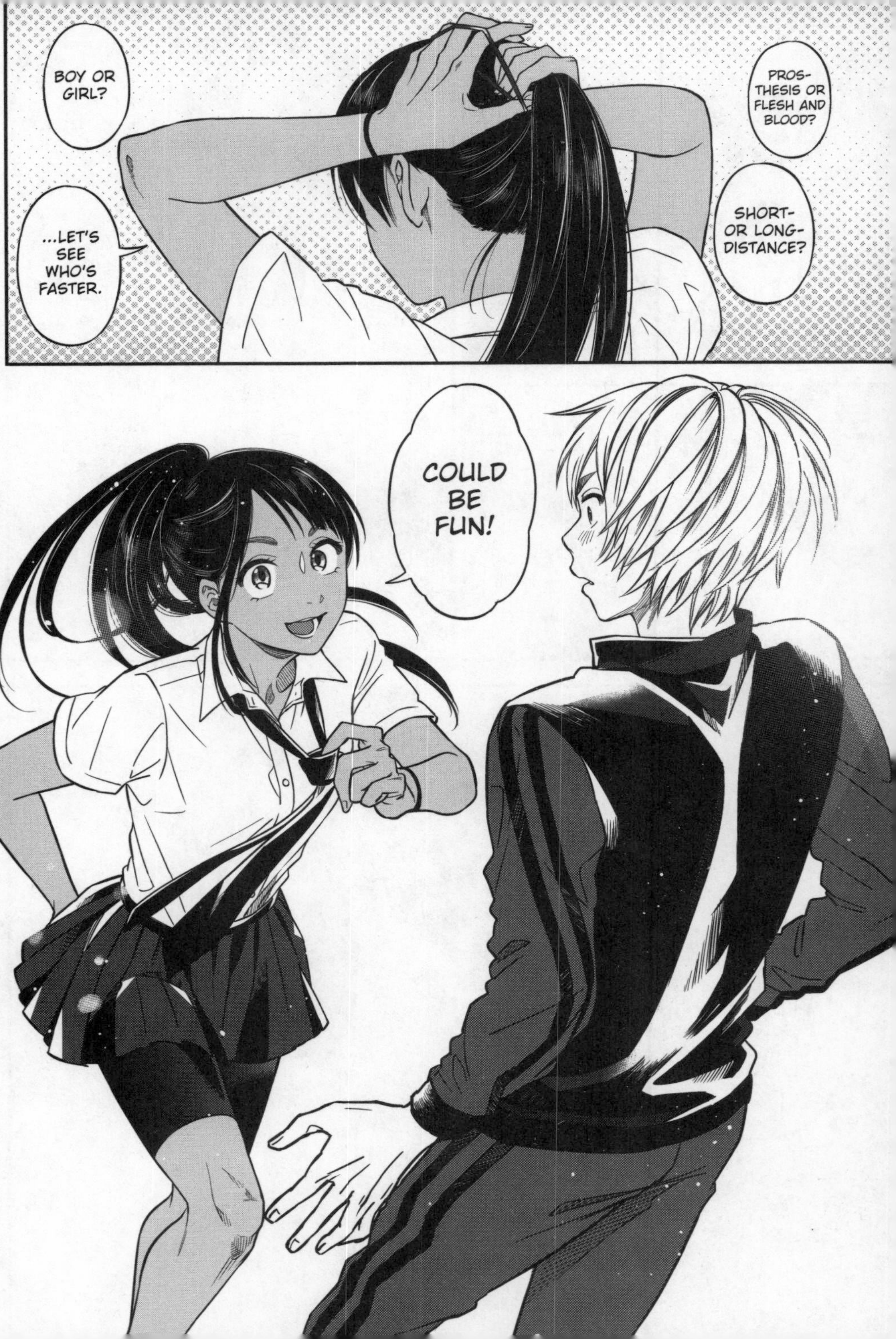
PROS-THESIS OR FLESH AND BLOOD?
BOY OR GIRL?
SHORT- OR LONG-DISTANCE?
...LET'S SEE WHO'S FASTER.
COULD BE FUN!

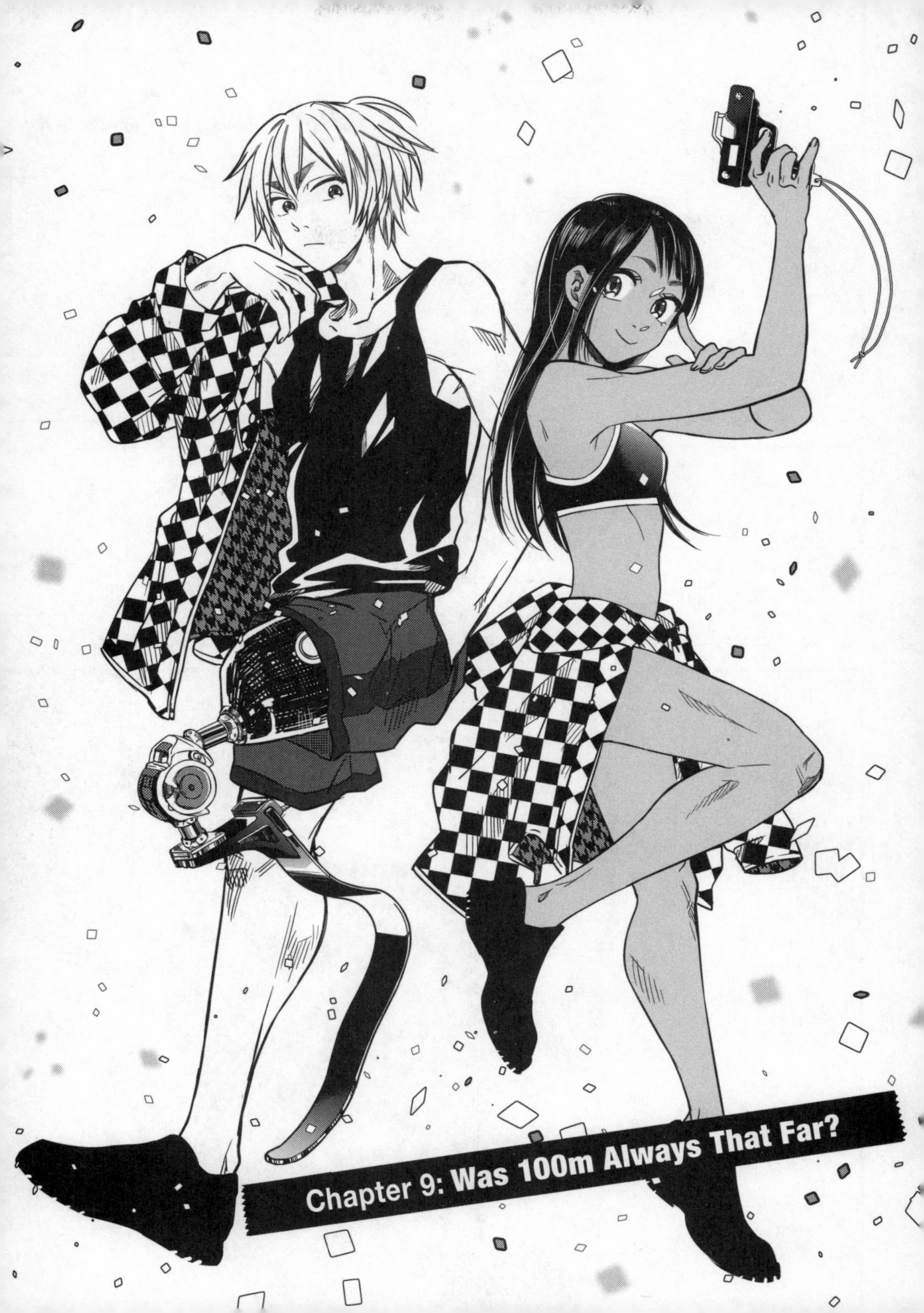
Chapter 9: Was 100m Always That Far?

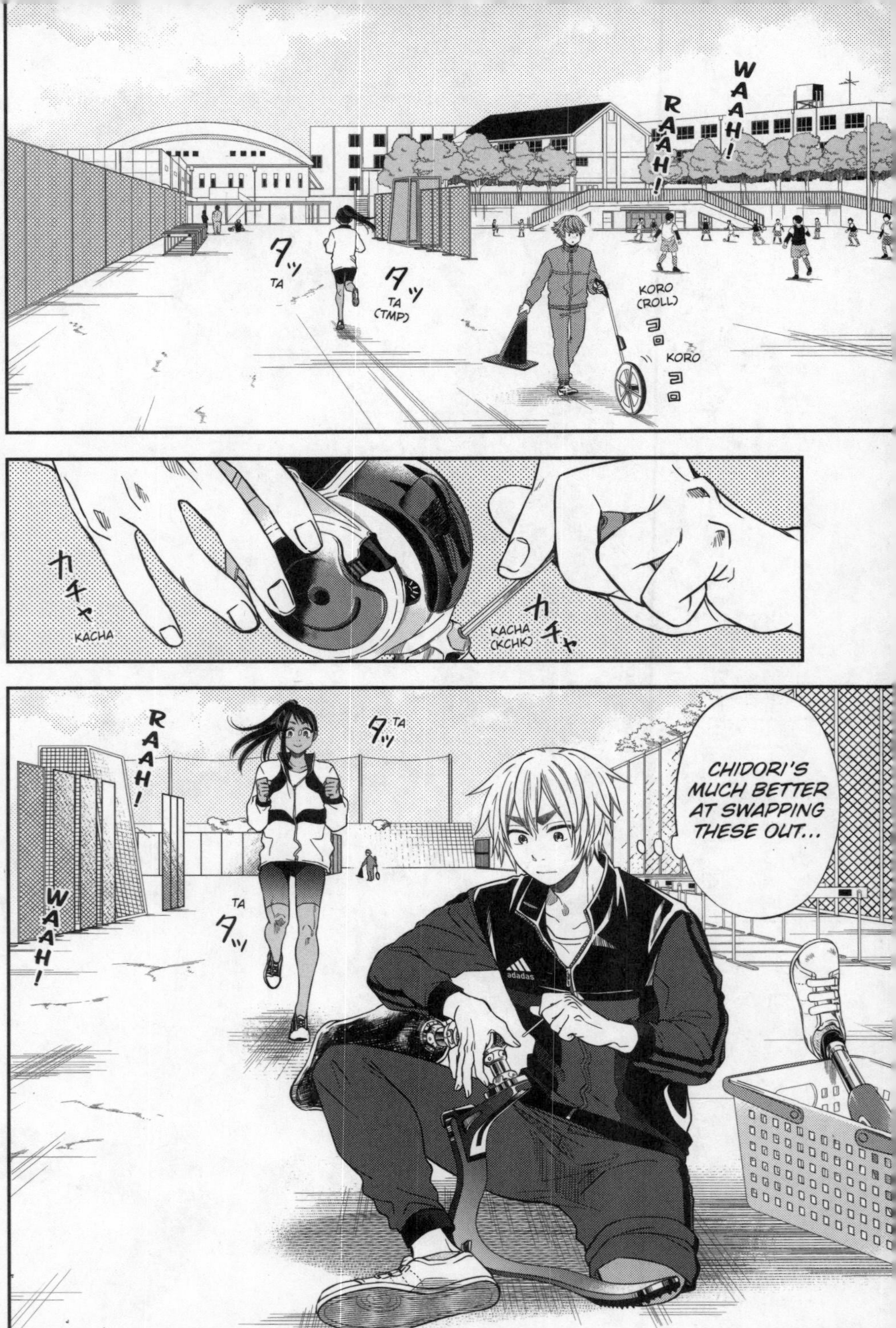
WAAAH!
RAAAH!
KORO (ROLL)
コロ
KORO
コロ
タッ
TA (TMP)
タッ
TA
カチャ
KACHA (KCHK)
カチャ
KACHA
CHIDORI'S MUCH BETTER AT SWAPPING THESE OUT...
タッ
TA
RAAAH!
TA
タッ
WAAAH!

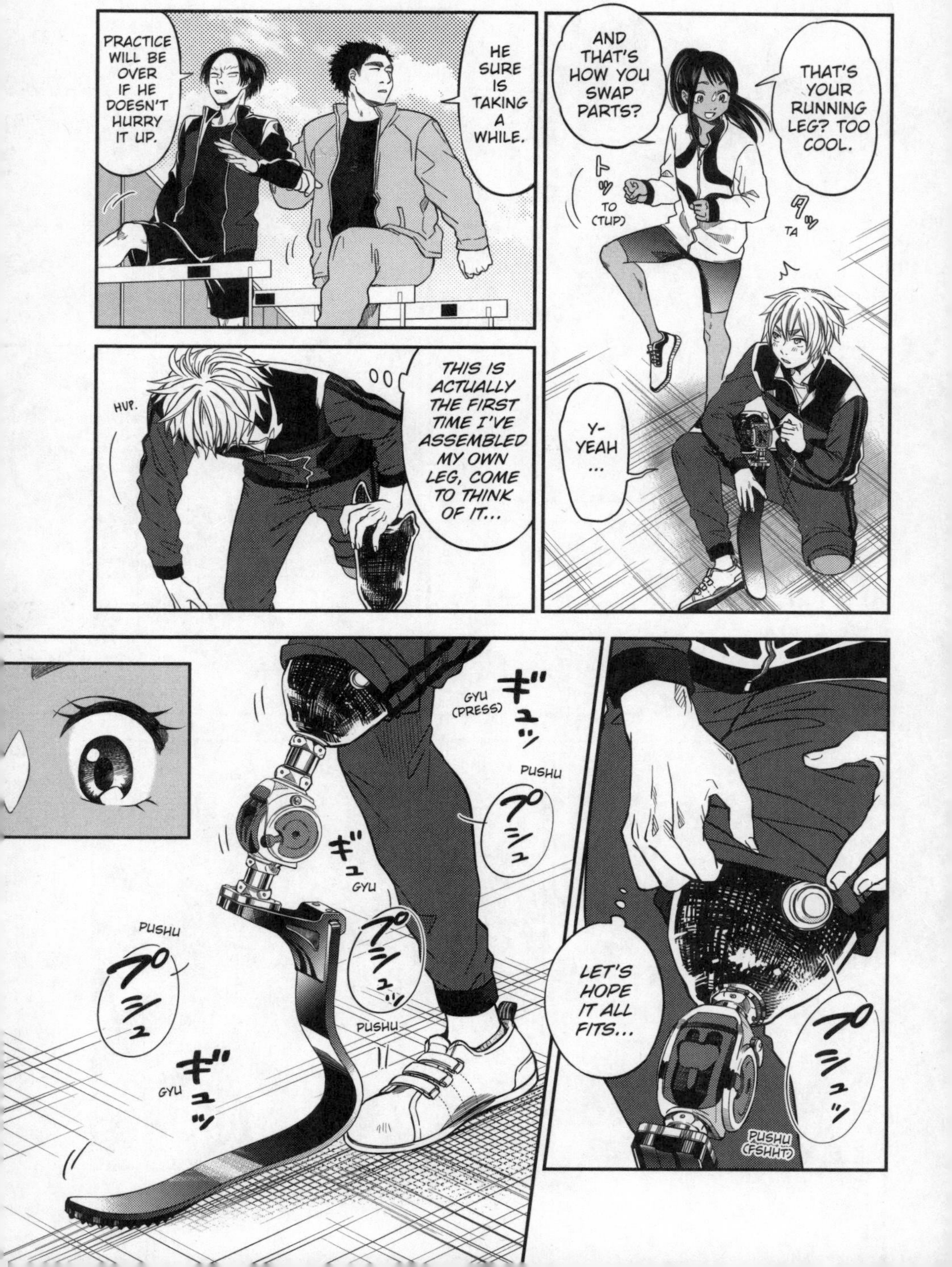
THAT'S YOUR RUNNING LEG? TOO COOL.
ダッ
TA
AND THAT'S HOW YOU SWAP PARTS?
トッ
TO (TUP)
Y-YEAH ...
HE SURE IS TAKING A WHILE.
PRACTICE WILL BE OVER IF HE DOESN'T HURRY IT UP.
THIS IS ACTUALLY THE FIRST TIME I'VE ASSEMBLED MY OWN LEG, COME TO THINK OF IT...
HUP.
LET'S HOPE IT ALL FITS...
プシュッ
PUSHU (FSHHT)
ギュッ
GYU (PRESS)
プシュ
PUSHU
ギュ
GYU
プシュッ
PUSHU
プシュ
PUSHU
ギュッ
GYU

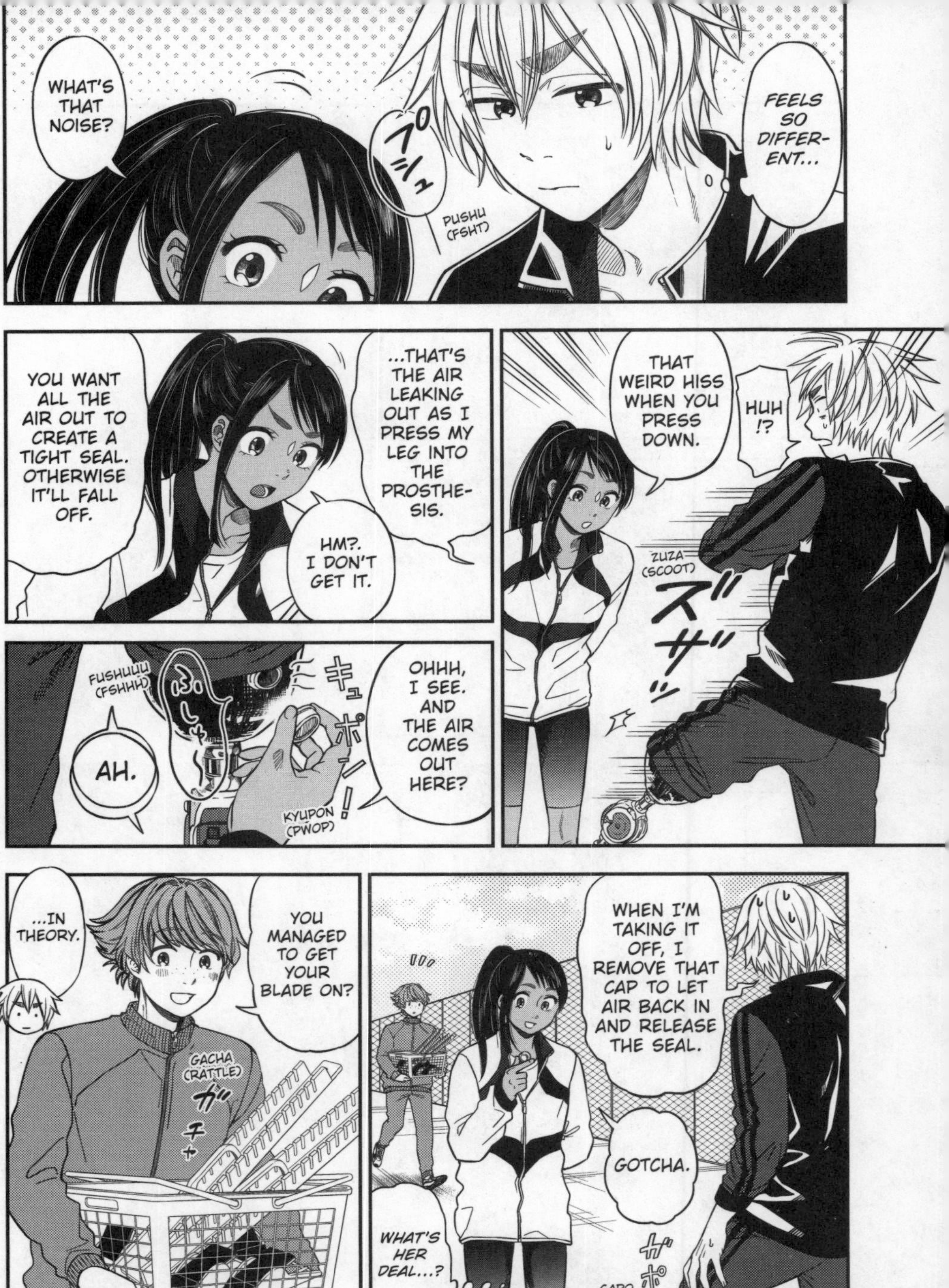
FEELS SO DIFFERENT...
プシュ
PUSHU (FSHT)
WHAT'S THAT NOISE?
HUH!?
THAT WEIRD HISS WHEN YOU PRESS DOWN.
ズザッ
ZUZA (SCOOT)
...THAT'S THE AIR LEAKING OUT AS I PRESS MY LEG INTO THE PROSTHESIS.
YOU WANT ALL THE AIR OUT TO CREATE A TIGHT SEAL. OTHERWISE IT'LL FALL OFF.
HM?. I DON'T GET IT.
OHHH, I SEE. AND THE AIR COMES OUT HERE?
キュポーン!
KYUPON (PWOP)
ふしゅ
FUSHUUU (FSHHH)
AH.
WHEN I'M TAKING IT OFF, I REMOVE THAT CAP TO LET AIR BACK IN AND RELEASE THE SEAL.
GOTCHA.
WHAT'S HER DEAL...?
ガポ
GAPO (PWOK)
YOU MANAGED TO GET YOUR BLADE ON?
...IN THEORY.
GACHA (RATTLE)
ガチャ

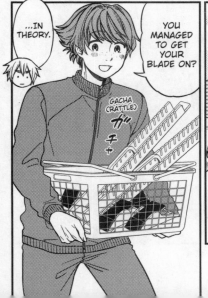

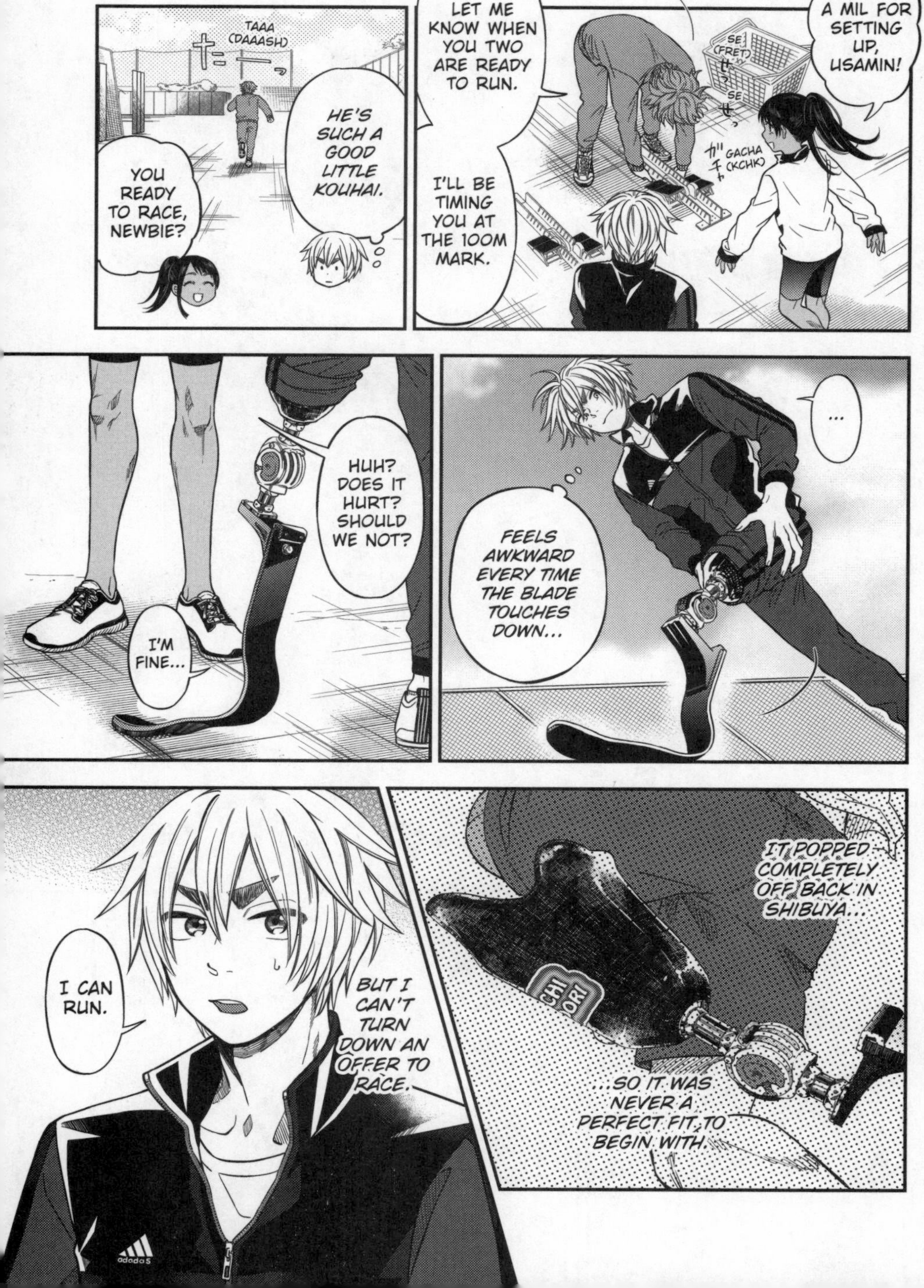
THANKS A MIL FOR SETTING UP, USAMIN!
SE (FRET) SE
GACHA (KCHK)
LET ME KNOW WHEN YOU TWO ARE READY TO RUN.
I'LL BE TIMING YOU AT THE 100M MARK.
TAAA (DAAASH)
HE'S SUCH A GOOD LITTLE KOUHAI.
YOU READY TO RACE, NEWBIE?
...
FEELS AWKWARD EVERY TIME THE BLADE TOUCHES DOWN...
HUH? DOES IT HURT? SHOULD WE NOT?
I'M FINE...
IT POPPED COMPLETELY OFF BACK IN SHIBUYA...
...SO IT WAS NEVER A PERFECT FIT TO BEGIN WITH.
BUT I CAN'T TURN DOWN AN OFFER TO RACE.
I CAN RUN.

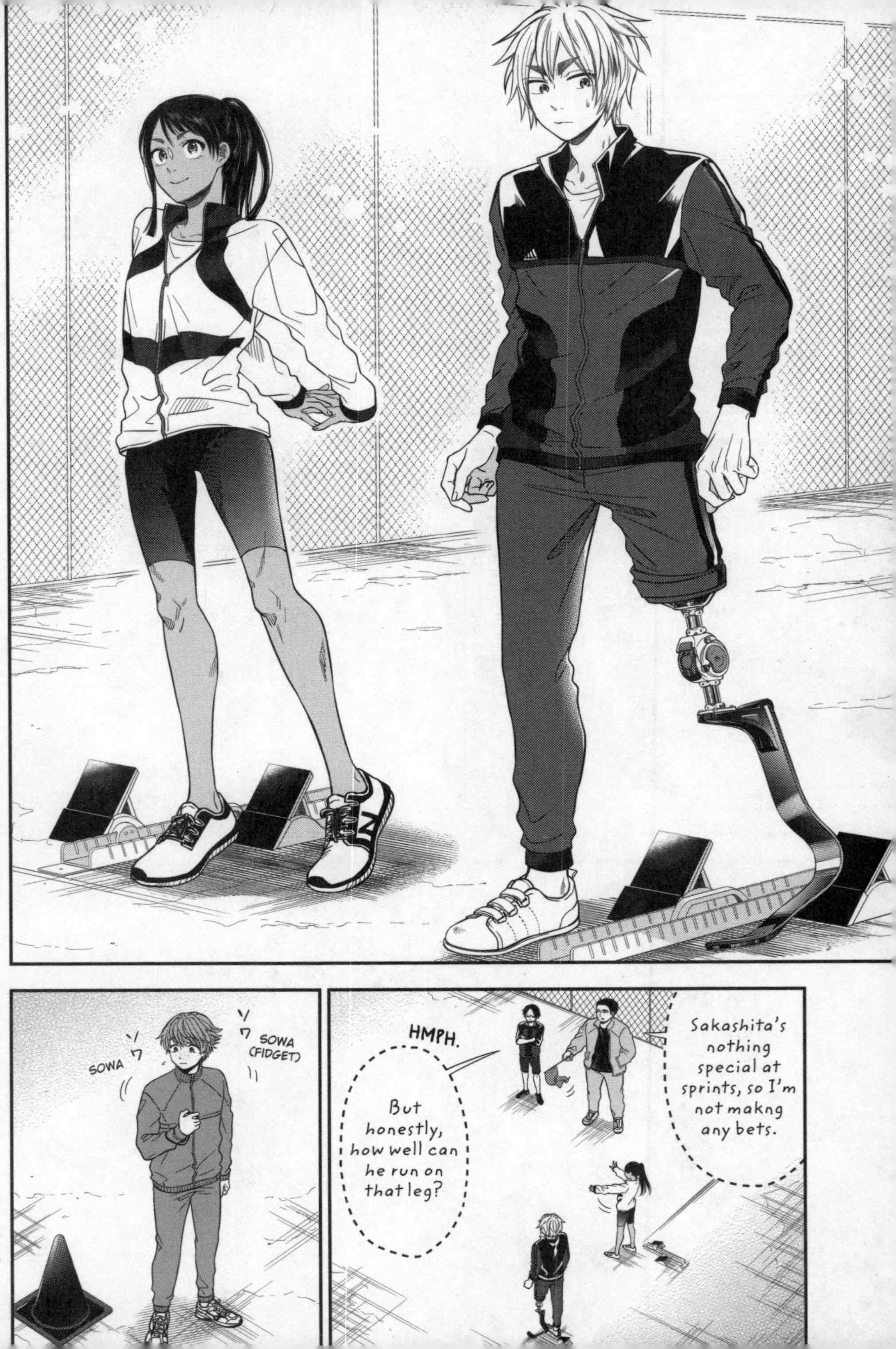
Sakashita's nothing special at sprints, so I'm not makng any bets.
HMPH.
But honestly, how well can he run on that leg?
SOWA (FIDGET)
SOWA

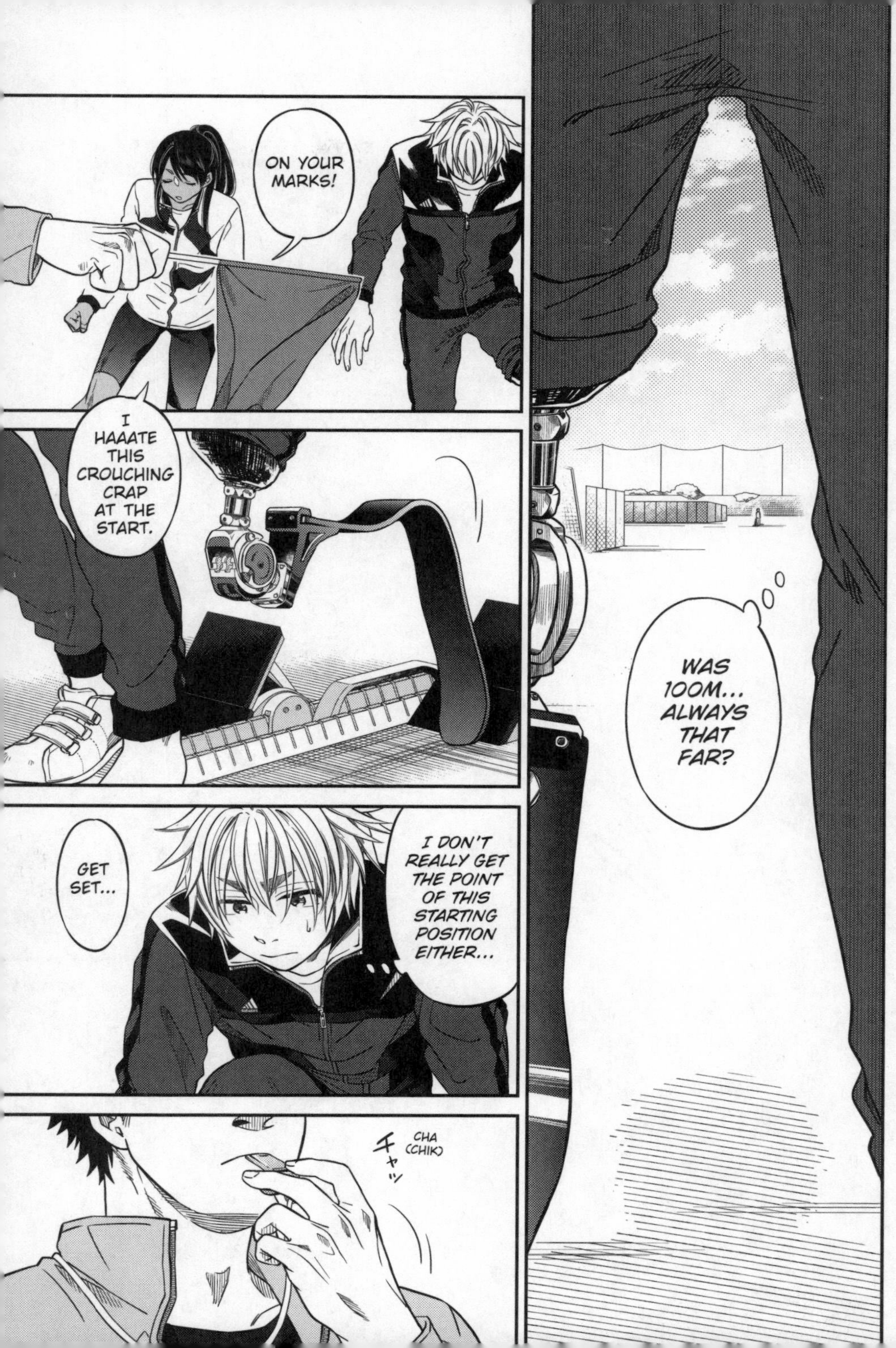
WAS 100M... ALWAYS THAT FAR?
ON YOUR MARKS!
I HAAATE THIS CROUCHING CRAP AT THE START.
I DON'T REALLY GET THE POINT OF THIS STARTING POSITION EITHER...
GET SET...
チャッ
CHA (CHIK)

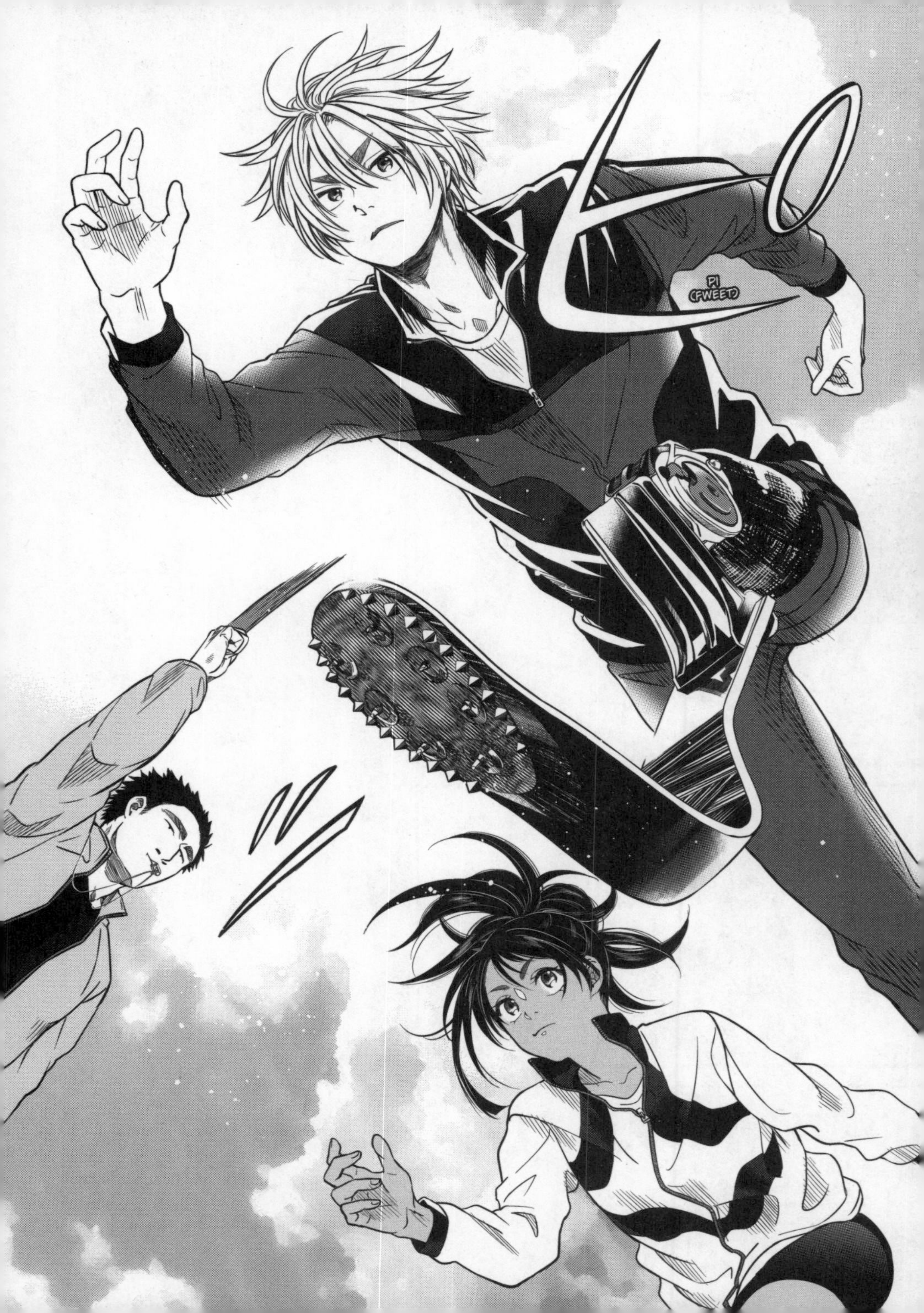
PI
(FWEET)

ZUSHI
(THROB)

GI
(KREEK)

DAN
(SLAM)

BA
(SWING)

DA
(TMP)

DA

DA

MY STUMP AND MY ASS...

...ARE FEELING THE PAIN WHERE THE SOCKET CONNECTS ...!

NHH ...!?

BIRI
(TINGLE)

BIRI

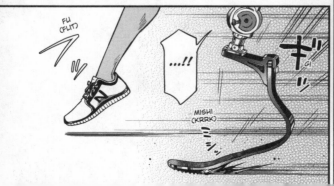

FU
(FLIT)

...!!

GI

MISHI
(KRRK)

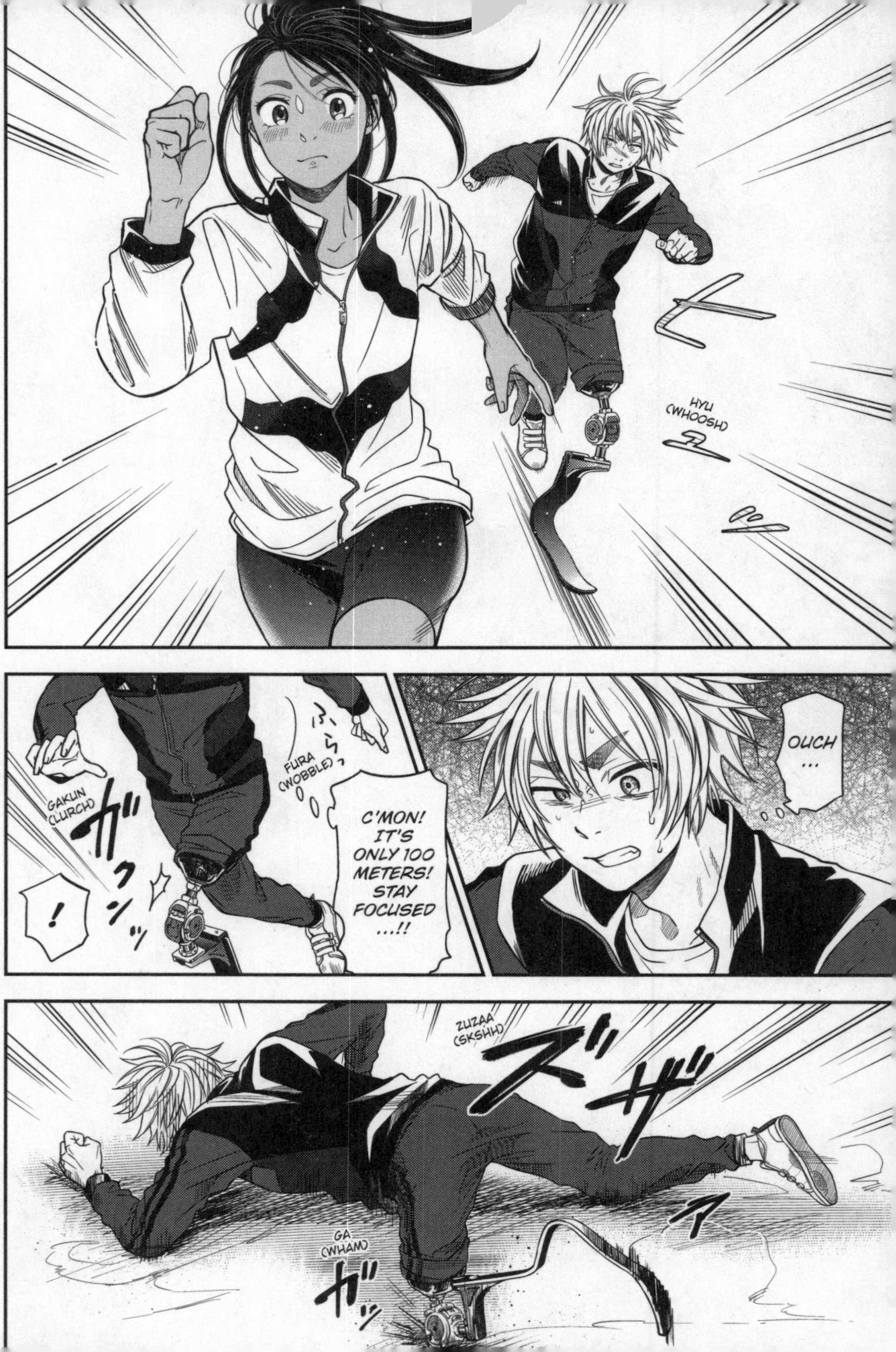
HYU (WHOOSH)
OUCH ...
FURA (WOBBLE)
C'MON! IT'S ONLY 100 METERS! STAY FOCUSED ...!!
GAKUN (LURCH)
!
ZUZAA (SKSHH)
GA (WHAM)

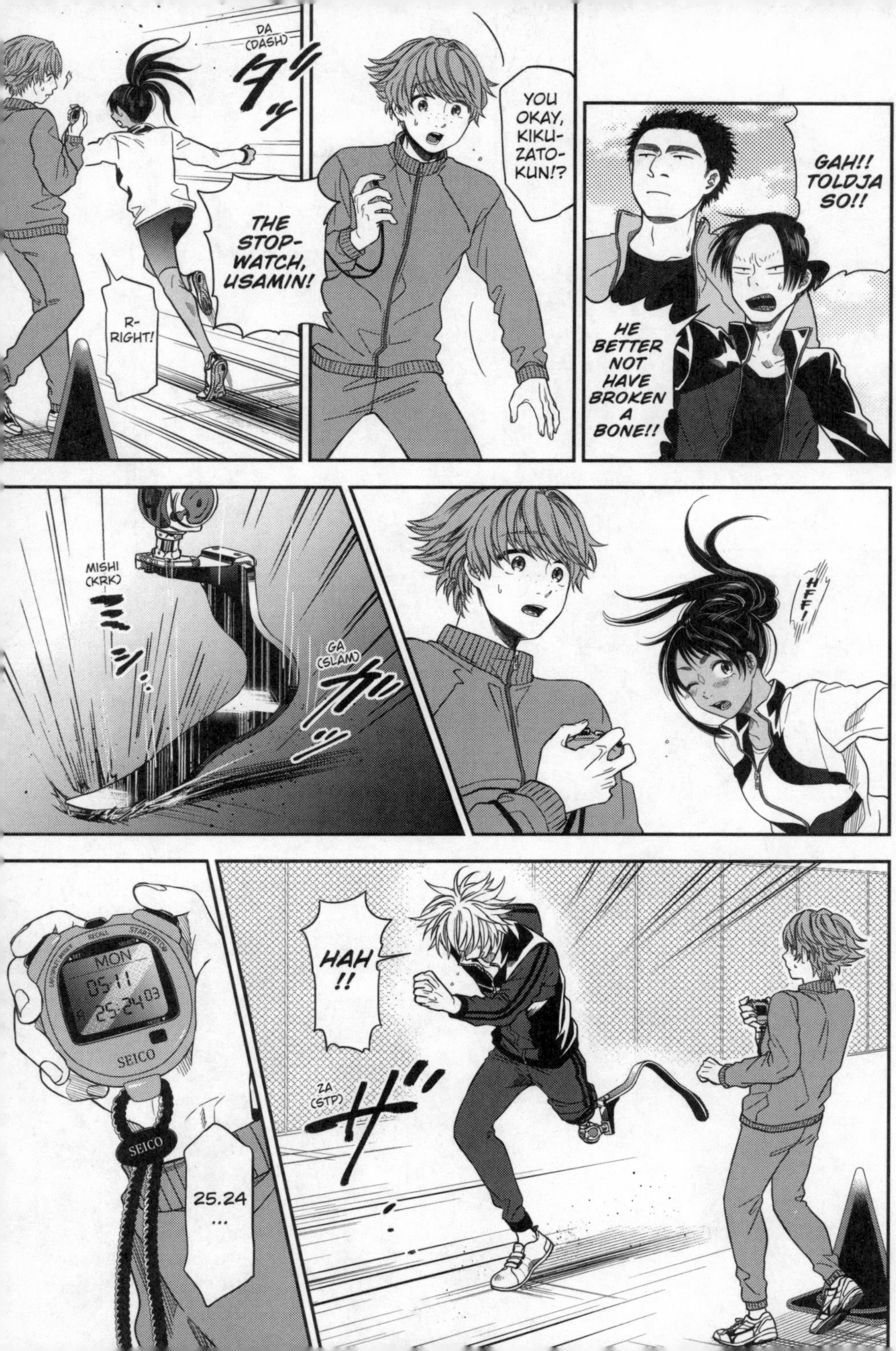
GAH!! TOLDJA SO!!
HE BETTER NOT HAVE BROKEN A BONE!!
YOU OKAY, KIKUZATO-KUN!?
THE STOP-WATCH, USAMIN!
DA (DASH)
R-RIGHT!
HFF!
MISHI (KRK)
GA (SLAM)
HAH!!
ZA (STP)
MON
05-11
25-24 03
SEICO
SEICO
25.24 ...

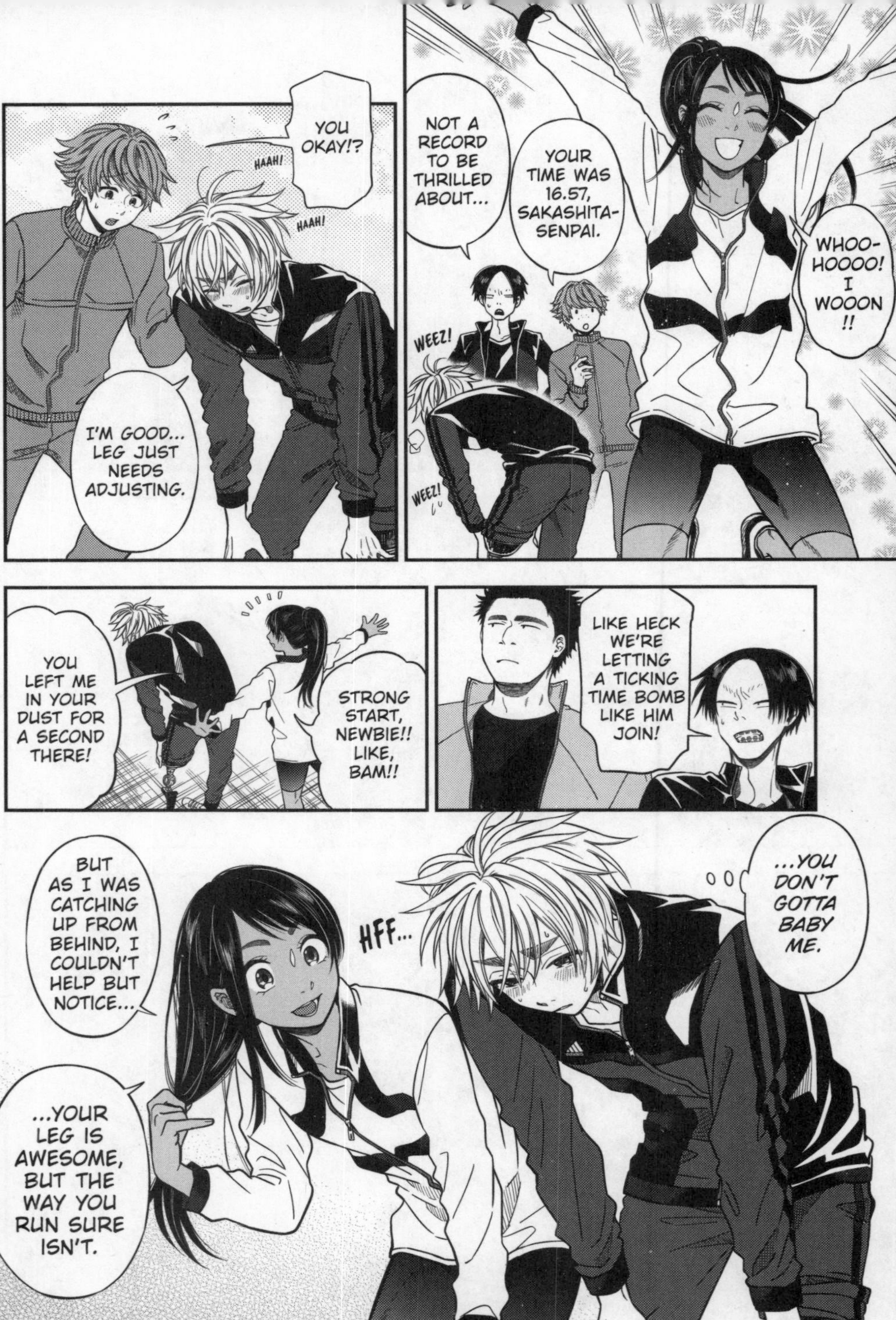
WHOO-HOOOO! I WOOON!!
YOUR TIME WAS 16.57, SAKASHITA-SENPAI.
NOT A RECORD TO BE THRILLED ABOUT...
WEEZ!
WEEZ!
YOU OKAY!?
HAAH!
HAAH!
I'M GOOD... LEG JUST NEEDS ADJUSTING.
LIKE HECK WE'RE LETTING A TICKING TIME BOMB LIKE HIM JOIN!
STRONG START, NEWBIE!! LIKE, BAM!!
YOU LEFT ME IN YOUR DUST FOR A SECOND THERE!
...YOU DON'T GOTTA BABY ME.
HFF...
BUT AS I WAS CATCHING UP FROM BEHIND, I COULDN'T HELP BUT NOTICE...
...YOUR LEG IS AWESOME, BUT THE WAY YOU RUN SURE ISN'T.

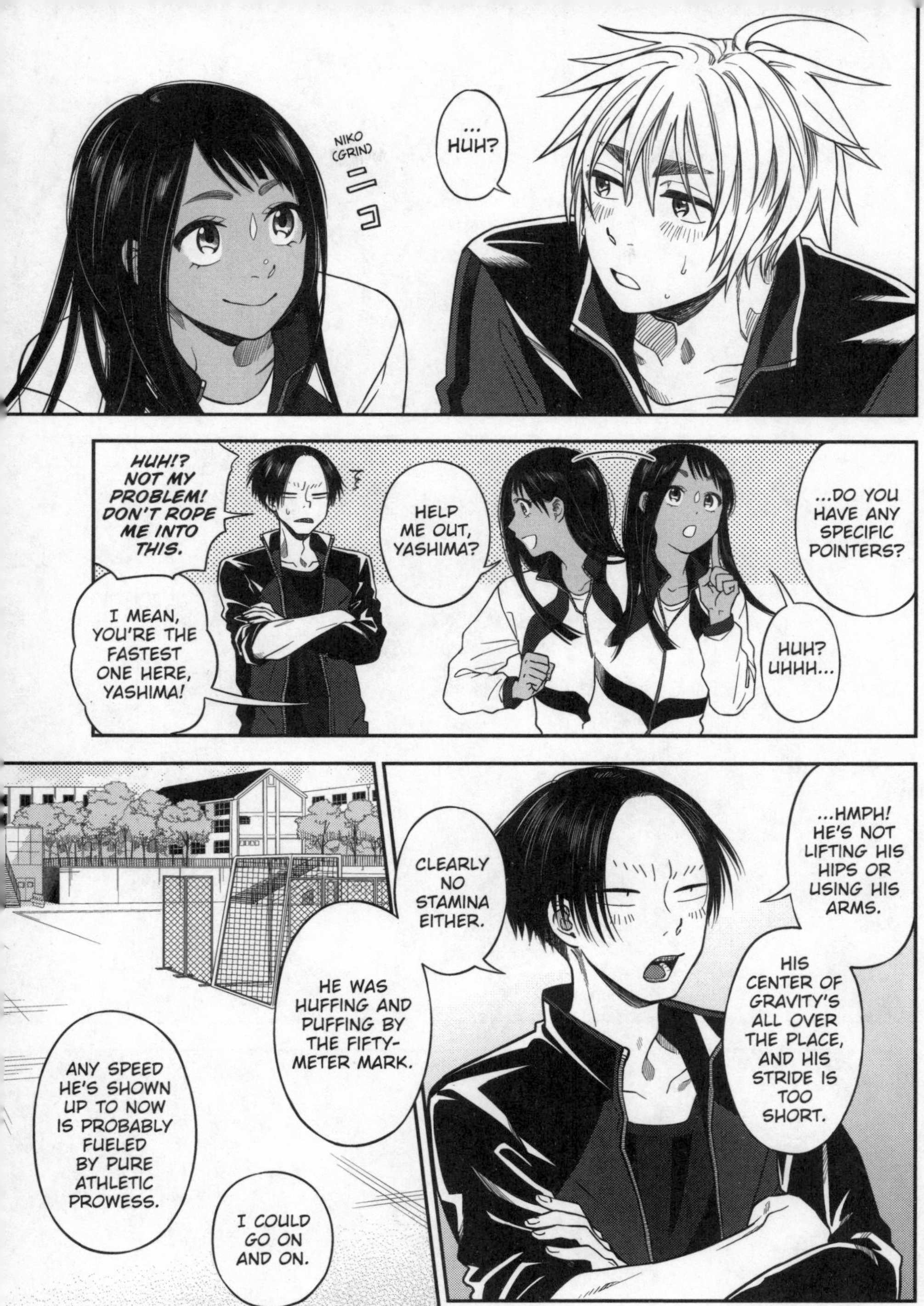
...HUH?
NIKO (GRIN)
ニコ
...DO YOU HAVE ANY SPECIFIC POINTERS?
HUH? UHHH...
HELP ME OUT, YASHIMA?
I MEAN, YOU'RE THE FASTEST ONE HERE, YASHIMA!
HUH!? NOT MY PROBLEM! DON'T ROPE ME INTO THIS.
...HMPH! HE'S NOT LIFTING HIS HIPS OR USING HIS ARMS.
HIS CENTER OF GRAVITY'S ALL OVER THE PLACE, AND HIS STRIDE IS TOO SHORT.
CLEARLY NO STAMINA EITHER.
HE WAS HUFFING AND PUFFING BY THE FIFTY-METER MARK.
ANY SPEED HE'S SHOWN UP TO NOW IS PROBABLY FUELED BY PURE ATHLETIC PROWESS.
I COULD GO ON AND ON.

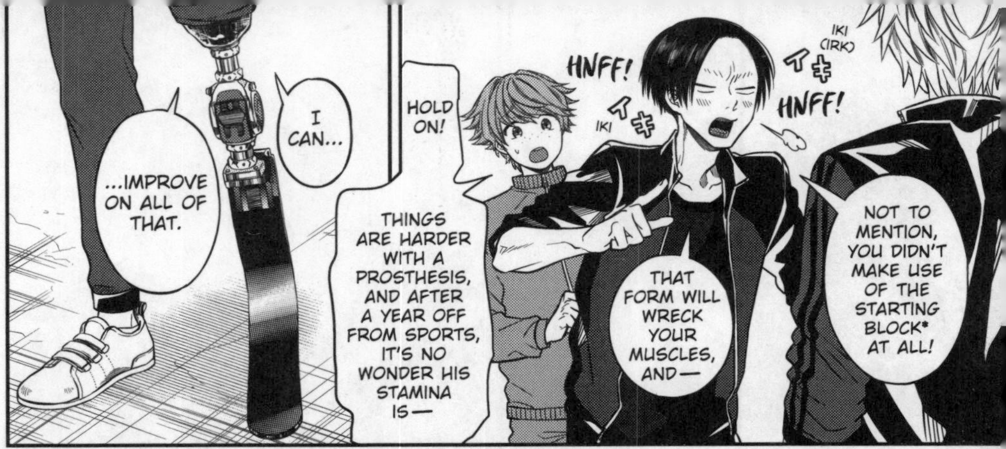
IKI (IRK)
イキ
HNFF!
NOT TO MENTION, YOU DIDN'T MAKE USE OF THE STARTING BLOCK* AT ALL!
HNFF!
イキ
IKI
THAT FORM WILL WRECK YOUR MUSCLES, AND—
HOLD ON!
THINGS ARE HARDER WITH A PROSTHESIS, AND AFTER A YEAR OFF FROM SPORTS, IT'S NO WONDER HIS STAMINA IS—
I CAN...
...IMPROVE ON ALL OF THAT.

*THE STARTING BLOCK IS USED FOR A CROUCHING START IN SHORT-DISTANCE RACING.

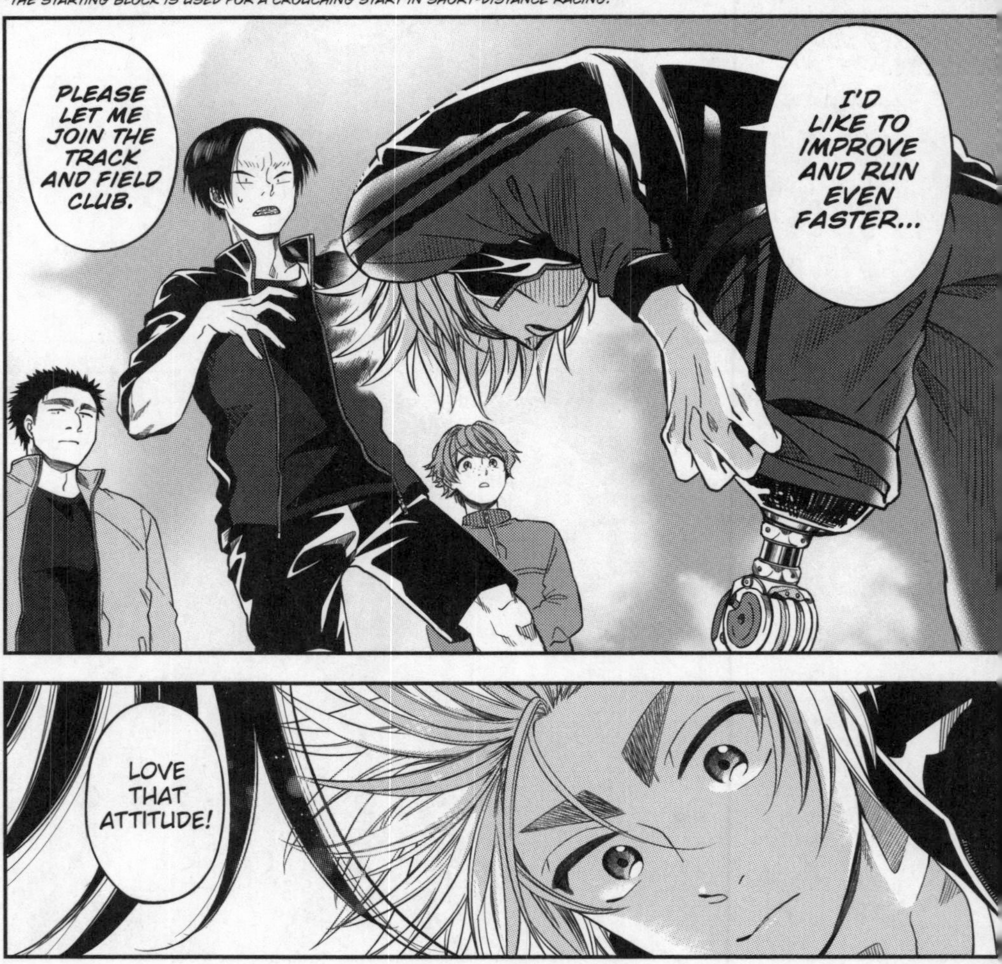
I'D LIKE TO IMPROVE AND RUN EVEN FASTER...
PLEASE LET ME JOIN THE TRACK AND FIELD CLUB.
LOVE THAT ATTITUDE!

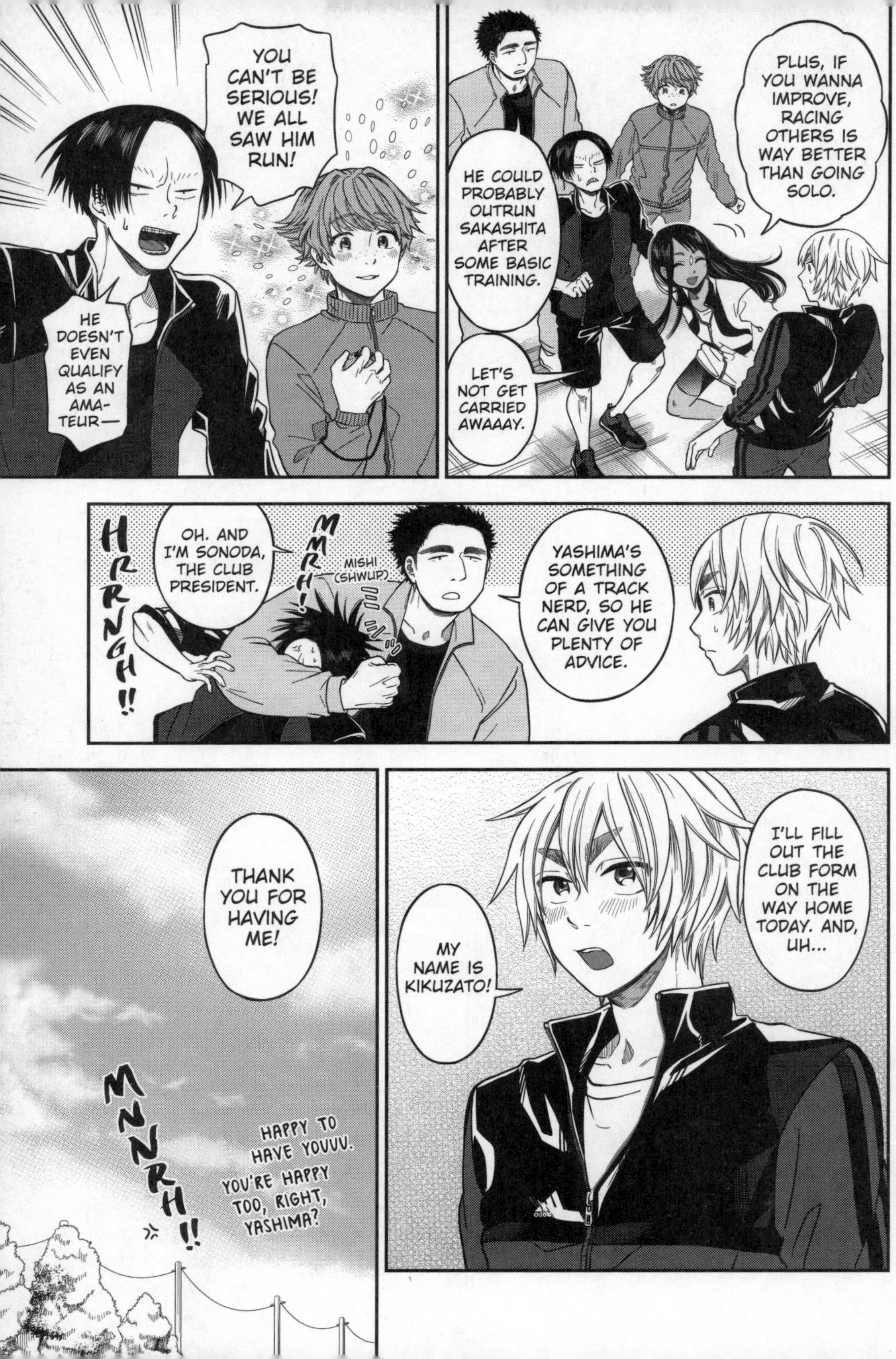
PLUS, IF YOU WANNA IMPROVE, RACING OTHERS IS WAY BETTER THAN GOING SOLO.
HE COULD PROBABLY OUTRUN SAKASHITA AFTER SOME BASIC TRAINING.
LET'S NOT GET CARRIED AWAAAY.
YOU CAN'T BE SERIOUS! WE ALL SAW HIM RUN!
HE DOESN'T EVEN QUALIFY AS AN AMA-TEUR—
YASHIMA'S SOMETHING OF A TRACK NERD, SO HE CAN GIVE YOU PLENTY OF ADVICE.
MMRH!
MISHI (SHWUP)
OH. AND I'M SONODA, THE CLUB PRESIDENT.
HRRNGH!!
I'LL FILL OUT THE CLUB FORM ON THE WAY HOME TODAY. AND, UH...
MY NAME IS KIKUZATO!
THANK YOU FOR HAVING ME!
HAPPY TO HAVE YOUUU.
YOU'RE HAPPY TOO, RIGHT, YASHIMA?
MNNRH!!

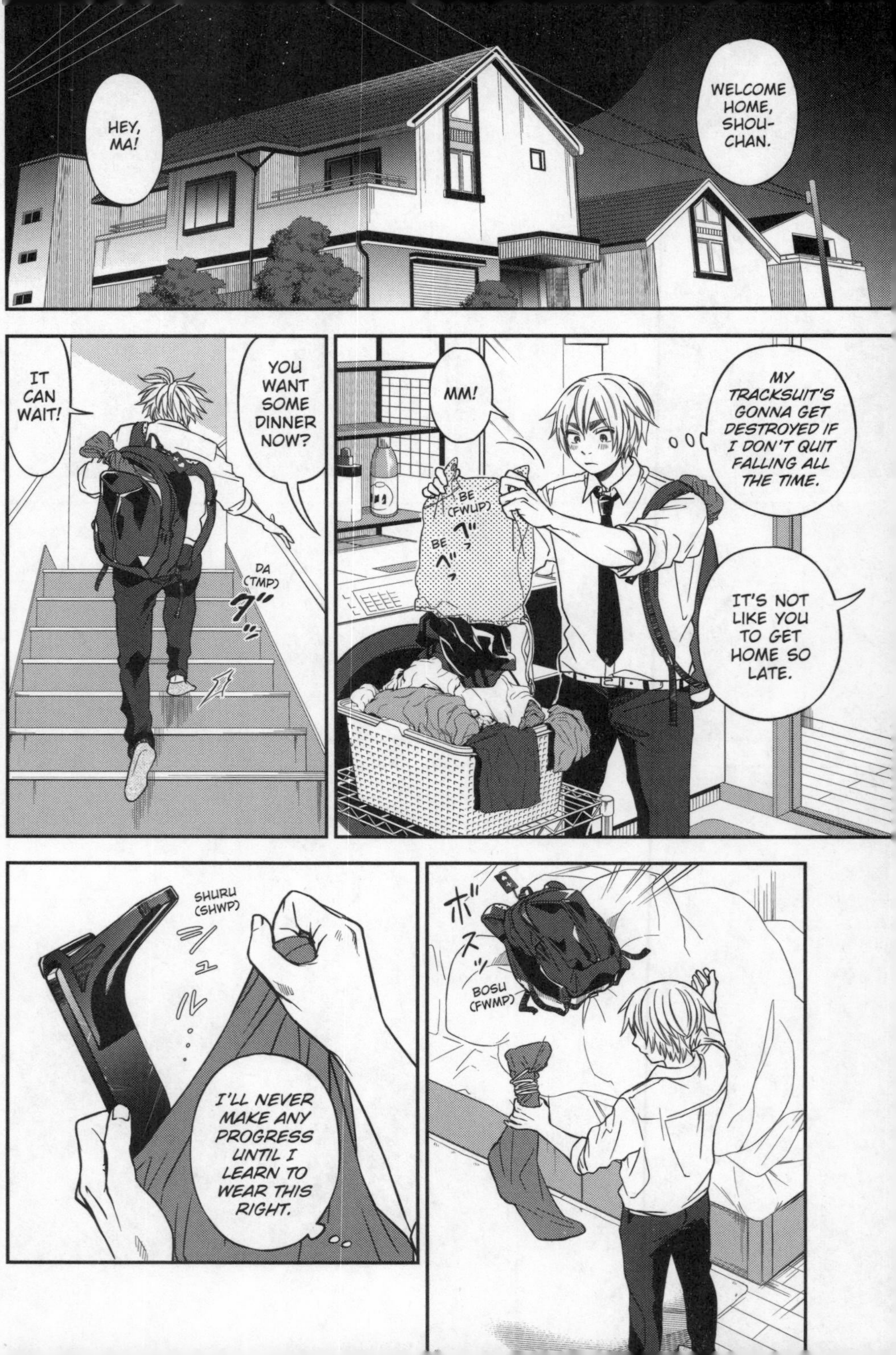
WELCOME HOME, SHOU-CHAN.
HEY, MA!
MY TRACKSUIT'S GONNA GET DESTROYED IF I DON'T QUIT FALLING ALL THE TIME.
MM!
IT'S NOT LIKE YOU TO GET HOME SO LATE.
BE (FWUP)
BE
YOU WANT SOME DINNER NOW?
IT CAN WAIT!
DA (TMP)
BOSU (FWMP)
SHURU (SHWP)
I'LL NEVER MAKE ANY PROGRESS UNTIL I LEARN TO WEAR THIS RIGHT.

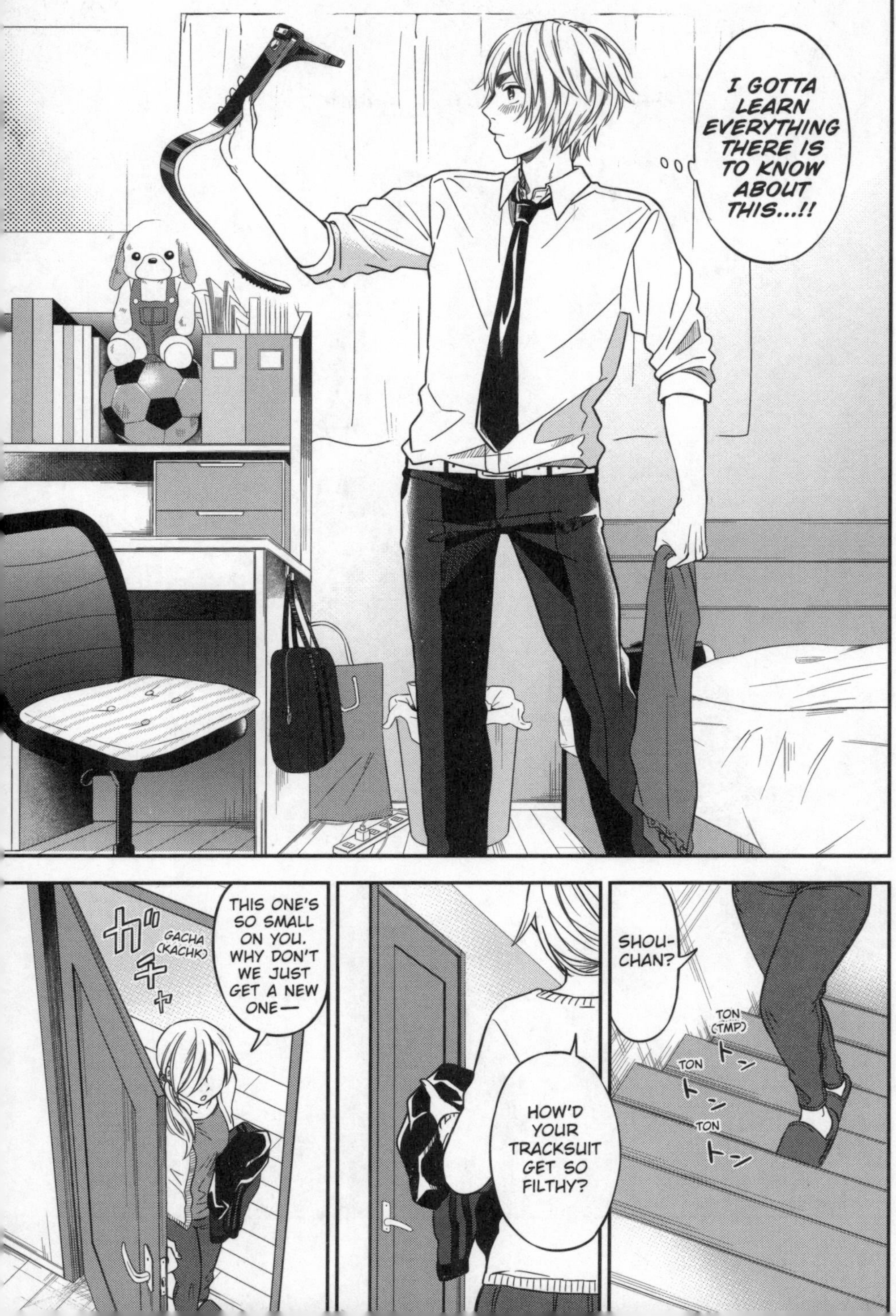
I GOTTA LEARN EVERYTHING THERE IS TO KNOW ABOUT THIS...!!
SHOU-CHAN?
トン TON (TMP)
トン TON
トン TON
HOW'D YOUR TRACKSUIT GET SO FILTHY?
THIS ONE'S SO SMALL ON YOU. WHY DON'T WE JUST GET A NEW ONE—
ガチャ GACHA (KACHK)

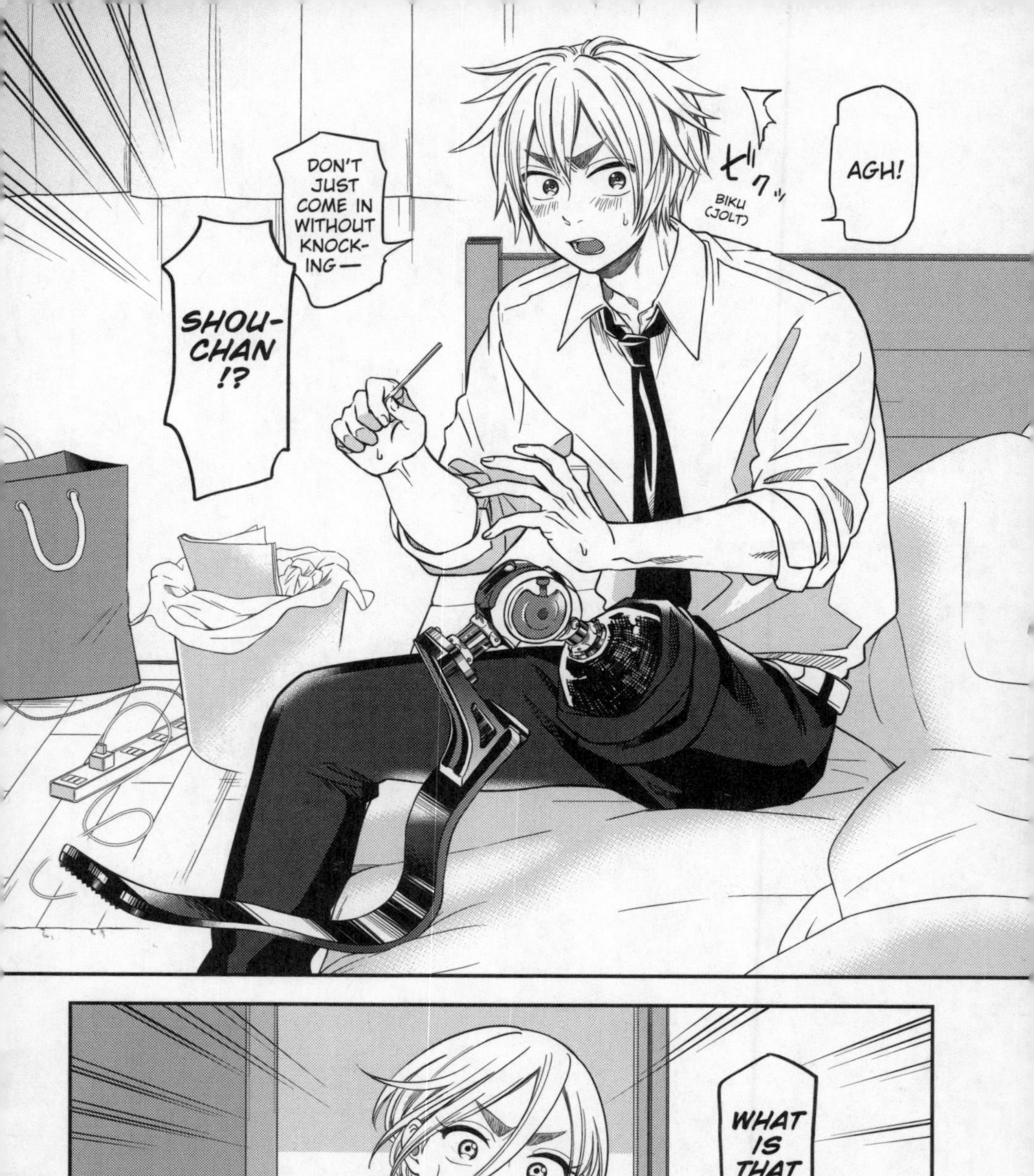
AGH!
ビクッ
BIKU (JOLT)
DON'T JUST COME IN WITHOUT KNOCKING—
SHOU-CHAN!?

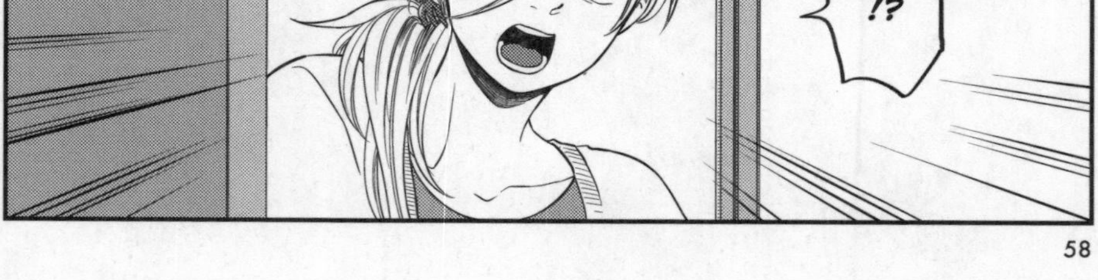
WHAT IS THAT!?

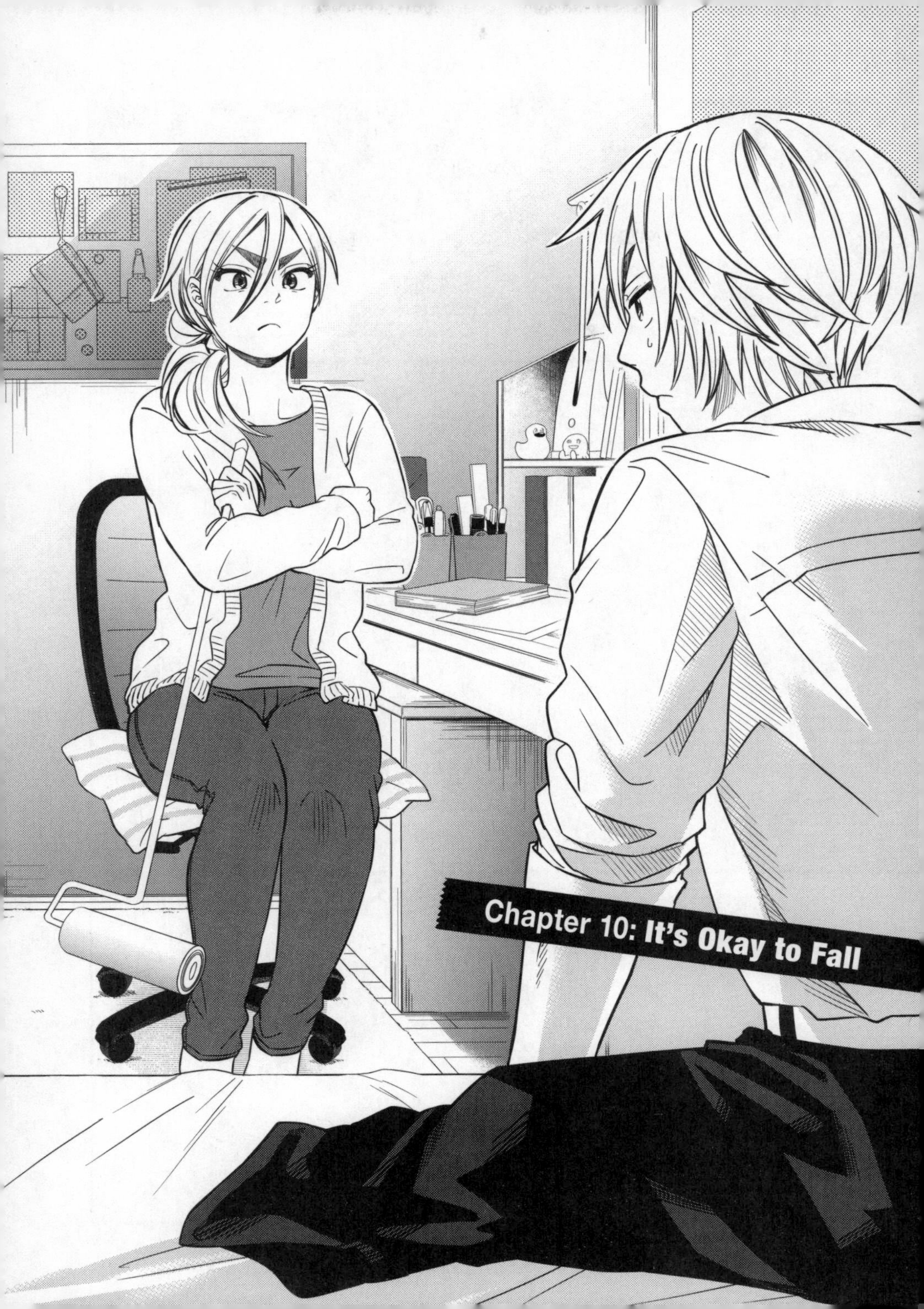
Chapter 10: It's Okay to Fall

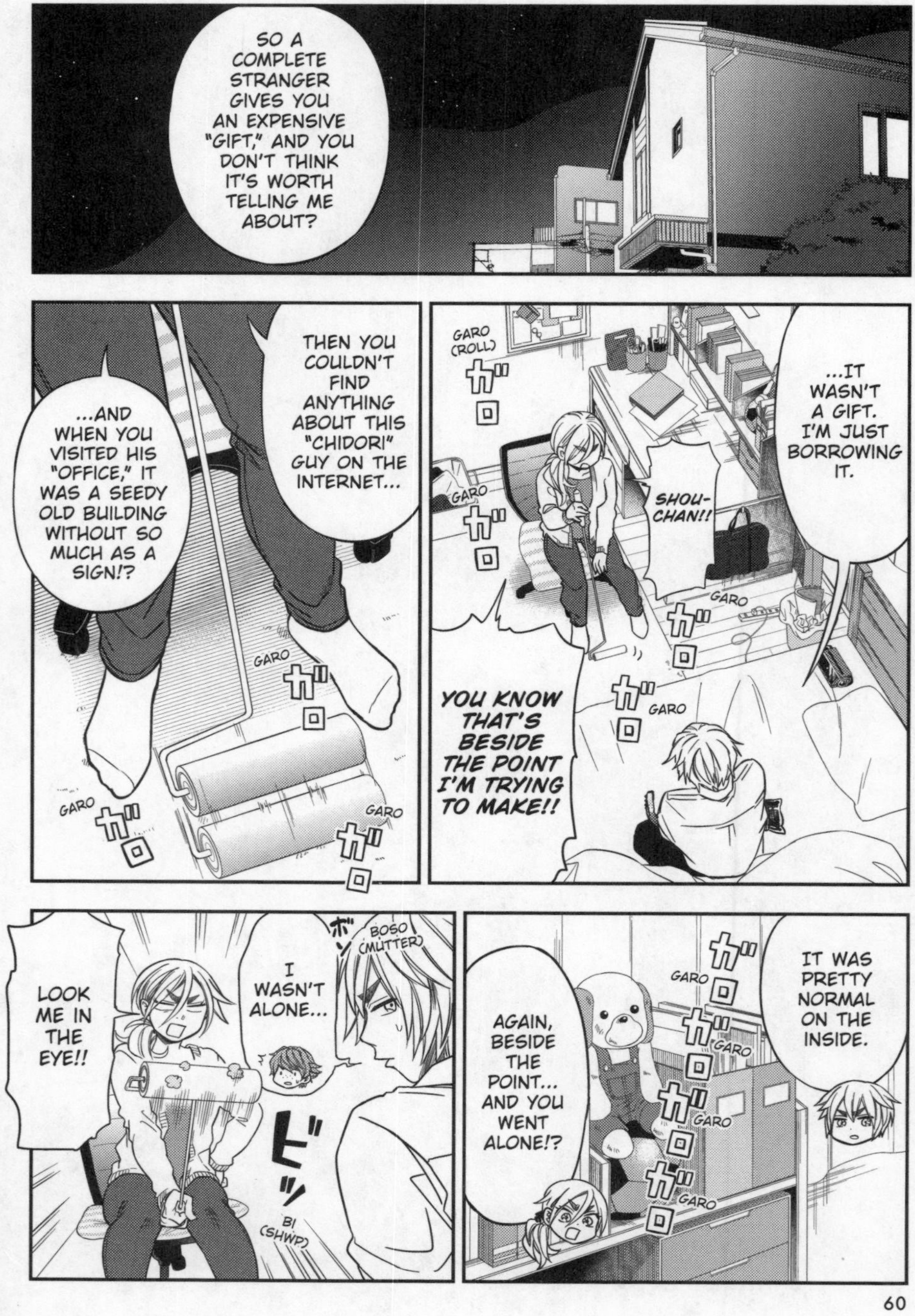
SO A COMPLETE STRANGER GIVES YOU AN EXPENSIVE "GIFT," AND YOU DON'T THINK IT'S WORTH TELLING ME ABOUT?
...IT WASN'T A GIFT. I'M JUST BORROWING IT.
GARO (ROLL)
GARO
SHOU-CHAN!!
GARO
GARO
YOU KNOW THAT'S BESIDE THE POINT I'M TRYING TO MAKE!!
THEN YOU COULDN'T FIND ANYTHING ABOUT THIS "CHIDORI" GUY ON THE INTERNET...
...AND WHEN YOU VISITED HIS "OFFICE," IT WAS A SEEDY OLD BUILDING WITHOUT SO MUCH AS A SIGN!?
GARO
GARO
GARO
IT WAS PRETTY NORMAL ON THE INSIDE.
GARO
GARO
GARO
GARO
AGAIN, BESIDE THE POINT... AND YOU WENT ALONE!?
BOSO (MUTTER)
I WASN'T ALONE...
BI (SHWP)
LOOK ME IN THE EYE!!

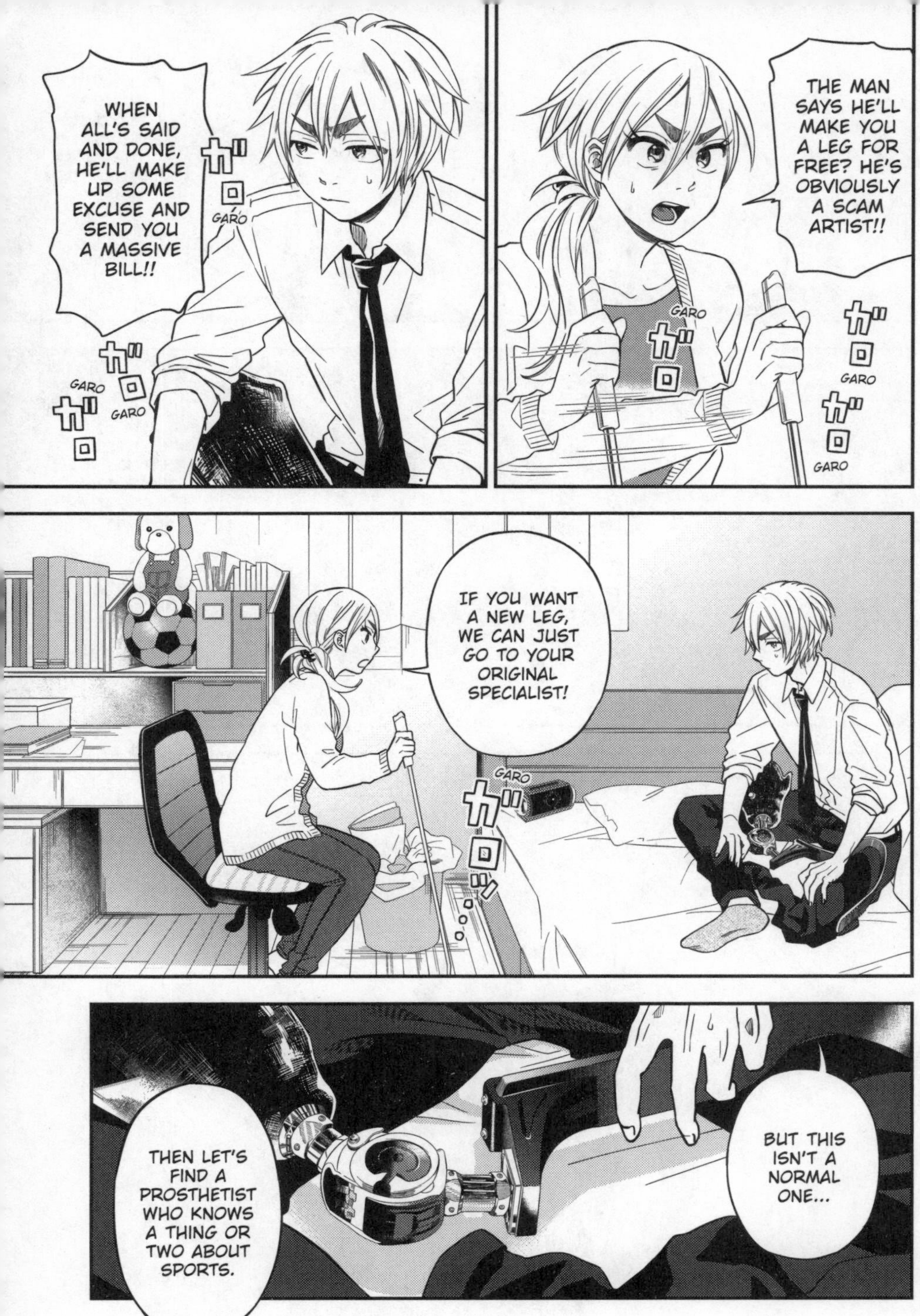
THE MAN SAYS HE'LL MAKE YOU A LEG FOR FREE? HE'S OBVIOUSLY A SCAM ARTIST!!
ガロ
GARO
ガロ
GARO
ガロ
GARO
WHEN ALL'S SAID AND DONE, HE'LL MAKE UP SOME EXCUSE AND SEND YOU A MASSIVE BILL!!
ガロ
GARO
ガロ
GARO
ガロ
GARO
IF YOU WANT A NEW LEG, WE CAN JUST GO TO YOUR ORIGINAL SPECIALIST!
GARO
ガロッ
BUT THIS ISN'T A NORMAL ONE...
THEN LET'S FIND A PROSTHETIST WHO KNOWS A THING OR TWO ABOUT SPORTS.

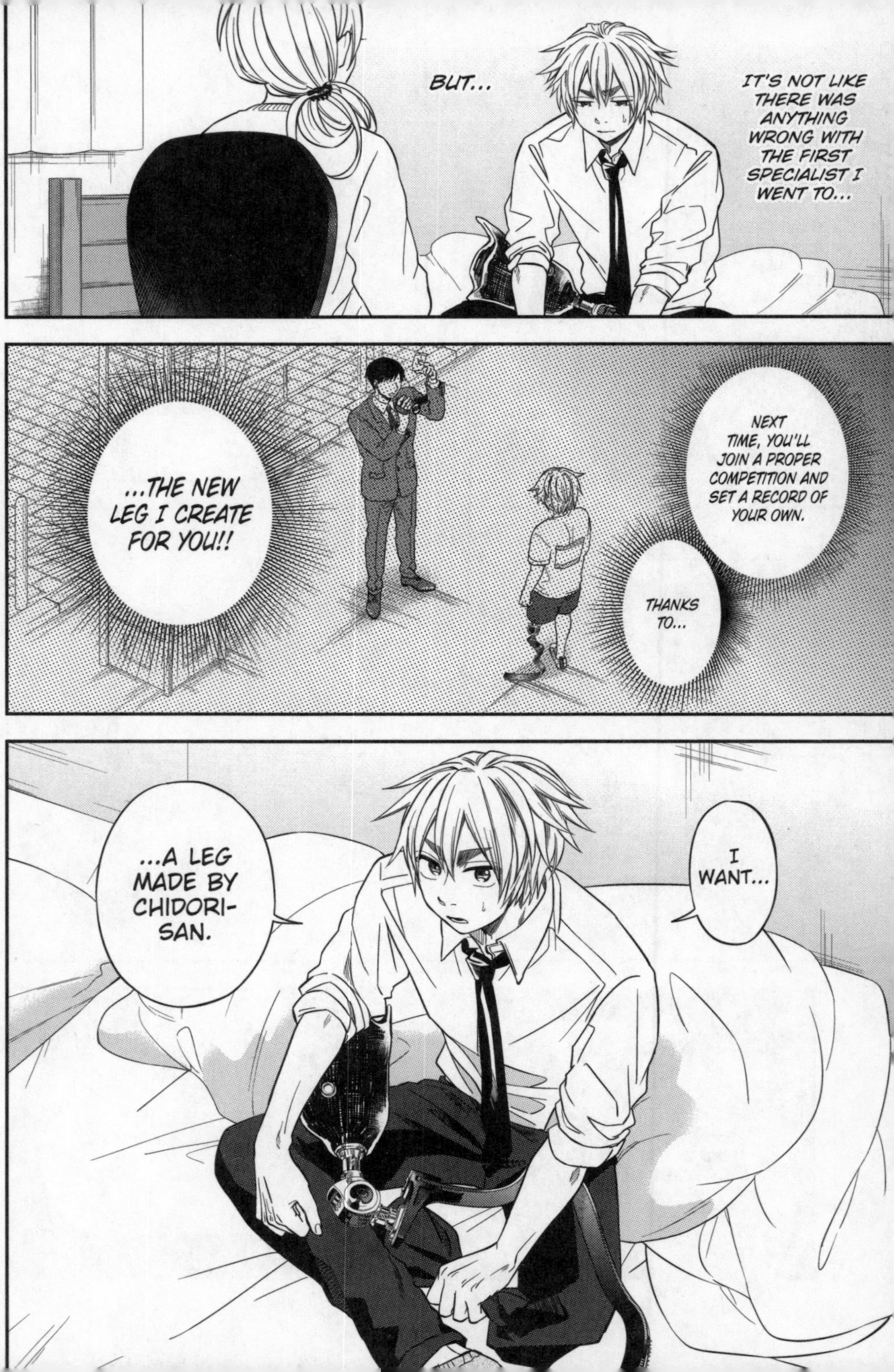
IT'S NOT LIKE THERE WAS ANYTHING WRONG WITH THE FIRST SPECIALIST I WENT TO...
BUT...
NEXT TIME, YOU'LL JOIN A PROPER COMPETITION AND SET A RECORD OF YOUR OWN.
THANKS TO...
...THE NEW LEG I CREATE FOR YOU!!
I WANT...
...A LEG MADE BY CHIDORI-SAN.

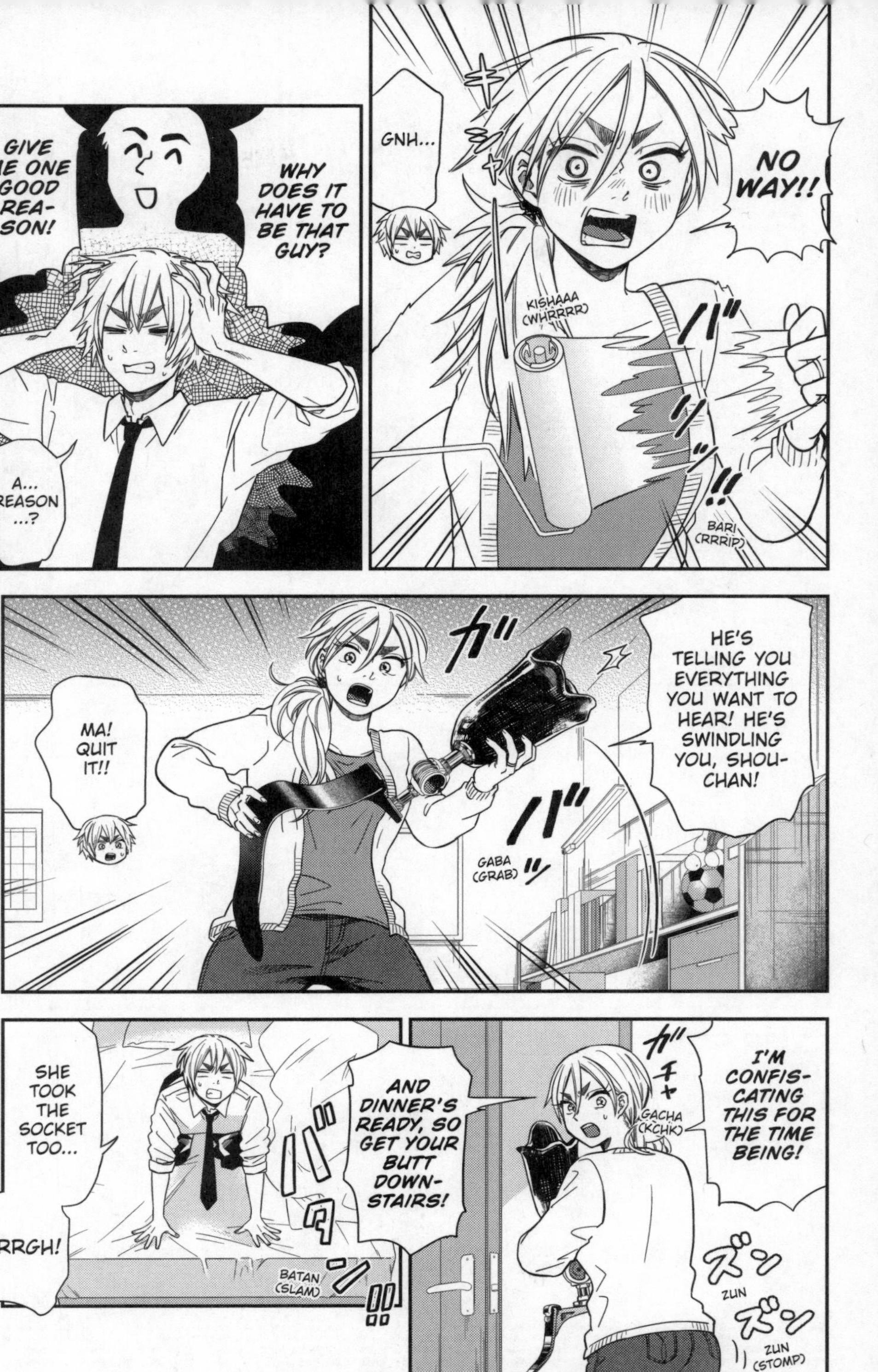
GNH...
NO WAY!!
KISHAA (WHRRRR)
BARI (RRRIP)
WHY DOES IT HAVE TO BE THAT GUY?
GIVE ME ONE GOOD REA-SON!
A... REASON ...?
HE'S TELLING YOU EVERYTHING YOU WANT TO HEAR! HE'S SWINDLING YOU, SHOU-CHAN!
GABA (GRAB)
MA! QUIT IT!!
I'M CONFIS-CATING THIS FOR THE TIME BEING!
GACHA (KCHK)
AND DINNER'S READY, SO GET YOUR BUTT DOWN-STAIRS!
ZUN
ZUN (STOMP)
SHE TOOK THE SOCKET TOO...
RRGH!
BATAN (SLAM)

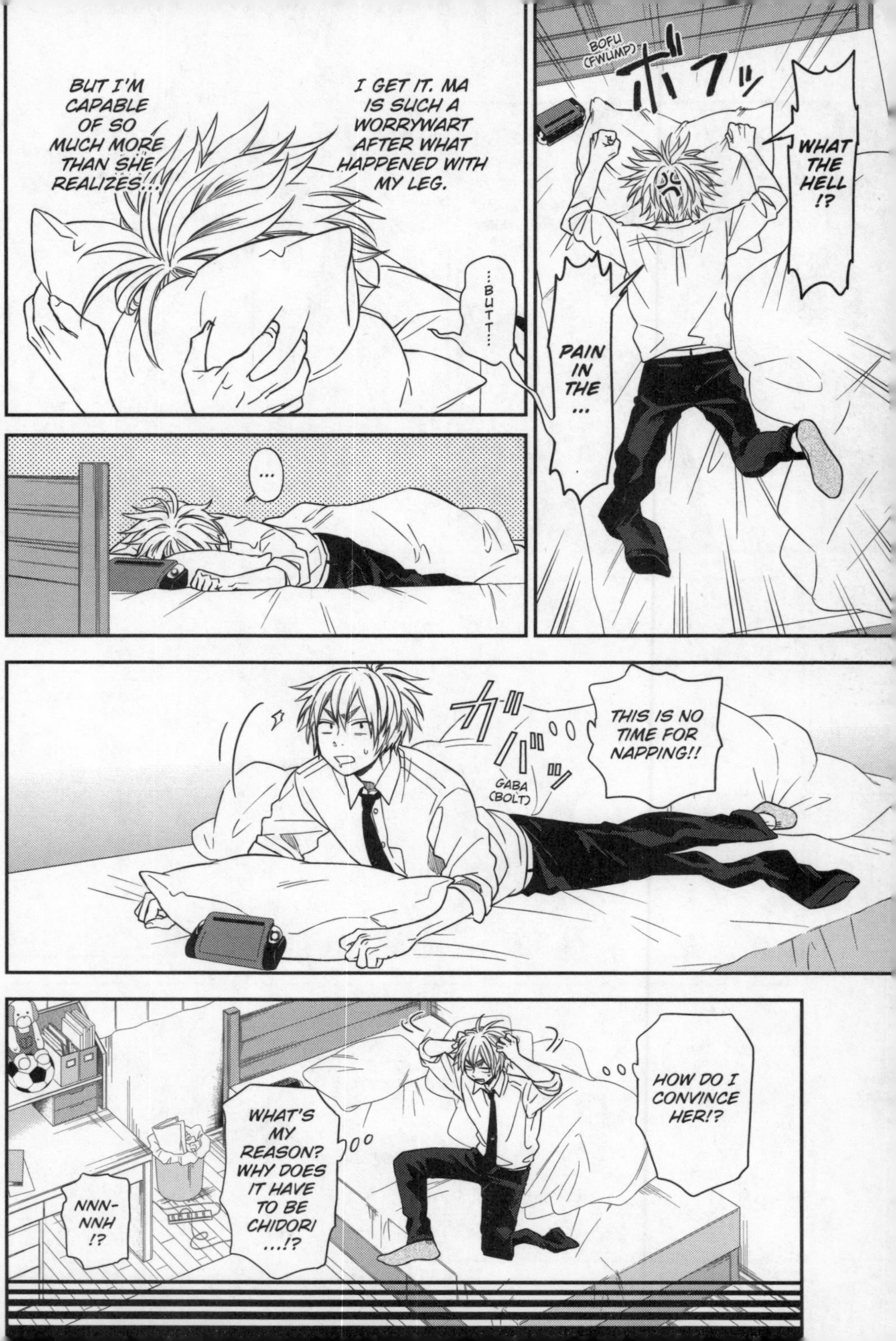
ボフッ
BOFU (FWUMP)
WHAT THE HELL!?
PAIN IN THE...
I GET IT. MA IS SUCH A WORRYWART AFTER WHAT HAPPENED WITH MY LEG.
BUT I'M CAPABLE OF SO MUCH MORE THAN SHE REALIZES...
...BUTT...
...
THIS IS NO TIME FOR NAPPING!!
ガバッ
GABA (BOLT)
HOW DO I CONVINCE HER!?
WHAT'S MY REASON? WHY DOES IT HAVE TO BE CHIDORI...!?
NNN-NNH!?

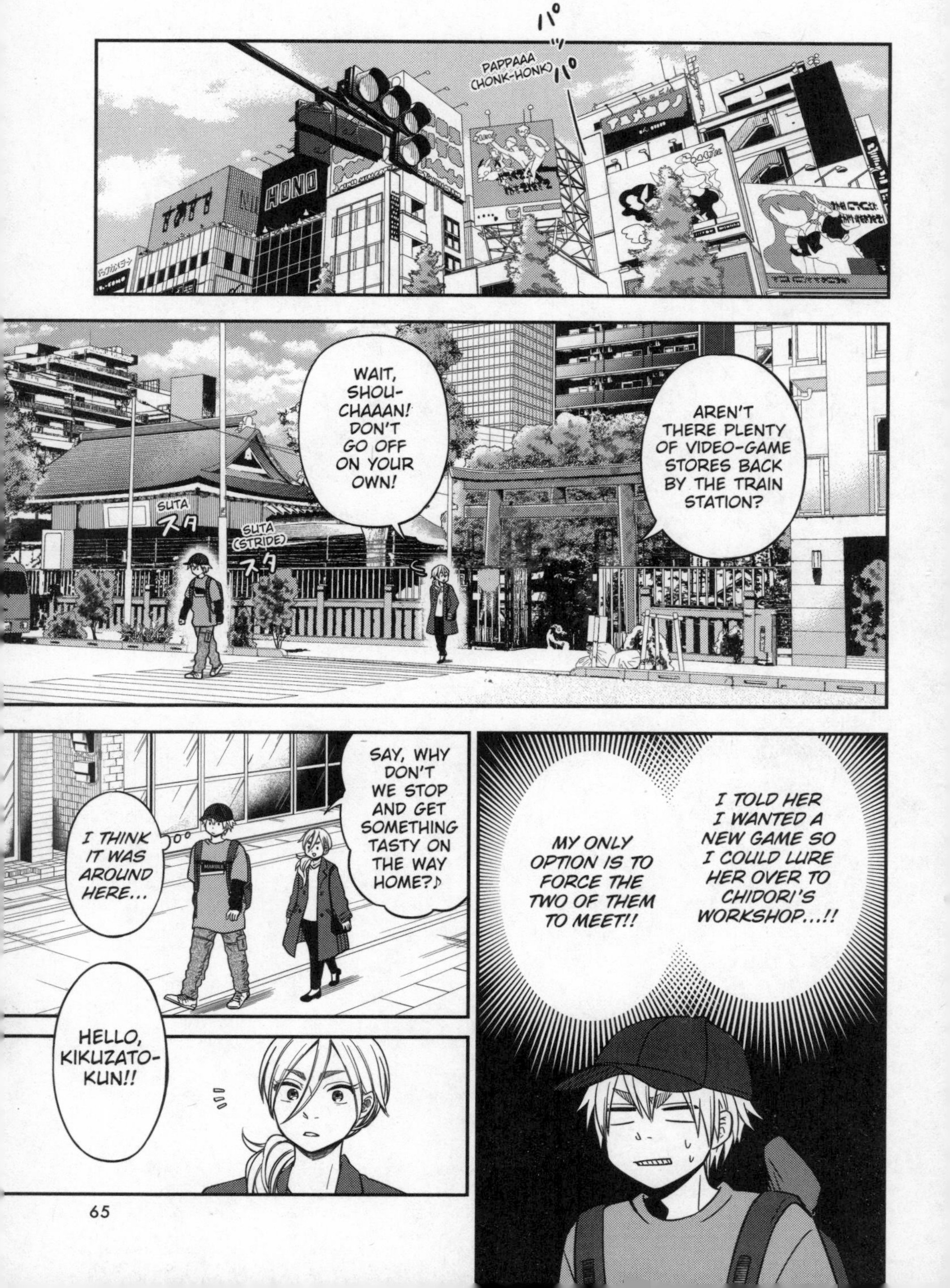
パ
ッ
パ
PAPPAAA (HONK-HONK)
WAIT, SHOU-CHAAAN! DON'T GO OFF ON YOUR OWN!
AREN'T THERE PLENTY OF VIDEO-GAME STORES BACK BY THE TRAIN STATION?
SUTA スタ
SUTA (STRIDE) スタ
I TOLD HER I WANTED A NEW GAME SO I COULD LURE HER OVER TO CHIDORI'S WORKSHOP...!!
MY ONLY OPTION IS TO FORCE THE TWO OF THEM TO MEET!!
SAY, WHY DON'T WE STOP AND GET SOMETHING TASTY ON THE WAY HOME?♪
I THINK IT WAS AROUND HERE...
HELLO, KIKUZATO-KUN!!

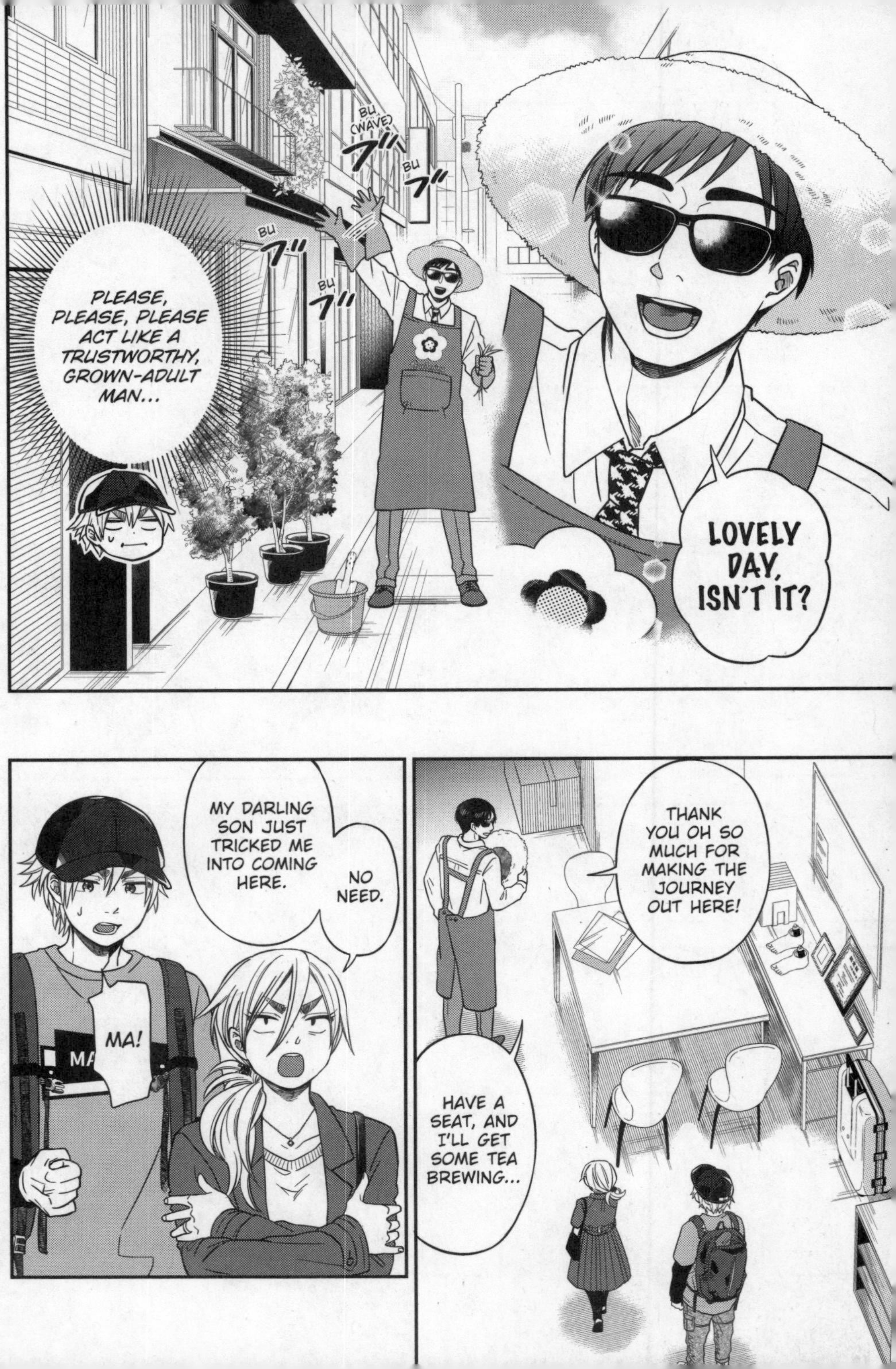
BU (WAVE)
BU
BU
BU
LOVELY DAY, ISN'T IT?
PLEASE, PLEASE, PLEASE ACT LIKE A TRUSTWORTHY, GROWN-ADULT MAN...
THANK YOU OH SO MUCH FOR MAKING THE JOURNEY OUT HERE!
HAVE A SEAT, AND I'LL GET SOME TEA BREWING...
MY DARLING SON JUST TRICKED ME INTO COMING HERE.
NO NEED.
MA!

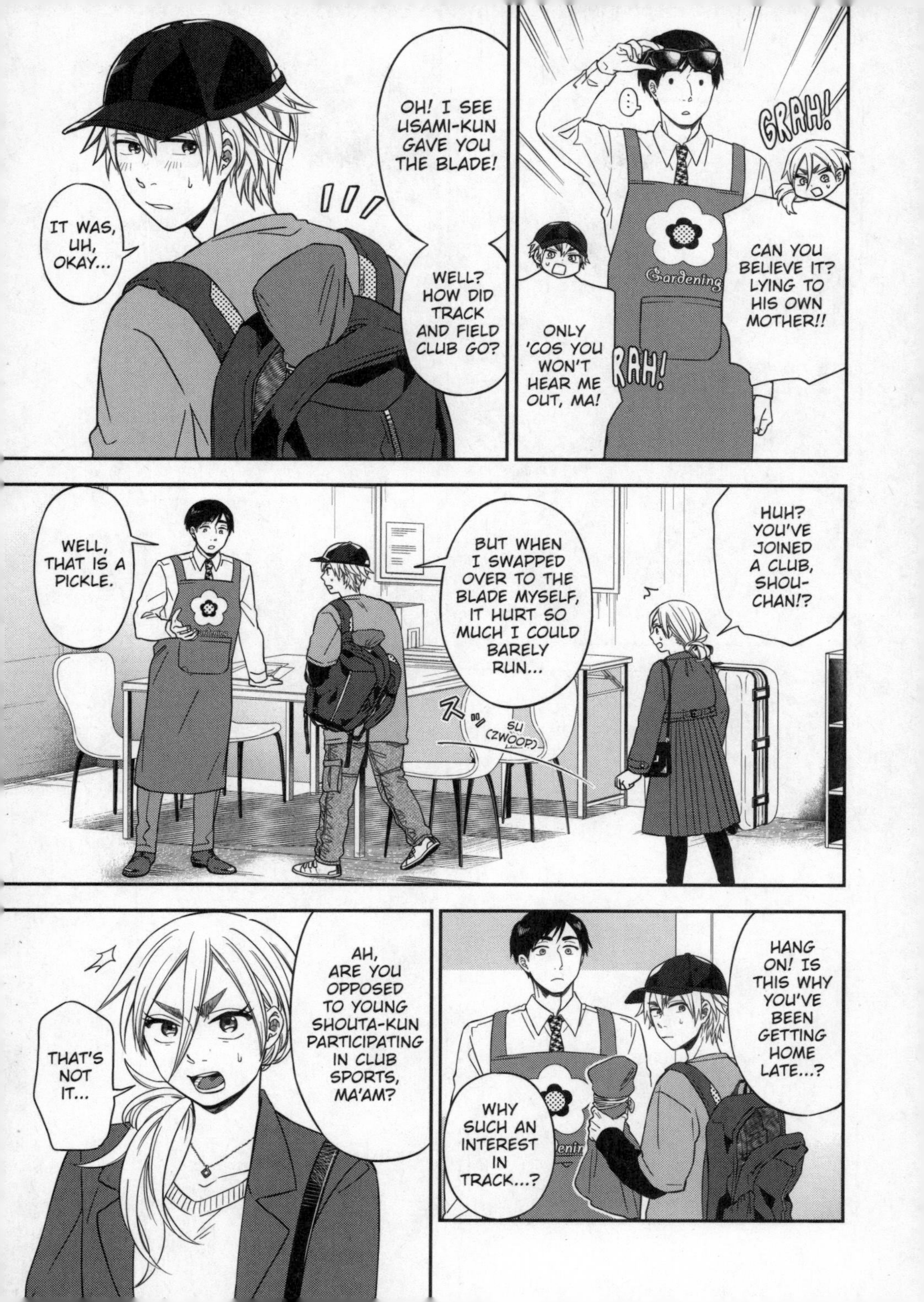
...
GRAH!
CAN YOU BELIEVE IT? LYING TO HIS OWN MOTHER!!
ONLY 'COS YOU WON'T HEAR ME OUT, MA!
RAH!
OH! I SEE USAMI-KUN GAVE YOU THE BLADE!
WELL? HOW DID TRACK AND FIELD CLUB GO?
IT WAS, UH, OKAY...
HUH? YOU'VE JOINED A CLUB, SHOU-CHAN!?
BUT WHEN I SWAPPED OVER TO THE BLADE MYSELF, IT HURT SO MUCH I COULD BARELY RUN...
SU (ZWOOP)
WELL, THAT IS A PICKLE.
HANG ON! IS THIS WHY YOU'VE BEEN GETTING HOME LATE...?
WHY SUCH AN INTEREST IN TRACK...?
AH, ARE YOU OPPOSED TO YOUNG SHOUTA-KUN PARTICIPATING IN CLUB SPORTS, MA'AM?
THAT'S NOT IT...

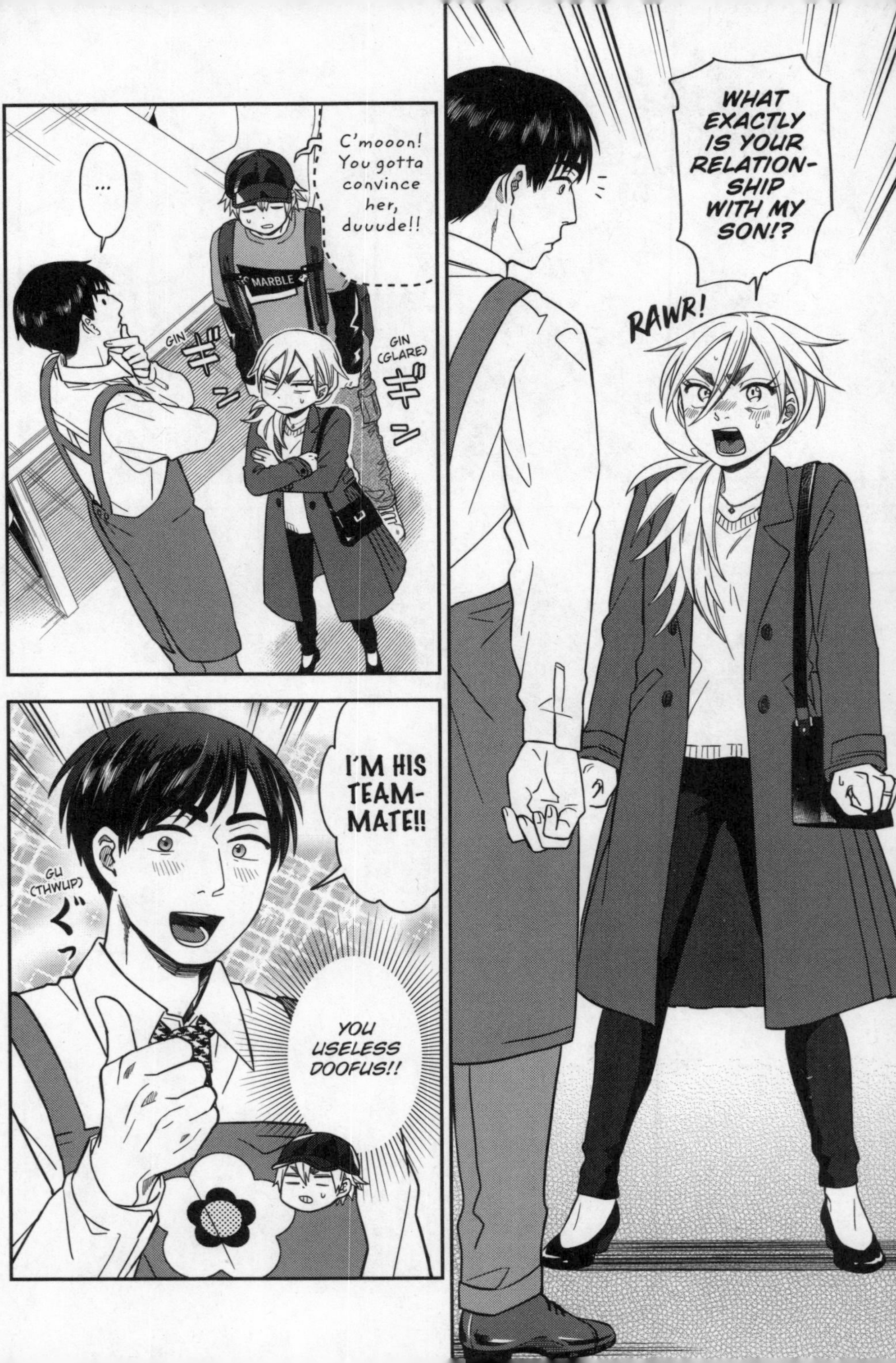
WHAT EXACTLY IS YOUR RELATION-SHIP WITH MY SON!?
RAWR!
C'mooon! You gotta convince her, duuude!!
...
GIN (GLARE)
ギン
GIN
ギン
I'M HIS TEAM-MATE!!
YOU USELESS DOOFUS!!
GU (THWUP)
ぐっ

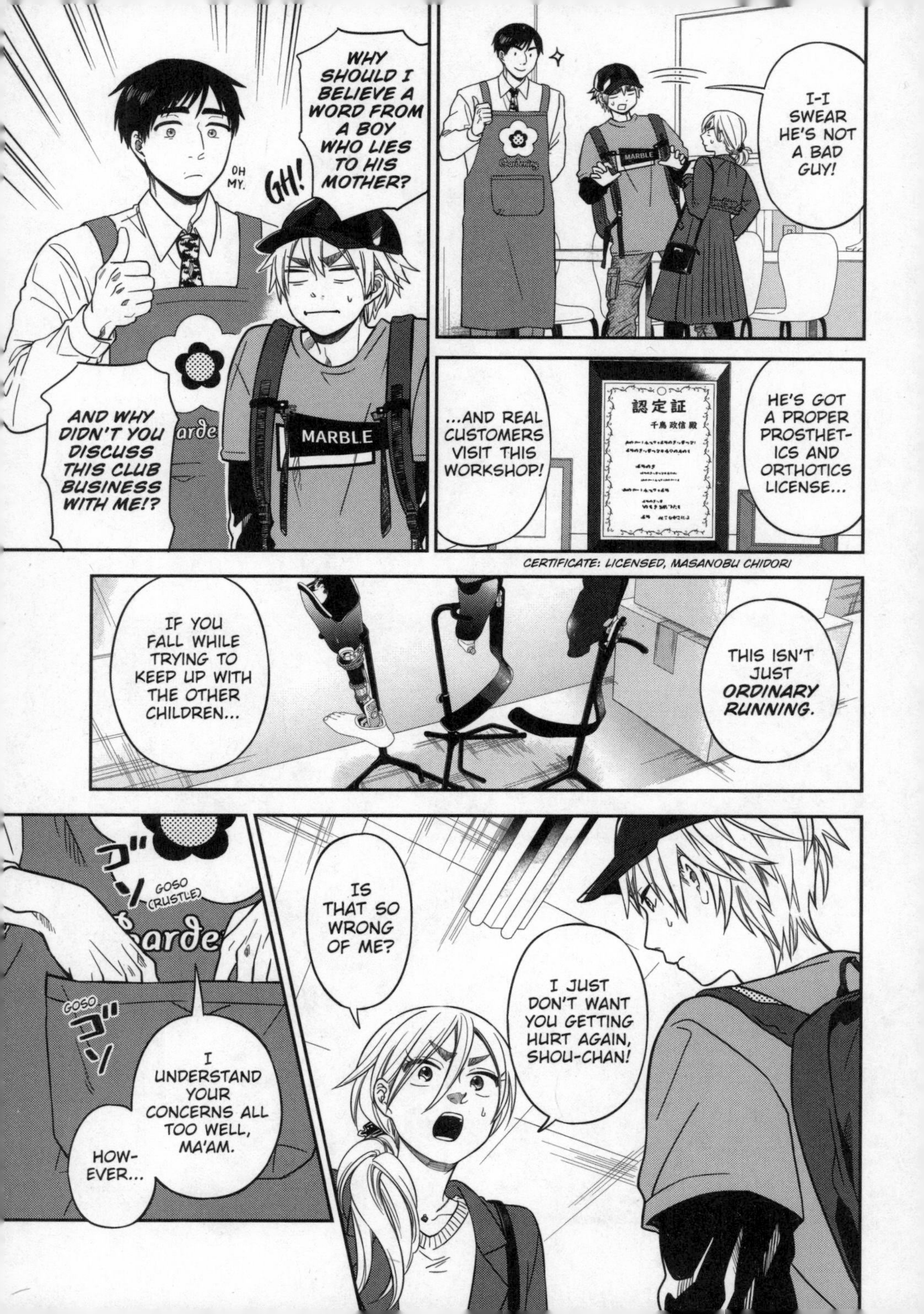
I-I SWEAR HE'S NOT A BAD GUY!
HE'S GOT A PROPER PROSTHETICS AND ORTHOTICS LICENSE...
認定証
千鳥 政信 殿
...AND REAL CUSTOMERS VISIT THIS WORKSHOP!
CERTIFICATE: LICENSED, MASANOBU CHIDORI
WHY SHOULD I BELIEVE A WORD FROM A BOY WHO LIES TO HIS MOTHER?
OH MY.
GH!
AND WHY DIDN'T YOU DISCUSS THIS CLUB BUSINESS WITH ME!?
THIS ISN'T JUST ORDINARY RUNNING.
IF YOU FALL WHILE TRYING TO KEEP UP WITH THE OTHER CHILDREN...
I JUST DON'T WANT YOU GETTING HURT AGAIN, SHOU-CHAN!
IS THAT SO WRONG OF ME?
ゴソ GOSO (RUSTLE)
ゴソ GOSO
I UNDERSTAND YOUR CONCERNS ALL TOO WELL, MA'AM.
HOW-EVER...

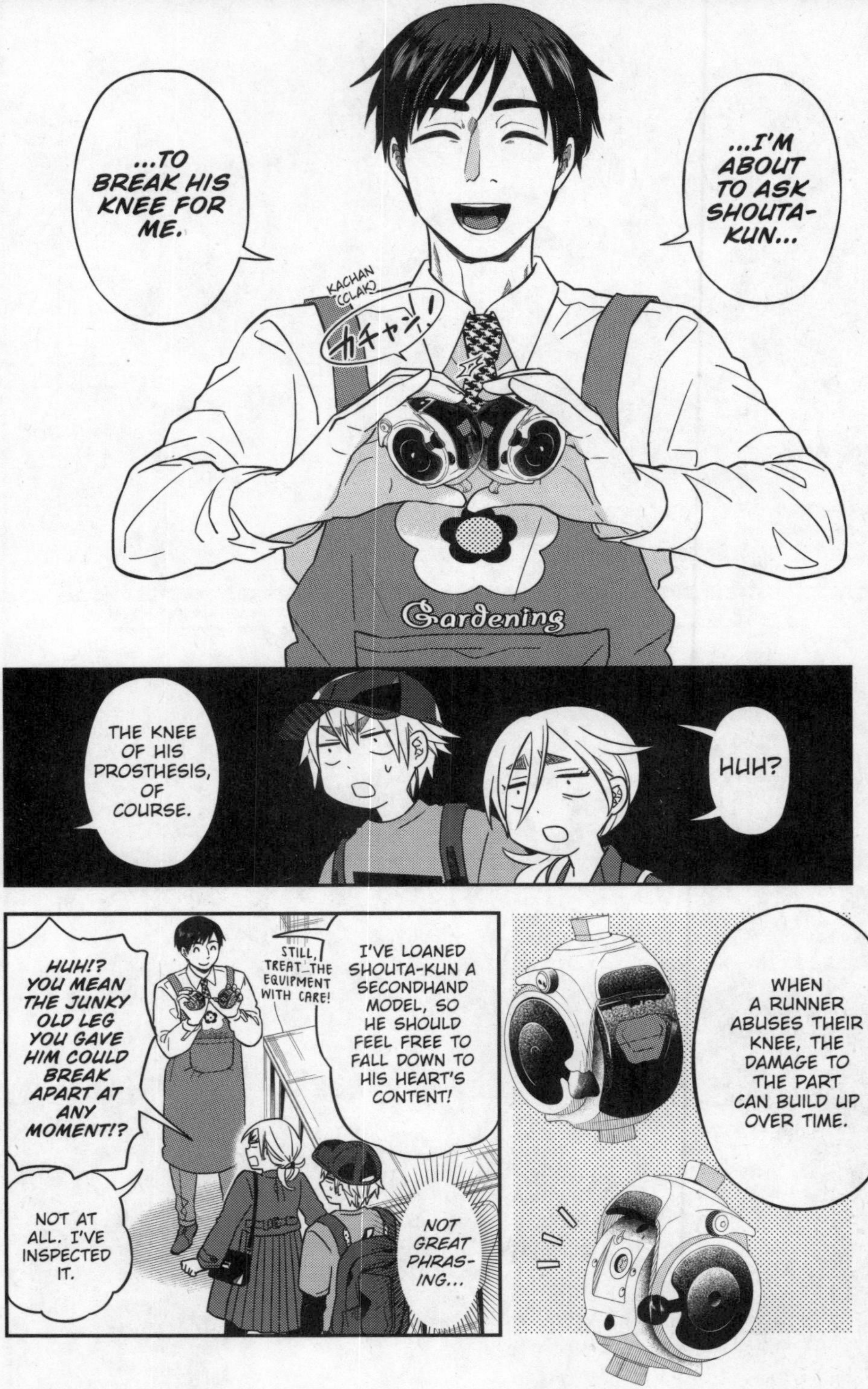
...I'M ABOUT TO ASK SHOUTA-KUN...
...TO BREAK HIS KNEE FOR ME.
カチャン!
KACHAN (CLAK)
Gardening
HUH?
THE KNEE OF HIS PROSTHESIS, OF COURSE.
WHEN A RUNNER ABUSES THEIR KNEE, THE DAMAGE TO THE PART CAN BUILD UP OVER TIME.
I'VE LOANED SHOUTA-KUN A SECONDHAND MODEL, SO HE SHOULD FEEL FREE TO FALL DOWN TO HIS HEART'S CONTENT!
STILL, TREAT THE EQUIPMENT WITH CARE!
HUH!? YOU MEAN THE JUNKY OLD LEG YOU GAVE HIM COULD BREAK APART AT ANY MOMENT!?
NOT GREAT PHRASING...
NOT AT ALL. I'VE INSPECTED IT.

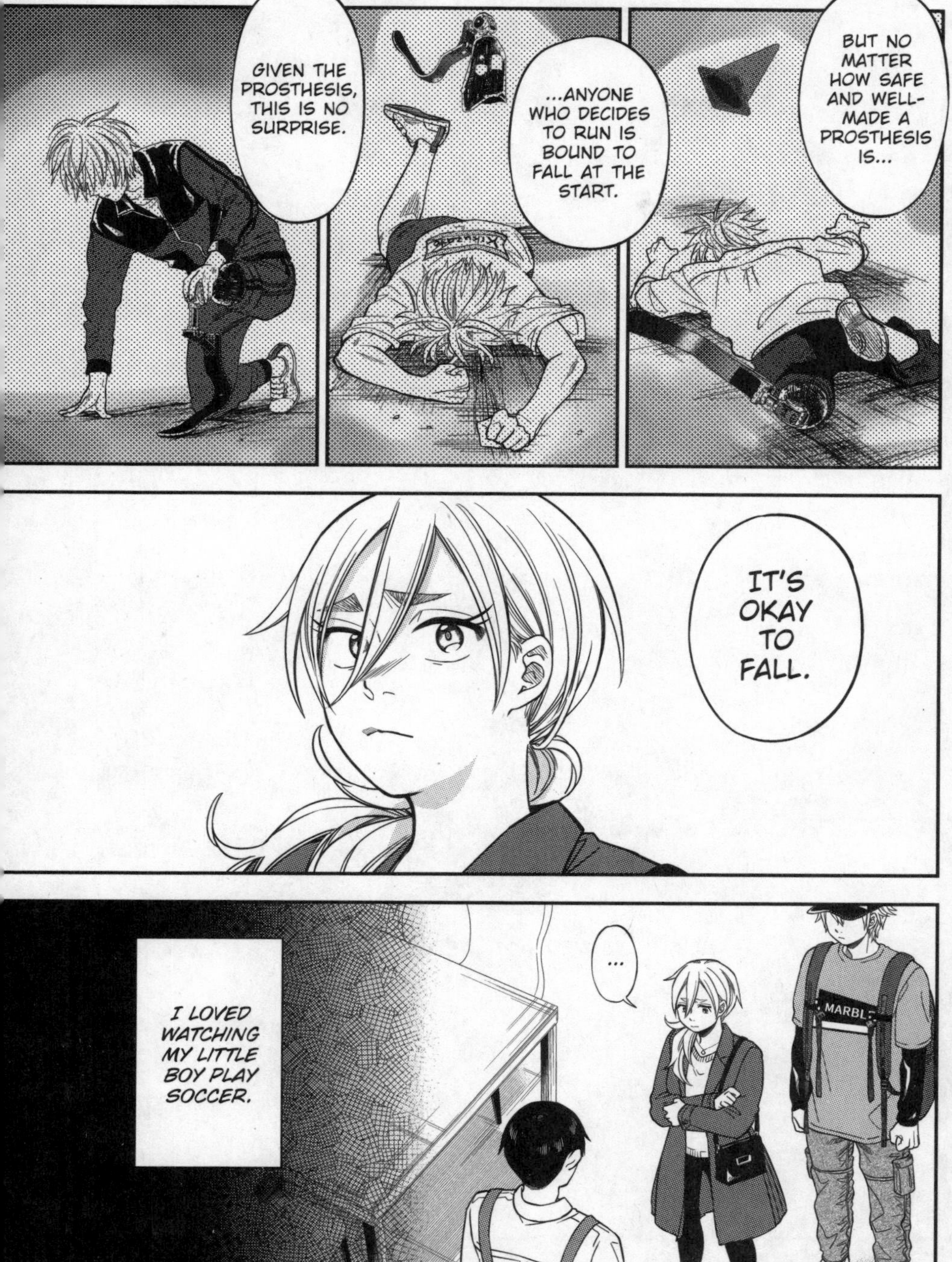
BUT NO MATTER HOW SAFE AND WELL-MADE A PROSTHESIS IS...
...ANYONE WHO DECIDES TO RUN IS BOUND TO FALL AT THE START.
GIVEN THE PROSTHESIS, THIS IS NO SURPRISE.
IT'S OKAY TO FALL.
...
I LOVED WATCHING MY LITTLE BOY PLAY SOCCER.

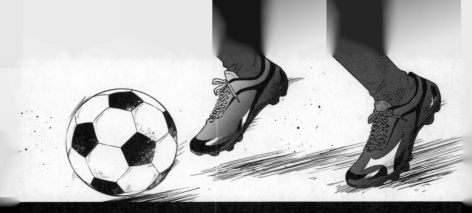

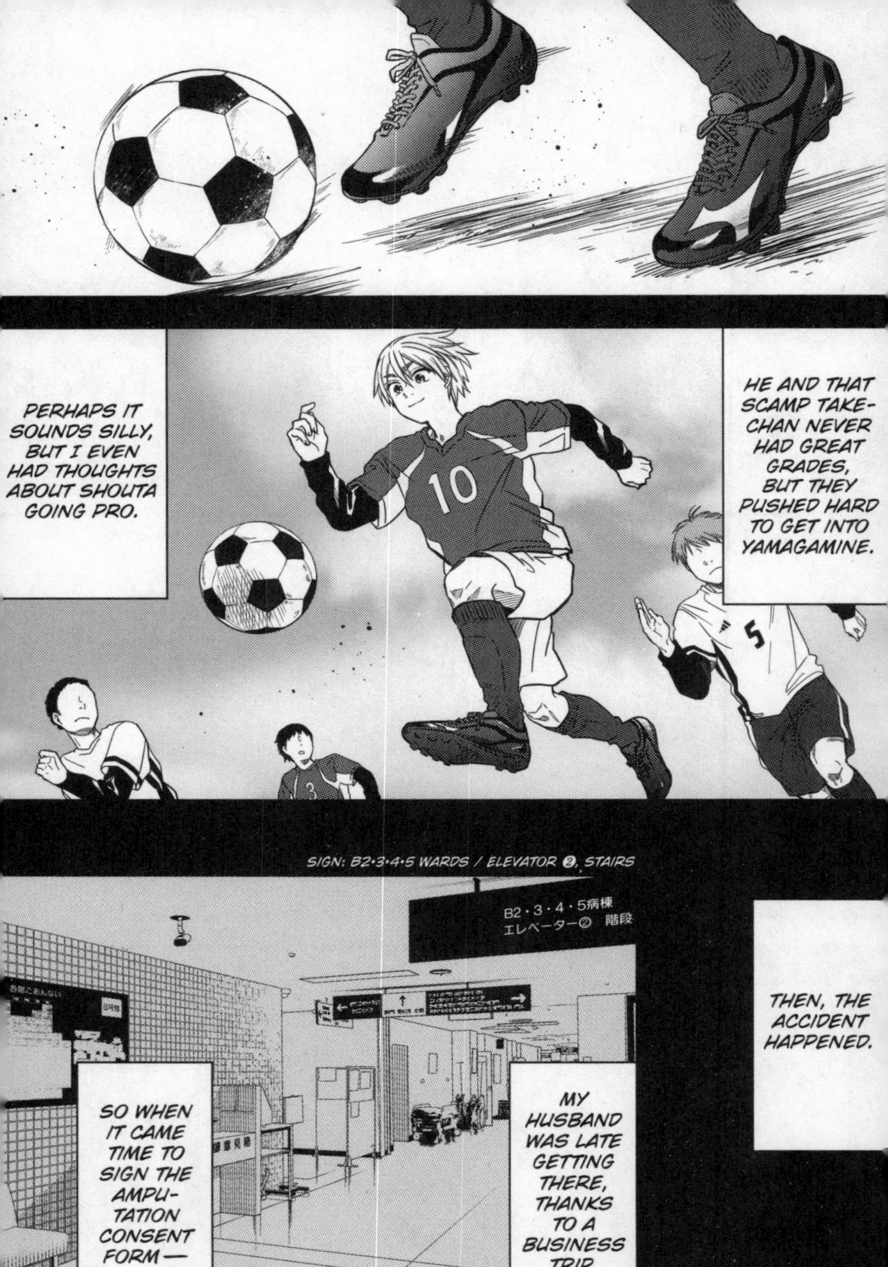
HE AND THAT SCAMP TAKE-CHAN NEVER HAD GREAT GRADES, BUT THEY PUSHED HARD TO GET INTO YAMAGAMINE.
PERHAPS IT SOUNDS SILLY, BUT I EVEN HAD THOUGHTS ABOUT SHOUTA GOING PRO.
SIGN: B2•3•4•5 WARDS / ELEVATOR ❷, STAIRS
THEN, THE ACCIDENT HAPPENED.
B2・3・4・5病棟
エレベーター② 階段
MY HUSBAND WAS LATE GETTING THERE, THANKS TO A BUSINESS TRIP.
SO WHEN IT CAME TIME TO SIGN THE AMPUTATION CONSENT FORM—

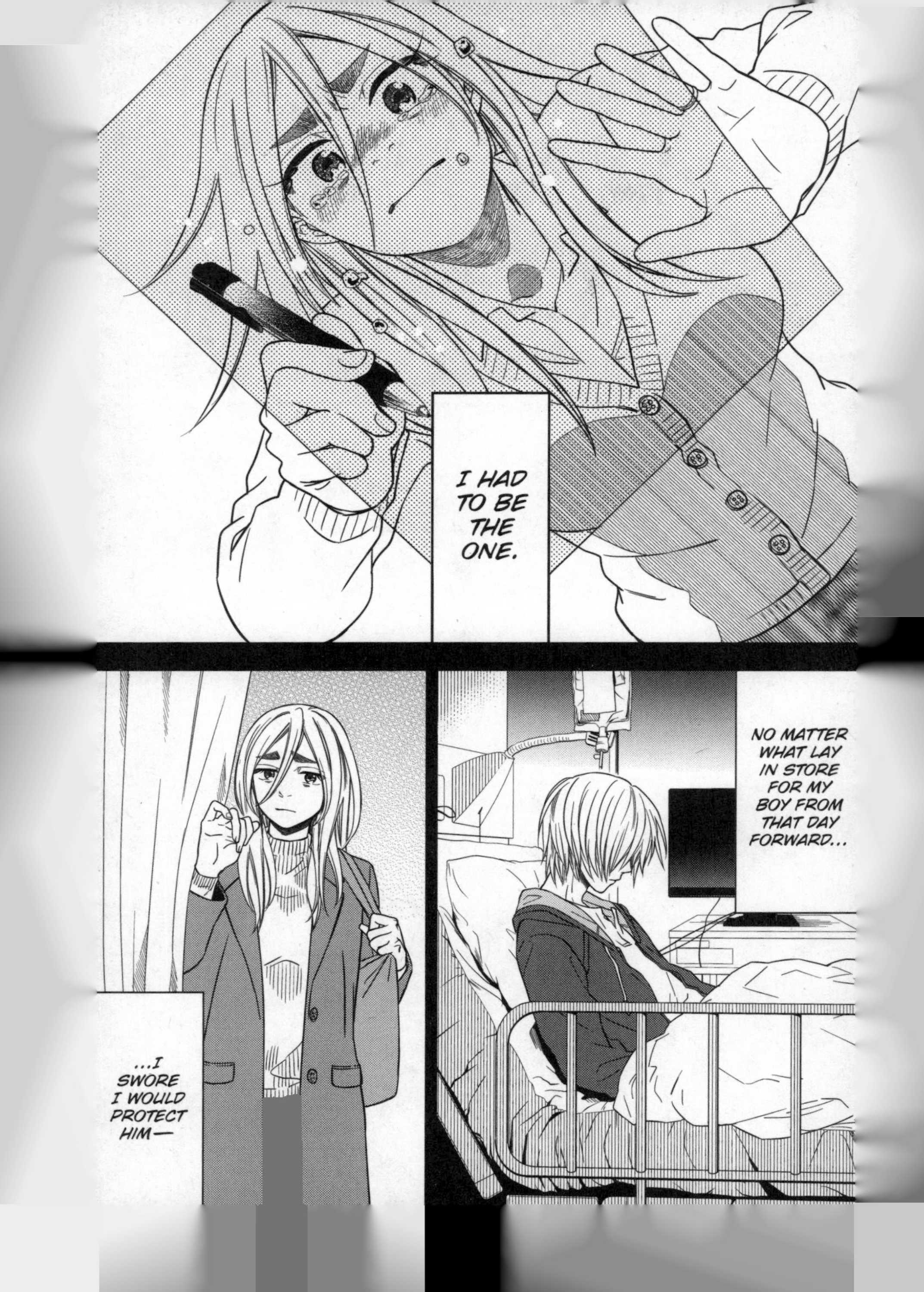
I HAD TO BE THE ONE.
NO MATTER WHAT LAY IN STORE FOR MY BOY FROM THAT DAY FORWARD...
...I SWORE I WOULD PROTECT HIM—

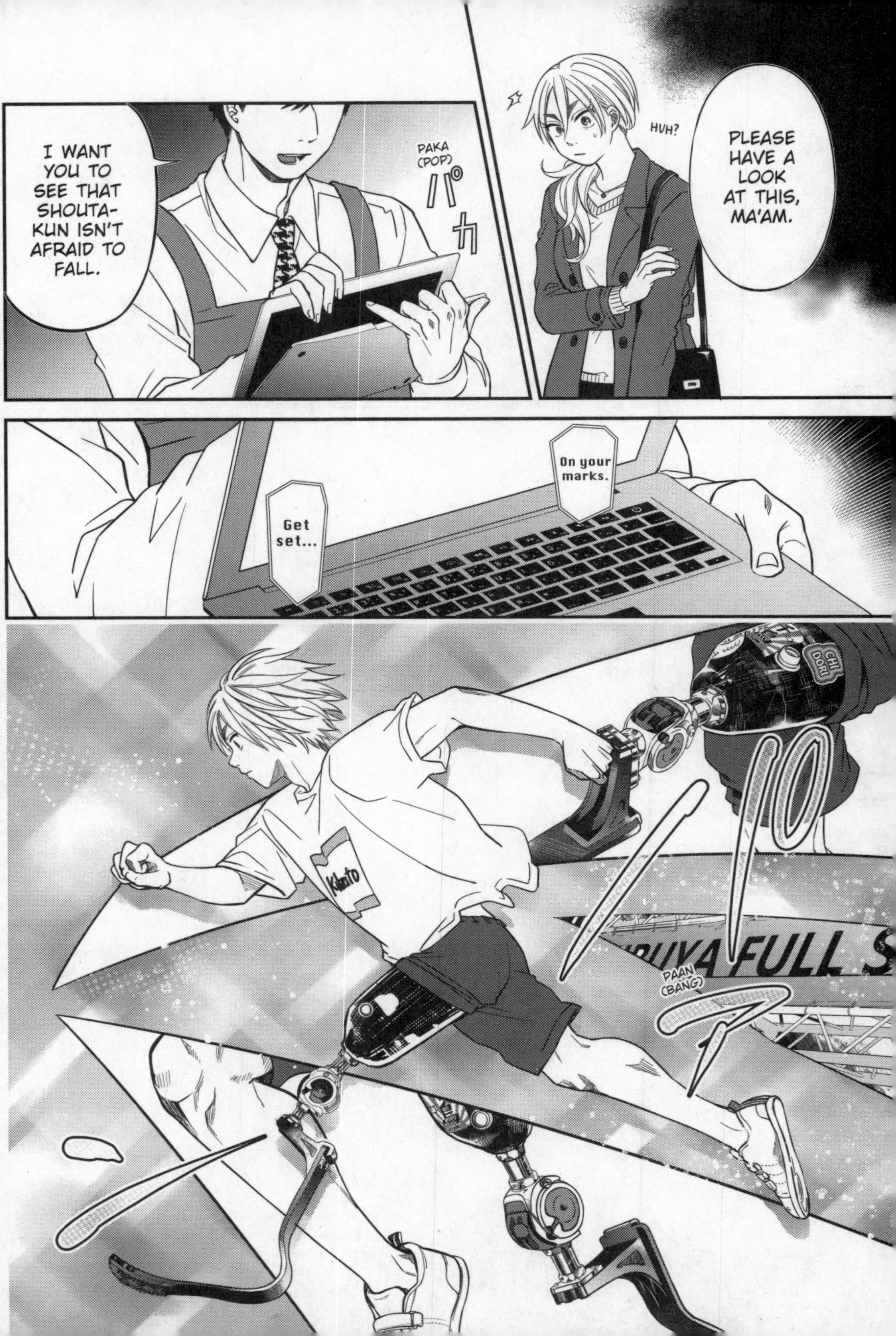
HUH?
PLEASE HAVE A LOOK AT THIS, MA'AM.
PAKA (POP)
I WANT YOU TO SEE THAT SHOUTA-KUN ISN'T AFRAID TO FALL.
On your marks.
Get set...
CHI DORI
FULL S
PAAN (BANG)

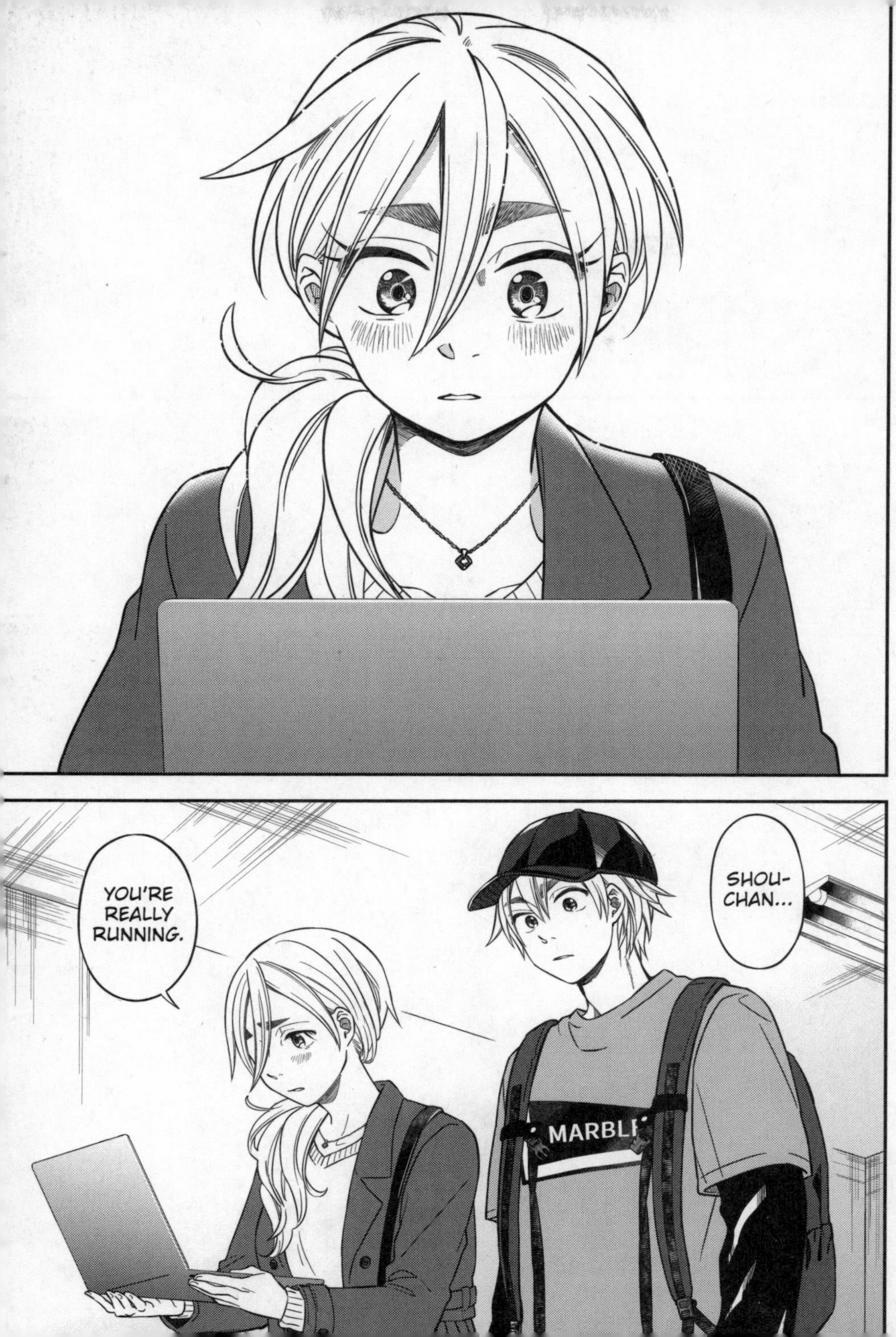
SHOU-CHAN...
YOU'RE REALLY RUNNING.

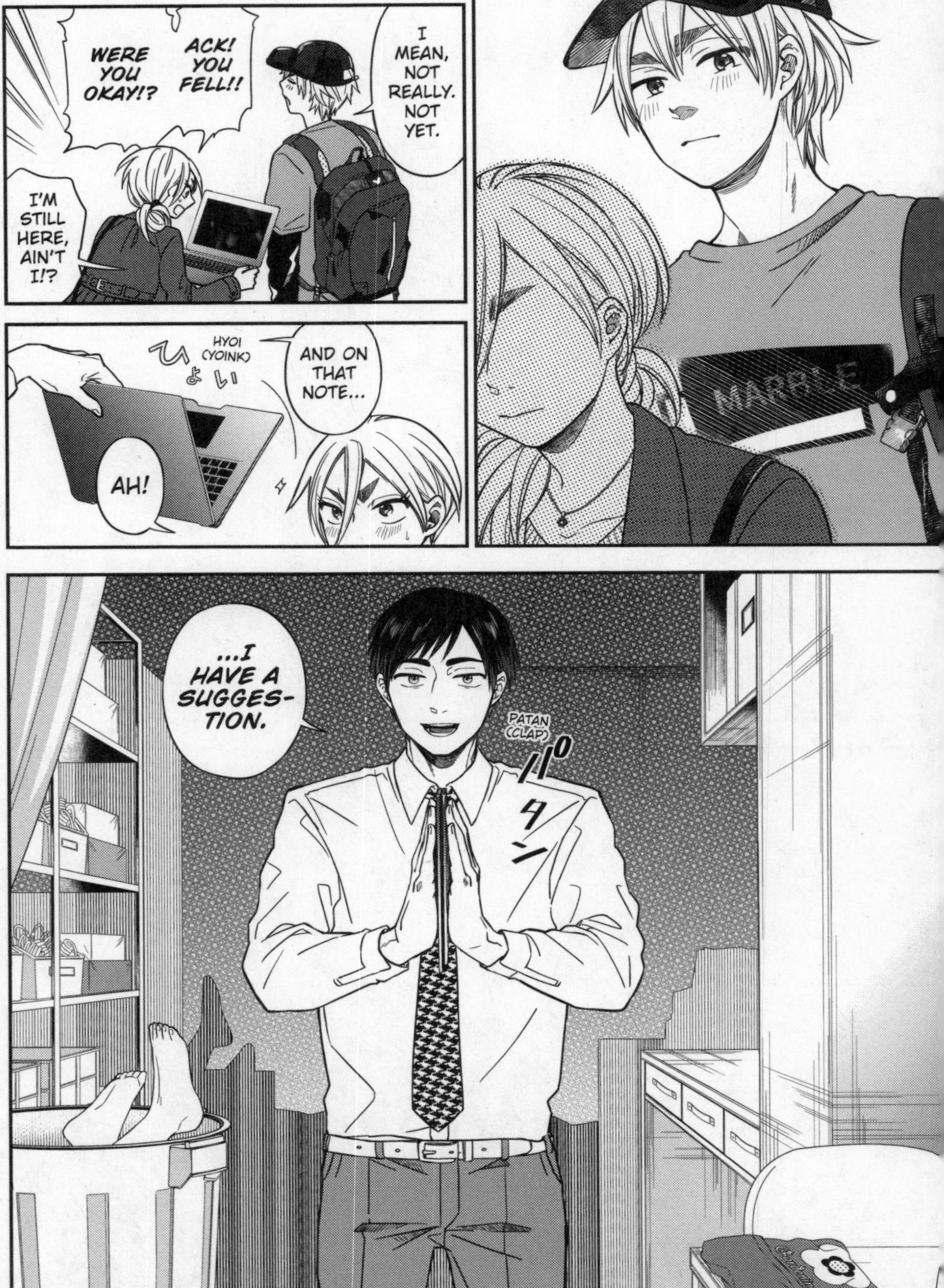
I MEAN, NOT REALLY. NOT YET.
ACK! YOU FELL!!
WERE YOU OKAY!?
I'M STILL HERE, AIN'T I!?
AND ON THAT NOTE...
HYOI (YOINK)
ひょい
AH!
...I HAVE A SUGGES-TION.
PATAN (CLAP)
パタン

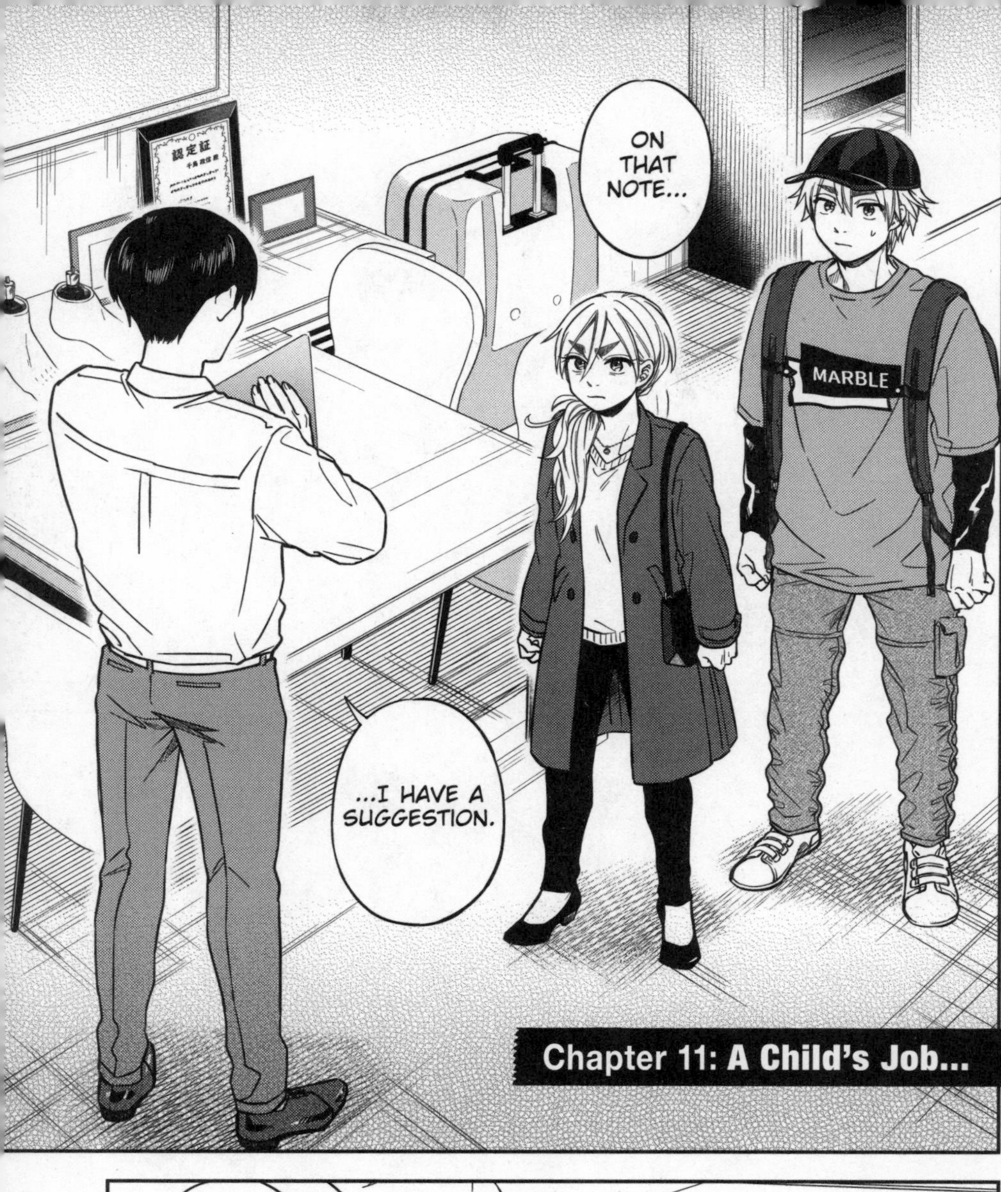
ON THAT NOTE...
...I HAVE A SUGGESTION.
MARBLE

Chapter 11: A Child's Job...

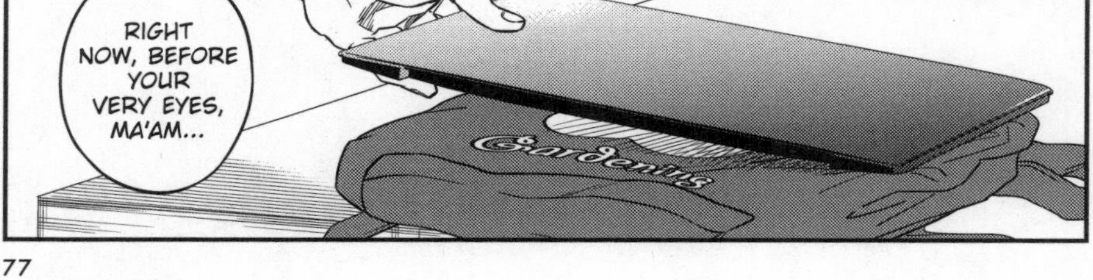
RIGHT NOW, BEFORE YOUR VERY EYES, MA'AM...
Gardening

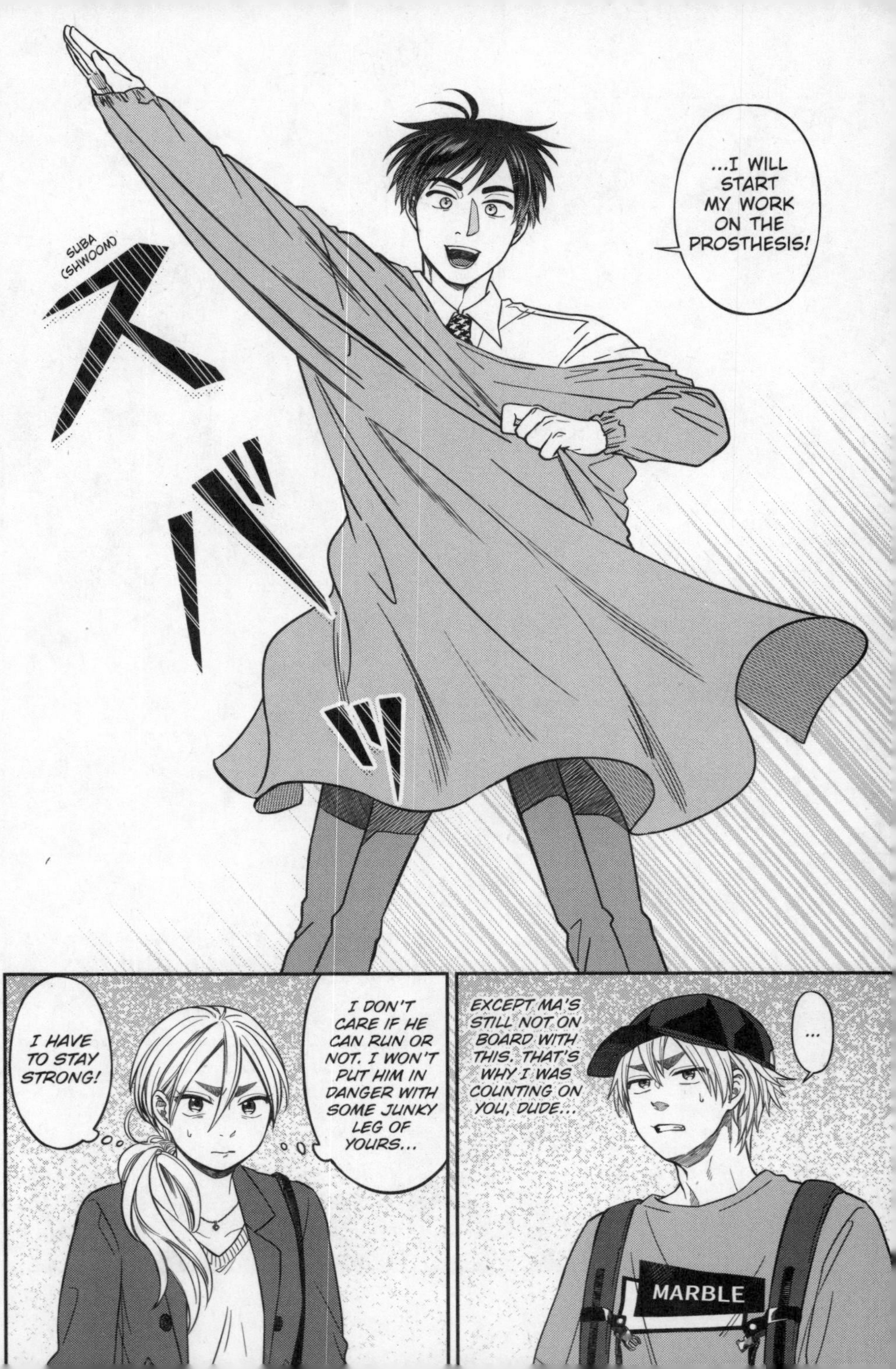
...I WILL START MY WORK ON THE PROSTHESIS!
SUBA (SHWOOM)
...
EXCEPT MA'S STILL NOT ON BOARD WITH THIS. THAT'S WHY I WAS COUNTING ON YOU, DUDE...
MARBLE
I DON'T CARE IF HE CAN RUN OR NOT. I WON'T PUT HIM IN DANGER WITH SOME JUNKY LEG OF YOURS...
I HAVE TO STAY STRONG!

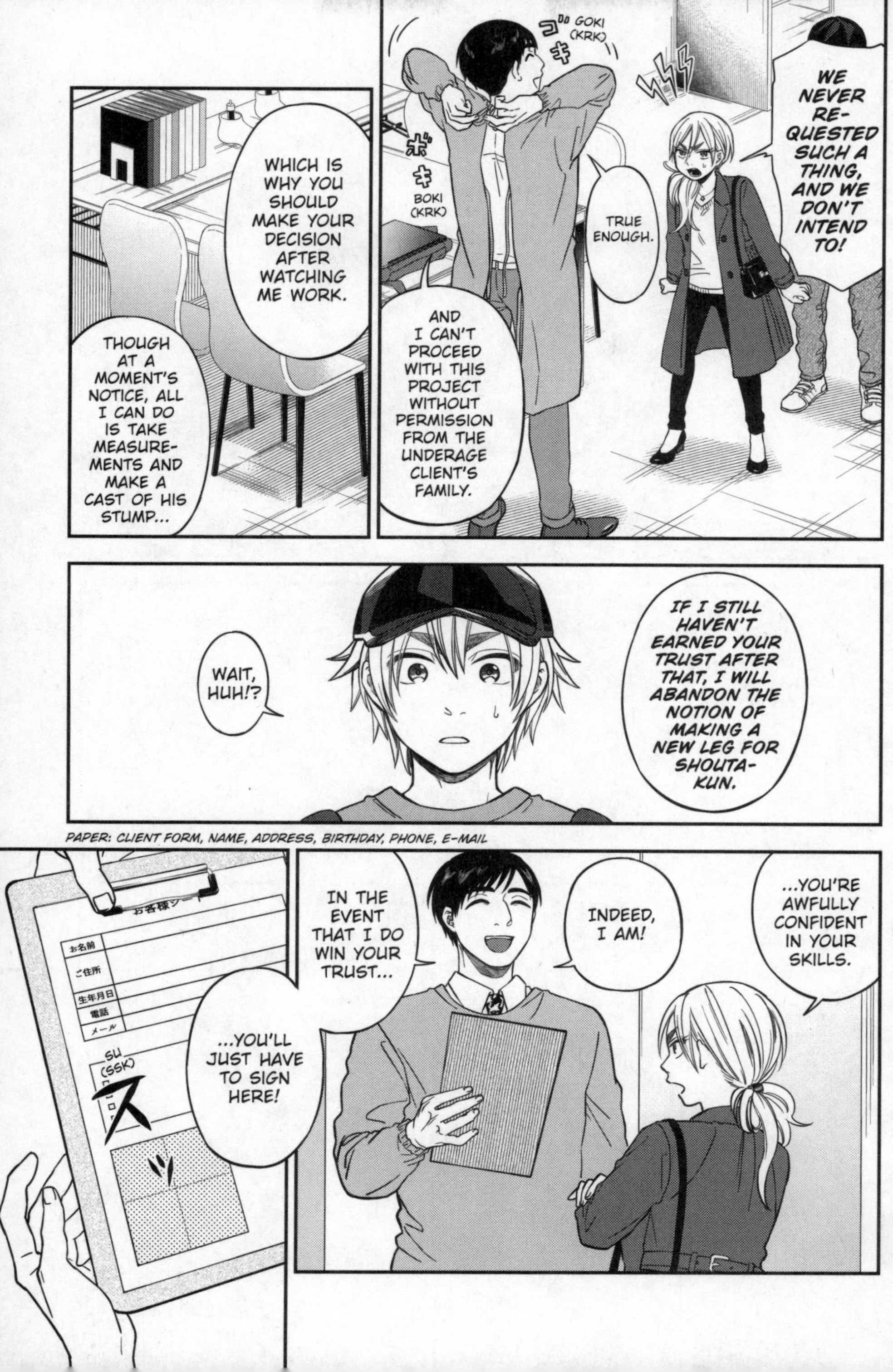
WE NEVER RE-QUESTED SUCH A THING, AND WE DON'T INTEND TO!
GOKI (KRK)
TRUE ENOUGH.
BOKI (KRK)
AND I CAN'T PROCEED WITH THIS PROJECT WITHOUT PERMISSION FROM THE UNDERAGE CLIENT'S FAMILY.
WHICH IS WHY YOU SHOULD MAKE YOUR DECISION AFTER WATCHING ME WORK.
THOUGH AT A MOMENT'S NOTICE, ALL I CAN DO IS TAKE MEASURE-MENTS AND MAKE A CAST OF HIS STUMP...
IF I STILL HAVEN'T EARNED YOUR TRUST AFTER THAT, I WILL ABANDON THE NOTION OF MAKING A NEW LEG FOR SHOUTA-KUN.
WAIT, HUH!?
PAPER: CLIENT FORM, NAME, ADDRESS, BIRTHDAY, PHONE, E-MAIL
...YOU'RE AWFULLY CONFIDENT IN YOUR SKILLS.
INDEED, I AM!
IN THE EVENT THAT I DO WIN YOUR TRUST...
...YOU'LL JUST HAVE TO SIGN HERE!
お名前
ご住所
生年月日
電話
メール
SU (SSK)

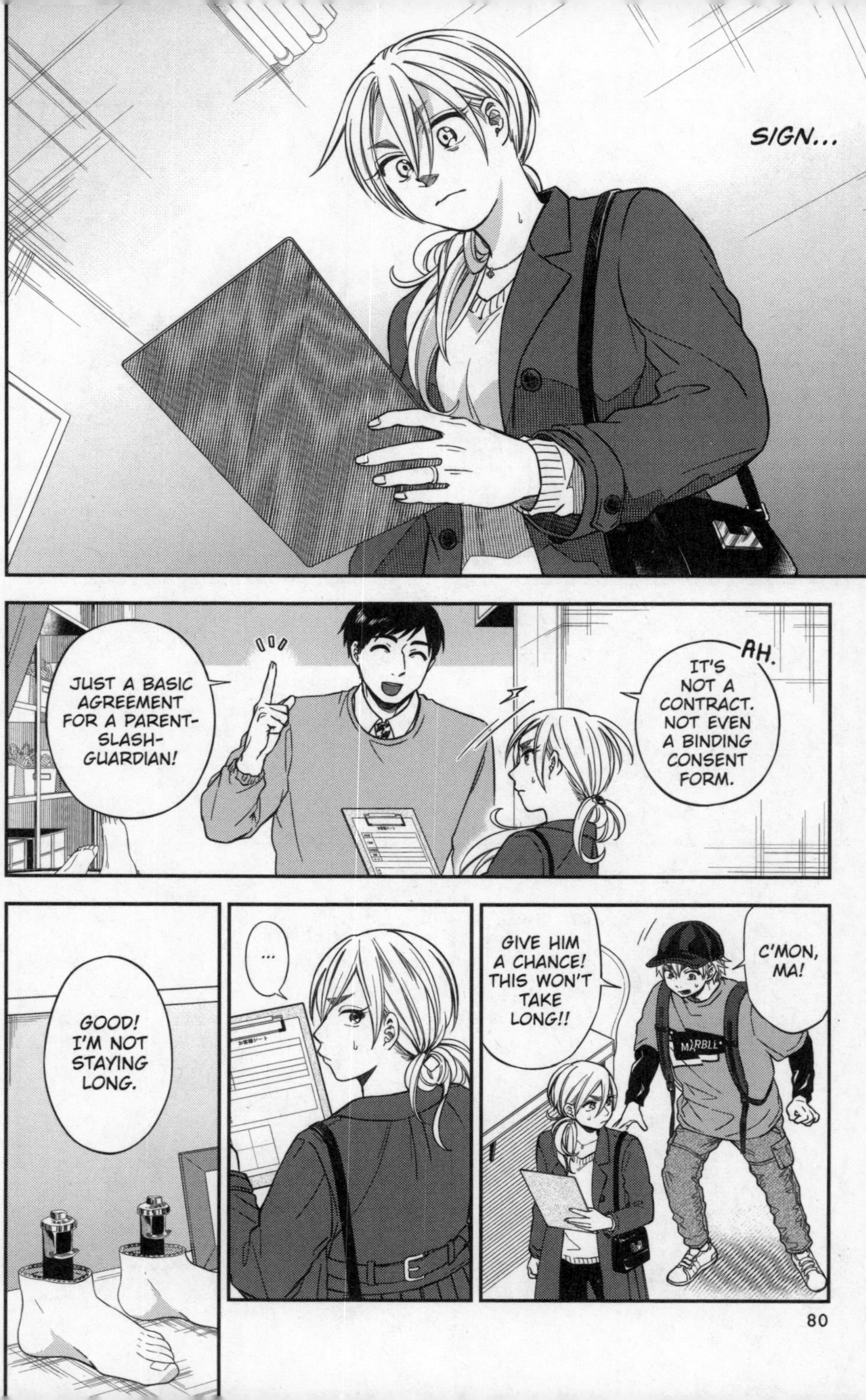
SIGN...
AH.
IT'S NOT A CONTRACT. NOT EVEN A BINDING CONSENT FORM.
JUST A BASIC AGREEMENT FOR A PARENT-SLASH-GUARDIAN!
C'MON, MA!
GIVE HIM A CHANCE! THIS WON'T TAKE LONG!!
...
GOOD! I'M NOT STAYING LONG.

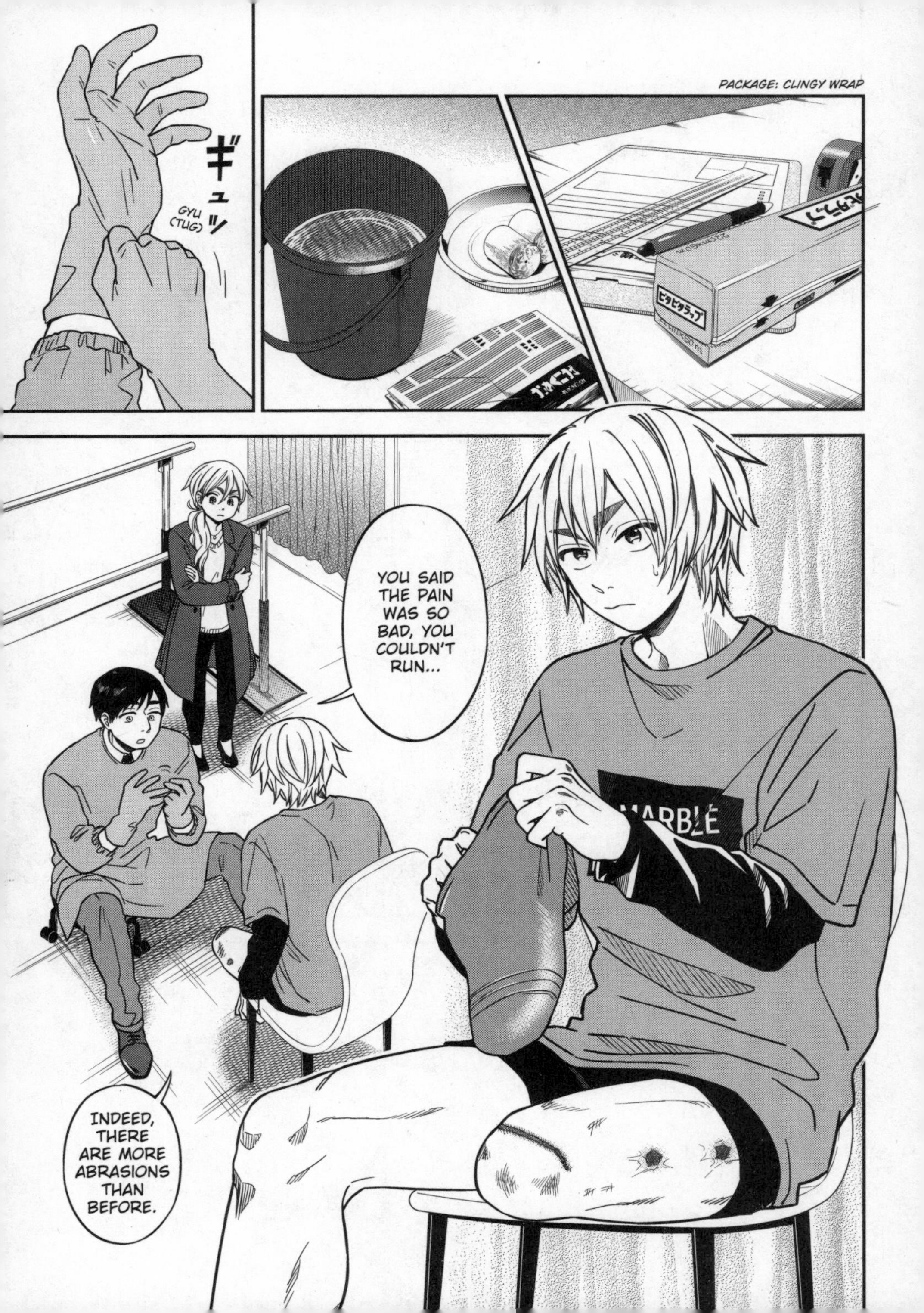
PACKAGE: CLINGY WRAP
ギュッ
GYU (TUG)
YOU SAID THE PAIN WAS SO BAD, YOU COULDN'T RUN...
INDEED, THERE ARE MORE ABRASIONS THAN BEFORE.

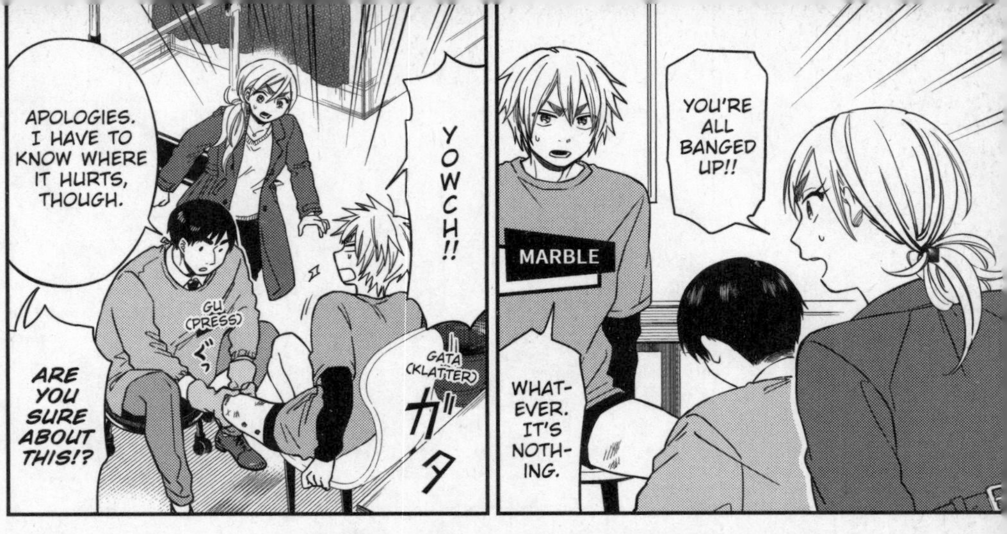
YOU'RE ALL BANGED UP!!
MARBLE
WHATEVER. IT'S NOTHING.
YOWCH!!
APOLOGIES. I HAVE TO KNOW WHERE IT HURTS, THOUGH.
GATA (KLATTER)
ガタ
GU (PRESS)
ぐっ
ARE YOU SURE ABOUT THIS!?

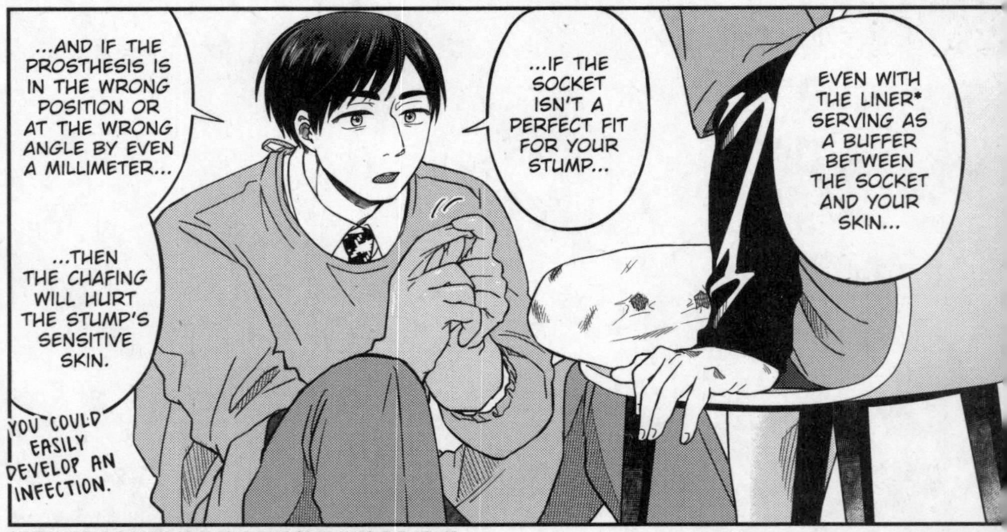
EVEN WITH THE LINER* SERVING AS A BUFFER BETWEEN THE SOCKET AND YOUR SKIN...
...IF THE SOCKET ISN'T A PERFECT FIT FOR YOUR STUMP...
...AND IF THE PROSTHESIS IS IN THE WRONG POSITION OR AT THE WRONG ANGLE BY EVEN A MILLIMETER...
...THEN THE CHAFING WILL HURT THE STUMP'S SENSITIVE SKIN.
YOU COULD EASILY DEVELOP AN INFECTION.

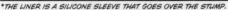

*THE LINER IS A SILICONE SLEEVE THAT GOES OVER THE STUMP.

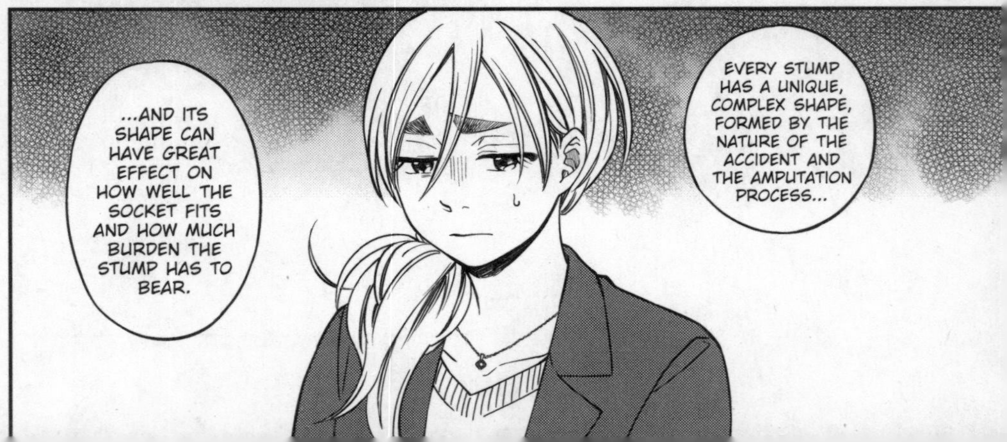
EVERY STUMP HAS A UNIQUE, COMPLEX SHAPE, FORMED BY THE NATURE OF THE ACCIDENT AND THE AMPUTATION PROCESS...
...AND ITS SHAPE CAN HAVE GREAT EFFECT ON HOW WELL THE SOCKET FITS AND HOW MUCH BURDEN THE STUMP HAS TO BEAR.

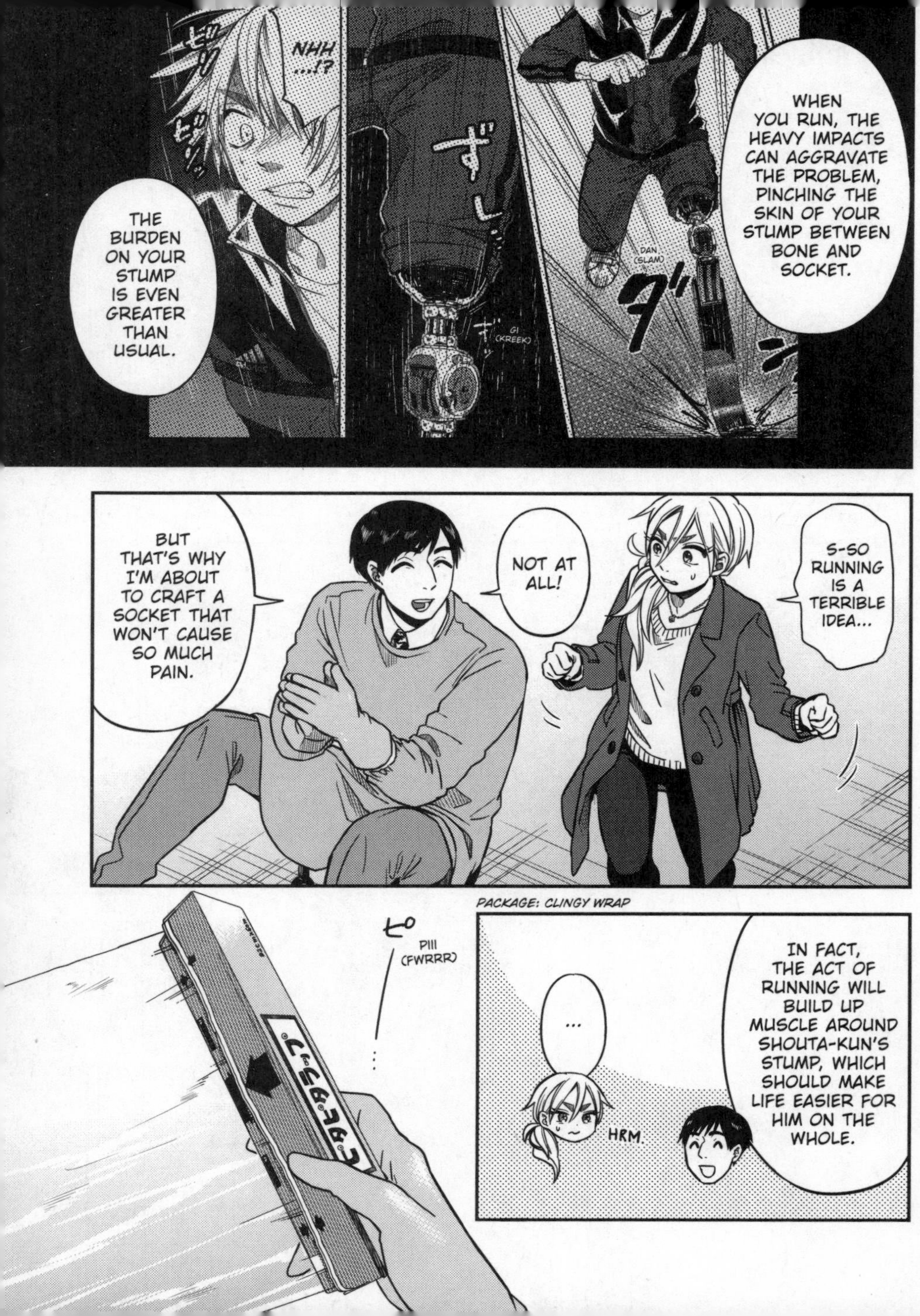
WHEN YOU RUN, THE HEAVY IMPACTS CAN AGGRAVATE THE PROBLEM, PINCHING THE SKIN OF YOUR STUMP BETWEEN BONE AND SOCKET.
DAN (SLAM)
GI (KREEK)
NHH ...!?
THE BURDEN ON YOUR STUMP IS EVEN GREATER THAN USUAL.
S-SO RUNNING IS A TERRIBLE IDEA...
NOT AT ALL!
BUT THAT'S WHY I'M ABOUT TO CRAFT A SOCKET THAT WON'T CAUSE SO MUCH PAIN.
IN FACT, THE ACT OF RUNNING WILL BUILD UP MUSCLE AROUND SHOUTA-KUN'S STUMP, WHICH SHOULD MAKE LIFE EASIER FOR HIM ON THE WHOLE.
...
HRM.
PACKAGE: CLINGY WRAP
PIII (FWRRR)

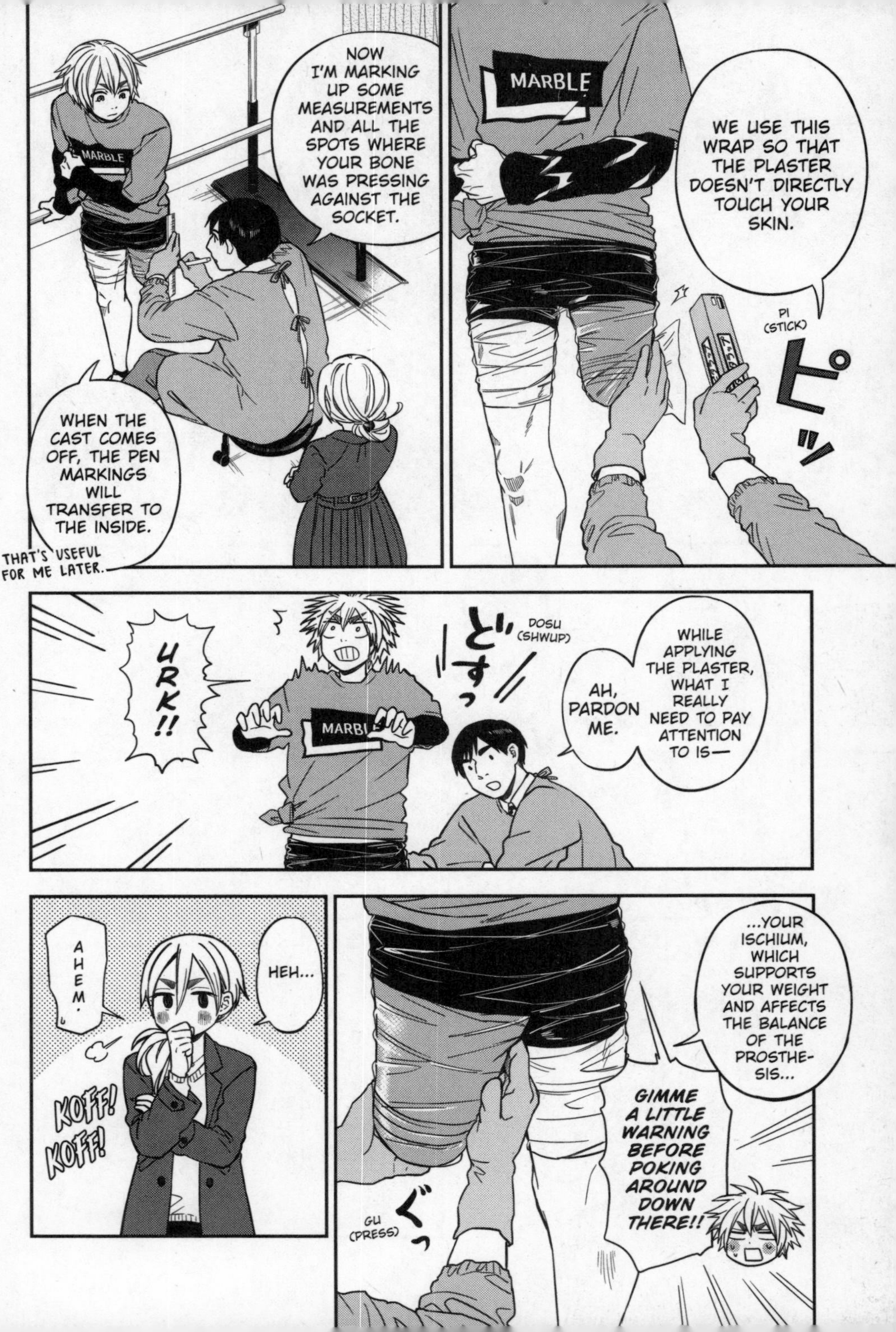
WE USE THIS WRAP SO THAT THE PLASTER DOESN'T DIRECTLY TOUCH YOUR SKIN.
PI (STICK)
ピッ
NOW I'M MARKING UP SOME MEASUREMENTS AND ALL THE SPOTS WHERE YOUR BONE WAS PRESSING AGAINST THE SOCKET.
WHEN THE CAST COMES OFF, THE PEN MARKINGS WILL TRANSFER TO THE INSIDE.
THAT'S USEFUL FOR ME LATER.
WHILE APPLYING THE PLASTER, WHAT I REALLY NEED TO PAY ATTENTION TO IS—
AH, PARDON ME.
DOSU (SHWUP)
どすっ
URK!!
...YOUR ISCHIUM, WHICH SUPPORTS YOUR WEIGHT AND AFFECTS THE BALANCE OF THE PROSTHE-SIS...
GIMME A LITTLE WARNING BEFORE POKING AROUND DOWN THERE!!
GU (PRESS)
ぐっ
HEH...
AHEM.
KOFF! KOFF!

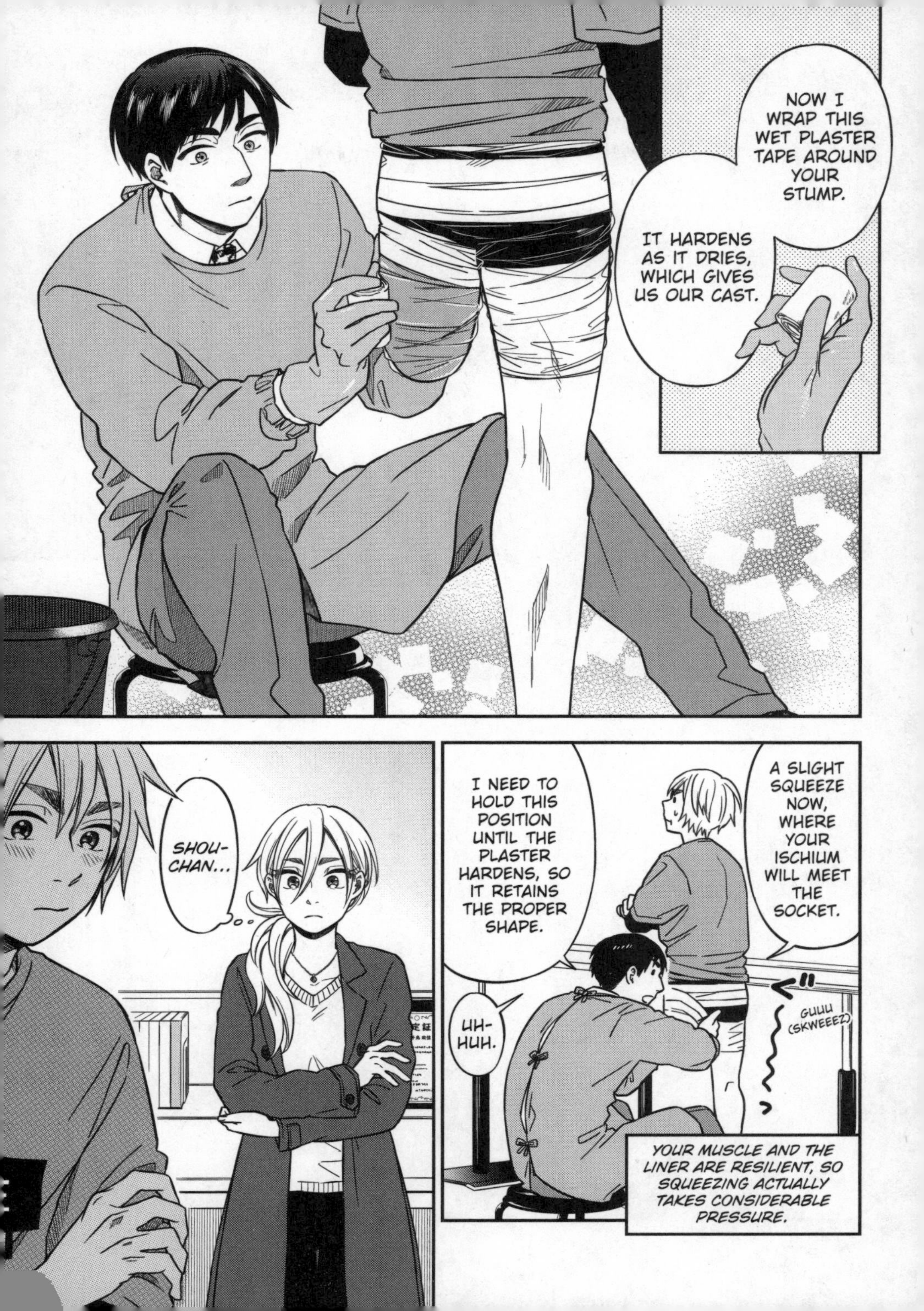
NOW I WRAP THIS WET PLASTER TAPE AROUND YOUR STUMP.
IT HARDENS AS IT DRIES, WHICH GIVES US OUR CAST.
A SLIGHT SQUEEZE NOW, WHERE YOUR ISCHIUM WILL MEET THE SOCKET.
I NEED TO HOLD THIS POSITION UNTIL THE PLASTER HARDENS, SO IT RETAINS THE PROPER SHAPE.
GUUU (SKWEEEZ)
UH-HUH.
YOUR MUSCLE AND THE LINER ARE RESILIENT, SO SQUEEZING ACTUALLY TAKES CONSIDERABLE PRESSURE.
SHOU-CHAN...

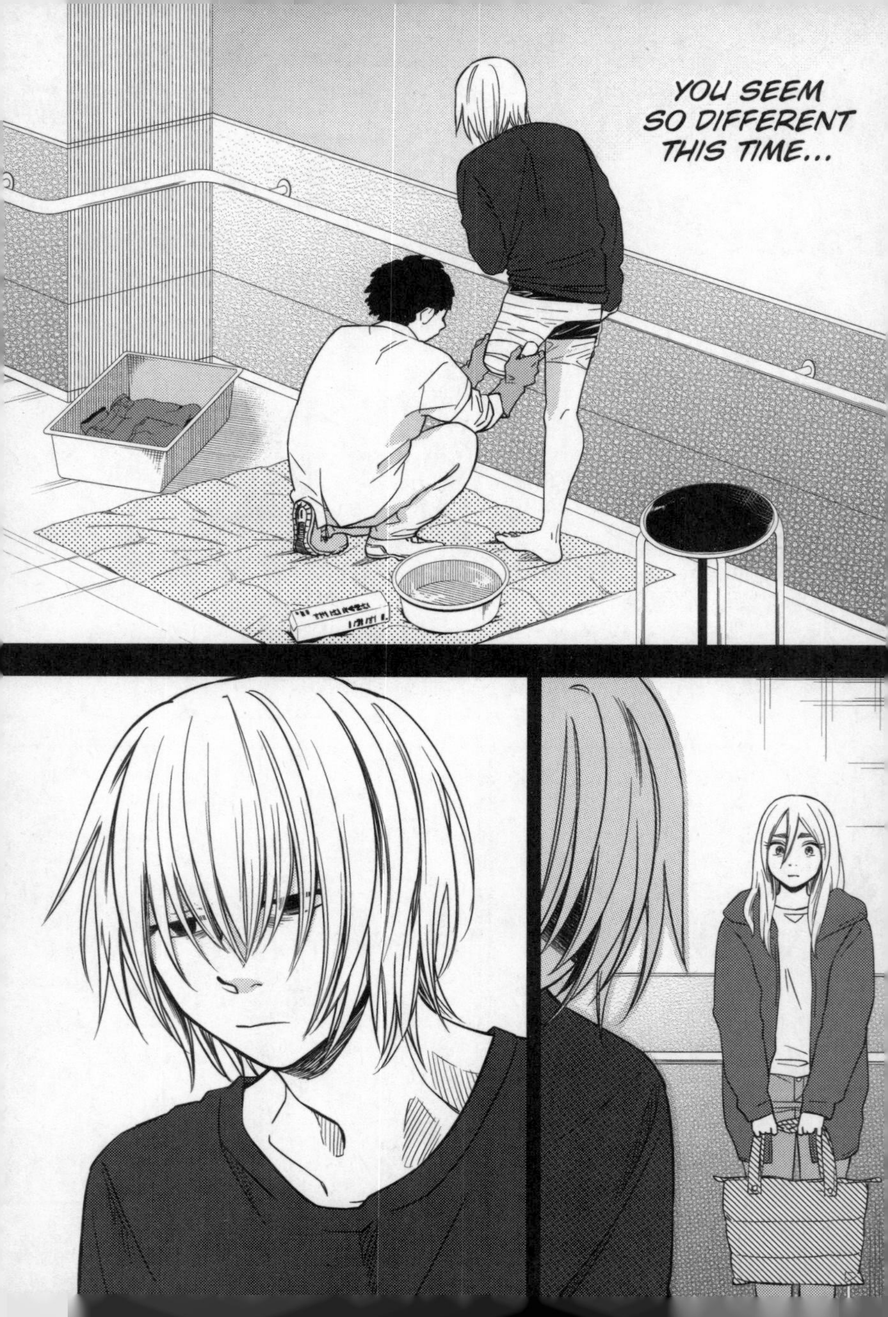
YOU SEEM SO DIFFERENT THIS TIME...

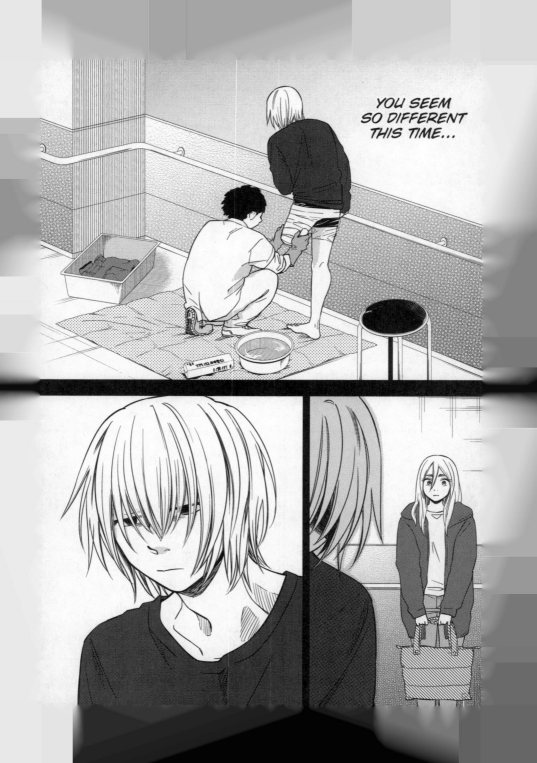

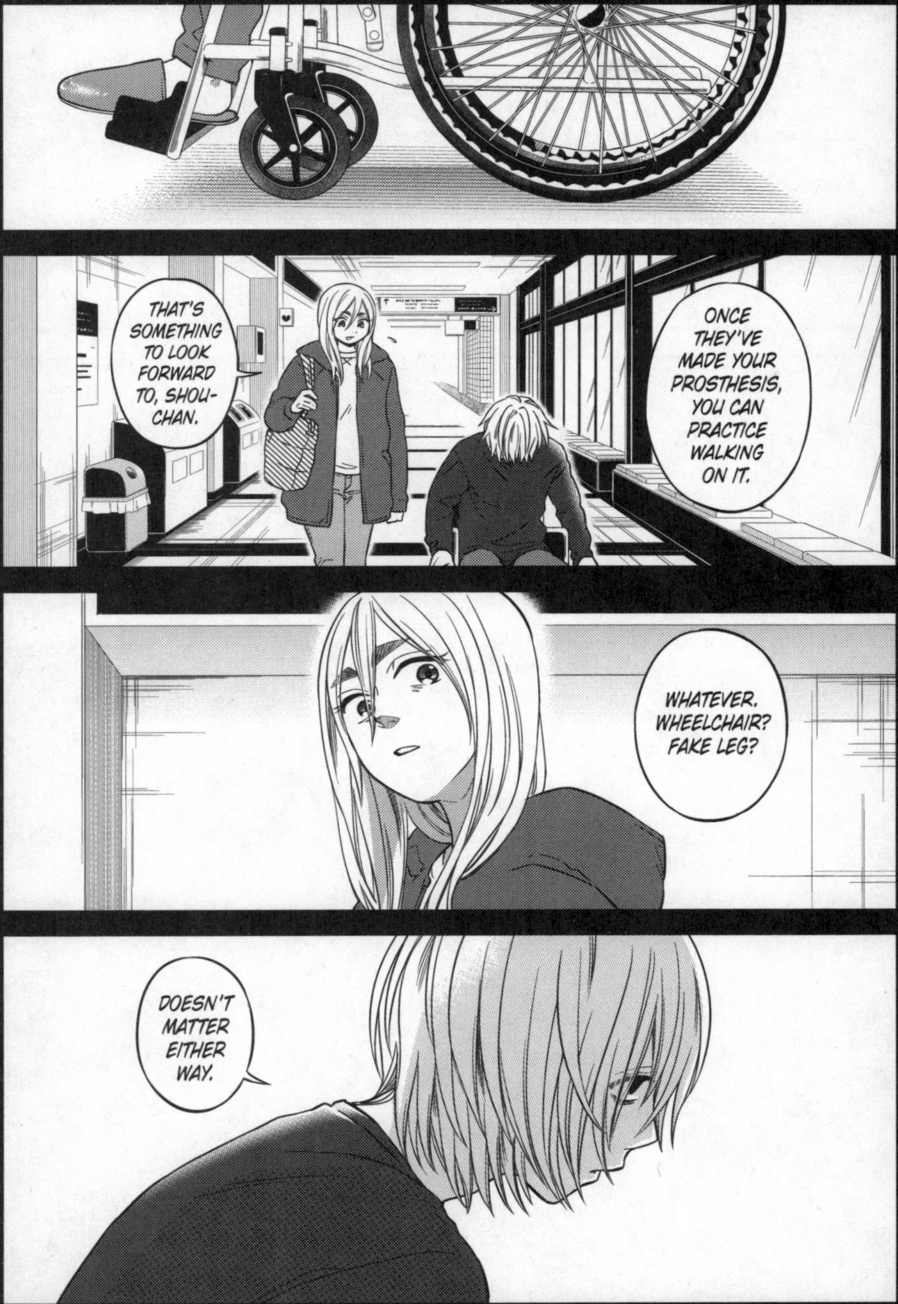
ONCE THEY'VE MADE YOUR PROSTHESIS, YOU CAN PRACTICE WALKING ON IT.
THAT'S SOMETHING TO LOOK FORWARD TO, SHOU-CHAN.
WHATEVER. WHEELCHAIR? FAKE LEG?
DOESN'T MATTER EITHER WAY.

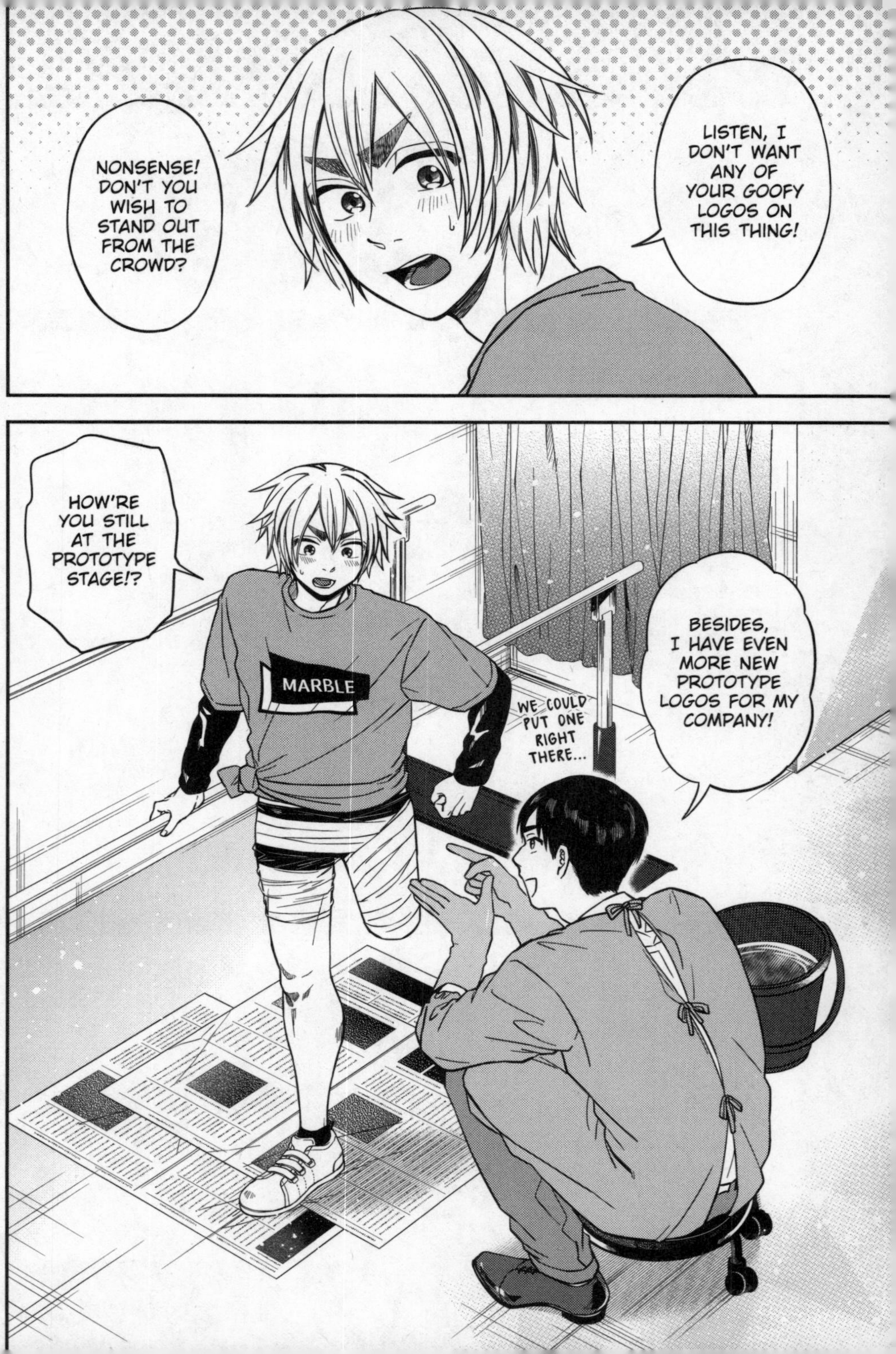
LISTEN, I DON'T WANT ANY OF YOUR GOOFY LOGOS ON THIS THING!
NONSENSE! DON'T YOU WISH TO STAND OUT FROM THE CROWD?
BESIDES, I HAVE EVEN MORE NEW PROTOTYPE LOGOS FOR MY COMPANY!
WE COULD PUT ONE RIGHT THERE...
MARBLE
HOW'RE YOU STILL AT THE PROTOTYPE STAGE!?

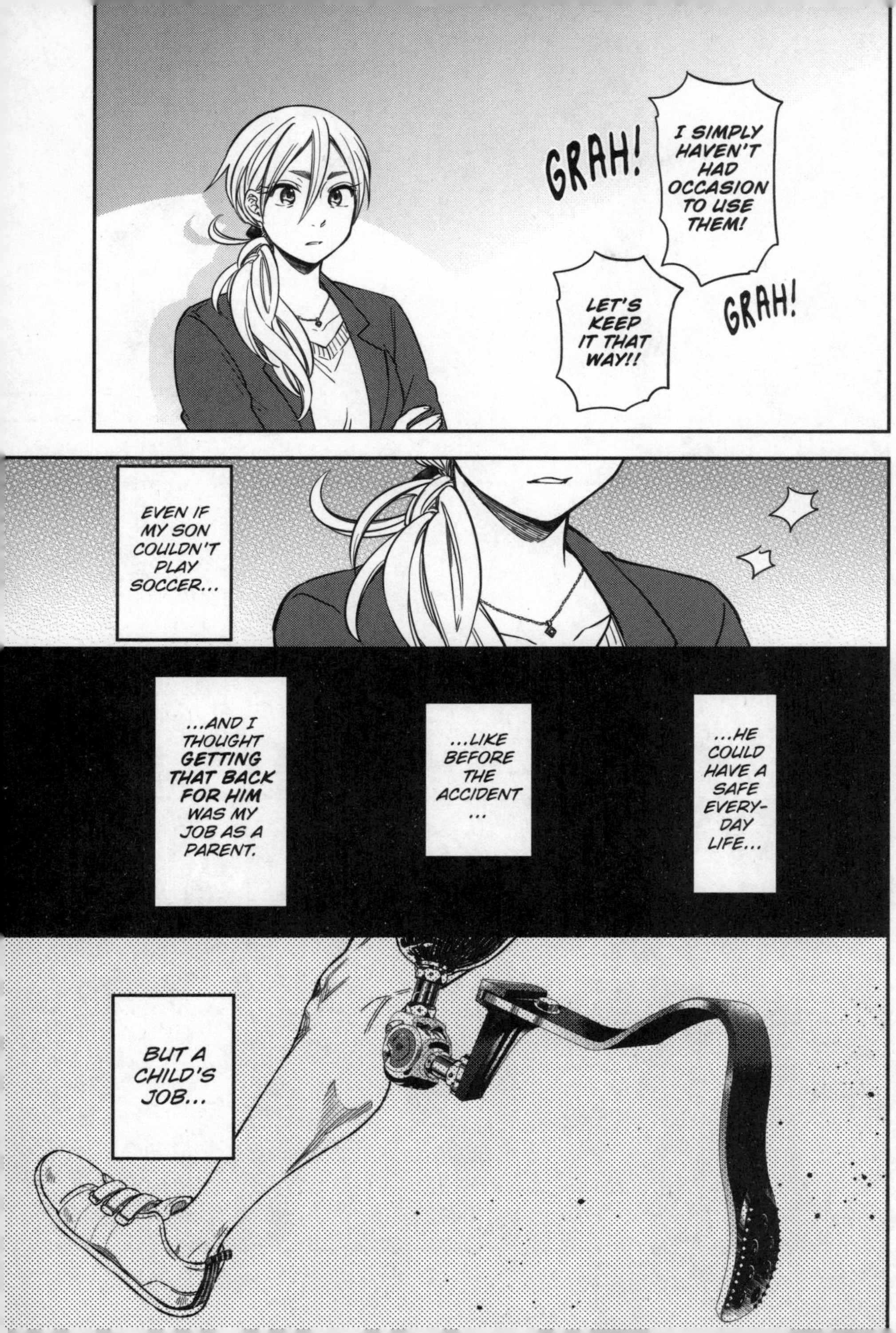
GRAH!
I SIMPLY HAVEN'T HAD OCCASION TO USE THEM!
GRAH!
LET'S KEEP IT THAT WAY!!
EVEN IF MY SON COULDN'T PLAY SOCCER...
...HE COULD HAVE A SAFE EVERY-DAY LIFE...
...LIKE BEFORE THE ACCIDENT...
...AND I THOUGHT GETTING THAT BACK FOR HIM WAS MY JOB AS A PARENT.
BUT A CHILD'S JOB...

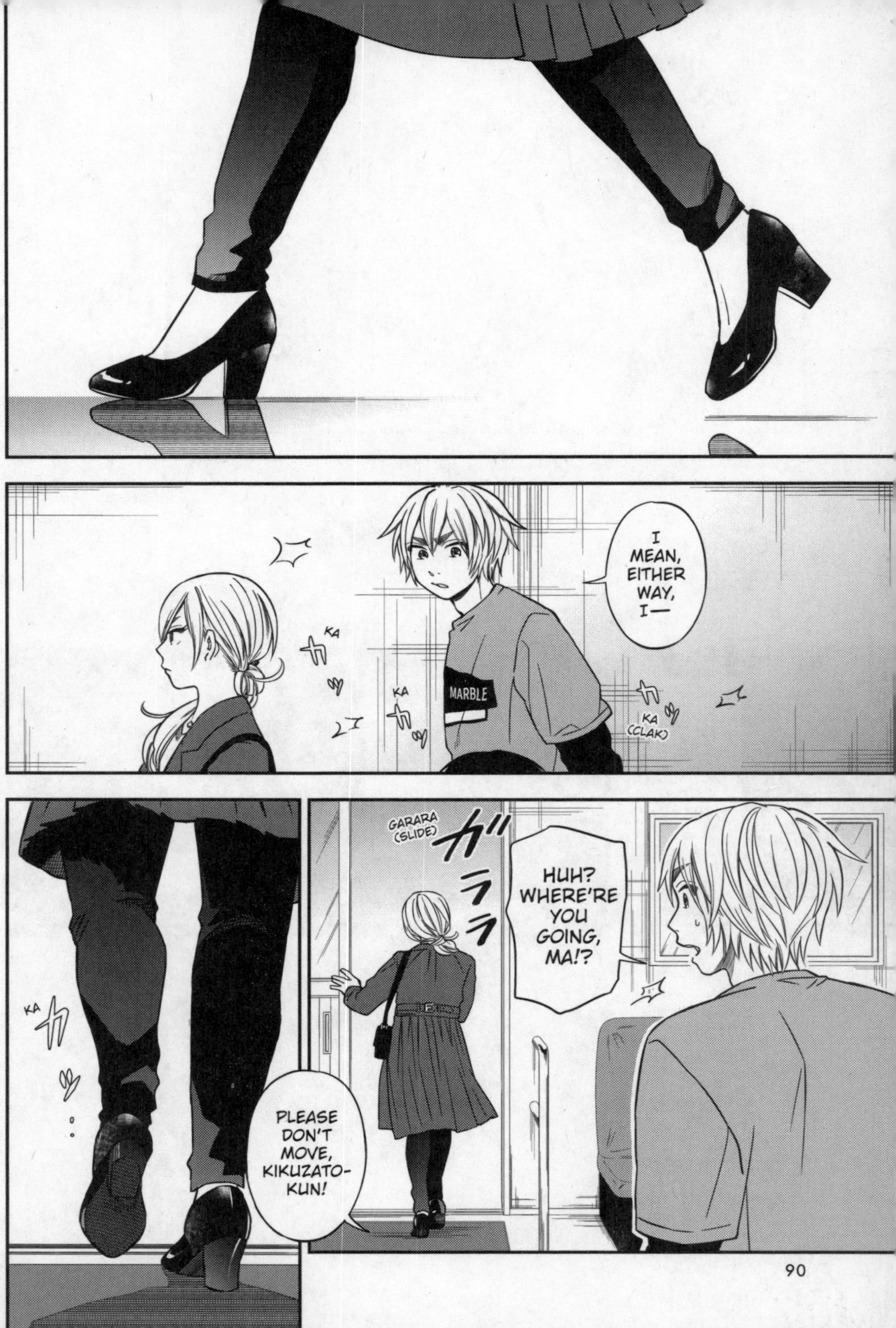
I MEAN, EITHER WAY, I—
KA
KA
KA (CLAK)
GARARA (SLIDE)
HUH? WHERE'RE YOU GOING, MA!?
PLEASE DON'T MOVE, KIKUZATO-KUN!
KA

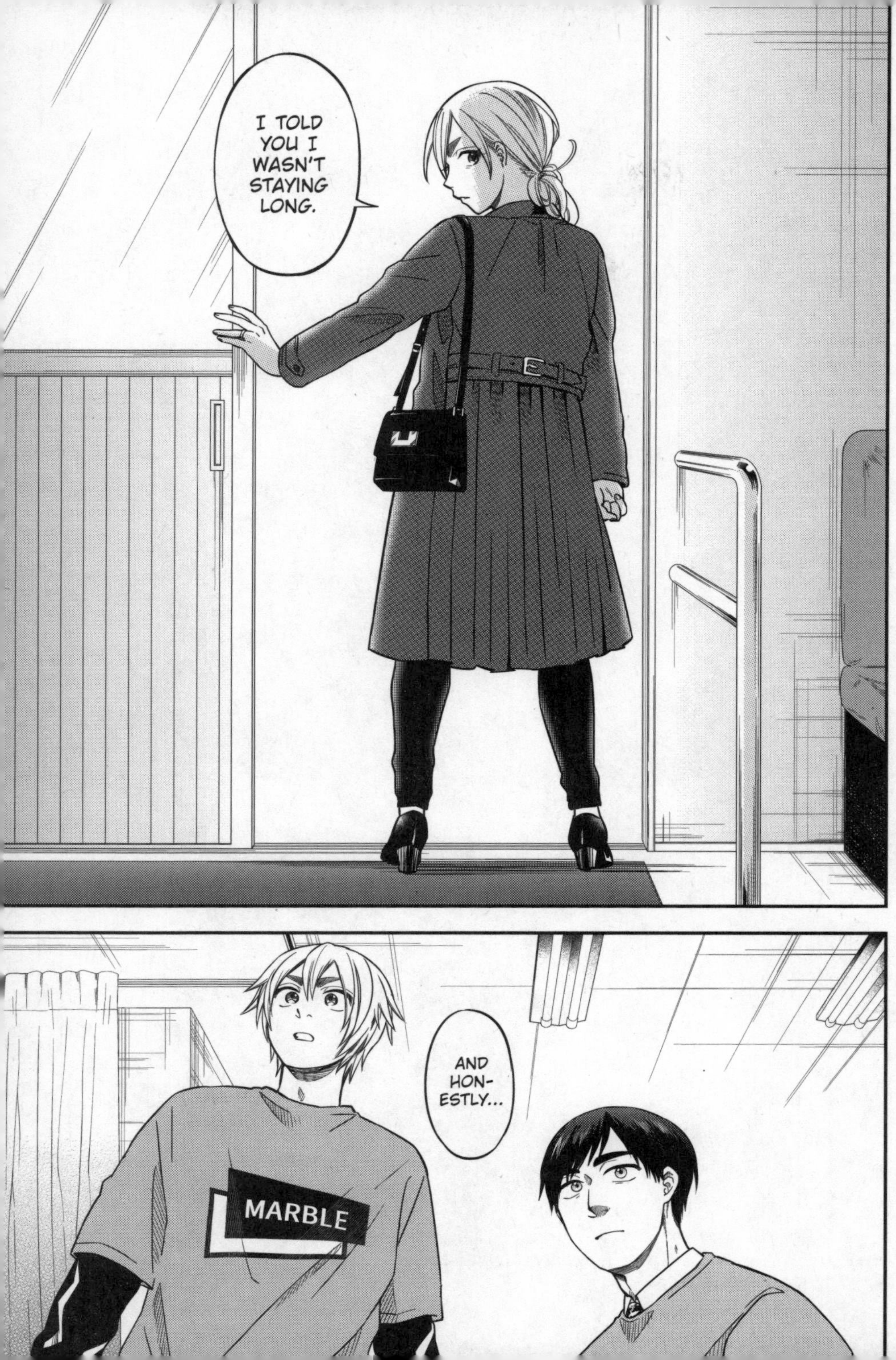
I TOLD YOU I WASN'T STAYING LONG.
AND HONESTLY...
MARBLE

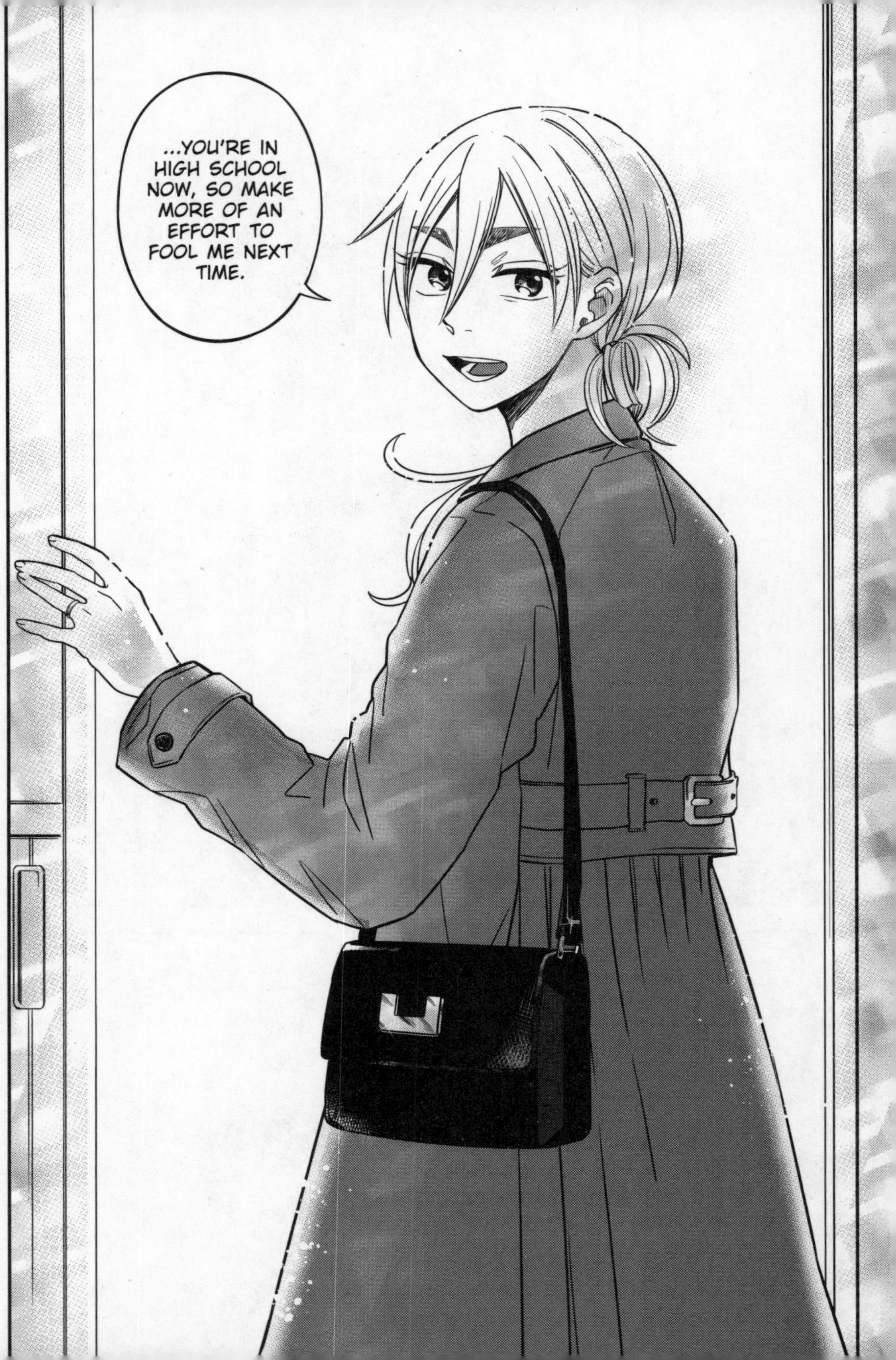
...YOU'RE IN HIGH SCHOOL NOW, SO MAKE MORE OF AN EFFORT TO FOOL ME NEXT TIME.

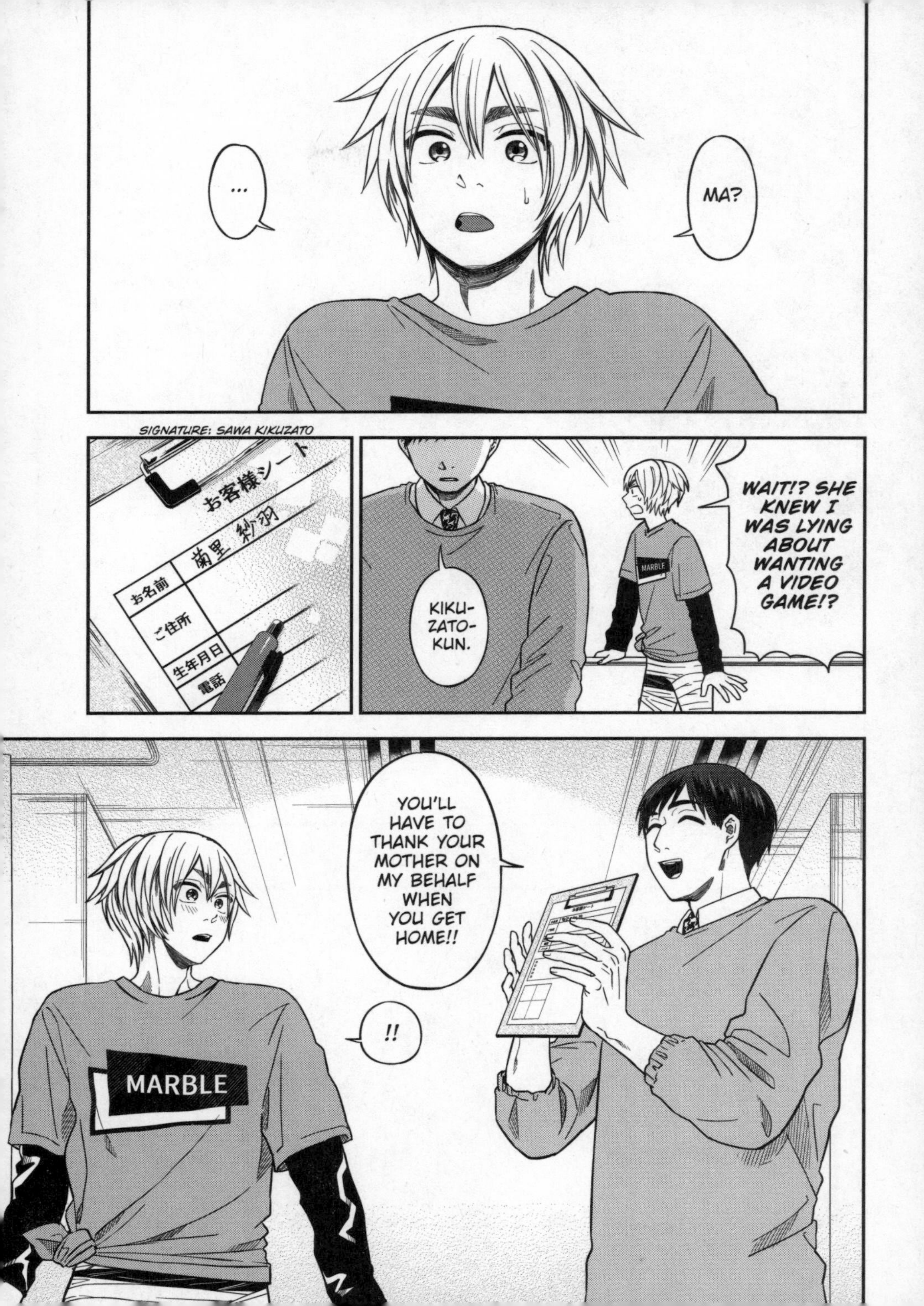
MA?
...
WAIT!? SHE KNEW I WAS LYING ABOUT WANTING A VIDEO GAME!?
KIKU-ZATO-KUN.
SIGNATURE: SAWA KIKUZATO
お客様シート
お名前
菊里 紗羽
ご住所
生年月日
電話
YOU'LL HAVE TO THANK YOUR MOTHER ON MY BEHALF WHEN YOU GET HOME!!
!!

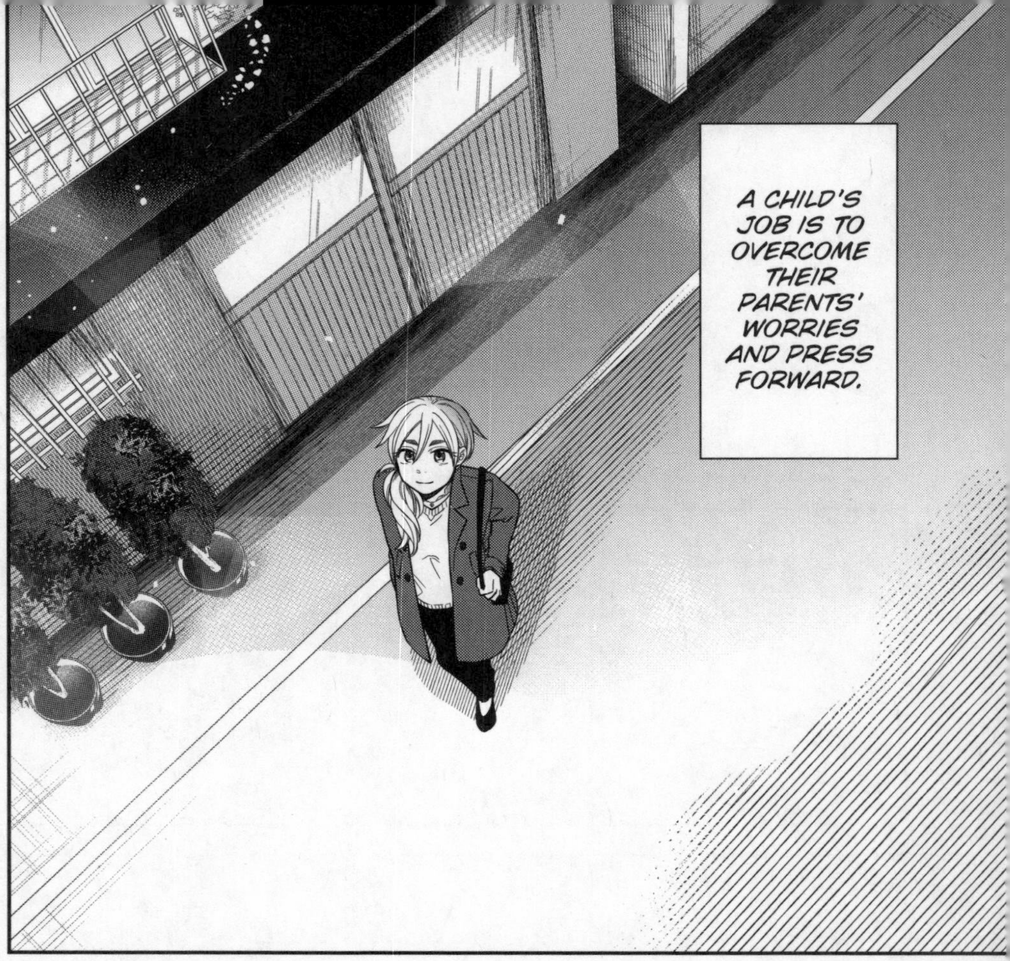
A CHILD'S JOB IS TO OVERCOME THEIR PARENTS' WORRIES AND PRESS FORWARD.

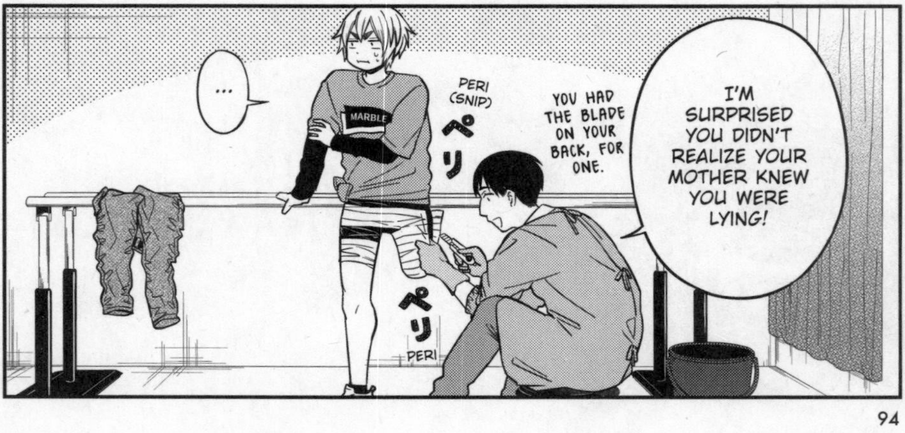
I'M SURPRISED YOU DIDN'T REALIZE YOUR MOTHER KNEW YOU WERE LYING!
YOU HAD THE BLADE ON YOUR BACK, FOR ONE.
ペリ
PERI (SNIP)
...
ペリ
PERI

RUN ON YOUR NEW LEGS

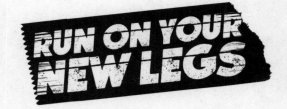

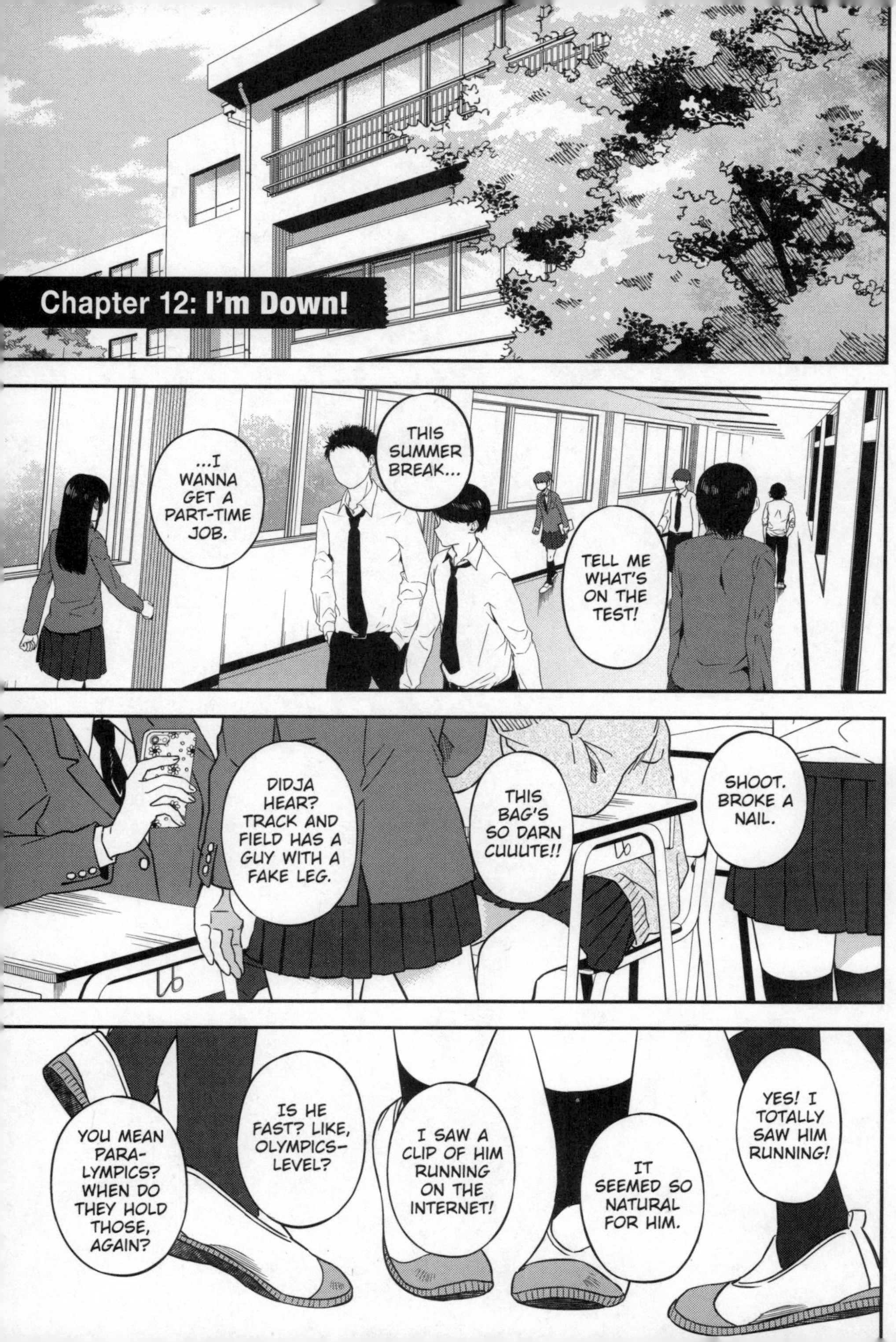
Chapter 12: I'm Down!
TELL ME WHAT'S ON THE TEST!
THIS SUMMER BREAK...
...I WANNA GET A PART-TIME JOB.
SHOOT. BROKE A NAIL.
THIS BAG'S SO DARN CUUUTE!!
DIDJA HEAR? TRACK AND FIELD HAS A GUY WITH A FAKE LEG.
YES! I TOTALLY SAW HIM RUNNING!
IT SEEMED SO NATURAL FOR HIM.
I SAW A CLIP OF HIM RUNNING ON THE INTERNET!
IS HE FAST? LIKE, OLYMPICS-LEVEL?
YOU MEAN PARA-LYMPICS? WHEN DO THEY HOLD THOSE, AGAIN?

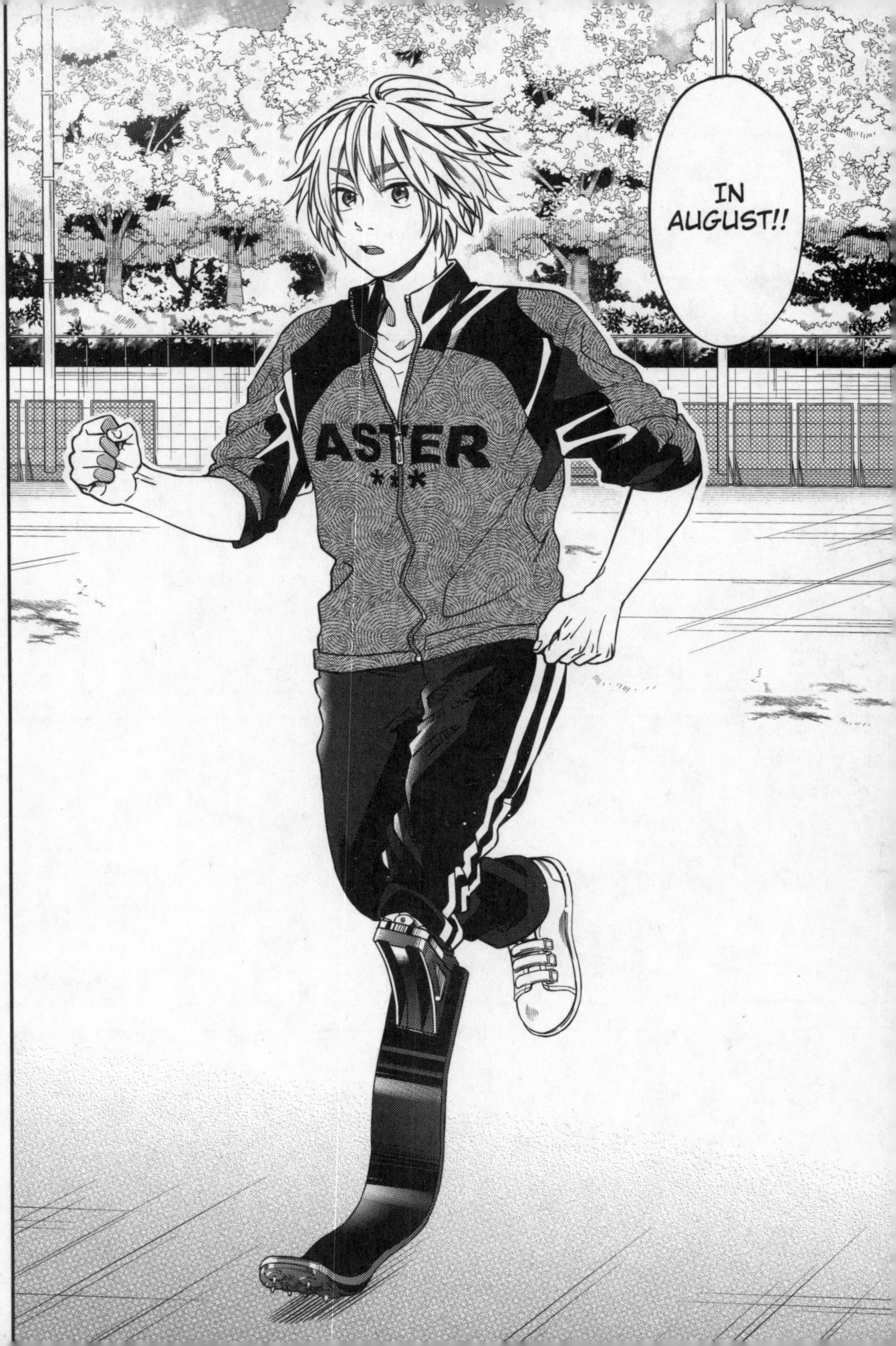
IN AUGUST!!
ASTER

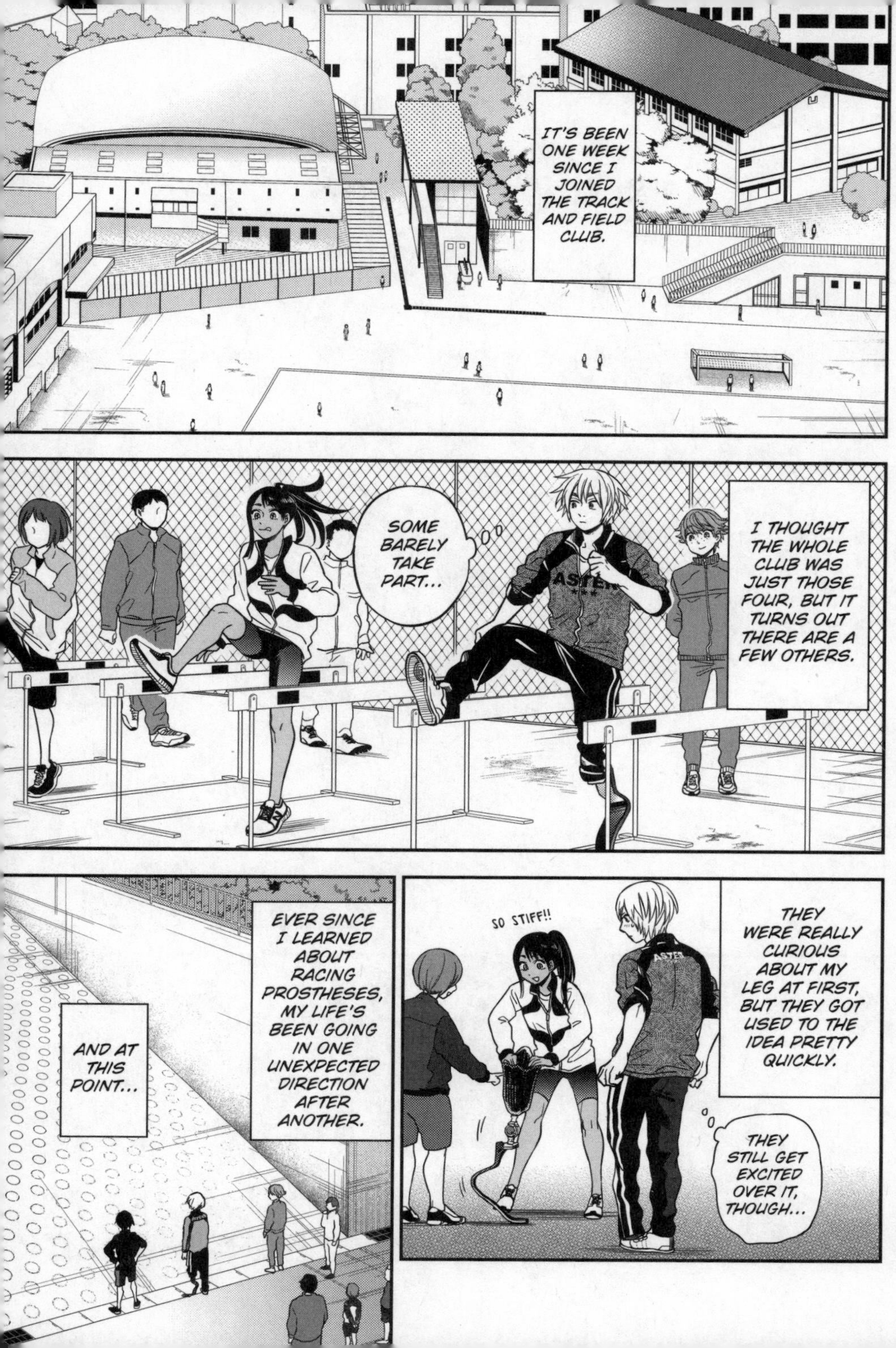
IT'S BEEN ONE WEEK SINCE I JOINED THE TRACK AND FIELD CLUB.
I THOUGHT THE WHOLE CLUB WAS JUST THOSE FOUR, BUT IT TURNS OUT THERE ARE A FEW OTHERS.
SOME BARELY TAKE PART...
ASTER
THEY WERE REALLY CURIOUS ABOUT MY LEG AT FIRST, BUT THEY GOT USED TO THE IDEA PRETTY QUICKLY.
SO STIFF!!
THEY STILL GET EXCITED OVER IT, THOUGH...
EVER SINCE I LEARNED ABOUT RACING PROSTHESES, MY LIFE'S BEEN GOING IN ONE UNEXPECTED DIRECTION AFTER ANOTHER.
AND AT THIS POINT...

...I'M HAVING A BLAST RUNNING.

PI
(FWEET)

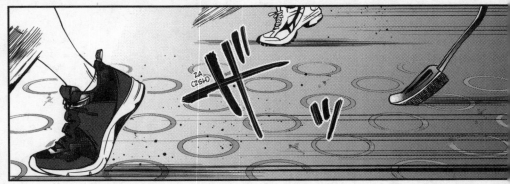

ZA
(ZSH)

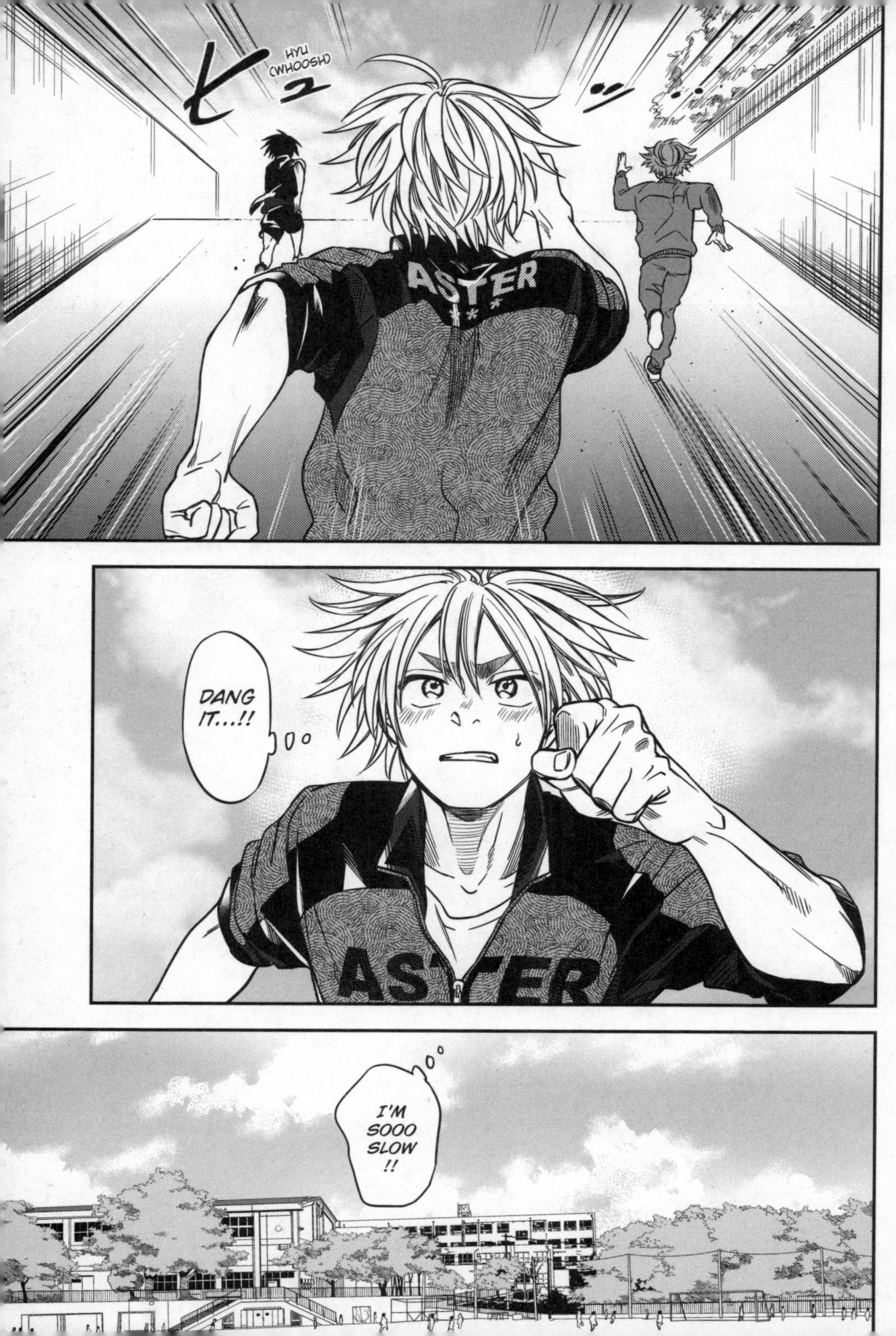

HYU (WHOOSH)
ASTER
DANG IT...!!
ASTER
I'M SOOO SLOW !!

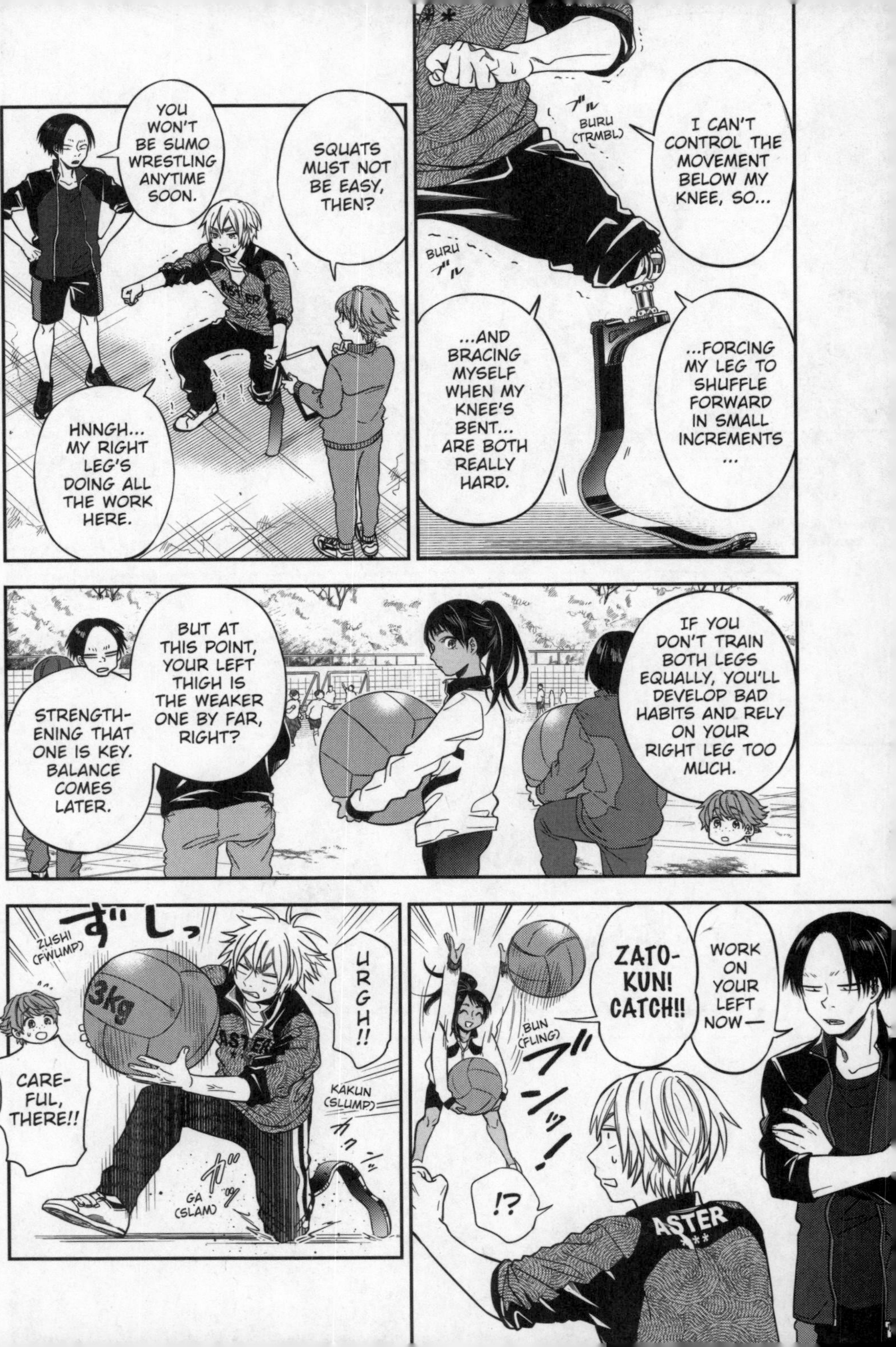
ブル
BURU (TRMBL)
I CAN'T CONTROL THE MOVEMENT BELOW MY KNEE, SO...
BURU
ブル
...FORCING MY LEG TO SHUFFLE FORWARD IN SMALL INCREMENTS...
...AND BRACING MYSELF WHEN MY KNEE'S BENT... ARE BOTH REALLY HARD.
SQUATS MUST NOT BE EASY, THEN?
YOU WON'T BE SUMO WRESTLING ANYTIME SOON.
HNNGH... MY RIGHT LEG'S DOING ALL THE WORK HERE.
IF YOU DON'T TRAIN BOTH LEGS EQUALLY, YOU'LL DEVELOP BAD HABITS AND RELY ON YOUR RIGHT LEG TOO MUCH.
BUT AT THIS POINT, YOUR LEFT THIGH IS THE WEAKER ONE BY FAR, RIGHT?
STRENGTH-ENING THAT ONE IS KEY. BALANCE COMES LATER.
WORK ON YOUR LEFT NOW—
ZATO-KUN! CATCH!!
BUN (FLING)
ブンッ!
!?
URGH!!
ずしっ
ZUSHI (FWUMP)
3kg
CARE-FUL, THERE!!
KAKUN (SLUMP)
カクン
GA (SLAM)
ガ

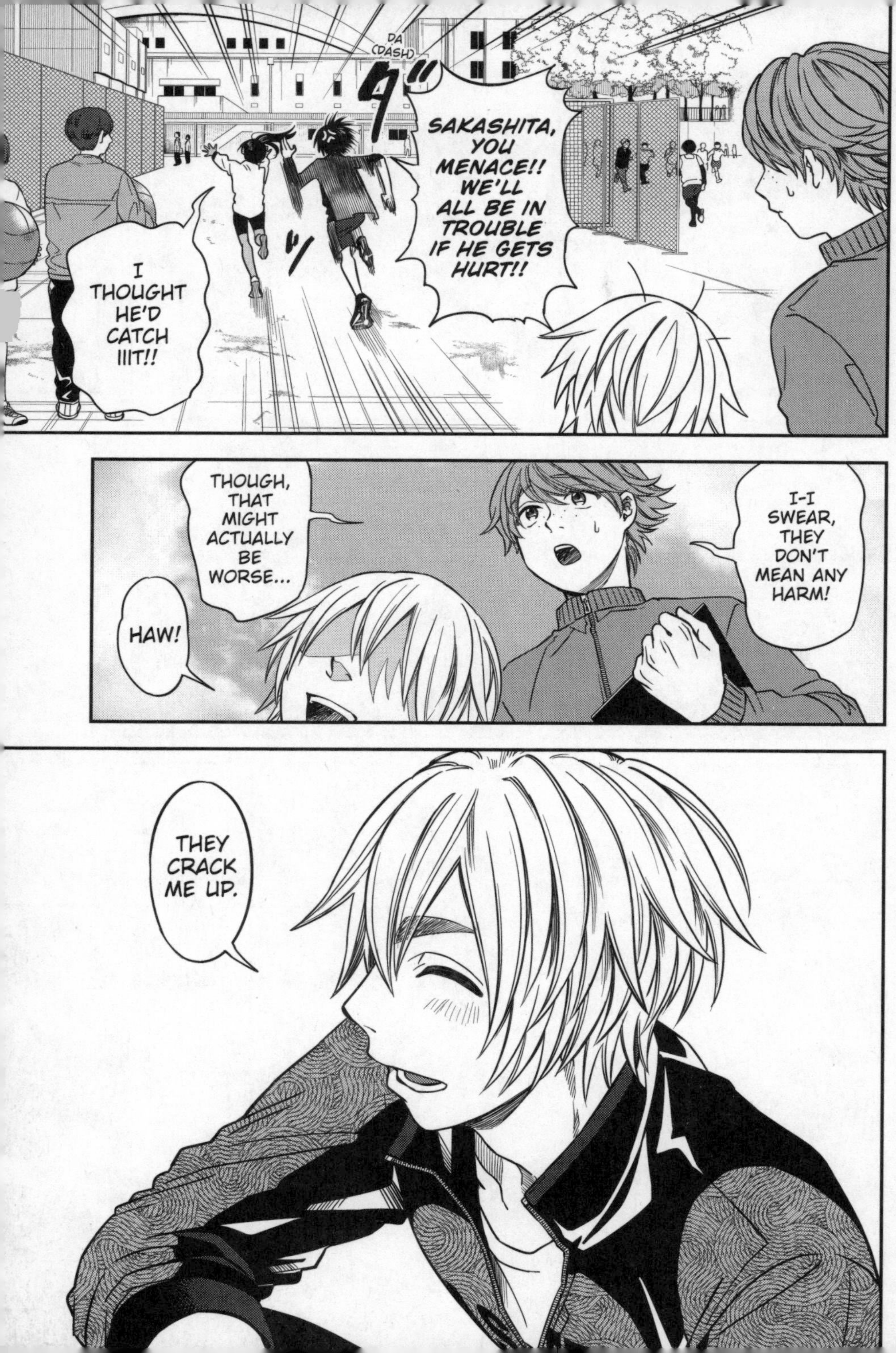
DA (DASH)
SAKASHITA, YOU MENACE!! WE'LL ALL BE IN TROUBLE IF HE GETS HURT!!
I THOUGHT HE'D CATCH IIIT!!
I-I SWEAR, THEY DON'T MEAN ANY HARM!
THOUGH, THAT MIGHT ACTUALLY BE WORSE...
HAW!
THEY CRACK ME UP.

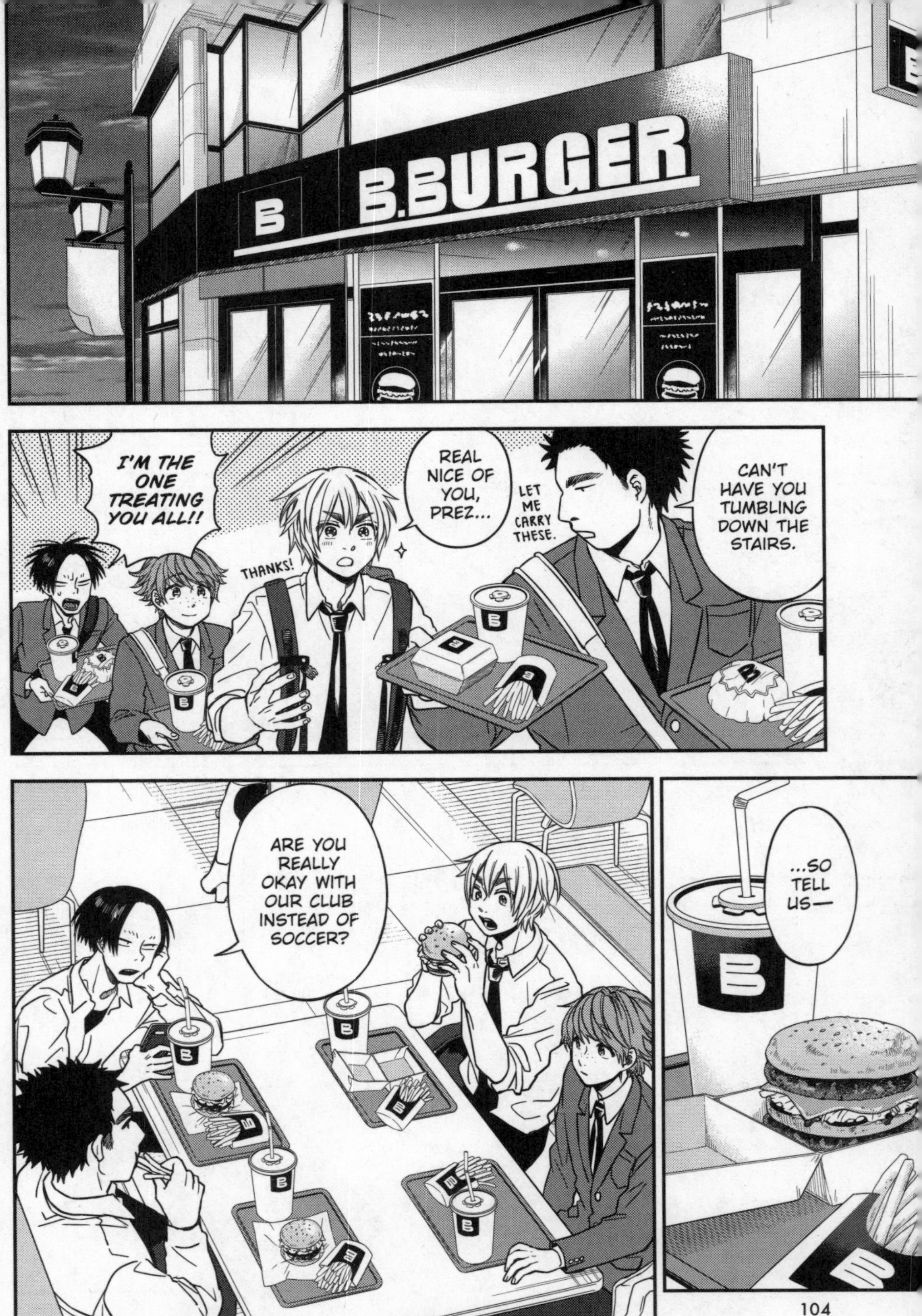
B.BURGER
CAN'T HAVE YOU TUMBLING DOWN THE STAIRS.
LET ME CARRY THESE.
REAL NICE OF YOU, PREZ...
THANKS!
I'M THE ONE TREATING YOU ALL!!
...SO TELL US—
ARE YOU REALLY OKAY WITH OUR CLUB INSTEAD OF SOCCER?

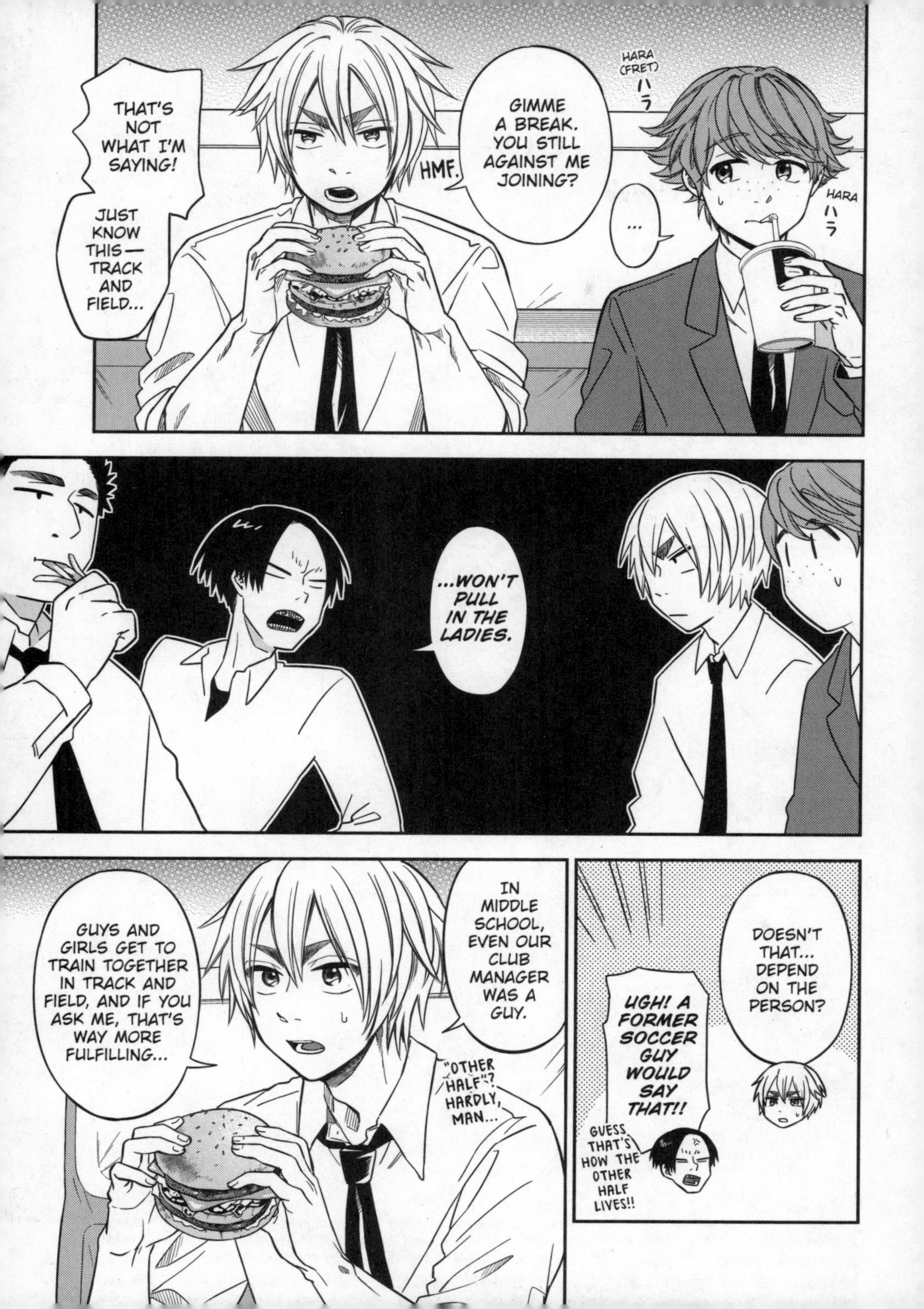
HARA (FRET) ハラ
HARA ハラ
...
GIMME A BREAK. YOU STILL AGAINST ME JOINING?
HMF.
THAT'S NOT WHAT I'M SAYING!
JUST KNOW THIS— TRACK AND FIELD...
...WON'T PULL IN THE LADIES.
DOESN'T THAT... DEPEND ON THE PERSON?
UGH! A FORMER SOCCER GUY WOULD SAY THAT!!
GUESS THAT'S HOW THE OTHER HALF LIVES!!
IN MIDDLE SCHOOL, EVEN OUR CLUB MANAGER WAS A GUY.
GUYS AND GIRLS GET TO TRAIN TOGETHER IN TRACK AND FIELD, AND IF YOU ASK ME, THAT'S WAY MORE FULFILLING...
"OTHER HALF"? HARDLY, MAN...

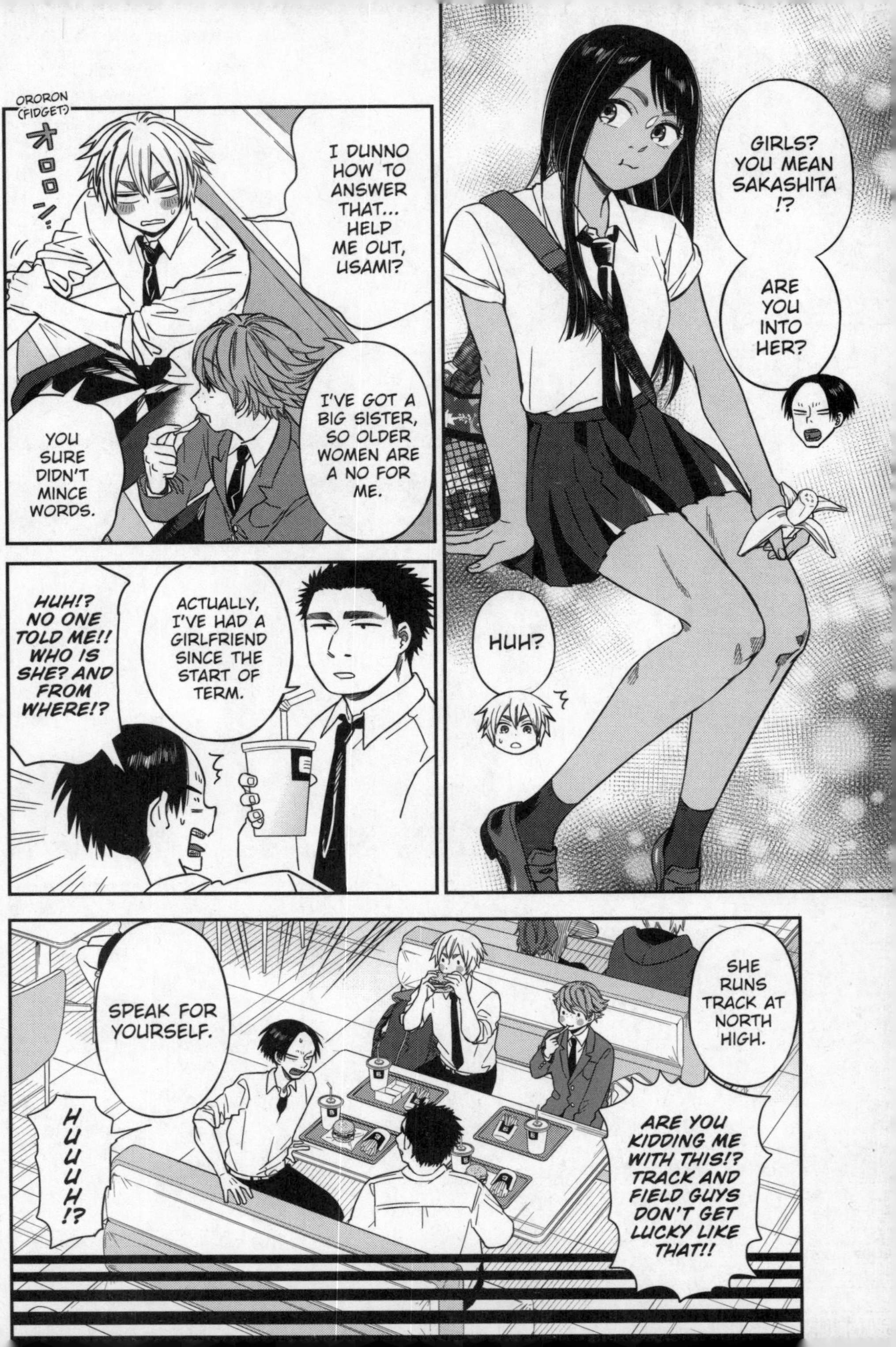

GIRLS? YOU MEAN SAKASHITA !?
ARE YOU INTO HER?
HUH?
I DUNNO HOW TO ANSWER THAT... HELP ME OUT, USAMI?
I'VE GOT A BIG SISTER, SO OLDER WOMEN ARE A NO FOR ME.
YOU SURE DIDN'T MINCE WORDS.
ORORON (FIDGET)
オロロン
ACTUALLY, I'VE HAD A GIRLFRIEND SINCE THE START OF TERM.
HUH!? NO ONE TOLD ME!! WHO IS SHE? AND FROM WHERE!?
SHE RUNS TRACK AT NORTH HIGH.
ARE YOU KIDDING ME WITH THIS!? TRACK AND FIELD GUYS DON'T GET LUCKY LIKE THAT!!
SPEAK FOR YOURSELF.
HUUUUH!?

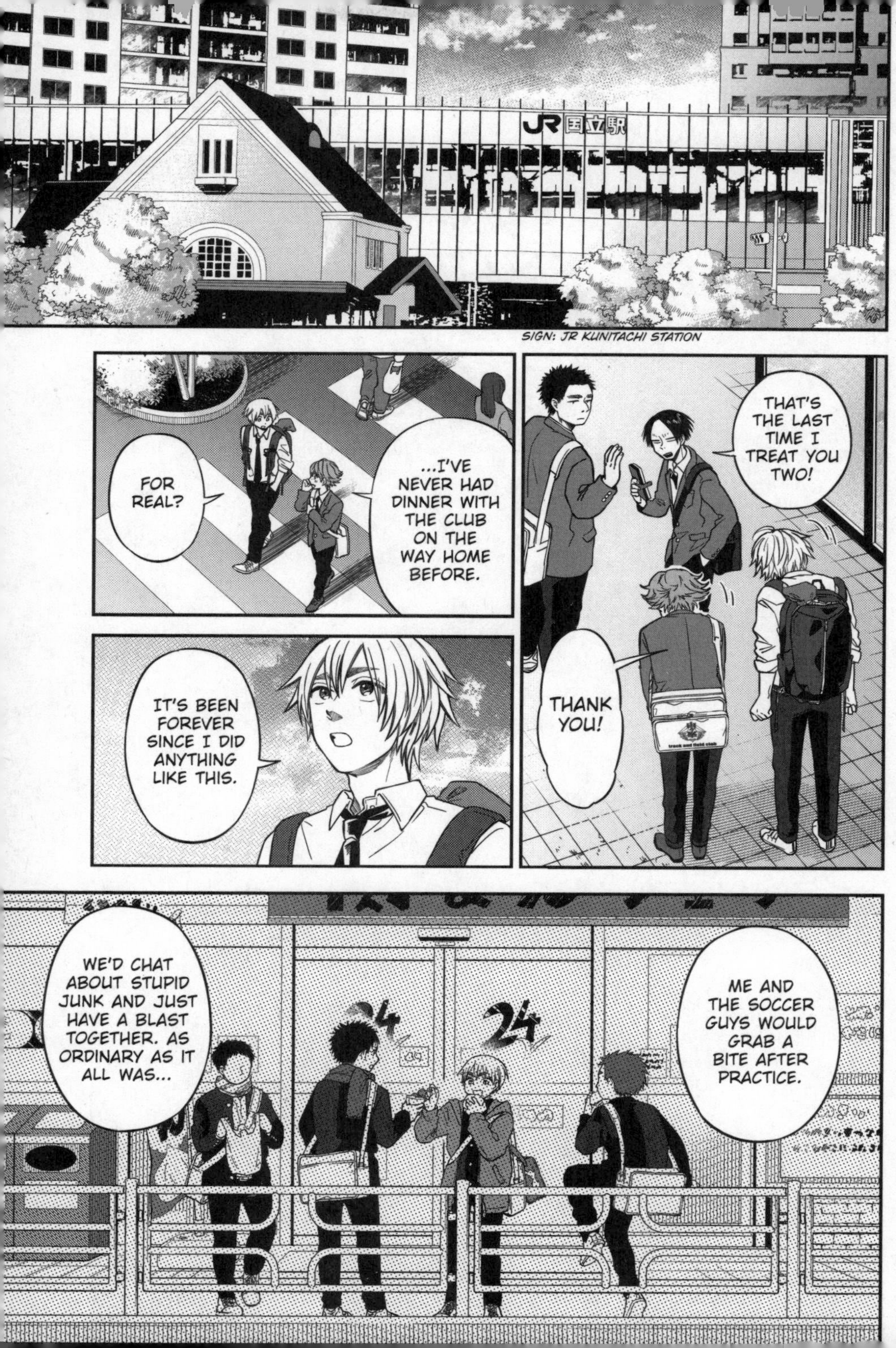
JR 国立駅
SIGN: JR KUNITACHI STATION
THAT'S THE LAST TIME I TREAT YOU TWO!
track and field club
THANK YOU!
...I'VE NEVER HAD DINNER WITH THE CLUB ON THE WAY HOME BEFORE.
FOR REAL?
IT'S BEEN FOREVER SINCE I DID ANYTHING LIKE THIS.
ME AND THE SOCCER GUYS WOULD GRAB A BITE AFTER PRACTICE.
WE'D CHAT ABOUT STUPID JUNK AND JUST HAVE A BLAST TOGETHER. AS ORDINARY AS IT ALL WAS...

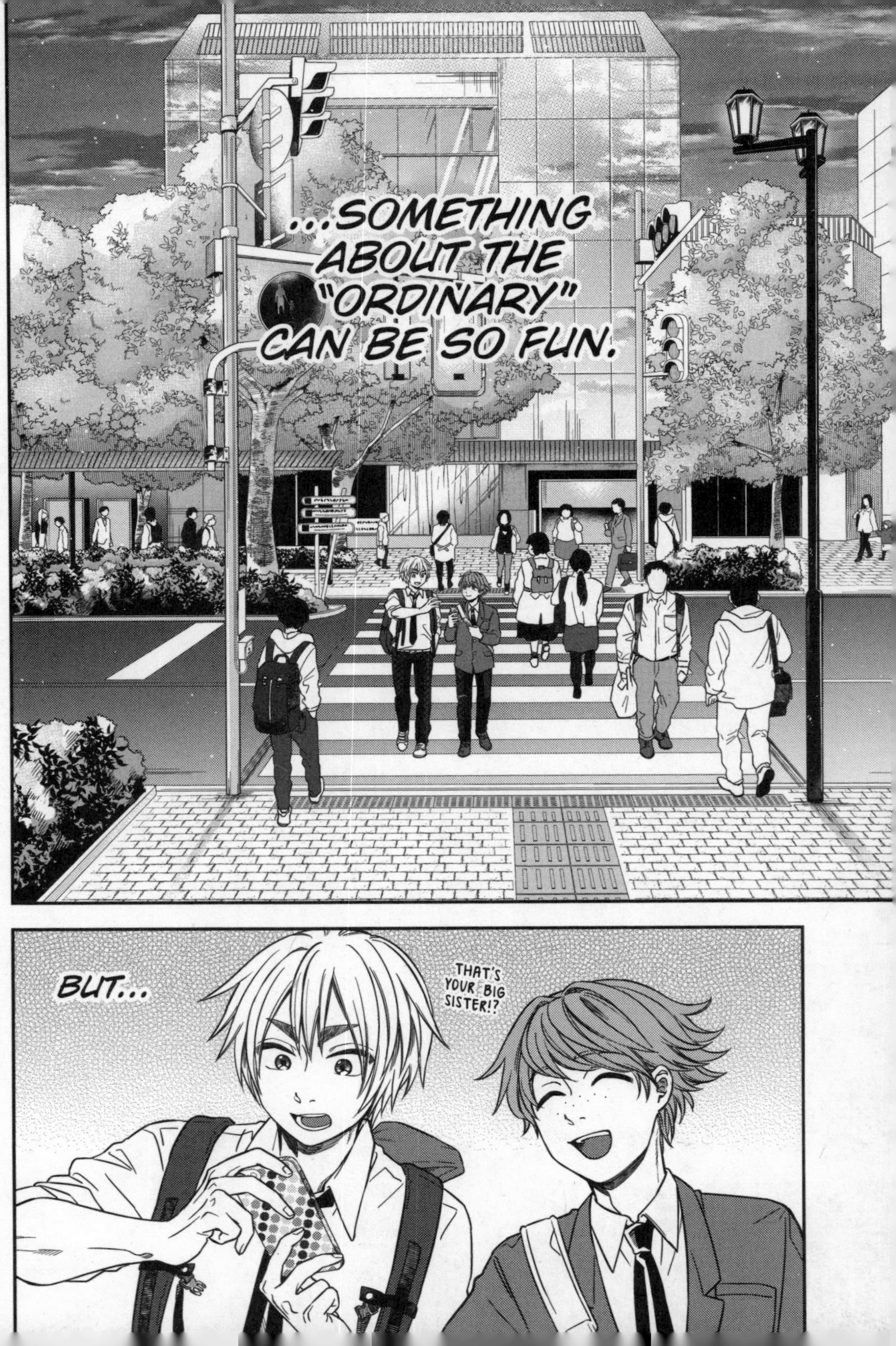
...SOMETHING ABOUT THE "ORDINARY" CAN BE SO FUN.
BUT...
THAT'S YOUR BIG SISTER!?

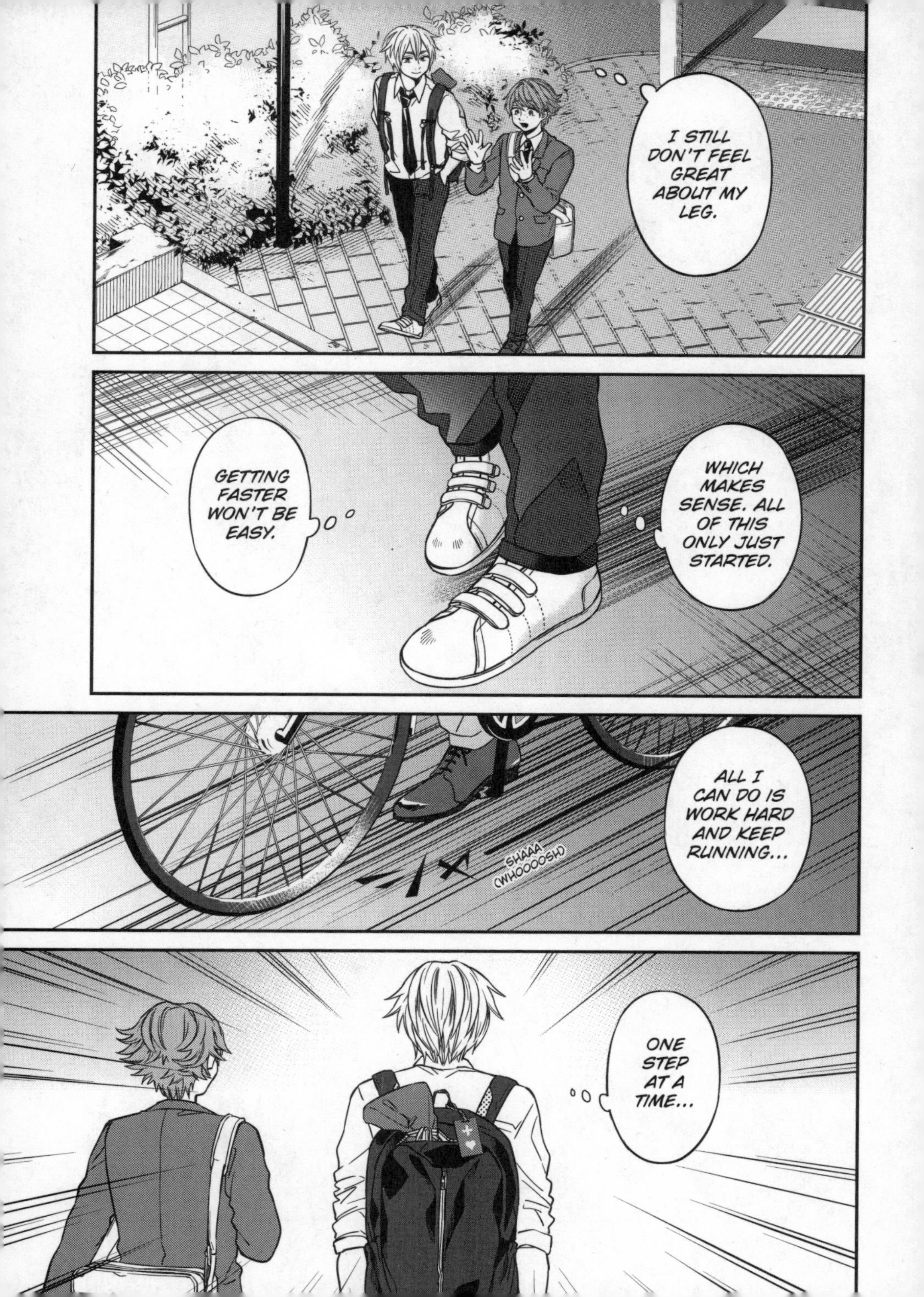
I STILL DON'T FEEL GREAT ABOUT MY LEG.
WHICH MAKES SENSE. ALL OF THIS ONLY JUST STARTED.
GETTING FASTER WON'T BE EASY.
ALL I CAN DO IS WORK HARD AND KEEP RUNNING...
SHAAA (WHOOOOSH)
ONE STEP AT A TIME...

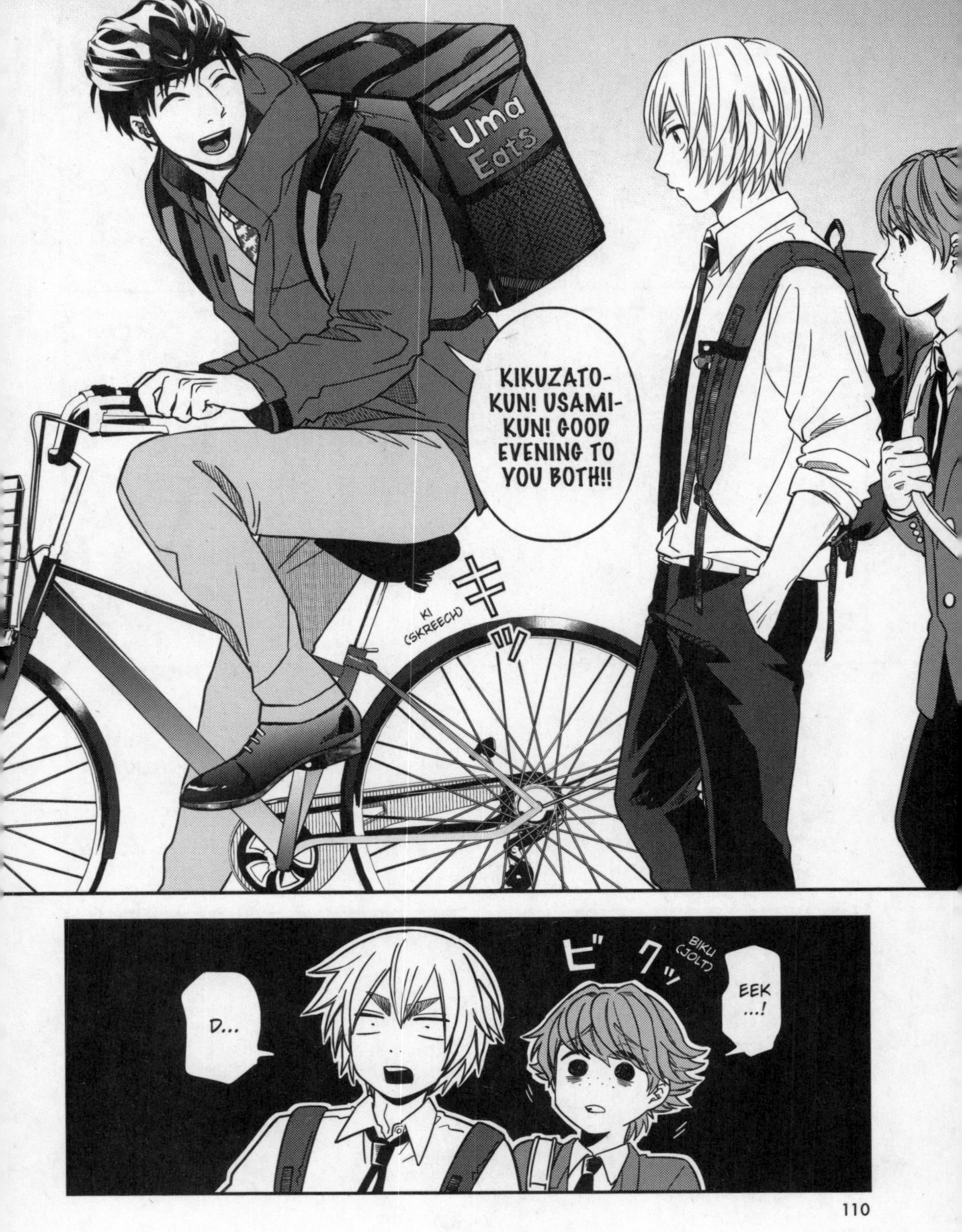

KIKUZATO-KUN! USAMI-KUN! GOOD EVENING TO YOU BOTH!!
キッ
KI (SKREECH)
ビクッ
BIKU (JOLT)
EEK ...!
D...

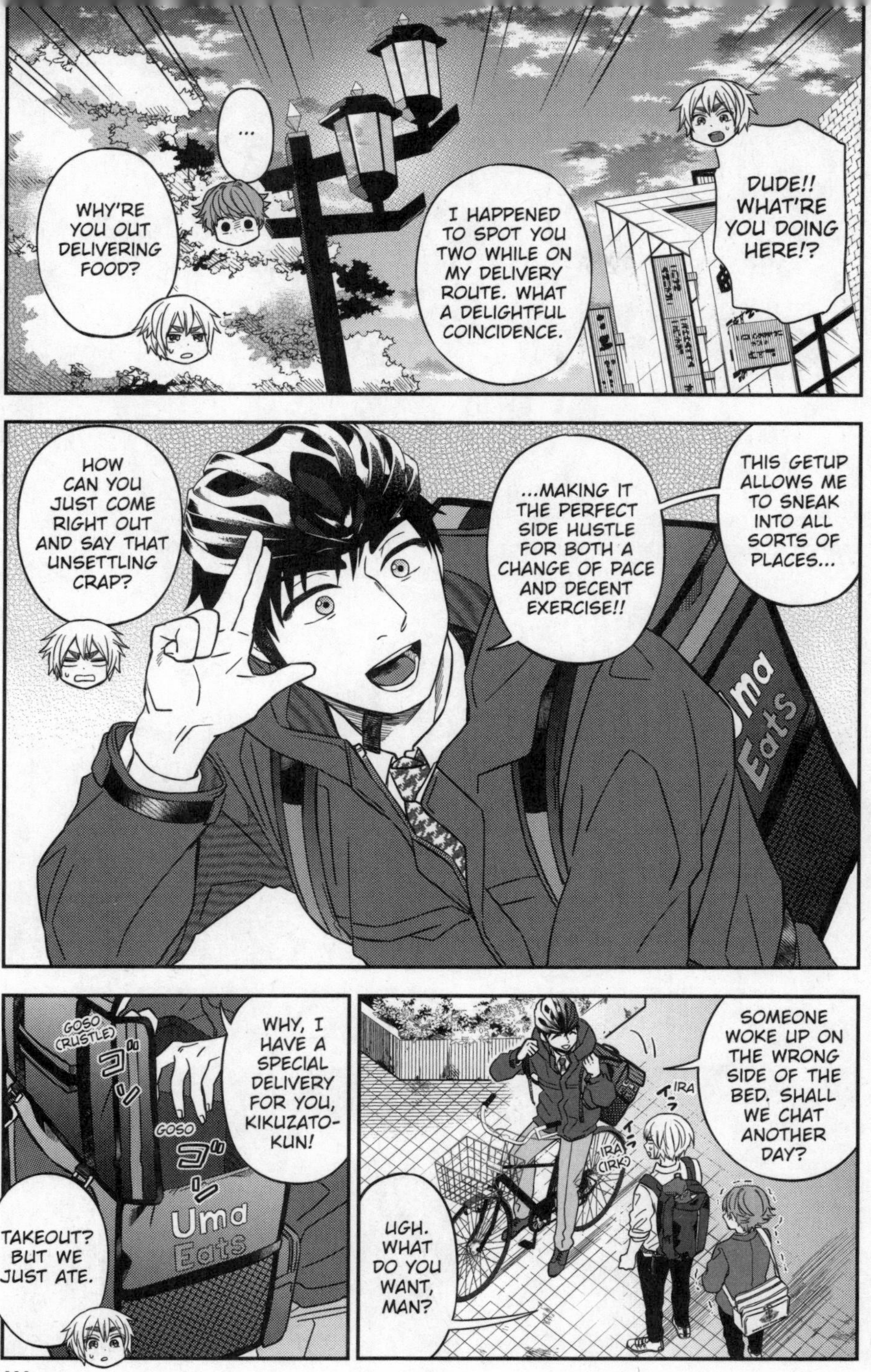
DUDE!! WHAT'RE YOU DOING HERE!?
I HAPPENED TO SPOT YOU TWO WHILE ON MY DELIVERY ROUTE. WHAT A DELIGHTFUL COINCIDENCE.
...
WHY'RE YOU OUT DELIVERING FOOD?
THIS GETUP ALLOWS ME TO SNEAK INTO ALL SORTS OF PLACES...
...MAKING IT THE PERFECT SIDE HUSTLE FOR BOTH A CHANGE OF PACE AND DECENT EXERCISE!!
Uma Eats
HOW CAN YOU JUST COME RIGHT OUT AND SAY THAT UNSETTLING CRAP?
SOMEONE WOKE UP ON THE WRONG SIDE OF THE BED. SHALL WE CHAT ANOTHER DAY?
IRA
IRA (IRK)
UGH. WHAT DO YOU WANT, MAN?
WHY, I HAVE A SPECIAL DELIVERY FOR YOU, KIKUZATO-KUN!
GOSO (RUSTLE)
GOSO
Uma Eats
TAKEOUT? BUT WE JUST ATE.

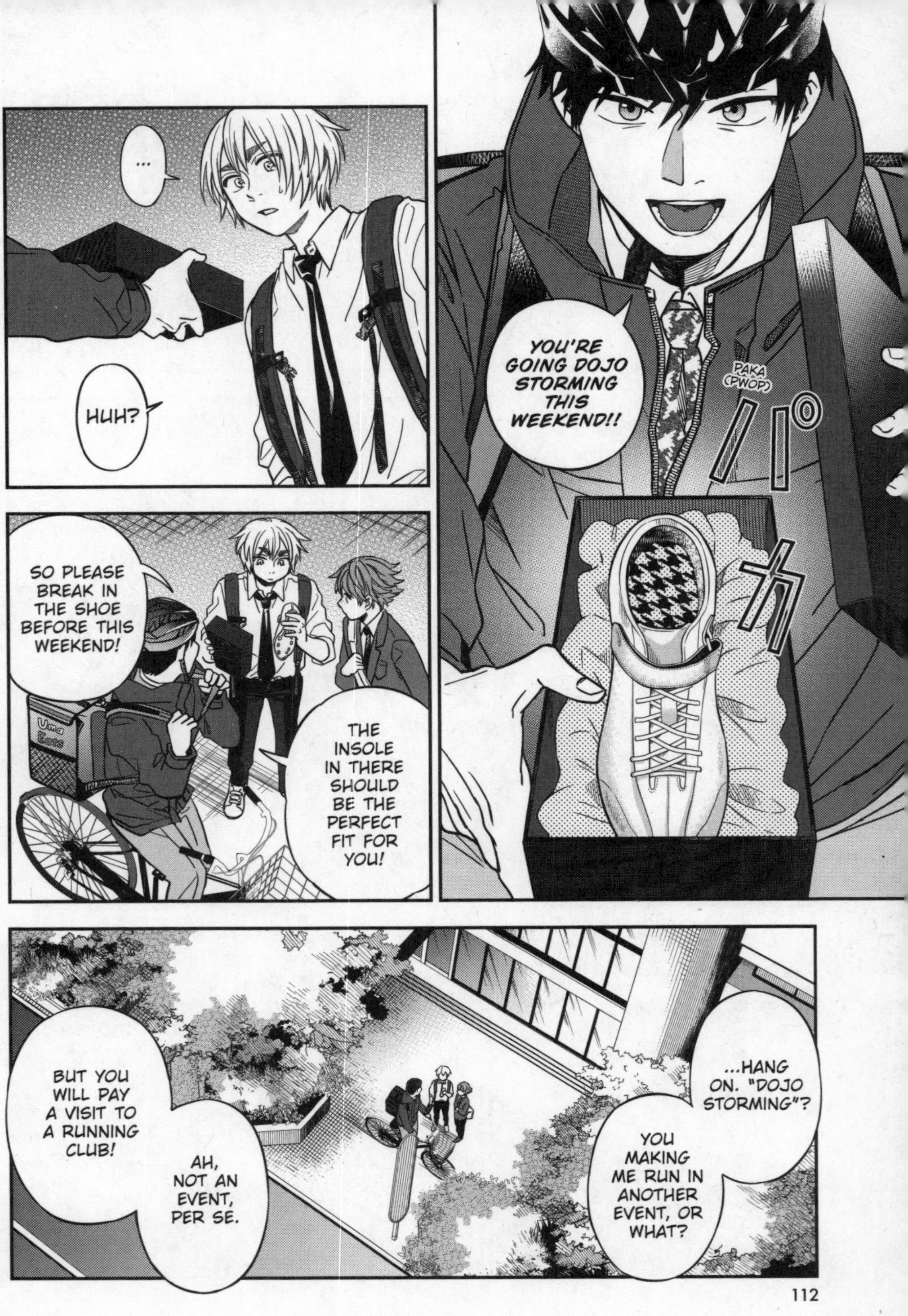
YOU'RE GOING DOJO STORMING THIS WEEKEND!!
PAKA (PWOP)
パ
カ
...
HUH?
SO PLEASE BREAK IN THE SHOE BEFORE THIS WEEKEND!
Uma Eats
THE INSOLE IN THERE SHOULD BE THE PERFECT FIT FOR YOU!
...HANG ON. "DOJO STORMING"?
YOU MAKING ME RUN IN ANOTHER EVENT, OR WHAT?
AH, NOT AN EVENT, PER SE.
BUT YOU WILL PAY A VISIT TO A RUNNING CLUB!

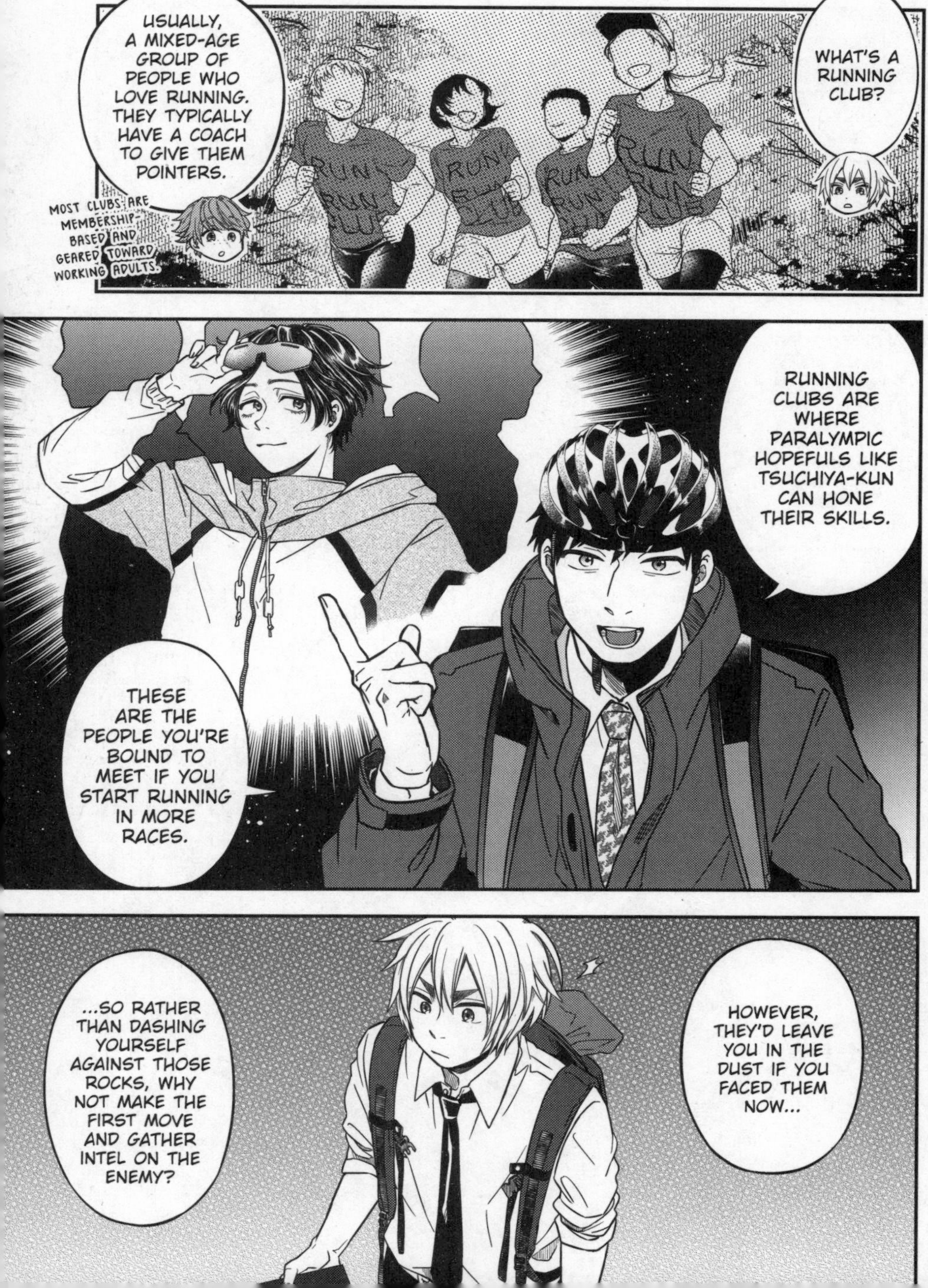
WHAT'S A RUNNING CLUB?
USUALLY, A MIXED-AGE GROUP OF PEOPLE WHO LOVE RUNNING. THEY TYPICALLY HAVE A COACH TO GIVE THEM POINTERS.
MOST CLUBS ARE MEMBERSHIP-BASED AND GEARED TOWARD WORKING ADULTS.
RUNNING CLUBS ARE WHERE PARALYMPIC HOPEFULS LIKE TSUCHIYA-KUN CAN HONE THEIR SKILLS.
THESE ARE THE PEOPLE YOU'RE BOUND TO MEET IF YOU START RUNNING IN MORE RACES.
HOWEVER, THEY'D LEAVE YOU IN THE DUST IF YOU FACED THEM NOW...
...SO RATHER THAN DASHING YOURSELF AGAINST THOSE ROCKS, WHY NOT MAKE THE FIRST MOVE AND GATHER INTEL ON THE ENEMY?

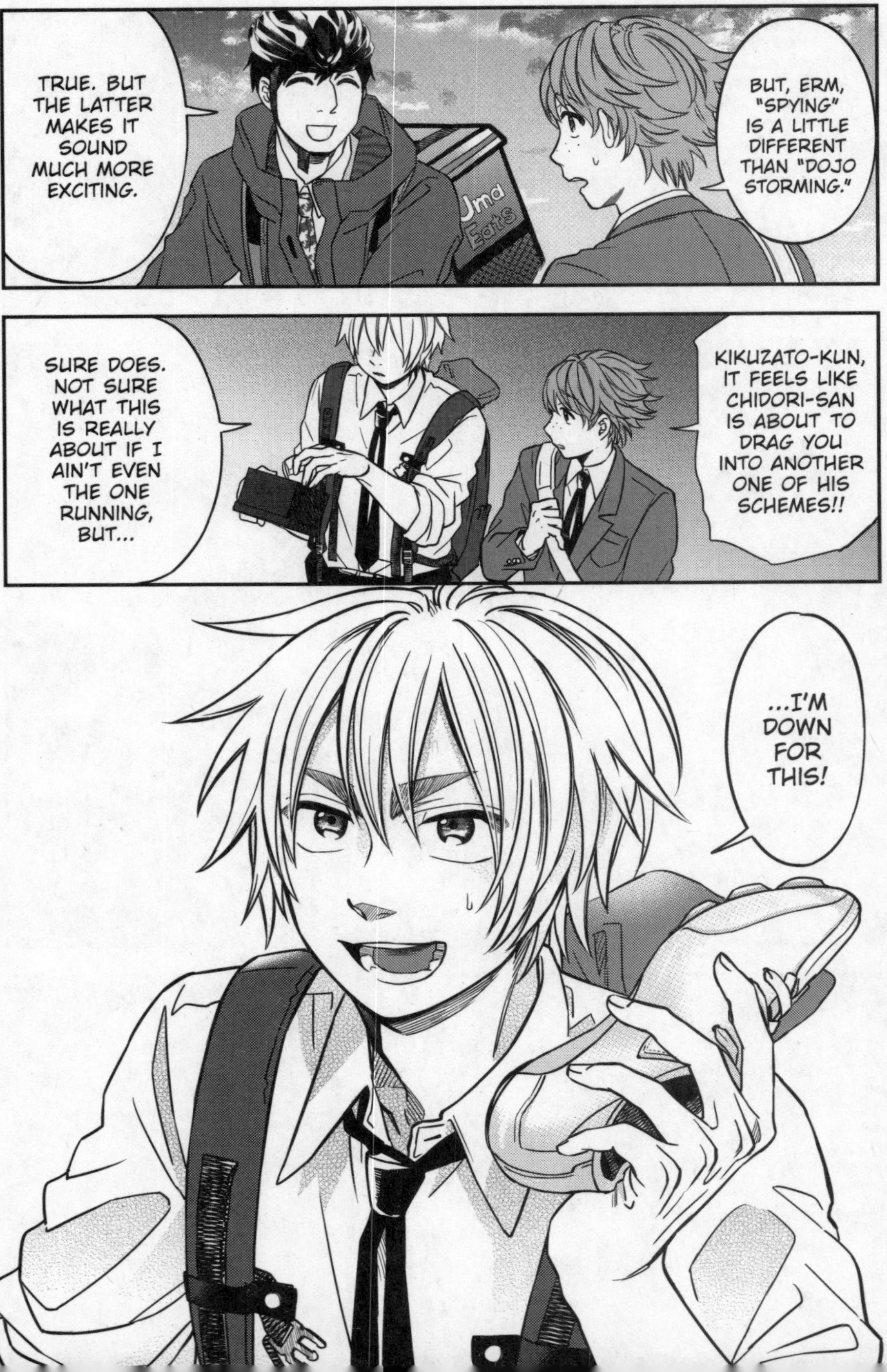
BUT, ERM, "SPYING" IS A LITTLE DIFFERENT THAN "DOJO STORMING."
TRUE. BUT THE LATTER MAKES IT SOUND MUCH MORE EXCITING.
Uma Eats
KIKUZATO-KUN, IT FEELS LIKE CHIDORI-SAN IS ABOUT TO DRAG YOU INTO ANOTHER ONE OF HIS SCHEMES!!
SURE DOES. NOT SURE WHAT THIS IS REALLY ABOUT IF I AIN'T EVEN THE ONE RUNNING, BUT...
...I'M DOWN FOR THIS!

Chapter 13: It's All About Play!

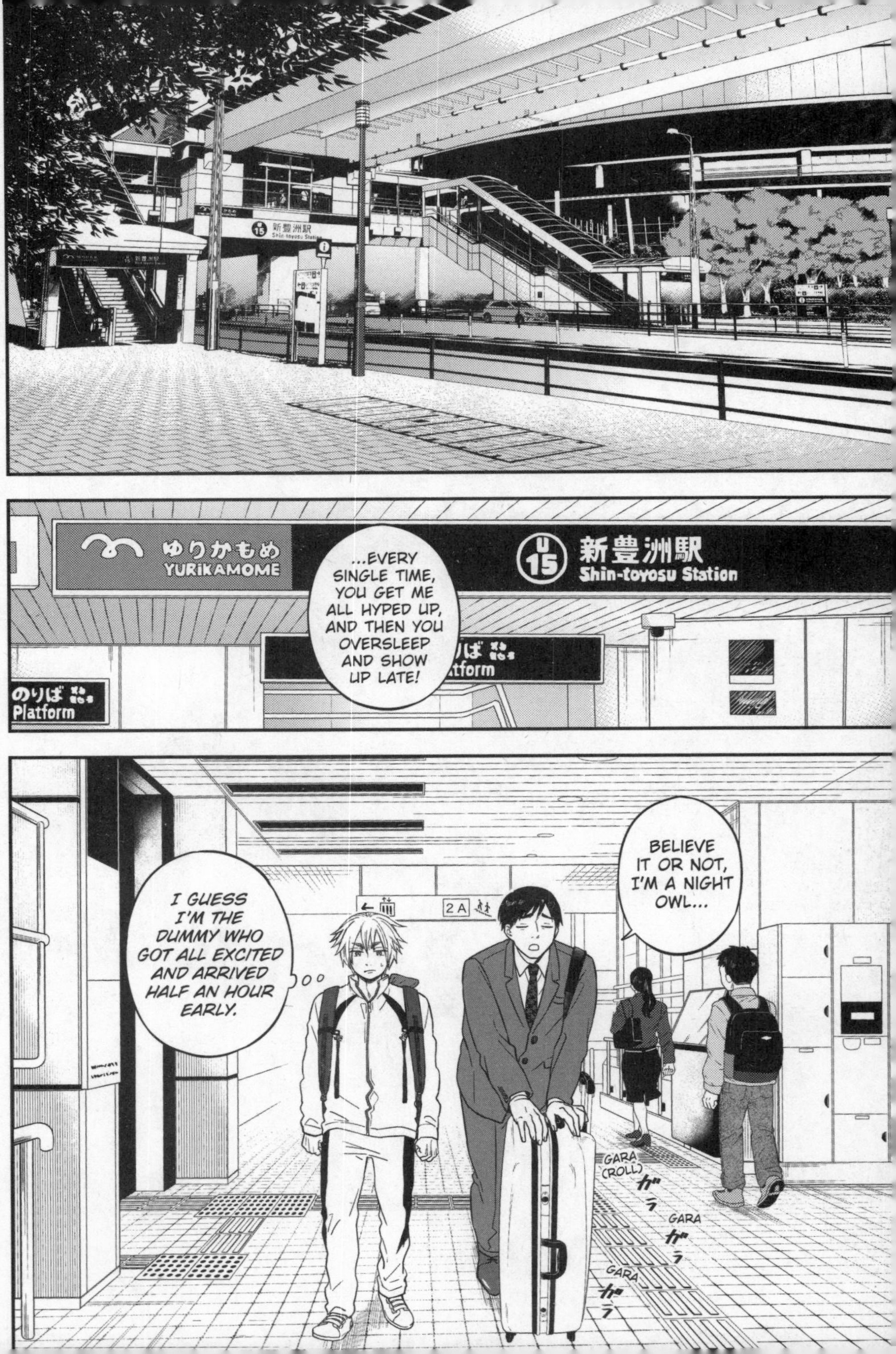
新豊洲駅
Shin-toyosu Station
ゆりかもめ
YURIKAMOME
...EVERY SINGLE TIME, YOU GET ME ALL HYPED UP, AND THEN YOU OVERSLEEP AND SHOW UP LATE!
のりば
Platform
BELIEVE IT OR NOT, I'M A NIGHT OWL...
I GUESS I'M THE DUMMY WHO GOT ALL EXCITED AND ARRIVED HALF AN HOUR EARLY.
2A
GARA (ROLL)
ガラ
GARA
ガラ
GARA
ガラ

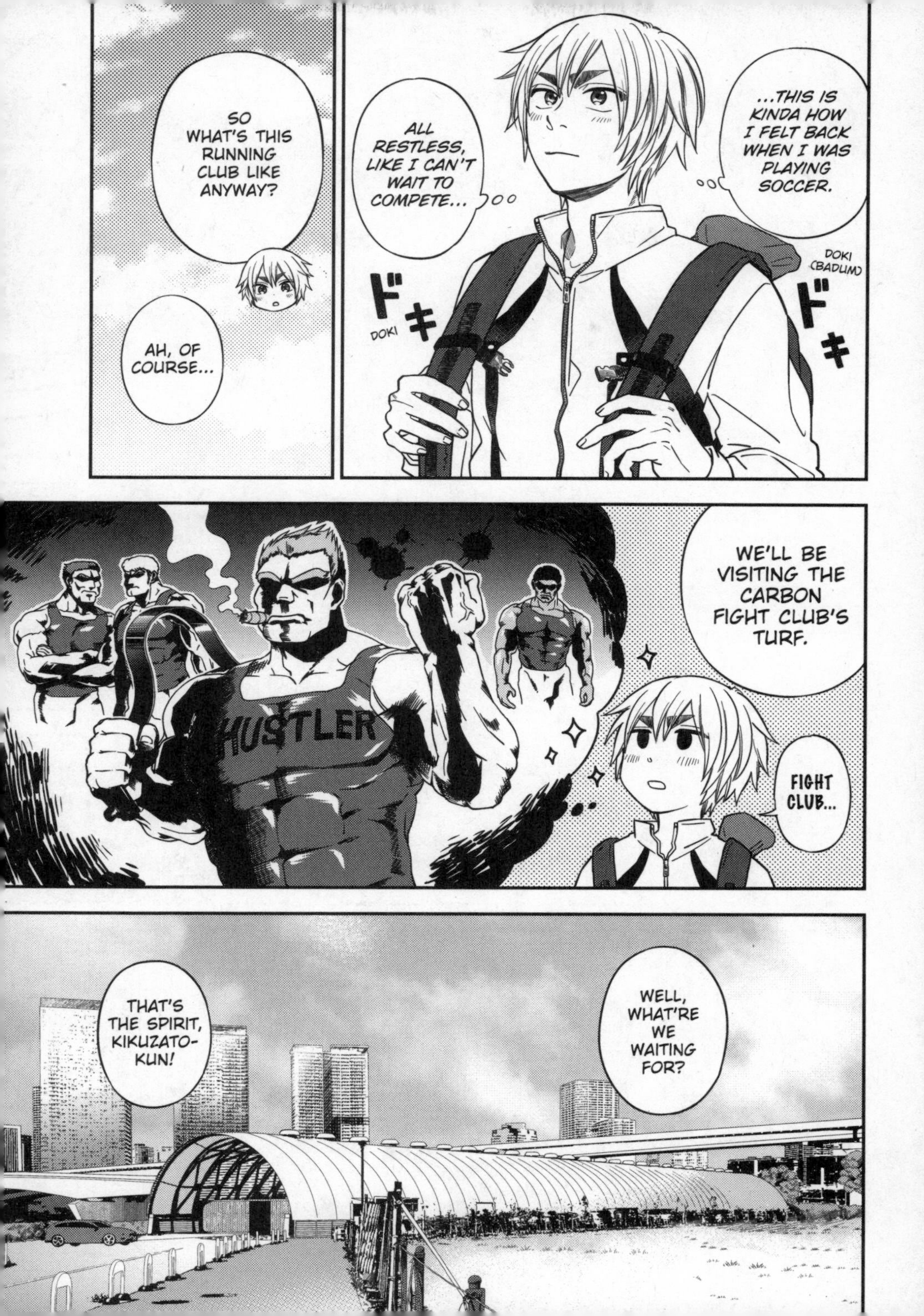
...THIS IS KINDA HOW I FELT BACK WHEN I WAS PLAYING SOCCER.
ALL RESTLESS, LIKE I CAN'T WAIT TO COMPETE...
DOKI (BADUM)
ドキ
DOKI
ドキ
SO WHAT'S THIS RUNNING CLUB LIKE ANYWAY?
AH, OF COURSE...
WE'LL BE VISITING THE CARBON FIGHT CLUB'S TURF.
HUSTLER
FIGHT CLUB...
WELL, WHAT'RE WE WAITING FOR?
THAT'S THE SPIRIT, KIKUZATO-KUN!

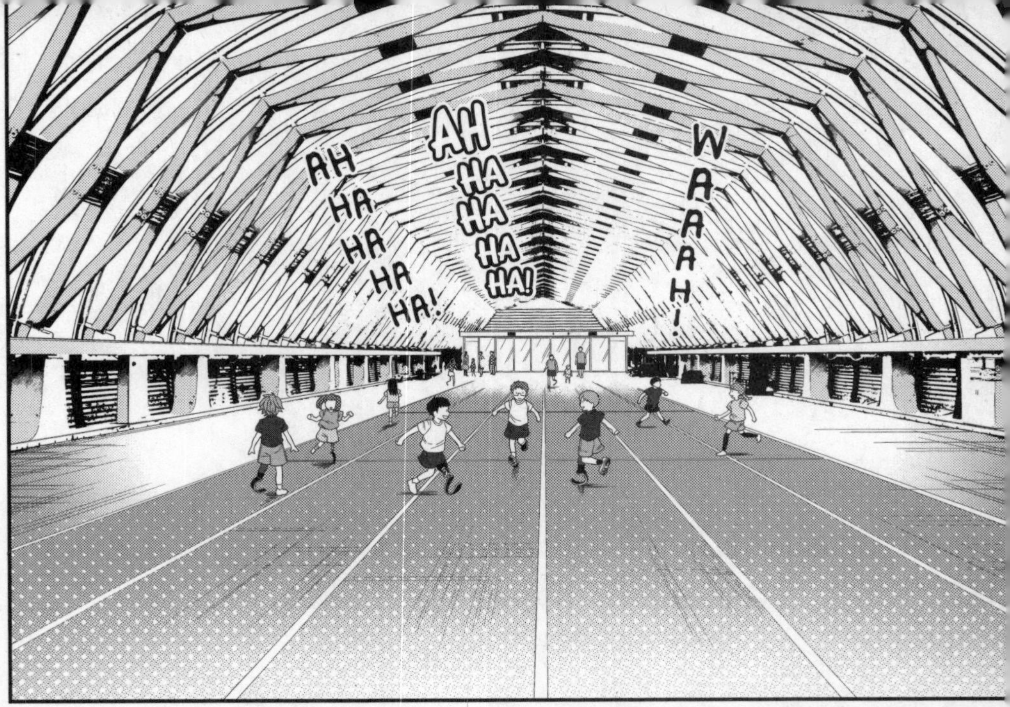
WAAAAH!
AH HA HA HA HA!
AH HA HA HA HA!

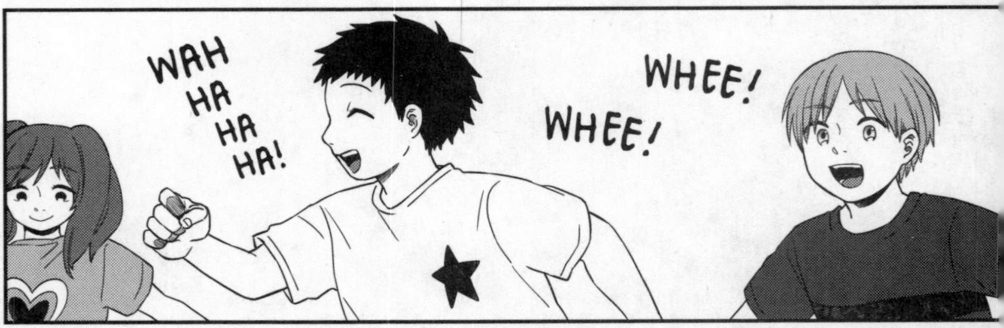
WHEE!
WHEE!
WAH HA HA HA!

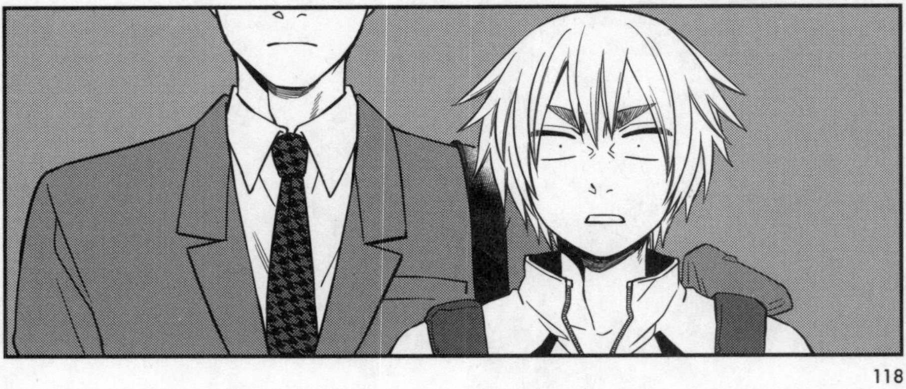

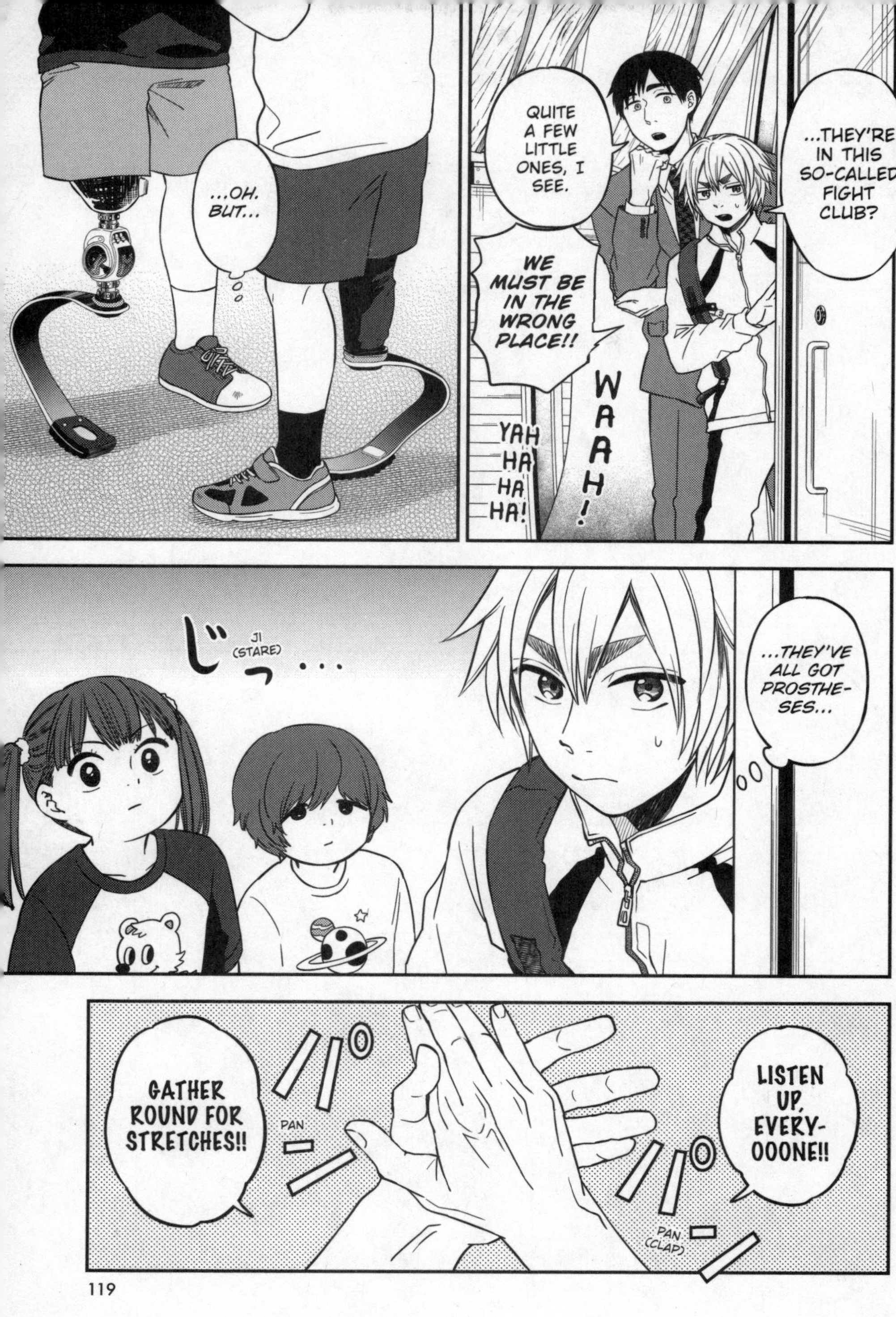
...THEY'RE IN THIS SO-CALLED FIGHT CLUB?
QUITE A FEW LITTLE ONES, I SEE.
WE MUST BE IN THE WRONG PLACE!!
WAAH!
YAH HA HA HA!
...OH. BUT...
...THEY'VE ALL GOT PROSTHESES...
じっ JI (STARE) ...
LISTEN UP, EVERY-OOONE!!
PAN (CLAP)
PAN
GATHER ROUND FOR STRETCHES!!

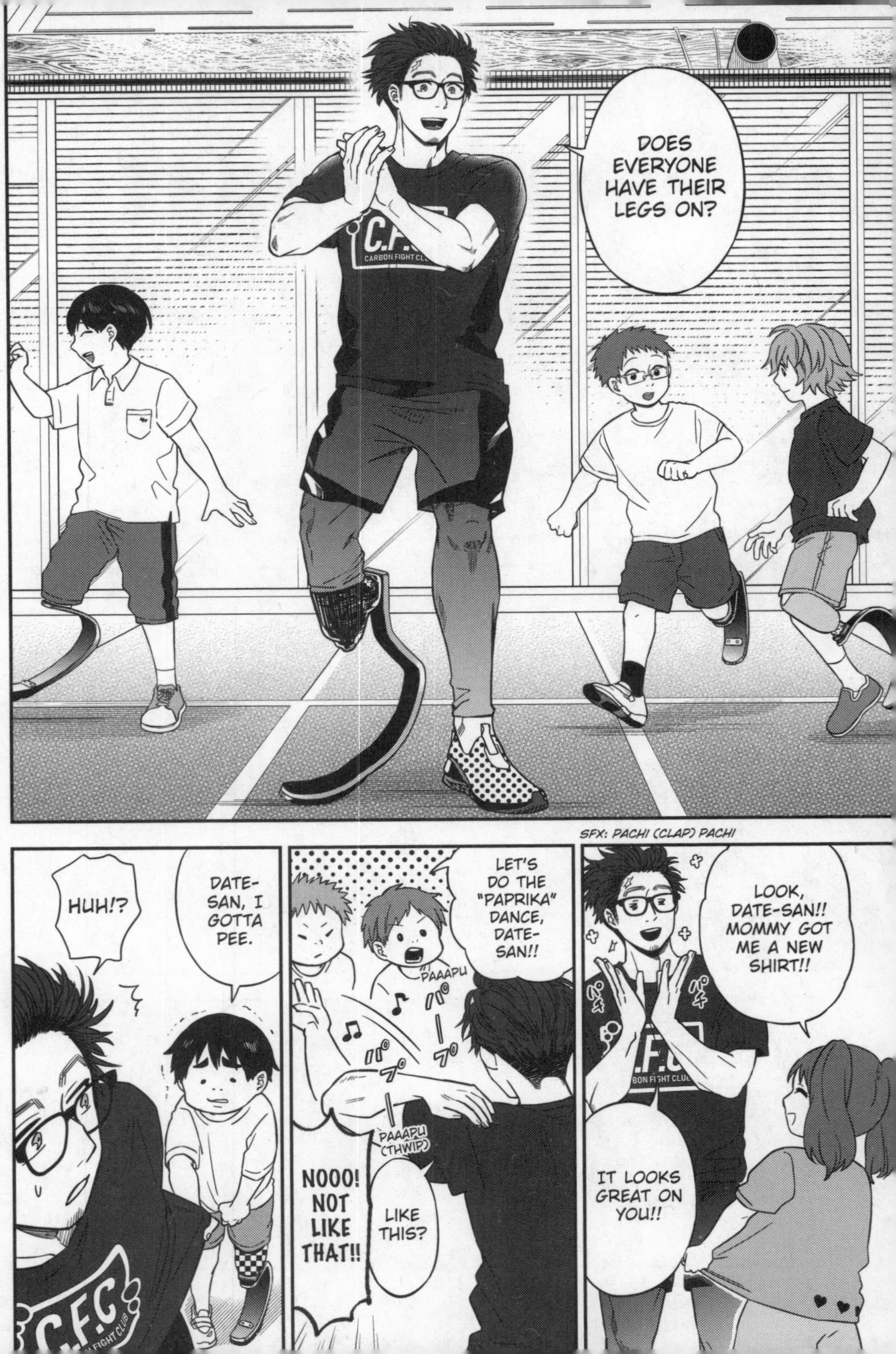
DOES EVERYONE HAVE THEIR LEGS ON?
SFX: PACHI (CLAP) PACHI
LOOK, DATE-SAN!! MOMMY GOT ME A NEW SHIRT!!
IT LOOKS GREAT ON YOU!!
LET'S DO THE "PAPRIKA" DANCE, DATE-SAN!!
PAAAPU
PAAAPU (THWIP)
LIKE THIS?
NOOO! NOT LIKE THAT!!
DATE-SAN, I GOTTA PEE.
HUH!?

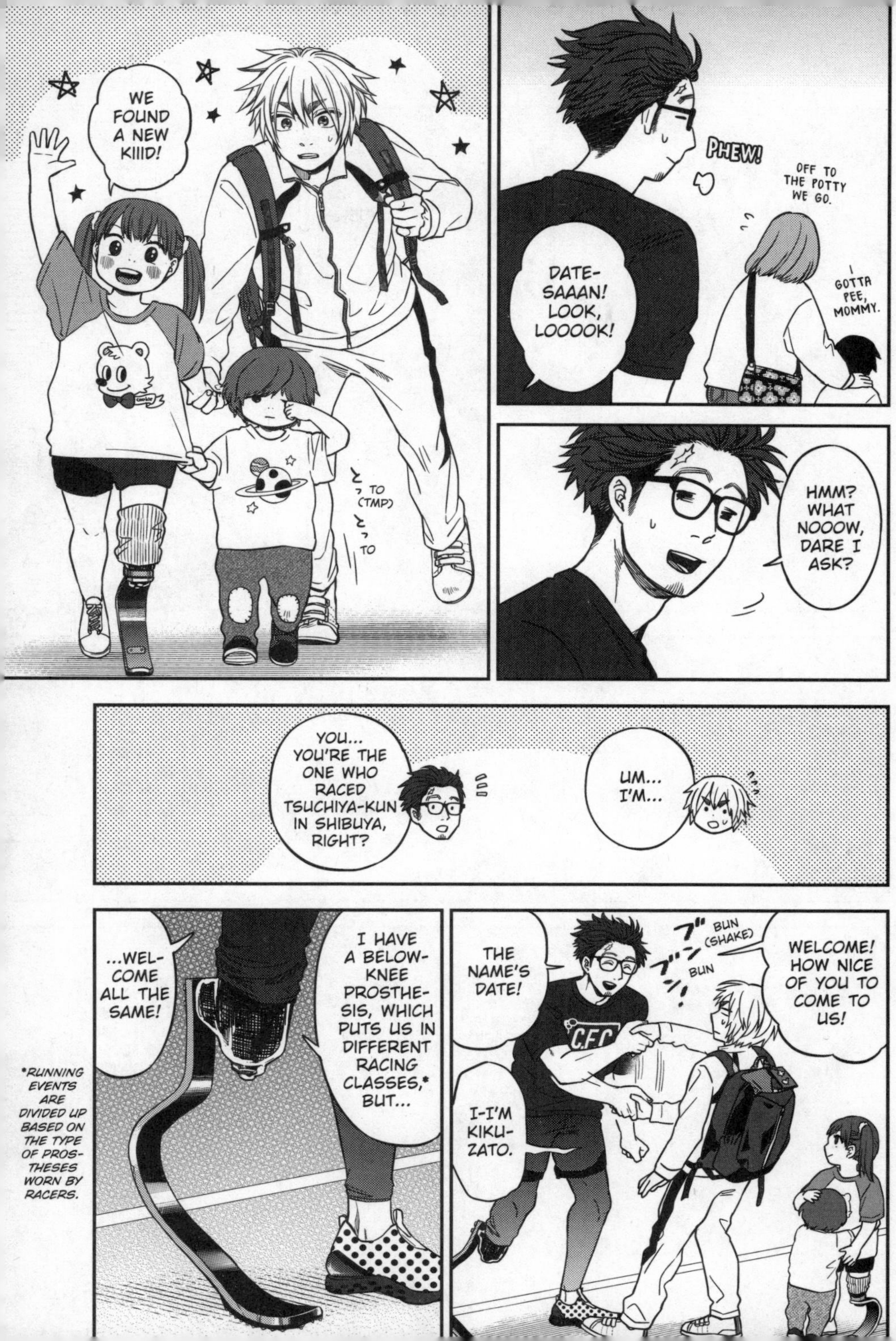
PHEW!
OFF TO THE POTTY WE GO.
I GOTTA PEE, MOMMY.
DATE-SAAAN! LOOK, LOOOOK!
HMM? WHAT NOOOW, DARE I ASK?
WE FOUND A NEW KIIID!
TO (TMP)
TO
UM... I'M...
YOU... YOU'RE THE ONE WHO RACED TSUCHIYA-KUN IN SHIBUYA, RIGHT?
WELCOME! HOW NICE OF YOU TO COME TO US!
BUN (SHAKE)
BUN
THE NAME'S DATE!
I-I'M KIKUZATO.
I HAVE A BELOW-KNEE PROSTHESIS, WHICH PUTS US IN DIFFERENT RACING CLASSES,* BUT...
...WELCOME ALL THE SAME!

*RUNNING EVENTS ARE DIVIDED UP BASED ON THE TYPE OF PROSTHESES WORN BY RACERS.

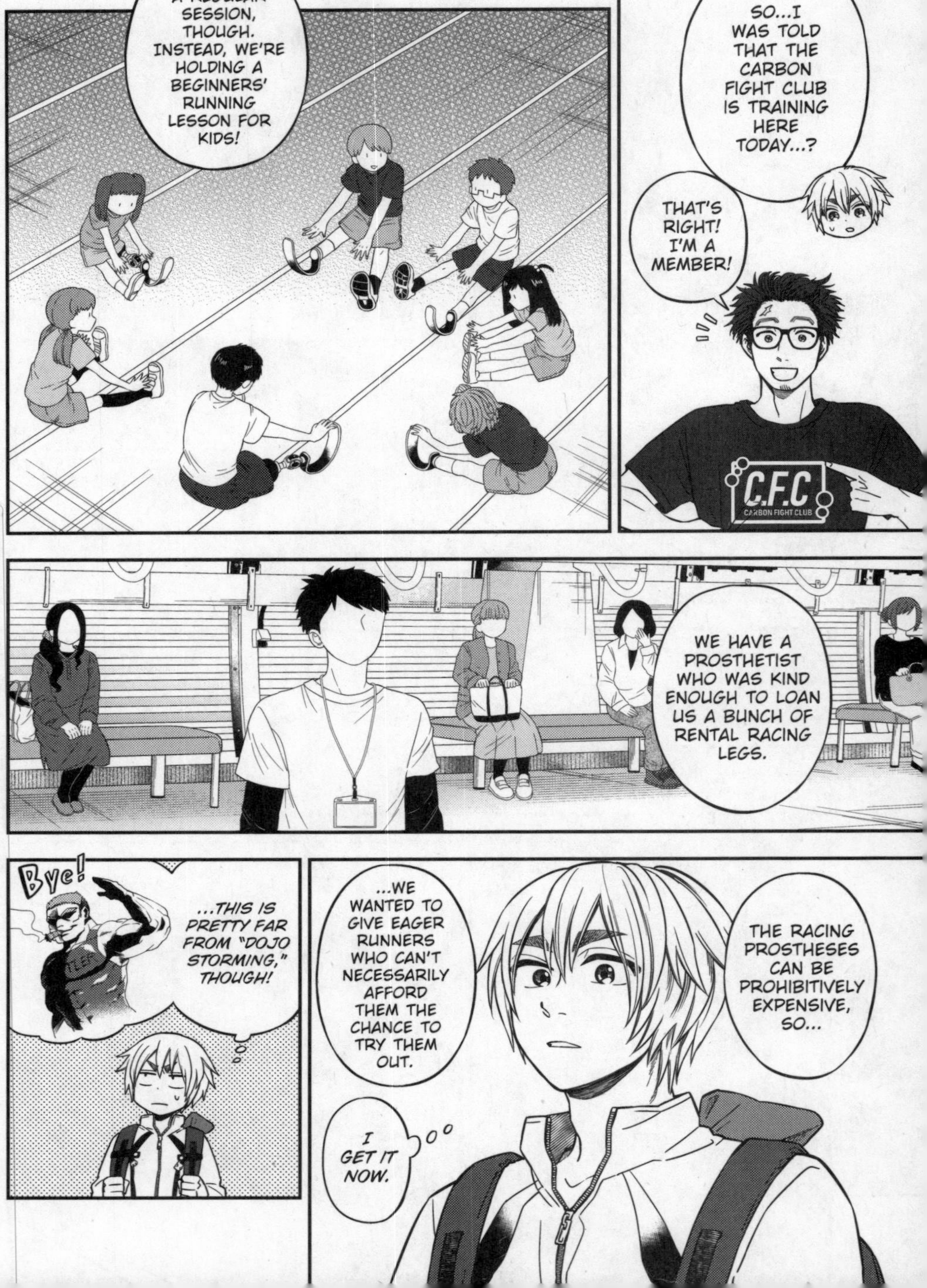
SO...I WAS TOLD THAT THE CARBON FIGHT CLUB IS TRAINING HERE TODAY...?
THAT'S RIGHT! I'M A MEMBER!
C.F.C
CARBON FIGHT CLUB
THIS ISN'T A REGULAR SESSION, THOUGH. INSTEAD, WE'RE HOLDING A BEGINNERS' RUNNING LESSON FOR KIDS!
WE HAVE A PROSTHETIST WHO WAS KIND ENOUGH TO LOAN US A BUNCH OF RENTAL RACING LEGS.
THE RACING PROSTHESES CAN BE PROHIBITIVELY EXPENSIVE, SO...
...WE WANTED TO GIVE EAGER RUNNERS WHO CAN'T NECESSARILY AFFORD THEM THE CHANCE TO TRY THEM OUT.
I GET IT NOW.
Bye!
...THIS IS PRETTY FAR FROM "DOJO STORMING," THOUGH!

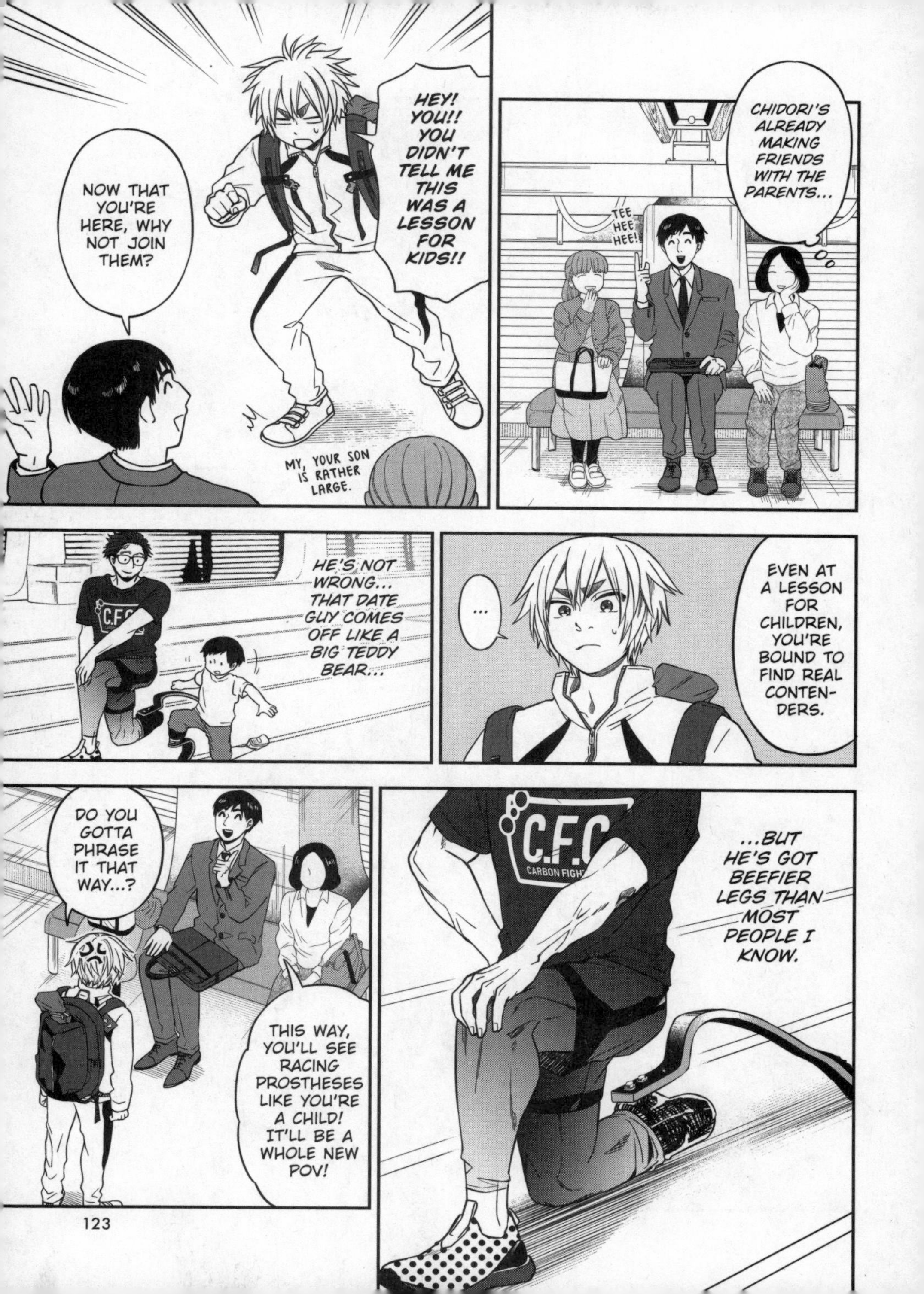
CHIDORI'S ALREADY MAKING FRIENDS WITH THE PARENTS...
TEE HEE HEE!
HEY! YOU!! YOU DIDN'T TELL ME THIS WAS A LESSON FOR KIDS!!
NOW THAT YOU'RE HERE, WHY NOT JOIN THEM?
MY, YOUR SON IS RATHER LARGE.
EVEN AT A LESSON FOR CHILDREN, YOU'RE BOUND TO FIND REAL CONTEN-DERS.
...
HE'S NOT WRONG... THAT DATE GUY COMES OFF LIKE A BIG TEDDY BEAR...
C.F.C
...BUT HE'S GOT BEEFIER LEGS THAN MOST PEOPLE I KNOW.
DO YOU GOTTA PHRASE IT THAT WAY...?
THIS WAY, YOU'LL SEE RACING PROSTHESES LIKE YOU'RE A CHILD! IT'LL BE A WHOLE NEW POV!

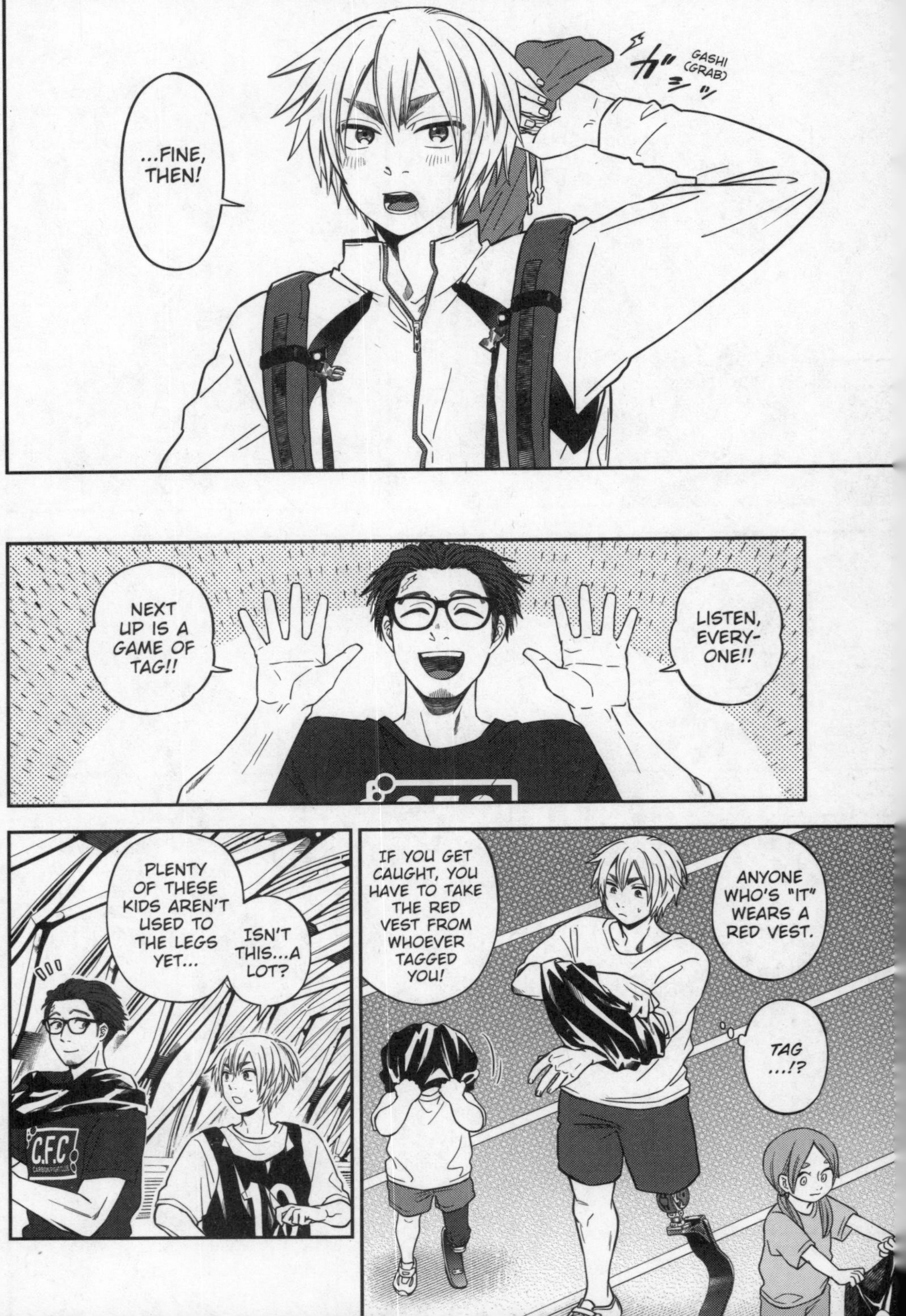
GASHI (GRAB)
...FINE, THEN!
LISTEN, EVERYONE!!
NEXT UP IS A GAME OF TAG!!
ANYONE WHO'S "IT" WEARS A RED VEST.
IF YOU GET CAUGHT, YOU HAVE TO TAKE THE RED VEST FROM WHOEVER TAGGED YOU!
TAG ...!?
ISN'T THIS...A LOT?
PLENTY OF THESE KIDS AREN'T USED TO THE LEGS YET...
C.F.C

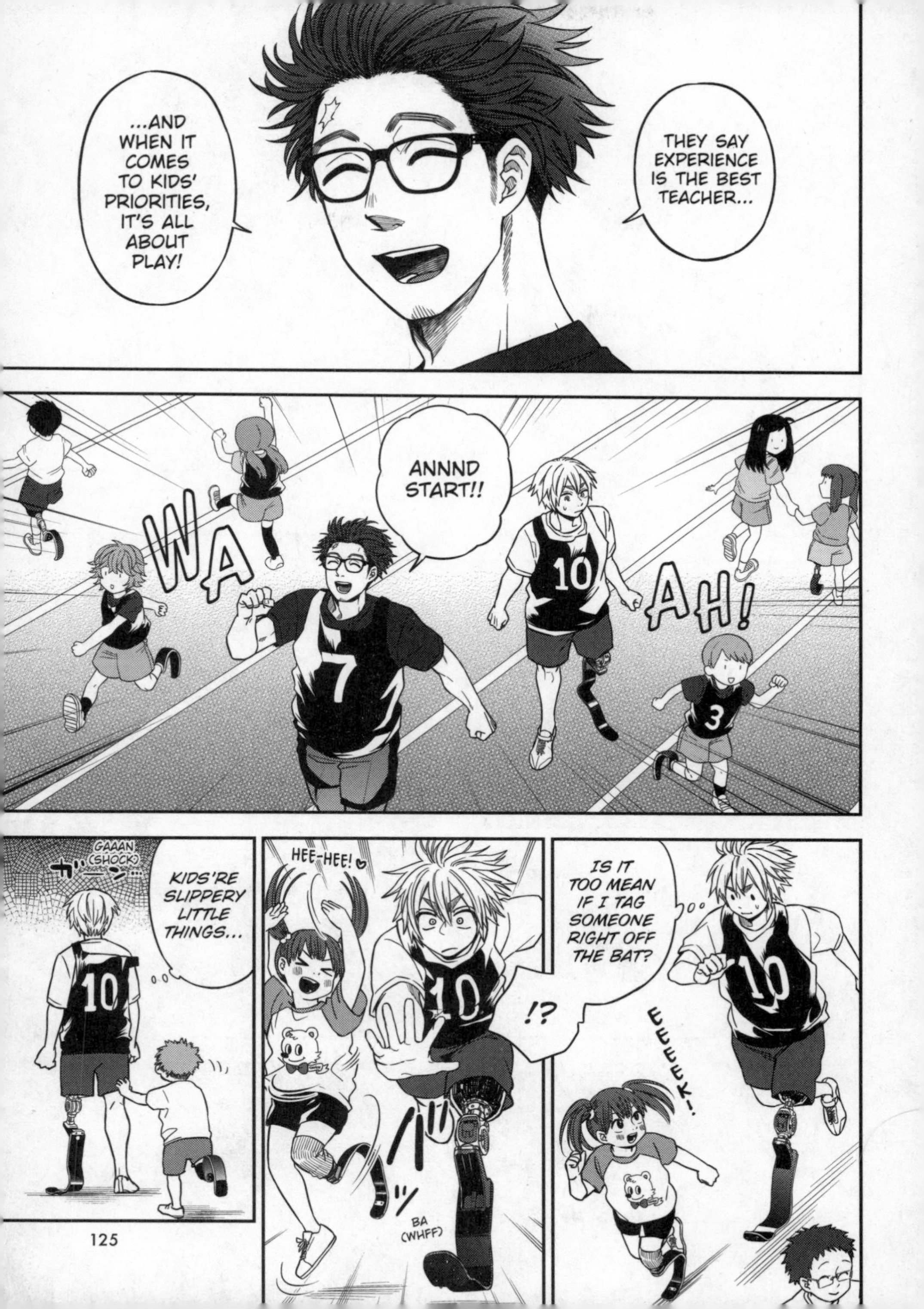
THEY SAY EXPERIENCE IS THE BEST TEACHER...
...AND WHEN IT COMES TO KIDS' PRIORITIES, IT'S ALL ABOUT PLAY!
AH!
ANNND START!!
WA
IS IT TOO MEAN IF I TAG SOMEONE RIGHT OFF THE BAT?
EEEEEK!
HEE-HEE!
!?
BA (WHFF)
GAAAN (SHOCK)
KIDS'RE SLIPPERY LITTLE THINGS...

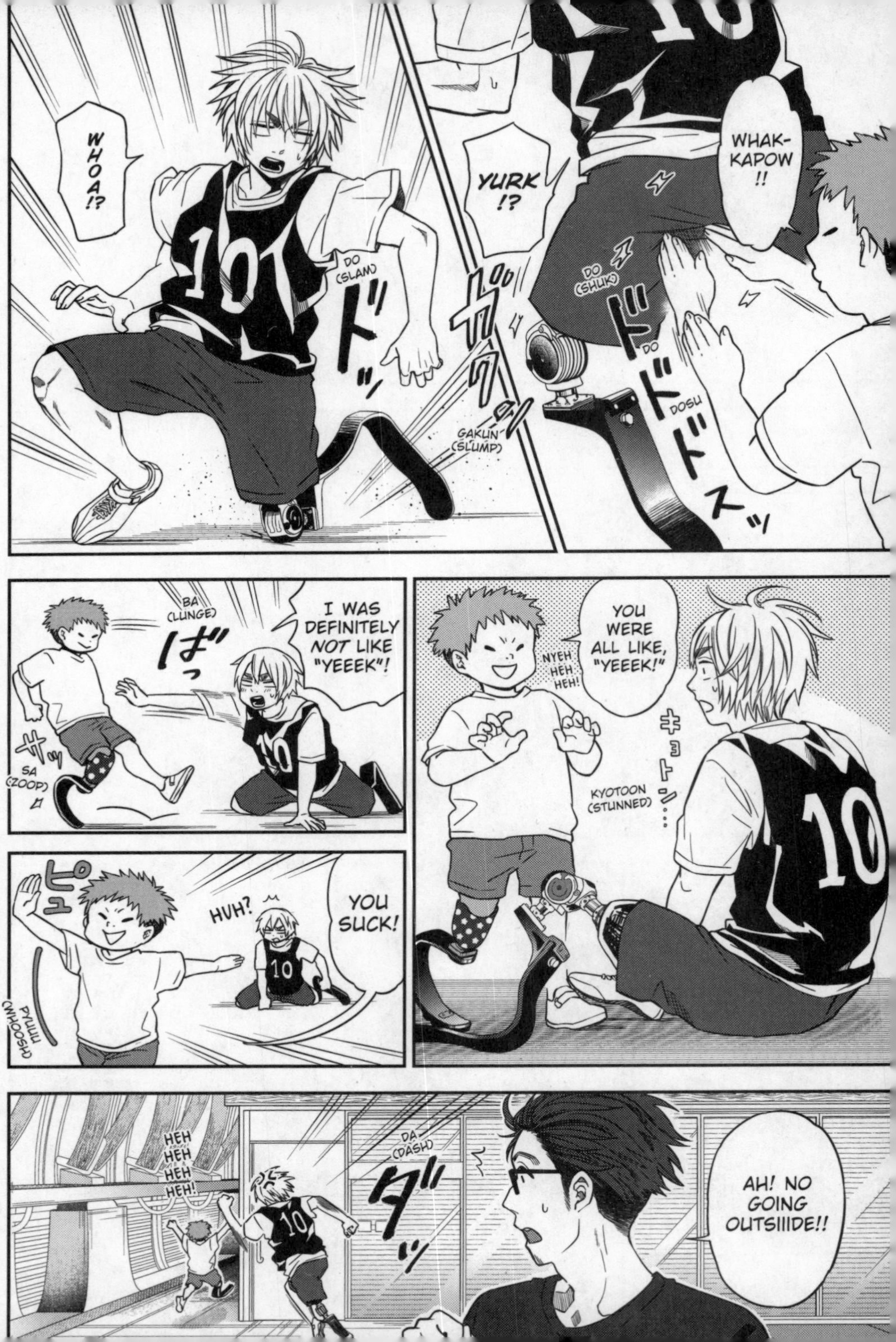
WHAK-KAPOW!!
YURK!?
DO (SHUK)
DO
DOSU
GAKUN (SLUMP)
WHOA!?
DO (SLAM)
YOU WERE ALL LIKE, "YEEEK!"
NYEH HEH HEH!
KYOTOON (STUNNED)
I WAS DEFINITELY *NOT* LIKE "YEEEK"!
BA (LUNGE)
SA (ZOOP)
YOU SUCK!
HUH?
PYUUU (WHOOSH)
AH! NO GOING OUTSIIIDE!!
DA (DASH)
HEH HEH HEH HEH!

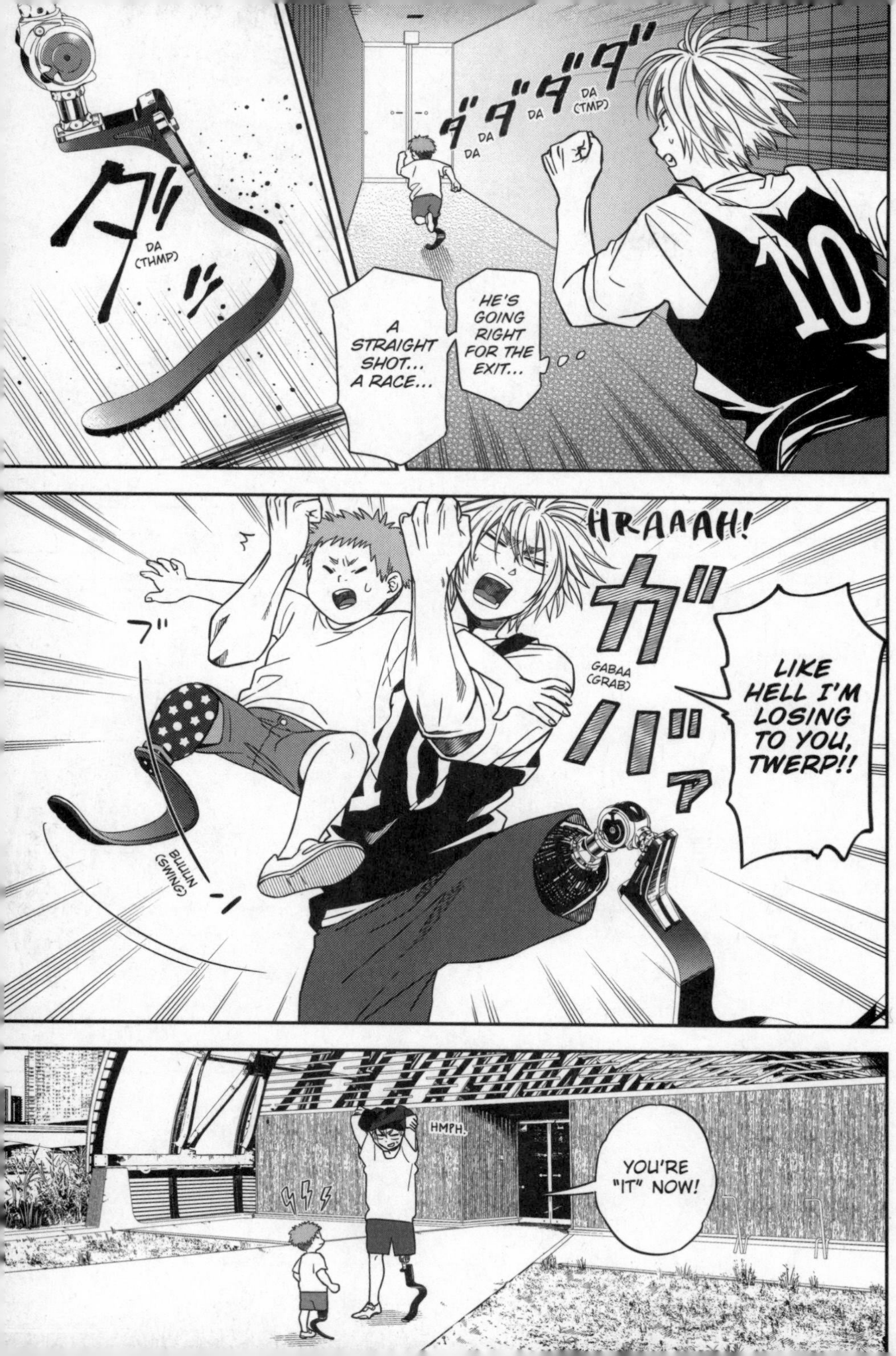

DA DA DA (TMP)
HE'S GOING RIGHT FOR THE EXIT...
A STRAIGHT SHOT... A RACE...
DA (THMP)
HRAAAH!
LIKE HELL I'M LOSING TO YOU, TWERP!!
GABAA (GRAB)
BULUN (SWING)
YOU'RE "IT" NOW!
HMPH.

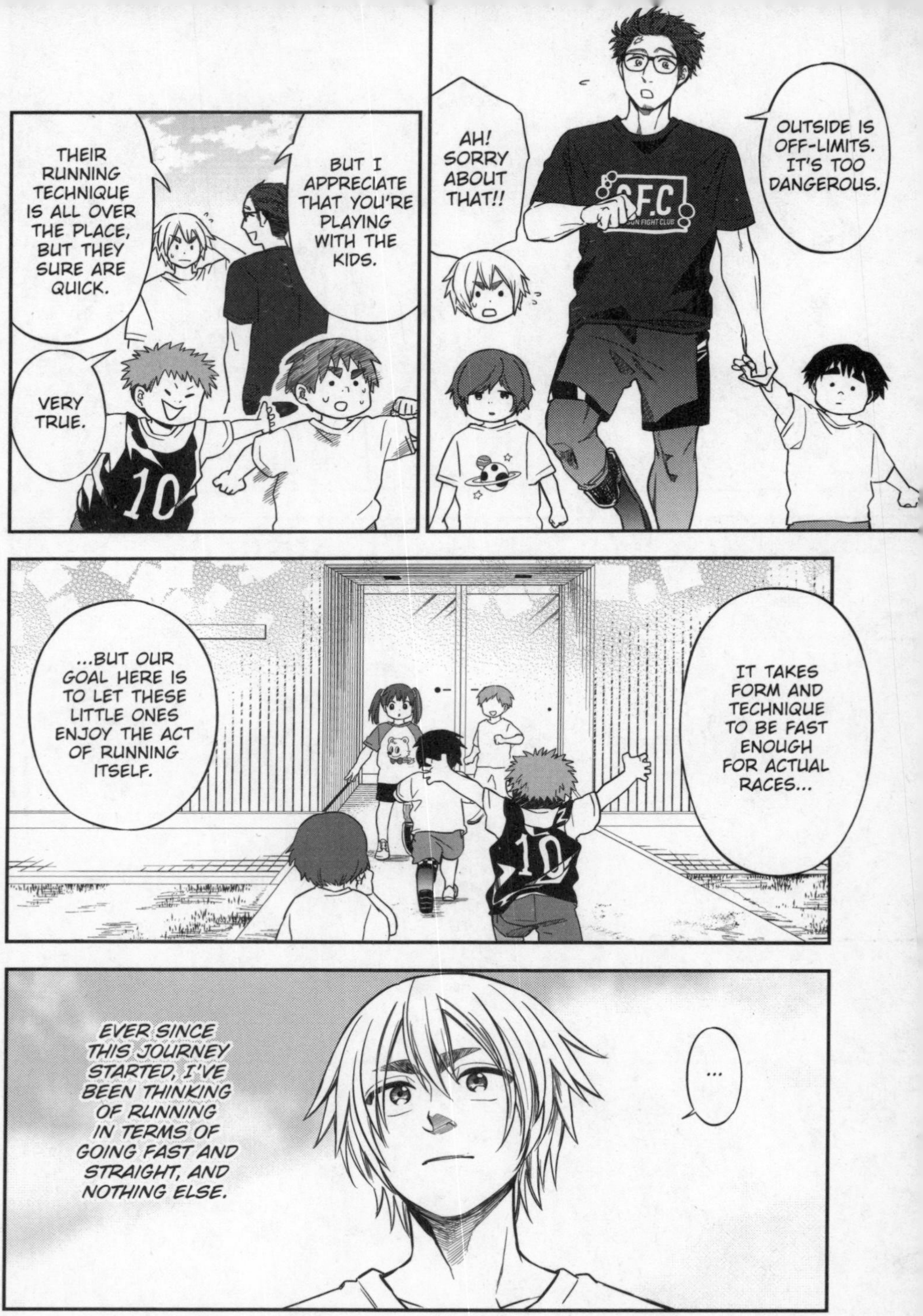
OUTSIDE IS OFF-LIMITS. IT'S TOO DANGEROUS.
AH! SORRY ABOUT THAT!!
BUT I APPRECIATE THAT YOU'RE PLAYING WITH THE KIDS.
THEIR RUNNING TECHNIQUE IS ALL OVER THE PLACE, BUT THEY SURE ARE QUICK.
VERY TRUE.
IT TAKES FORM AND TECHNIQUE TO BE FAST ENOUGH FOR ACTUAL RACES...
...BUT OUR GOAL HERE IS TO LET THESE LITTLE ONES ENJOY THE ACT OF RUNNING ITSELF.
...
EVER SINCE THIS JOURNEY STARTED, I'VE BEEN THINKING OF RUNNING IN TERMS OF GOING FAST AND STRAIGHT, AND NOTHING ELSE.

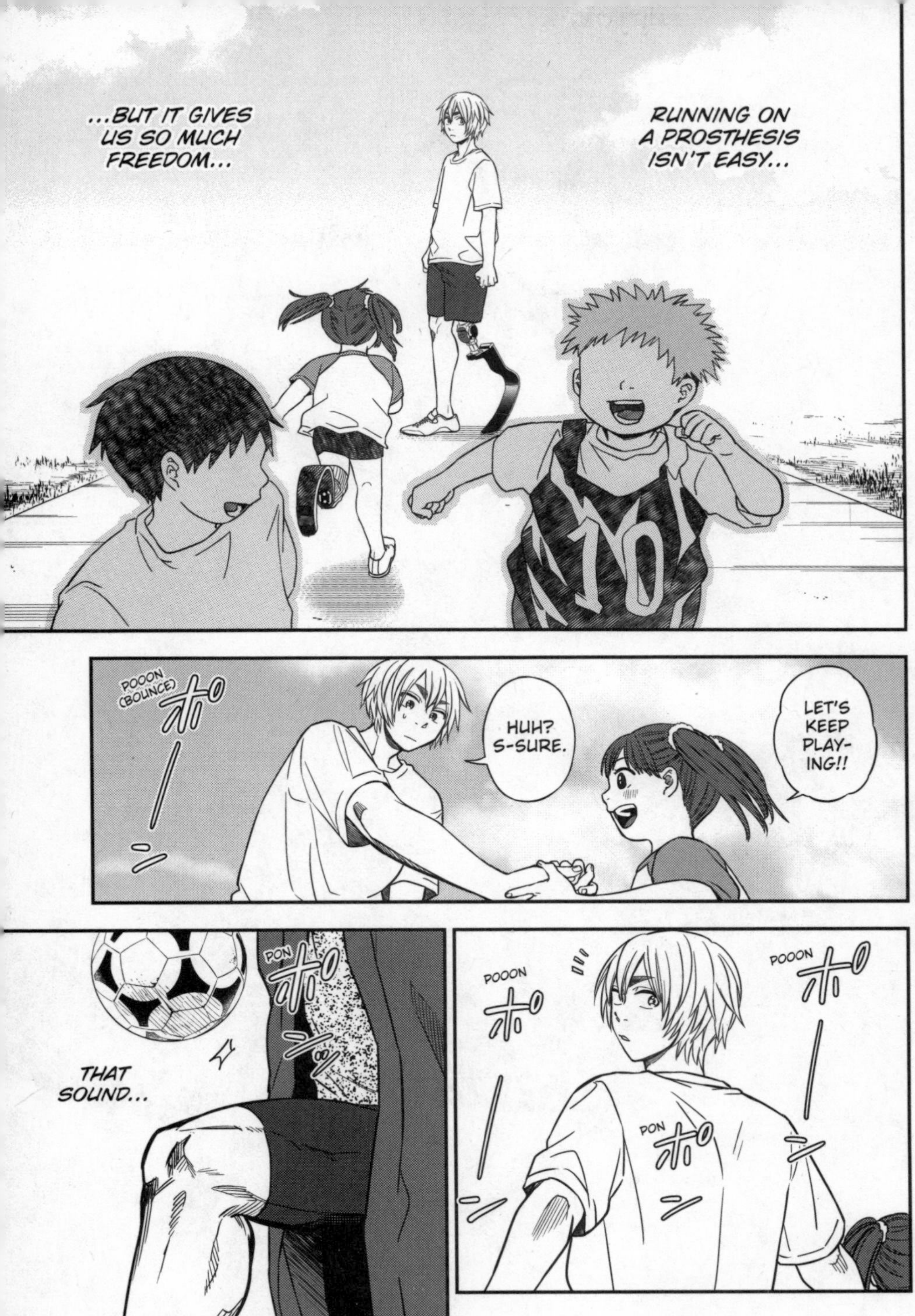
RUNNING ON A PROSTHESIS ISN'T EASY...
...BUT IT GIVES US SO MUCH FREEDOM...
LET'S KEEP PLAYING!!
HUH? S-SURE.
POOON (BOUNCE)
POOON
PON
POOON
PON
THAT SOUND...

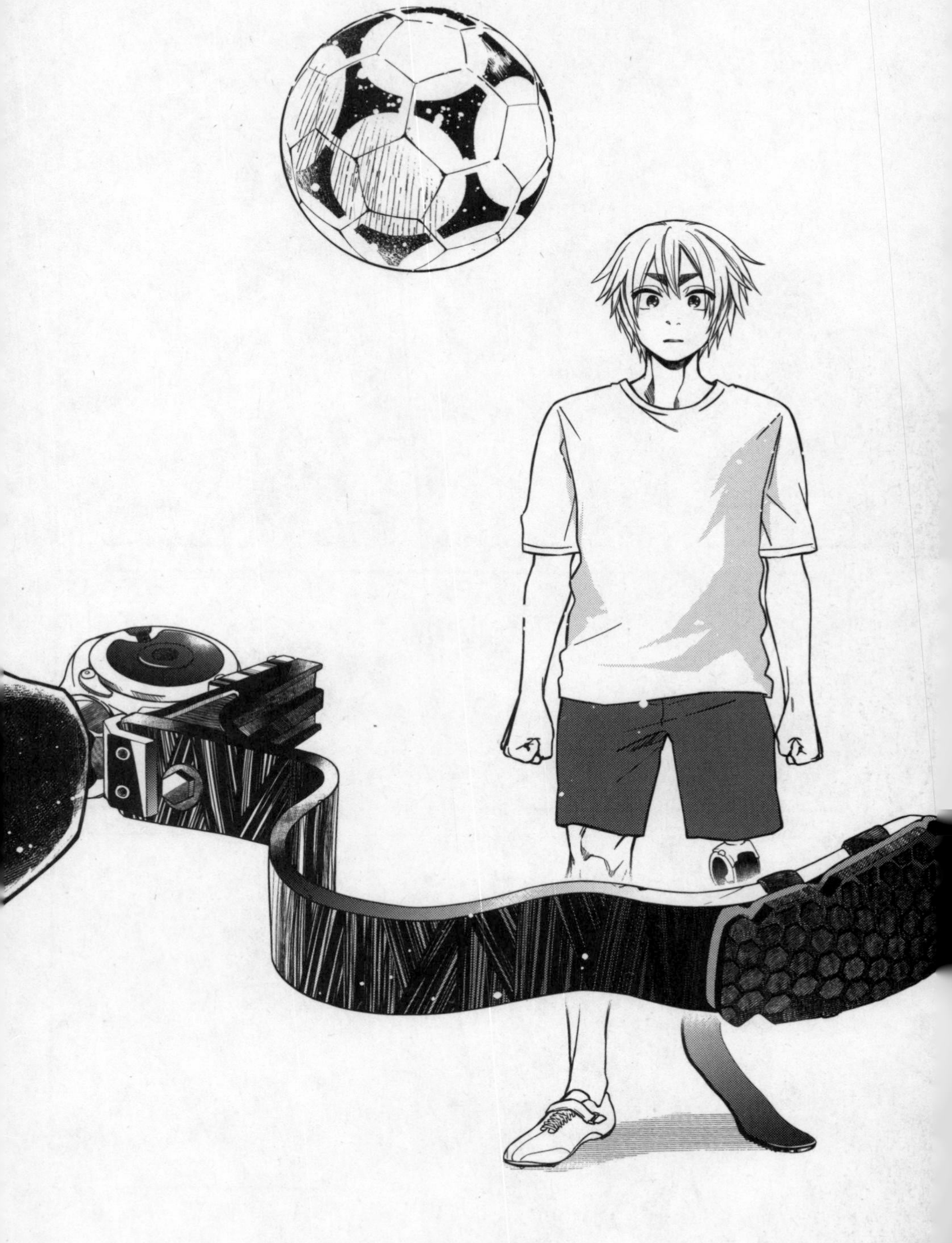

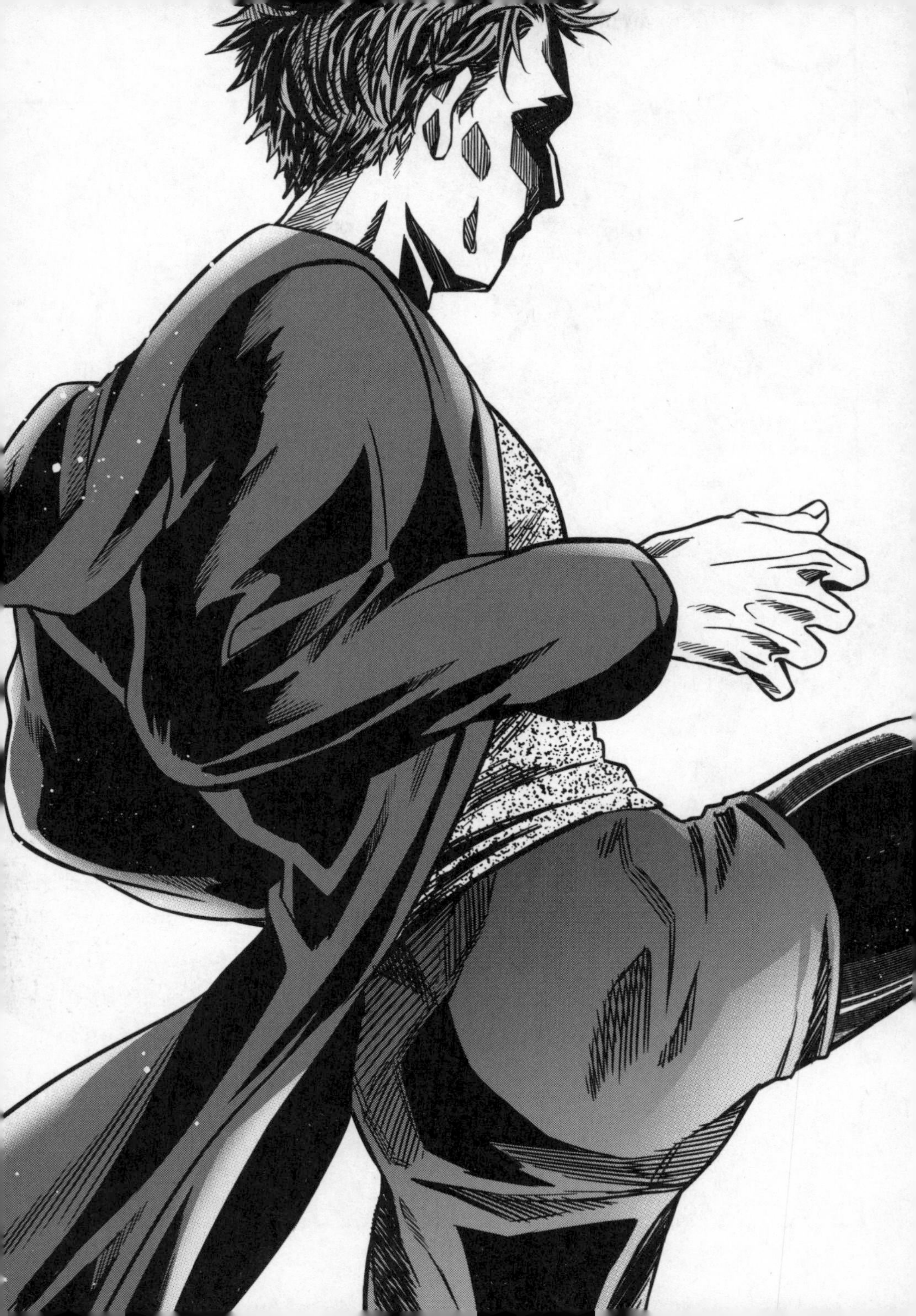

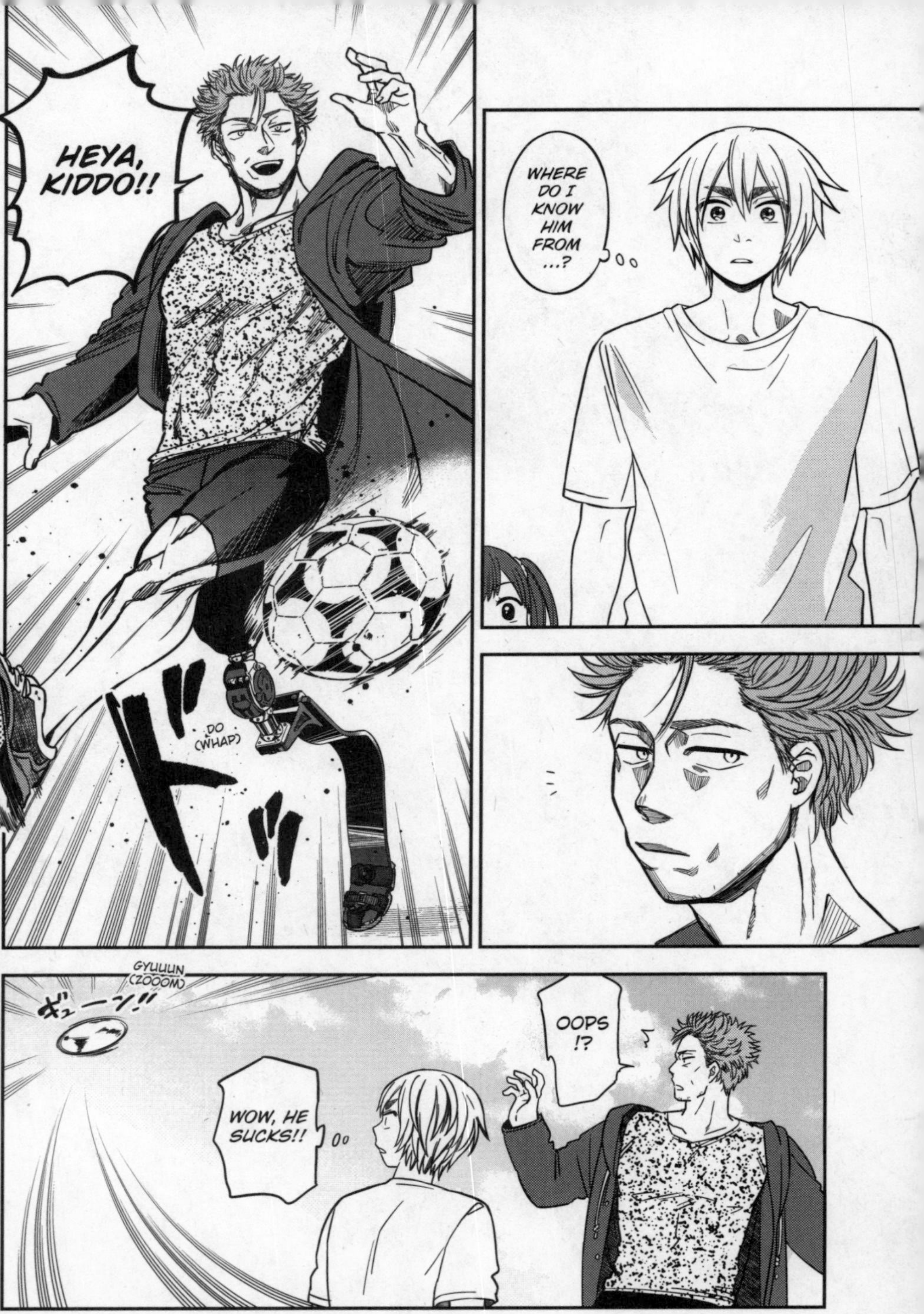
WHERE DO I KNOW HIM FROM ...?
HEYA, KIDDO!!
DO (WHAP)
OOPS !?
WOW, HE SUCKS!!
GYUUUN (ZOOOM)
ギューン!!

Chapter 14: Wanna Be Part of That World

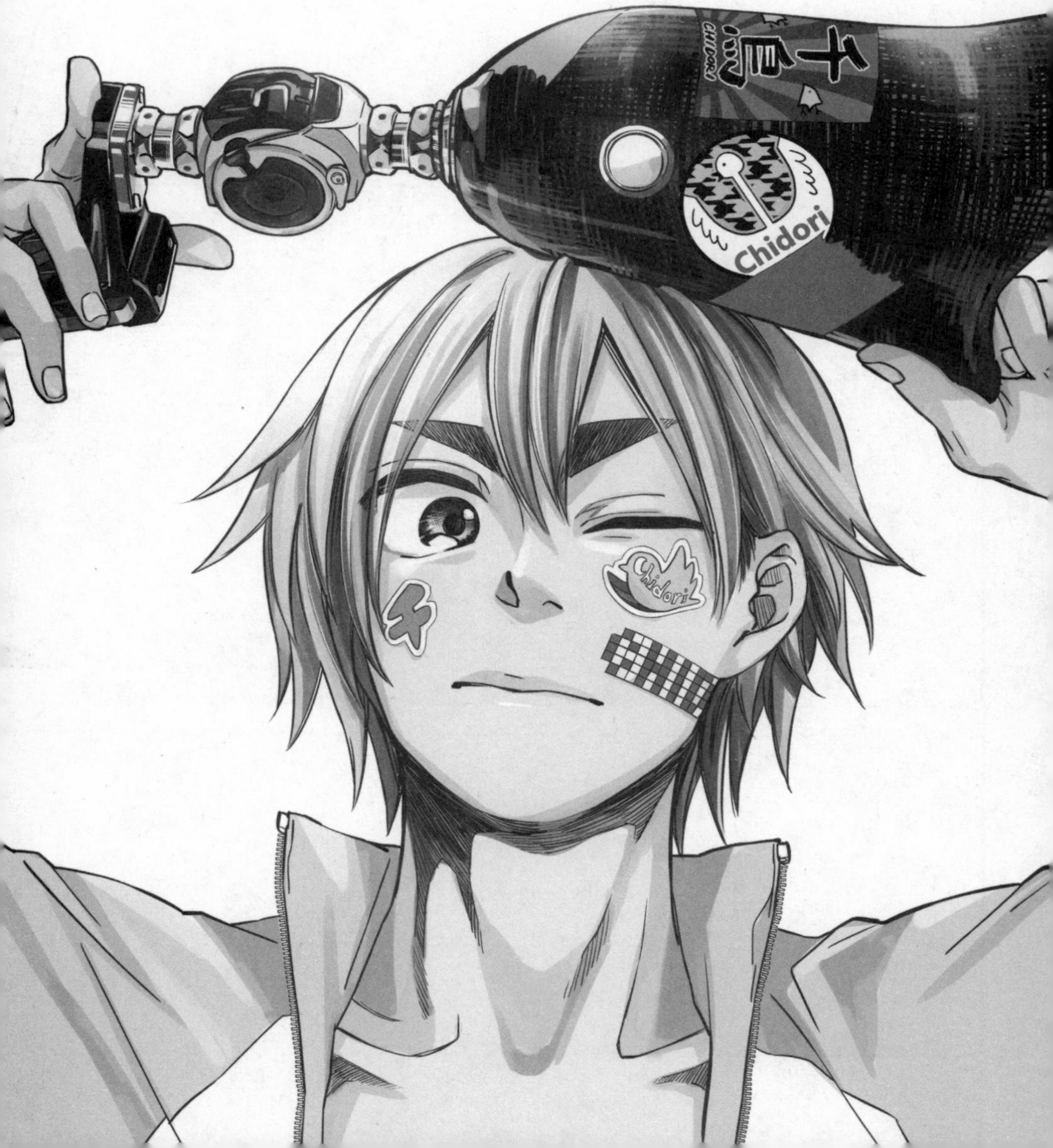
CHIDORI
Chidori
Chidori

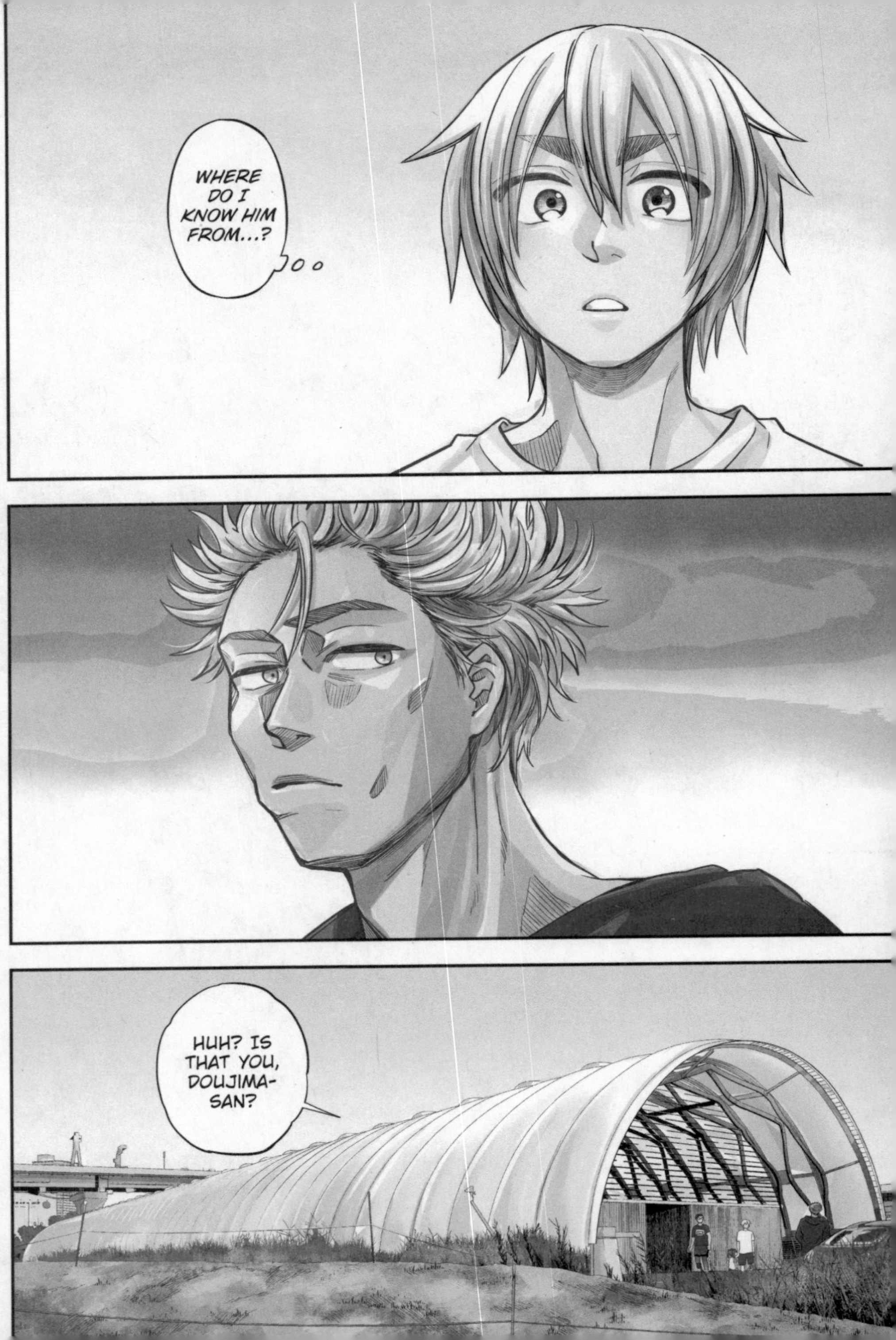
WHERE DO I KNOW HIM FROM...?
HUH? IS THAT YOU, DOUJIMA-SAN?

WHAT BRINGS YOU HERE?

FILMING A SPORTS SPECIAL.

...NOW I REMEMBER!

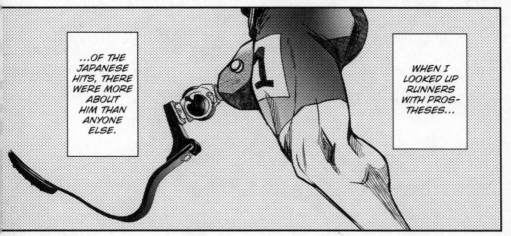

WHEN I LOOKED UP RUNNERS WITH PROSTHESES...

...OF THE JAPANESE HITS, THERE WERE MORE ABOUT HIM THAN ANYONE ELSE.

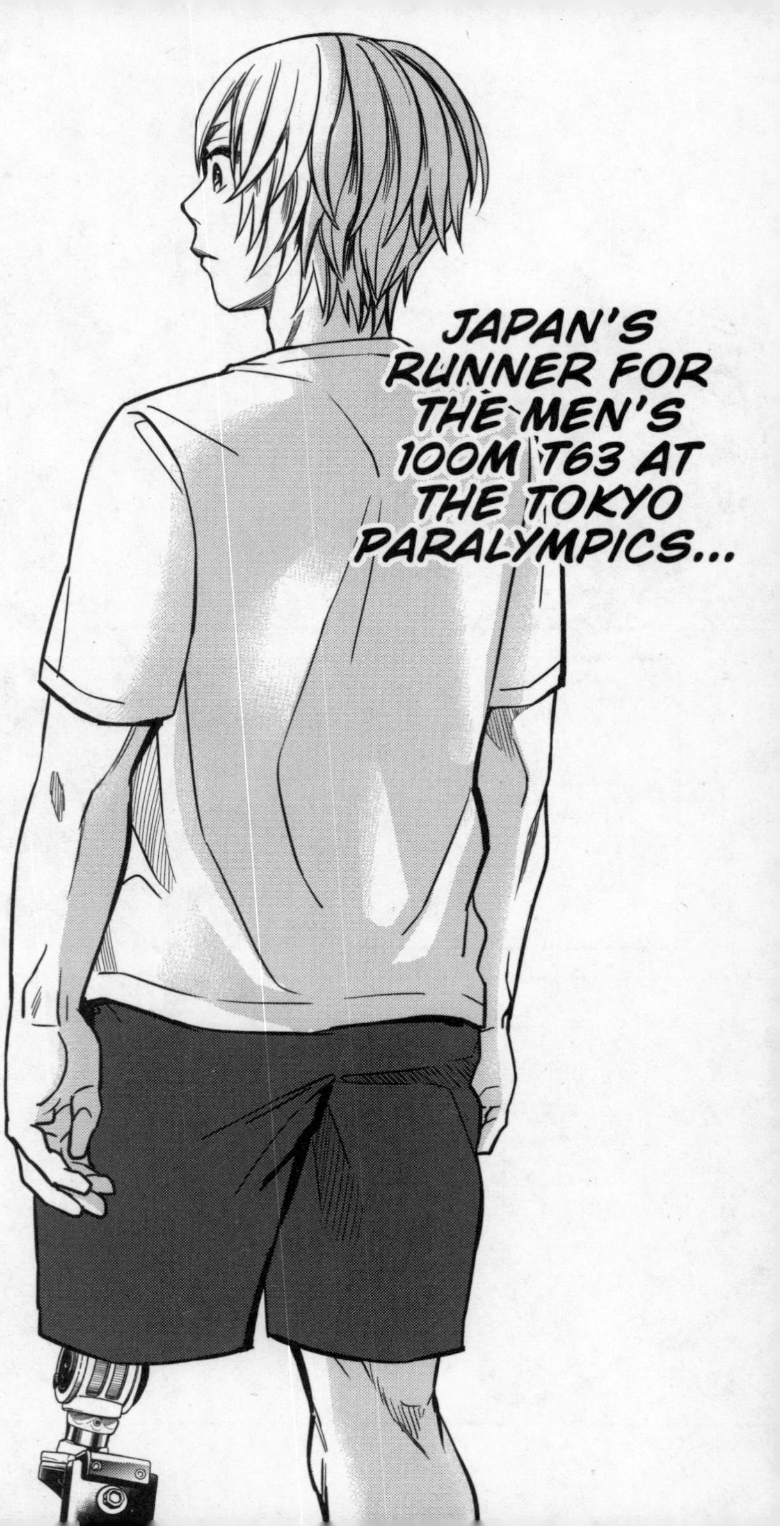
JAPAN'S RUNNER FOR THE MEN'S 100M T63 AT THE TOKYO PARALYMPICS...

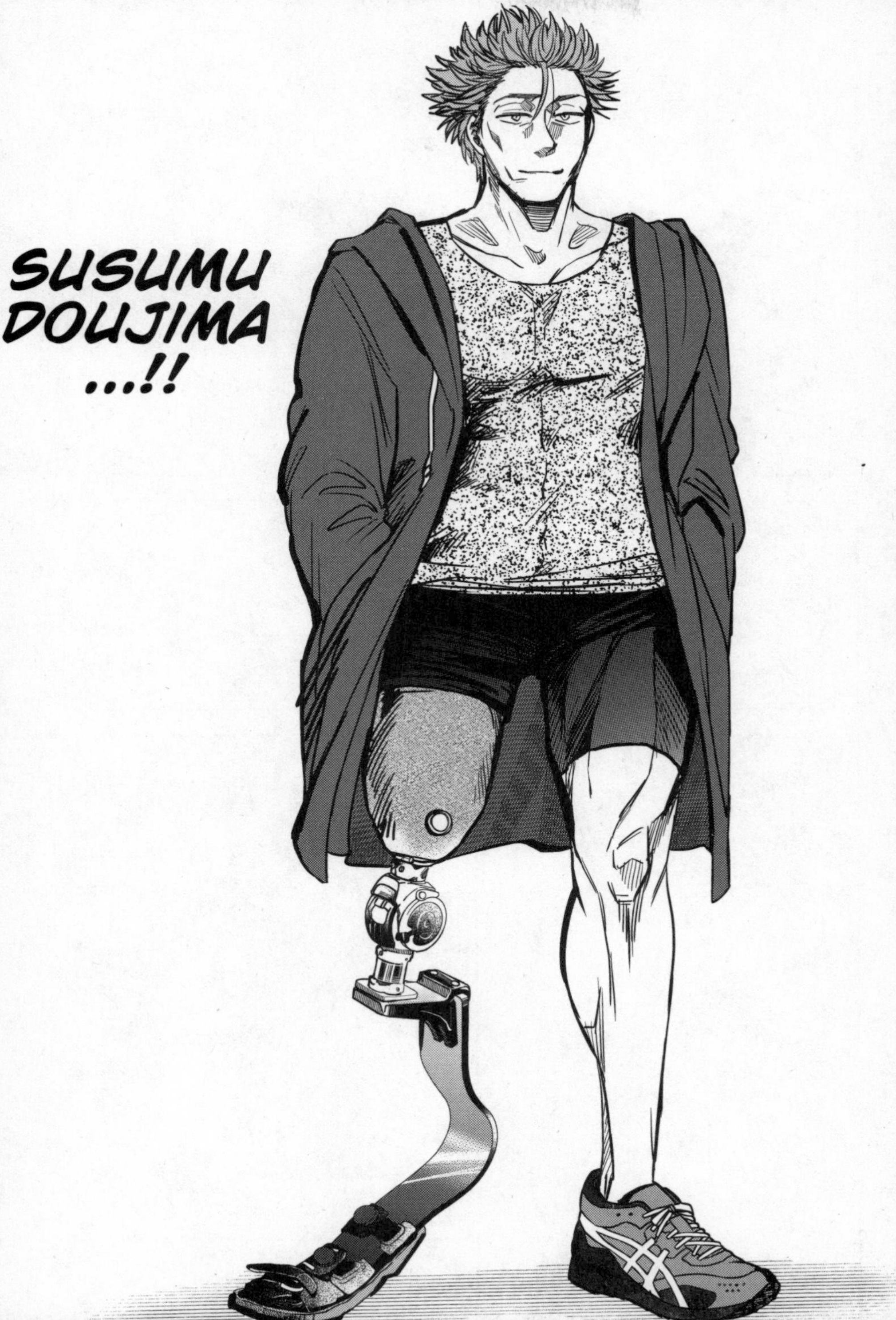
SUSUMU DOUJIMA ...!!

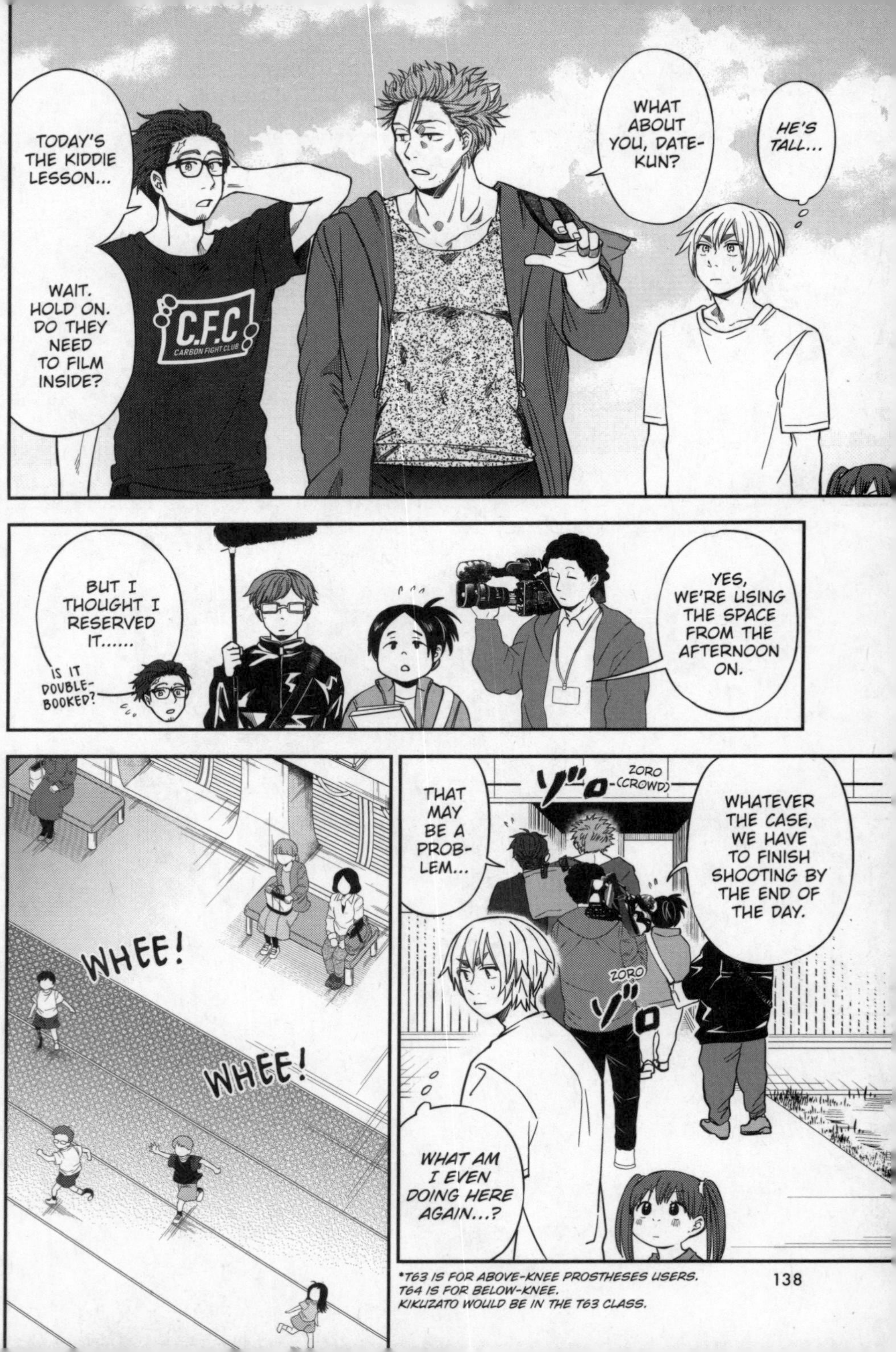
HE'S TALL...
WHAT ABOUT YOU, DATE-KUN?
TODAY'S THE KIDDIE LESSON...
WAIT. HOLD ON. DO THEY NEED TO FILM INSIDE?
YES, WE'RE USING THE SPACE FROM THE AFTERNOON ON.
BUT I THOUGHT I RESERVED IT......
IS IT DOUBLE-BOOKED?
ZORO (CROWD)
WHATEVER THE CASE, WE HAVE TO FINISH SHOOTING BY THE END OF THE DAY.
THAT MAY BE A PROBLEM...
ZORO
WHAT AM I EVEN DOING HERE AGAIN...?
WHEE!
WHEE!

*T63 IS FOR ABOVE-KNEE PROSTHESES USERS.
T64 IS FOR BELOW-KNEE.
KIKUZATO WOULD BE IN THE T63 CLASS.

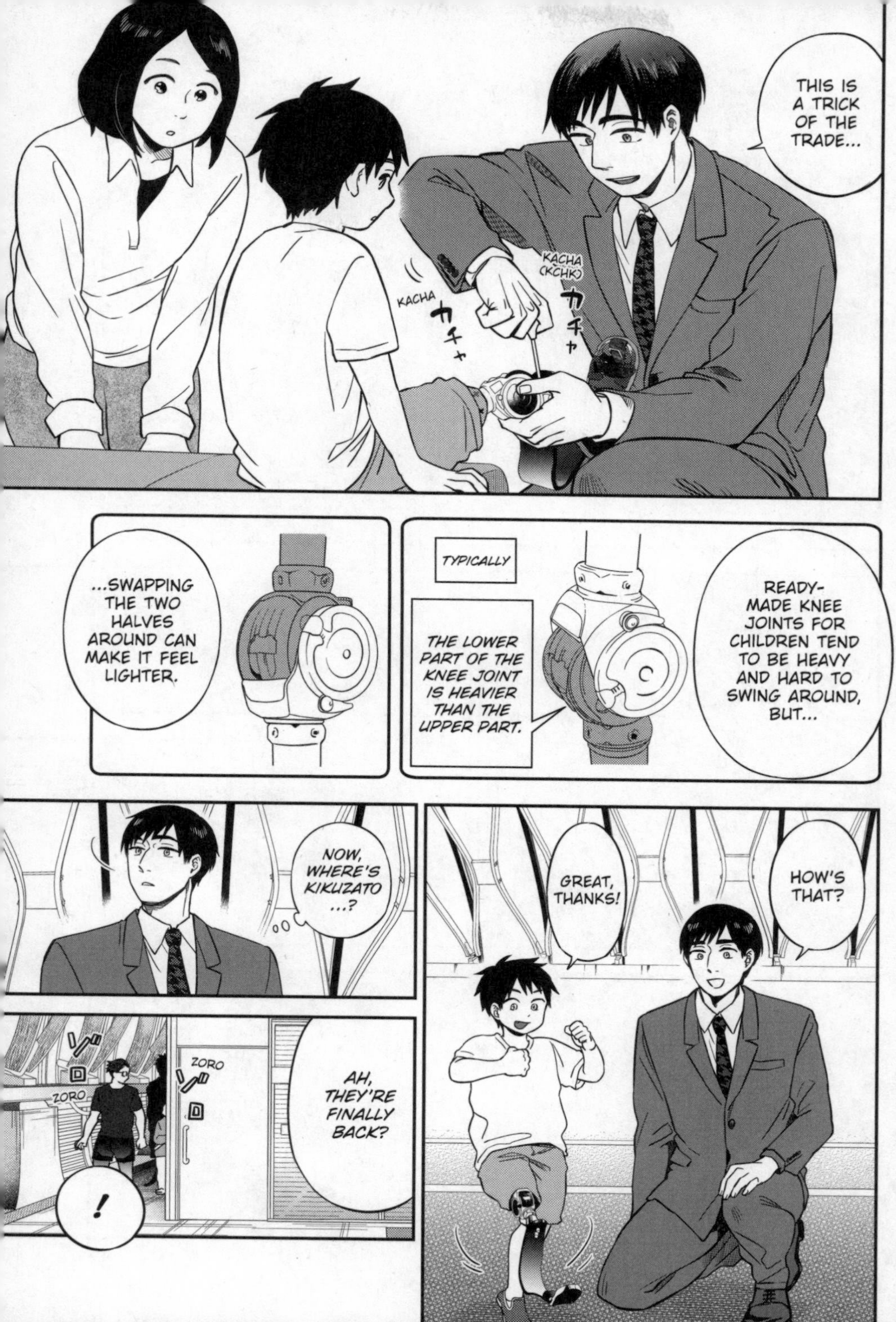
THIS IS A TRICK OF THE TRADE...
KACHA (KCHK)
カチャ
KACHA
カチャ
READY-MADE KNEE JOINTS FOR CHILDREN TEND TO BE HEAVY AND HARD TO SWING AROUND, BUT...
TYPICALLY
THE LOWER PART OF THE KNEE JOINT IS HEAVIER THAN THE UPPER PART.
...SWAPPING THE TWO HALVES AROUND CAN MAKE IT FEEL LIGHTER.
HOW'S THAT?
GREAT, THANKS!
NOW, WHERE'S KIKUZATO ...?
AH, THEY'RE FINALLY BACK?
ZORO
ゾロ
ZORO
ゾロ
!

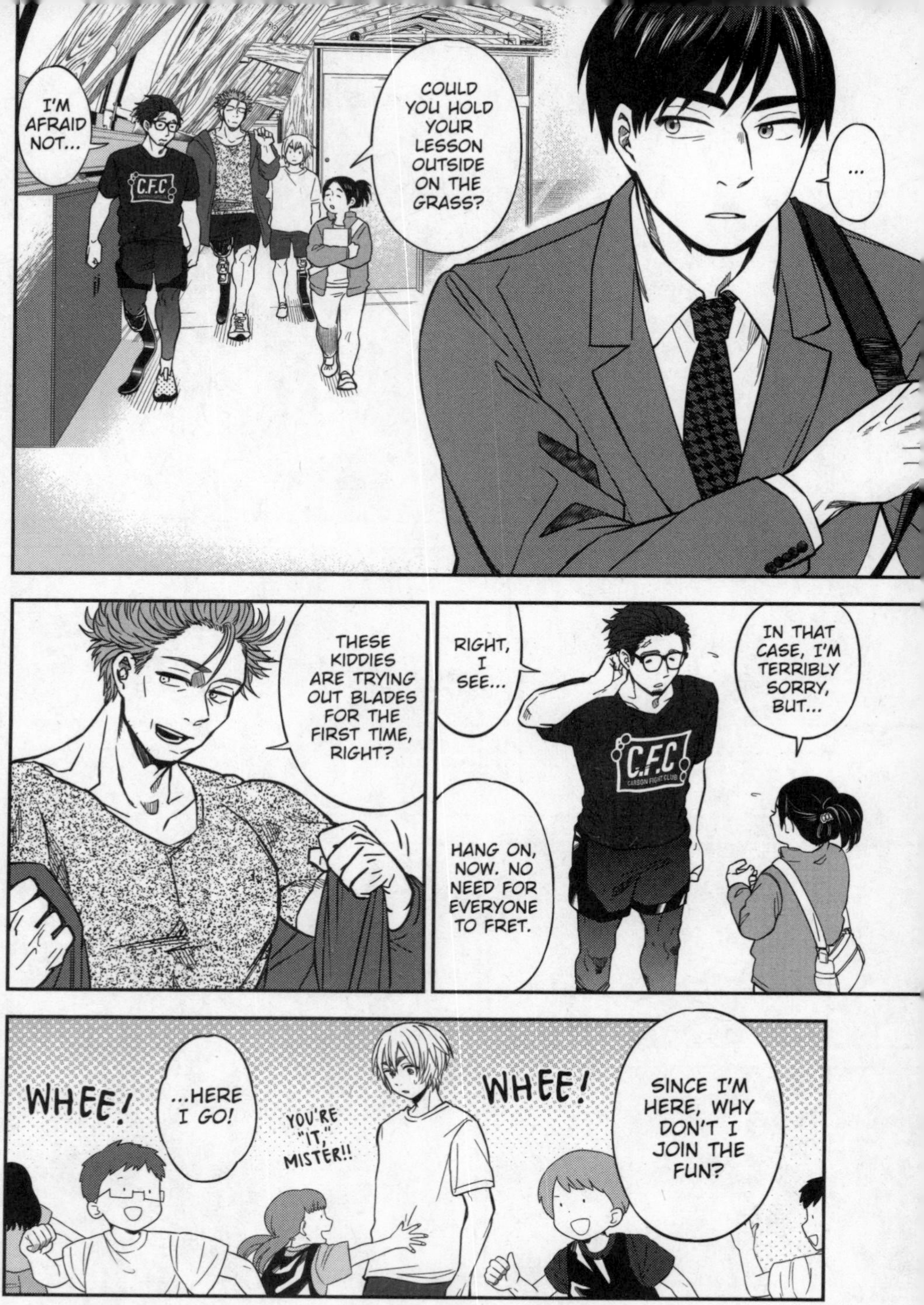
...
COULD YOU HOLD YOUR LESSON OUTSIDE ON THE GRASS?
I'M AFRAID NOT...
IN THAT CASE, I'M TERRIBLY SORRY, BUT...
RIGHT, I SEE...
HANG ON, NOW. NO NEED FOR EVERYONE TO FRET.
THESE KIDDIES ARE TRYING OUT BLADES FOR THE FIRST TIME, RIGHT?
SINCE I'M HERE, WHY DON'T I JOIN THE FUN?
WHEE!
YOU'RE "IT," MISTER!!
...HERE I GO!
WHEE!

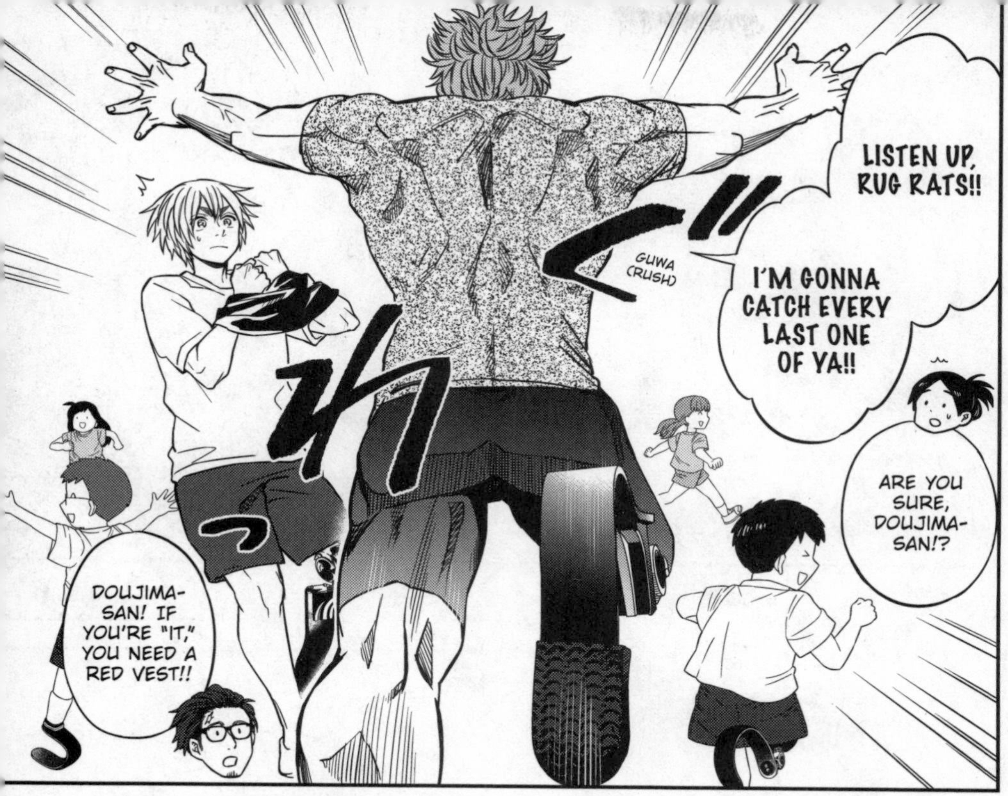
LISTEN UP, RUG RATS!!
I'M GONNA CATCH EVERY LAST ONE OF YA!!
GUWA (RUSH)
ARE YOU SURE, DOUJIMA-SAN!?
DOUJIMA-SAN! IF YOU'RE "IT," YOU NEED A RED VEST!!

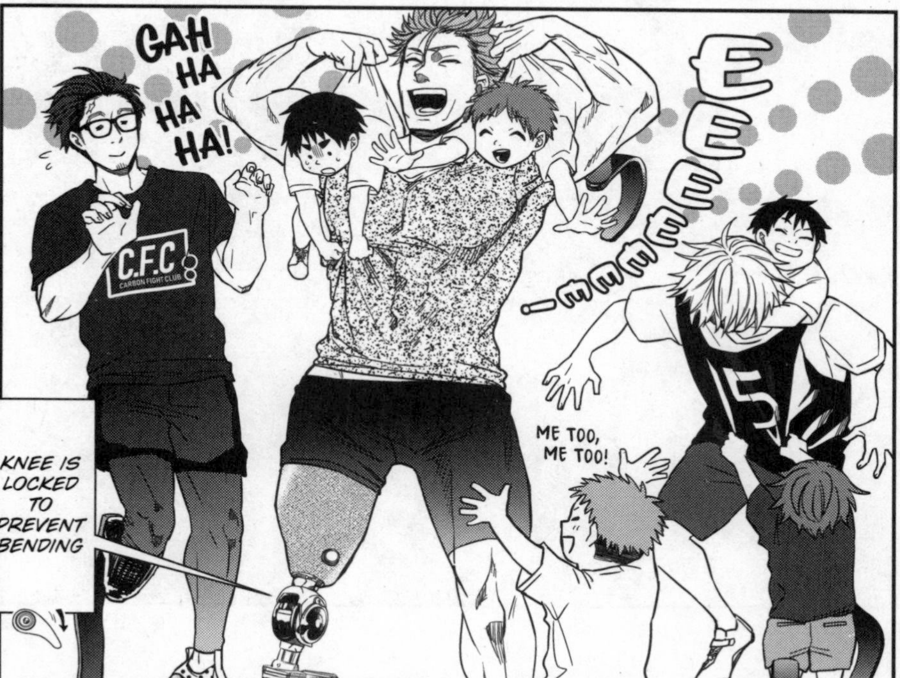
EEEEEEEEE—
GAH HA HA HA!
ME TOO, ME TOO!
C.F.C
CARBON FIGHT CLUB
KNEE IS LOCKED TO PREVENT BENDING

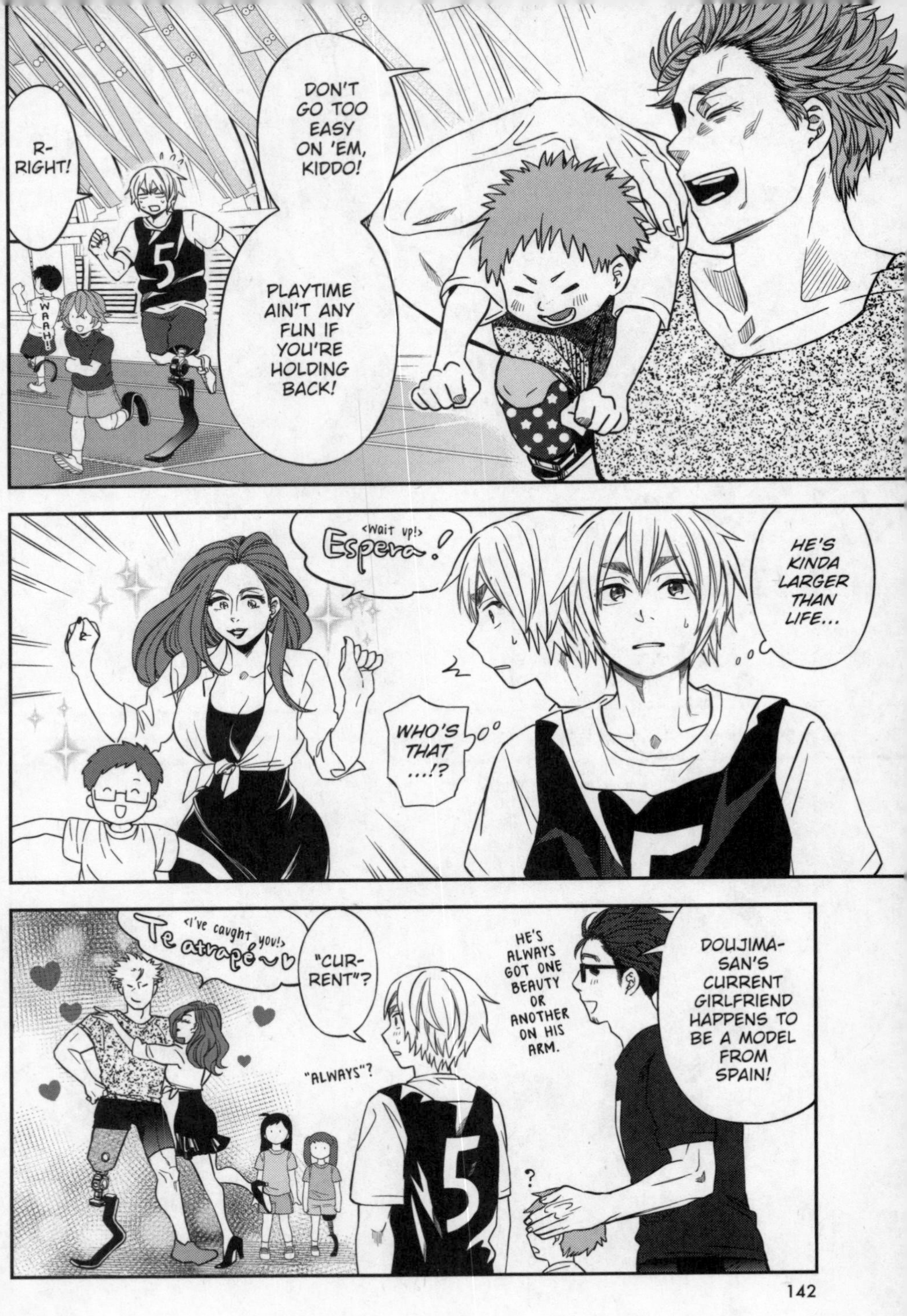
DON'T GO TOO EASY ON 'EM, KIDDO!
PLAYTIME AIN'T ANY FUN IF YOU'RE HOLDING BACK!
R-RIGHT!
WAAAH!
HE'S KINDA LARGER THAN LIFE...
<Wait up!>
Espera!
WHO'S THAT ...!?
DOUJIMA-SAN'S CURRENT GIRLFRIEND HAPPENS TO BE A MODEL FROM SPAIN!
HE'S ALWAYS GOT ONE BEAUTY OR ANOTHER ON HIS ARM.
"CUR-RENT"?
<I've caught you!>
Te atrapé~♡
"ALWAYS"?
?

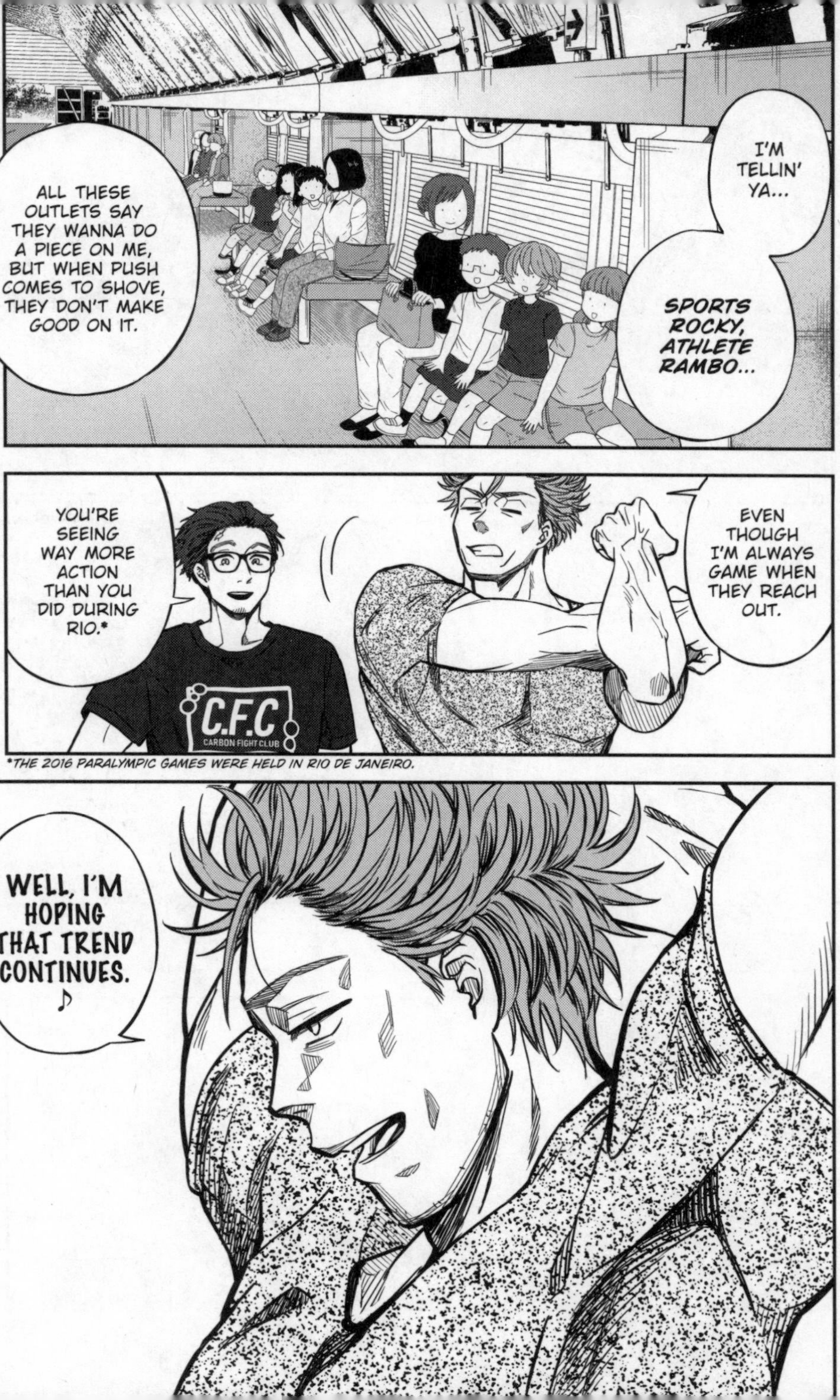
I'M TELLIN' YA...
SPORTS ROCKY, ATHLETE RAMBO...
ALL THESE OUTLETS SAY THEY WANNA DO A PIECE ON ME, BUT WHEN PUSH COMES TO SHOVE, THEY DON'T MAKE GOOD ON IT.
EVEN THOUGH I'M ALWAYS GAME WHEN THEY REACH OUT.
YOU'RE SEEING WAY MORE ACTION THAN YOU DID DURING RIO.*
WELL, I'M HOPING THAT TREND CONTINUES. ♪

*THE 2016 PARALYMPIC GAMES WERE HELD IN RIO DE JANEIRO.

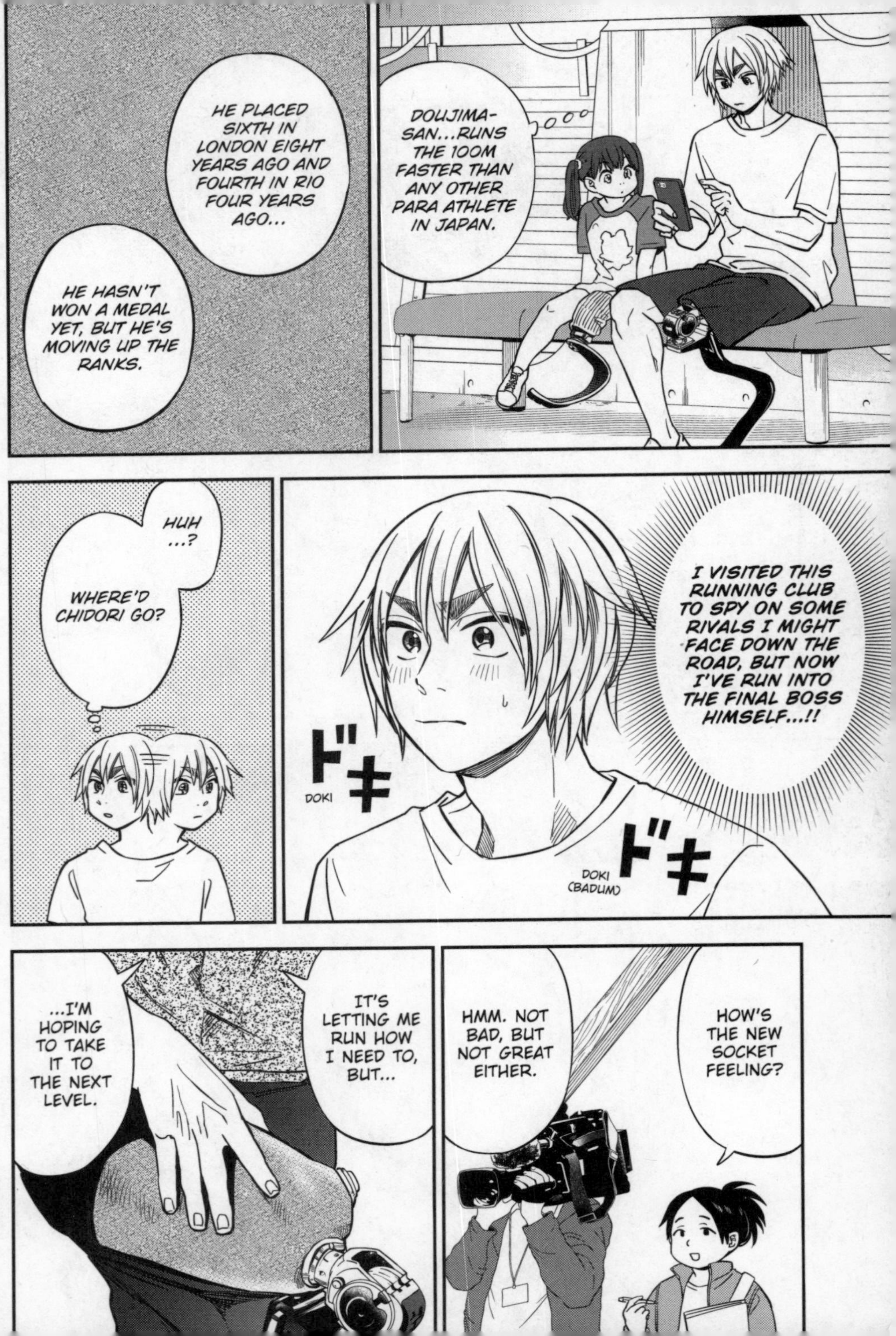
DOUJIMA-SAN...RUNS THE 100M FASTER THAN ANY OTHER PARA ATHLETE IN JAPAN.
HE PLACED SIXTH IN LONDON EIGHT YEARS AGO AND FOURTH IN RIO FOUR YEARS AGO...
HE HASN'T WON A MEDAL YET, BUT HE'S MOVING UP THE RANKS.
I VISITED THIS RUNNING CLUB TO SPY ON SOME RIVALS I MIGHT FACE DOWN THE ROAD, BUT NOW I'VE RUN INTO THE FINAL BOSS HIMSELF...!!
ドキ
DOKI
ドキ
DOKI (BADUM)
HUH ...?
WHERE'D CHIDORI GO?
HOW'S THE NEW SOCKET FEELING?
HMM. NOT BAD, BUT NOT GREAT EITHER.
IT'S LETTING ME RUN HOW I NEED TO, BUT...
...I'M HOPING TO TAKE IT TO THE NEXT LEVEL.

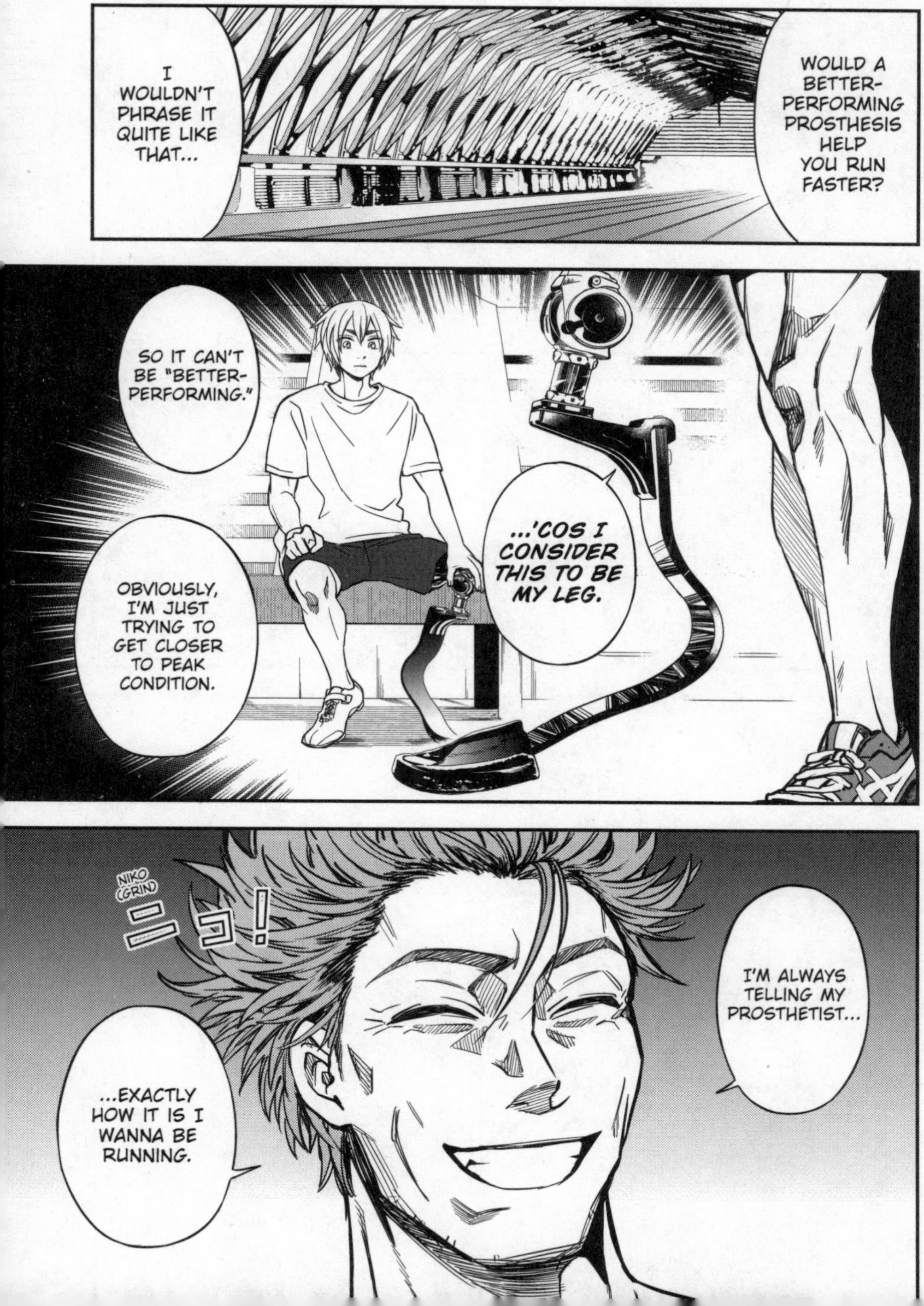
WOULD A BETTER-PERFORMING PROSTHESIS HELP YOU RUN FASTER?
I WOULDN'T PHRASE IT QUITE LIKE THAT...
...'COS I CONSIDER THIS TO BE MY LEG.
SO IT CAN'T BE "BETTER-PERFORMING."
OBVIOUSLY, I'M JUST TRYING TO GET CLOSER TO PEAK CONDITION.
NIKO (GRIN)
ニッ!
I'M ALWAYS TELLING MY PROSTHETIST...
...EXACTLY HOW IT IS I WANNA BE RUNNING.

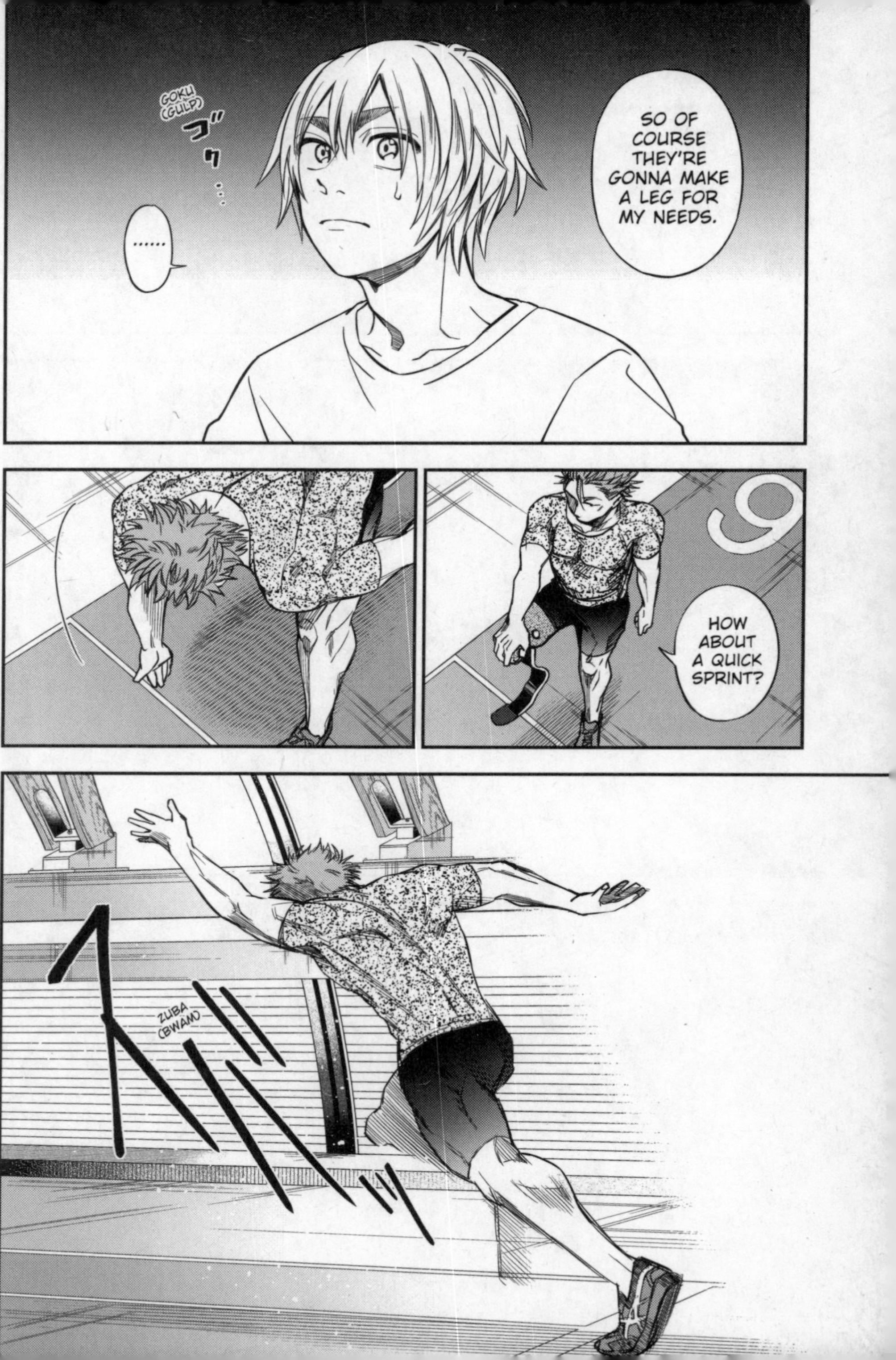
SO OF COURSE THEY'RE GONNA MAKE A LEG FOR MY NEEDS.
GOKU (GULP)
ゴク
......
HOW ABOUT A QUICK SPRINT?
ZUBA (BWAM)

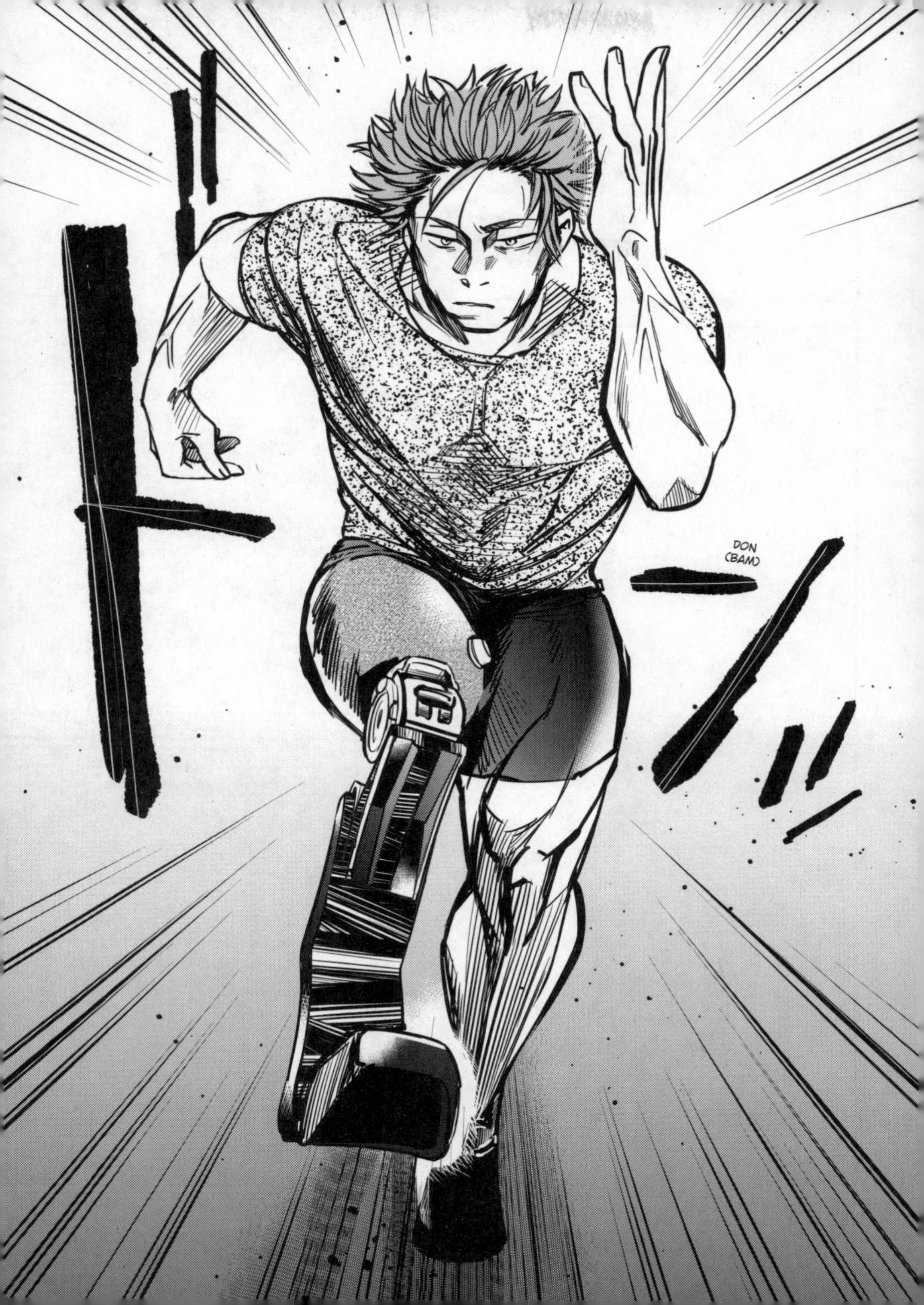
DON
(BAM)

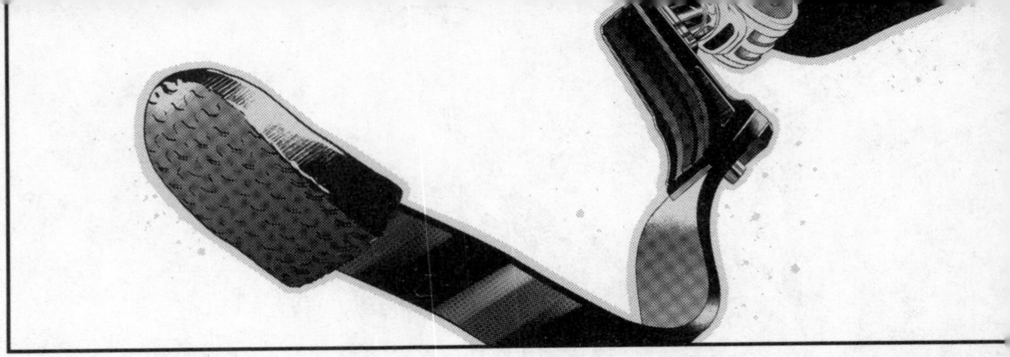
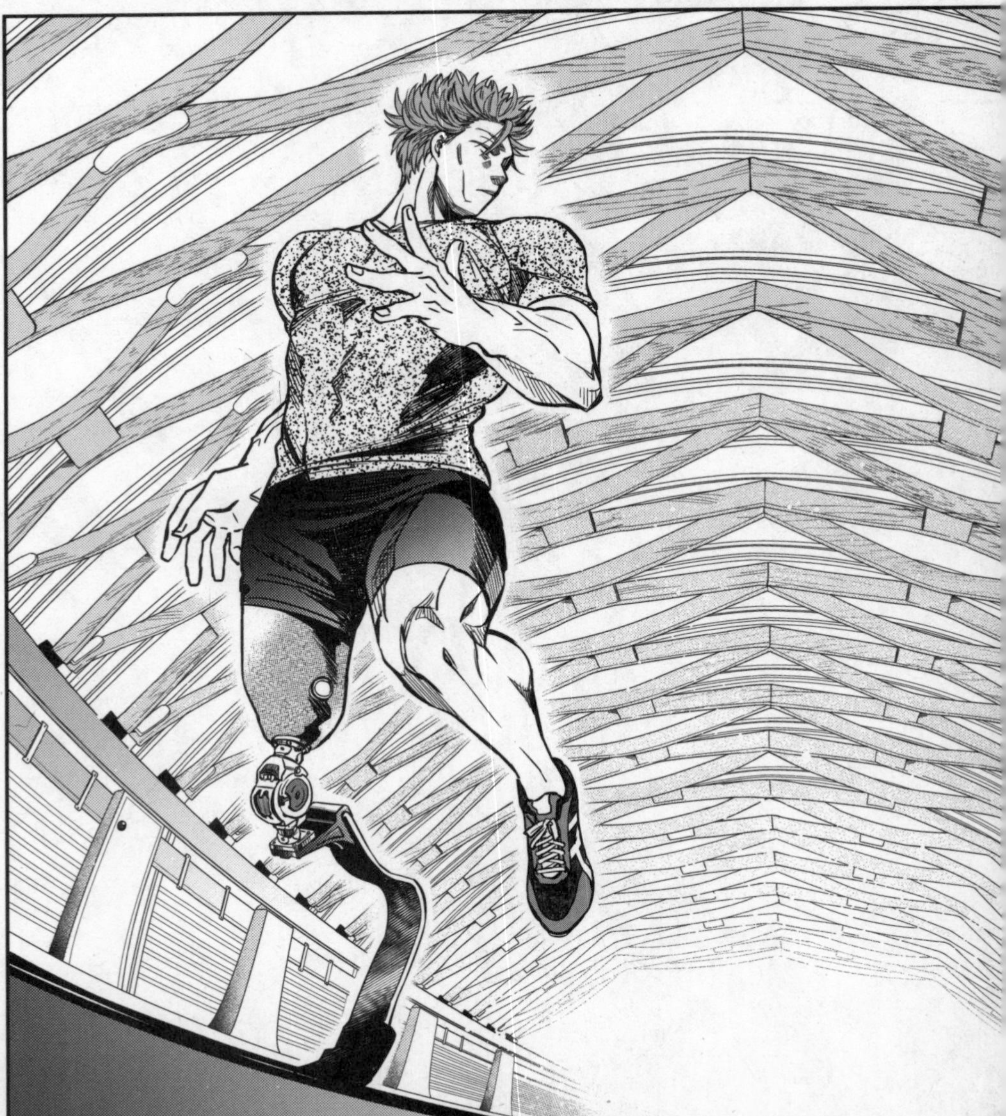

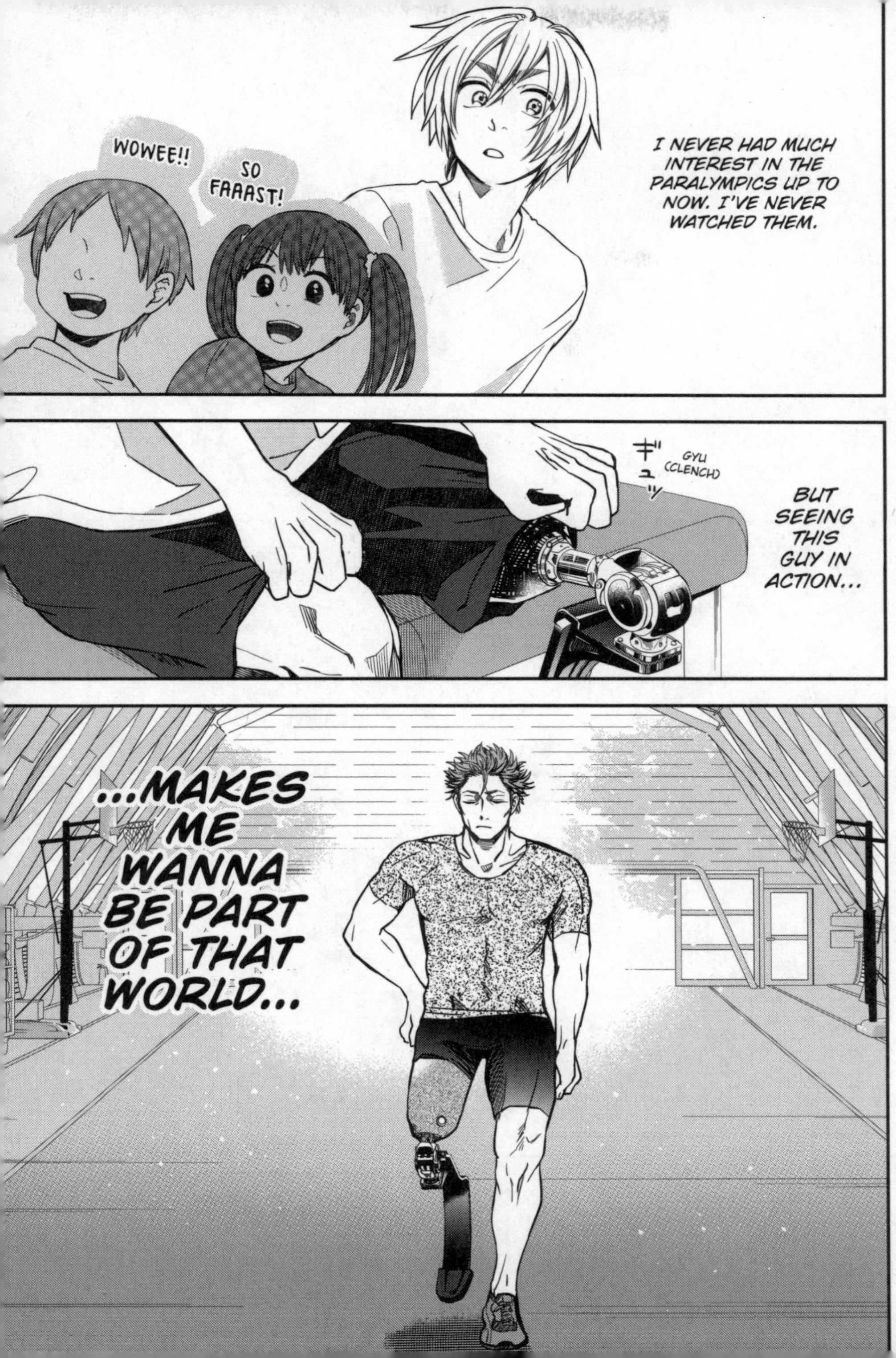

I NEVER HAD MUCH INTEREST IN THE PARALYMPICS UP TO NOW. I'VE NEVER WATCHED THEM.
SO FAAAST!
WOWEE!!
BUT SEEING THIS GUY IN ACTION...
ギュッ
GYU (CLENCH)
...MAKES ME WANNA BE PART OF THAT WORLD...

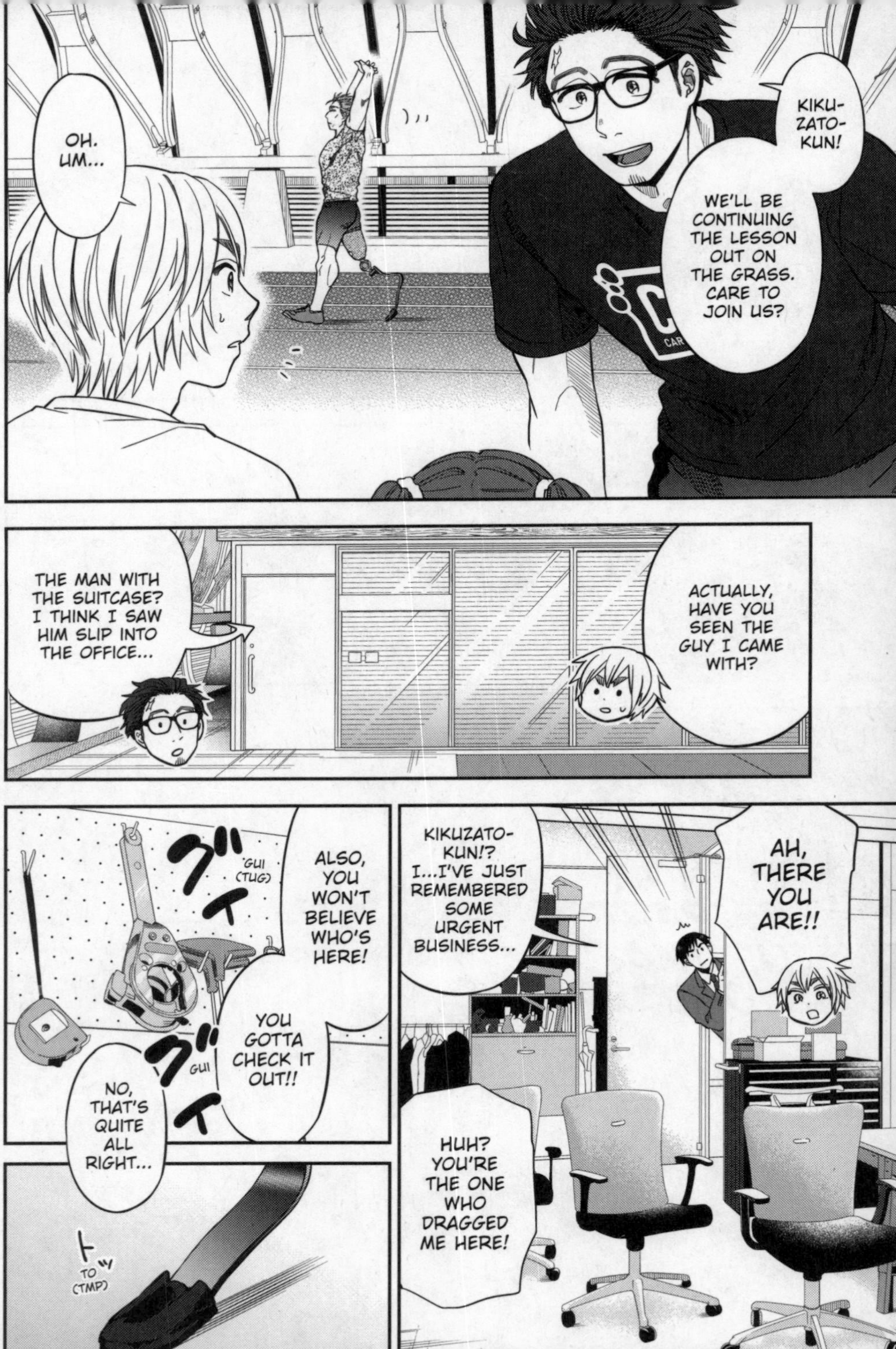
KIKU-ZATO-KUN!
WE'LL BE CONTINUING THE LESSON OUT ON THE GRASS. CARE TO JOIN US?
OH. UM...
ACTUALLY, HAVE YOU SEEN THE GUY I CAME WITH?
THE MAN WITH THE SUITCASE? I THINK I SAW HIM SLIP INTO THE OFFICE...
AH, THERE YOU ARE!!
KIKUZATO-KUN!? I...I'VE JUST REMEMBERED SOME URGENT BUSINESS...
HUH? YOU'RE THE ONE WHO DRAGGED ME HERE!
ALSO, YOU WON'T BELIEVE WHO'S HERE!
グイ
GUI (TUG)
YOU GOTTA CHECK IT OUT!!
グイ
GUI
NO, THAT'S QUITE ALL RIGHT...
トッ
TO (TMP)

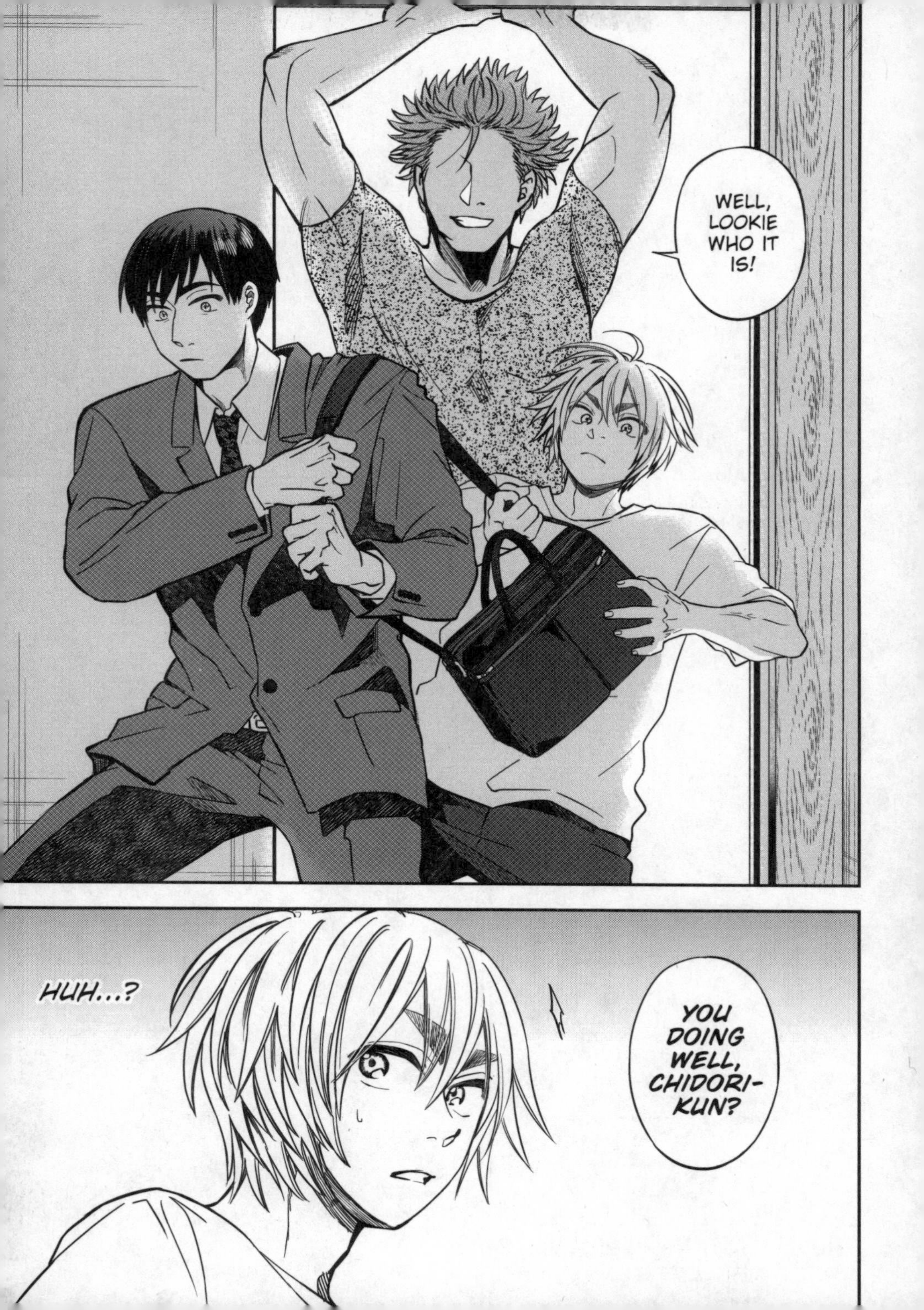
WELL, LOOKIE WHO IT IS!
YOU DOING WELL, CHIDORI-KUN?
HUH...?

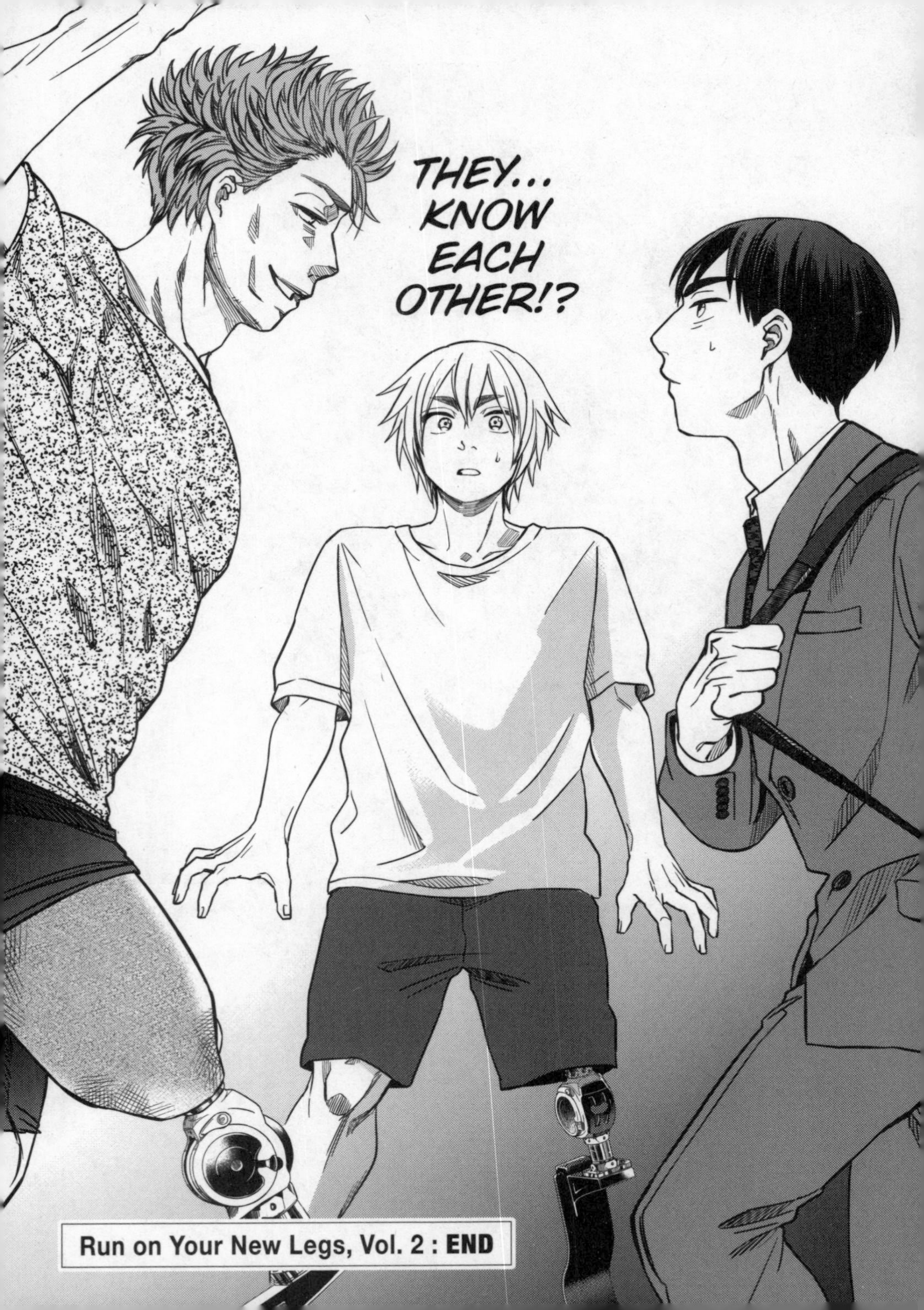
THEY... KNOW EACH OTHER!?
Run on Your New Legs, Vol. 2 : END

TRANSLATION NOTES

COMMON HONORIFICS

no honorific: Indicates familiarity or closeness; if used without permission or reason, addressing someone in this manner would constitute an insult.

-san: The Japanese equivalent of Mr./Mrs./Ms. This is the fail-safe honorific if politeness is required.

-kun: Used most often when referring to boys, this honorific indicates affection or familiarity. Occasionally used by older men among their peers, but it may also be used by anyone referring to a person of lower standing.

-chan: Affectionate honorific indicating familiarity used mostly in reference to girls; also used in reference to cute persons or animals of any gender.

-senpai: A suffix used when addressing upperclassmen or more senior coworkers.

-sensei: A respectful term for teachers, artists, or high-level professionals.

-sama: An honorific conveying great respect.

CURRENCY CONVERSION

While exchange rates fluctuate daily, a good approximation is ¥100 to 1 USD.

Page 45: The term *kouhai* is used for underclassmen or junior coworkers.

Page 112: The phrase Chidori uses, **dojo storming**, is *dojo yaburi*—the act of storming a rival martial arts dojo and challenging its members until they've all been beaten. It's a dramatic way to describe visiting the kiddie running lesson but very in-character for Chidori.

Page 120: The **Paprika** dance comes from a 2018 video featuring the children's dance troupe Foorin performing to the song "Paprika" by Kenshi Yonezu.

Special thanks
to all my consultants

Atsushi Yamamoto (Shin Nihon Jusetsu)
Junta Kosuda (Open House)
Mikio Ikeda (Digital Advertising Consortium)
Tomoki Yoshida (Nippon Sport Science University)

Xiborg
Otto Bock Japan
Okino Sports Prosthetics & Orthotics (Atsuo Okino)
D'ACTION (Shuji Miyake)
Naoto Yoshida (Writer)

Thank you to everyone else who
contributed to this book!

Turntable
THIS PART—THE TURNTABLE—LETS ME SWIVEL MY KNEE AROUND...
...WHICH MAKES IT EASIER TO PUT PANTS AND SHOES ON.

BONUS

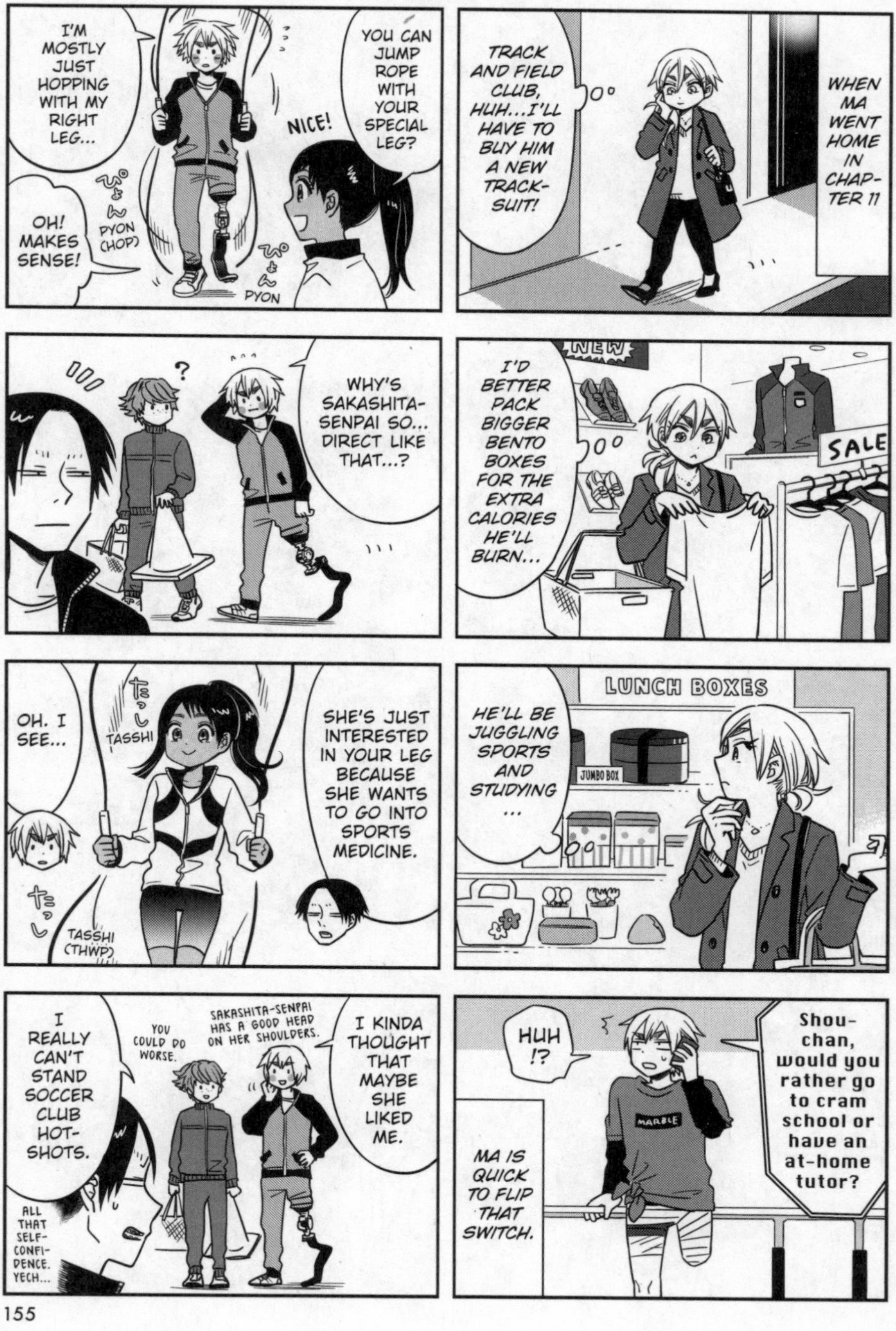
WHEN MA WENT HOME IN CHAPTER 11
TRACK AND FIELD CLUB, HUH...I'LL HAVE TO BUY HIM A NEW TRACKSUIT!
I'D BETTER PACK BIGGER BENTO BOXES FOR THE EXTRA CALORIES HE'LL BURN...
NEW
SALE
LUNCH BOXES
HE'LL BE JUGGLING SPORTS AND STUDYING ...
JUMBO BOX
Shou-chan, would you rather go to cram school or have an at-home tutor?
HUH !?
MA IS QUICK TO FLIP THAT SWITCH.
MARBLE
YOU CAN JUMP ROPE WITH YOUR SPECIAL LEG?
NICE!
I'M MOSTLY JUST HOPPING WITH MY RIGHT LEG...
OH! MAKES SENSE!
ぴょん
PYON (HOP)
ぴょん
PYON
WHY'S SAKASHITA-SENPAI SO... DIRECT LIKE THAT...?
?
SHE'S JUST INTERESTED IN YOUR LEG BECAUSE SHE WANTS TO GO INTO SPORTS MEDICINE.
OH. I SEE...
たっし
TASSHI
たっし
TASSHI (THWP)
I KINDA THOUGHT THAT MAYBE SHE LIKED ME.
SAKASHITA-SENPAI HAS A GOOD HEAD ON HER SHOULDERS.
YOU COULD DO WORSE.
I REALLY CAN'T STAND SOCCER CLUB HOT-SHOTS.
ALL THAT SELF-CONFIDENCE. YECH...

BY MORUNGA-SAN (SERIES ASSISTANT)

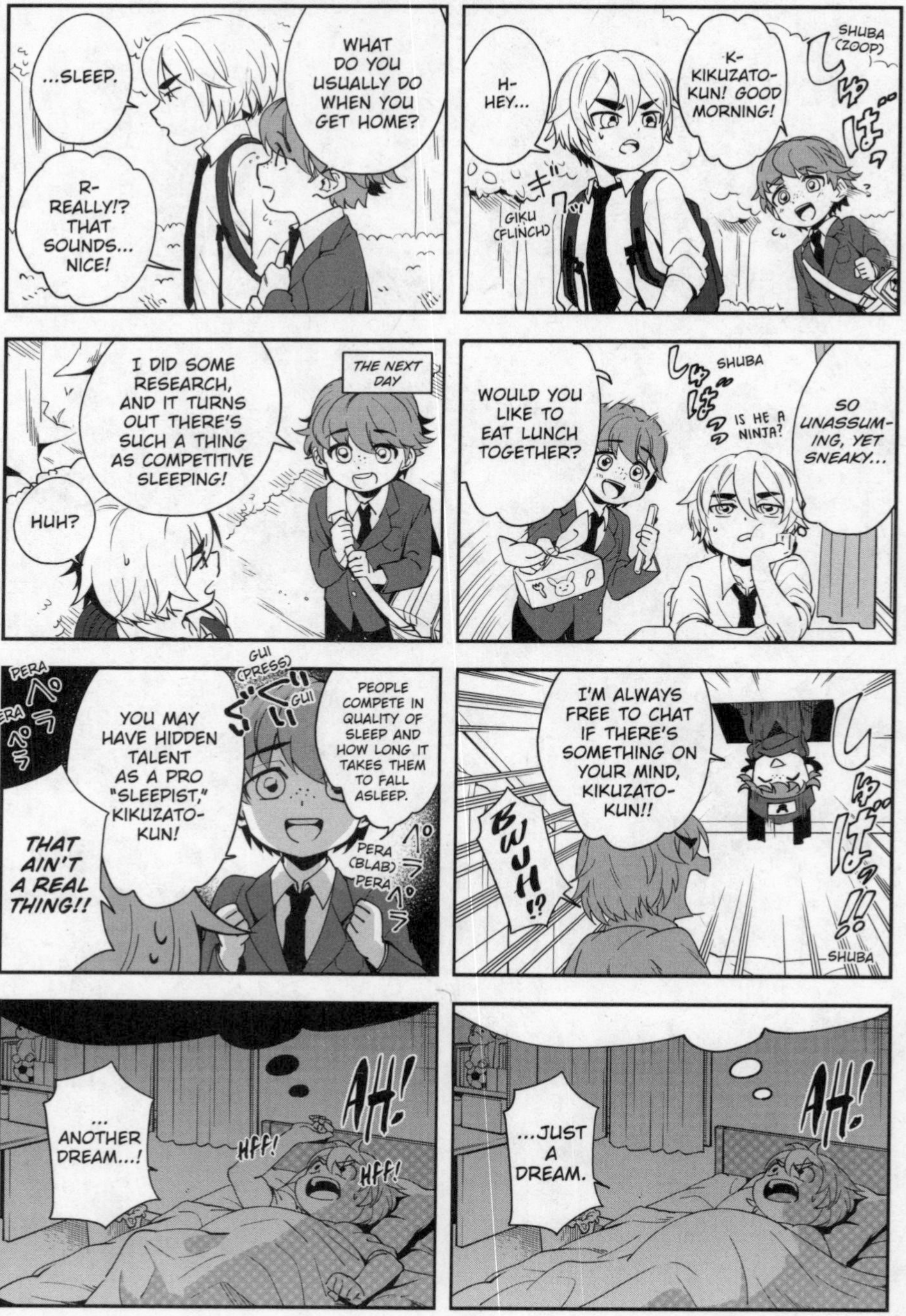
SHUBA (ZOOP)
K-KIKUZATO-KUN! GOOD MORNING!
H-HEY...
GIKU (FLINCH)
WHAT DO YOU USUALLY DO WHEN YOU GET HOME?
...SLEEP.
R-REALLY!? THAT SOUNDS... NICE!
SHUBA
IS HE A NINJA?
SO UNASSUMING, YET SNEAKY...
WOULD YOU LIKE TO EAT LUNCH TOGETHER?
THE NEXT DAY
I DID SOME RESEARCH, AND IT TURNS OUT THERE'S SUCH A THING AS COMPETITIVE SLEEPING!
HUH?
I'M ALWAYS FREE TO CHAT IF THERE'S SOMETHING ON YOUR MIND, KIKUZATO-KUN!!
BWUH!?
SHUBA
GUI (PRESS)
GUI
PEOPLE COMPETE IN QUALITY OF SLEEP AND HOW LONG IT TAKES THEM TO FALL ASLEEP.
YOU MAY HAVE HIDDEN TALENT AS A PRO "SLEEPIST," KIKUZATO-KUN!
PERA
PERA
PERA (BLAB) PERA
THAT AIN'T A REAL THING!!
AH!
...JUST A DREAM.
AH!
HFF!
HFF!
... ANOTHER DREAM...!

BY HIDEO NAKAJIMA-SAN (SERIES ASSISTANT)

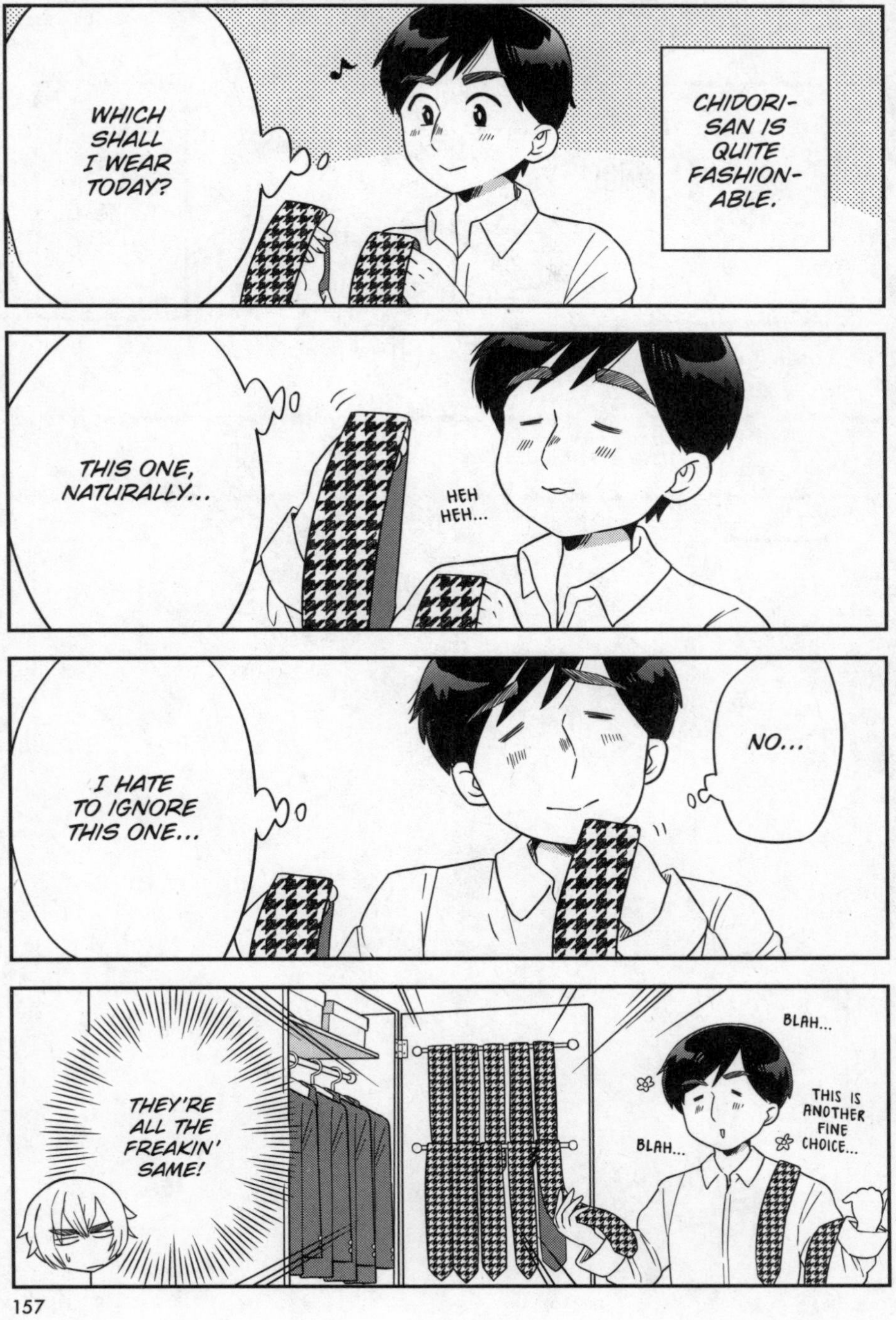
CHIDORI-SAN IS QUITE FASHION-ABLE.
WHICH SHALL I WEAR TODAY?
HEH HEH...
THIS ONE, NATURALLY...
NO...
I HATE TO IGNORE THIS ONE...
BLAH...
THIS IS ANOTHER FINE CHOICE...
BLAH...
THEY'RE ALL THE FREAKIN' SAME!

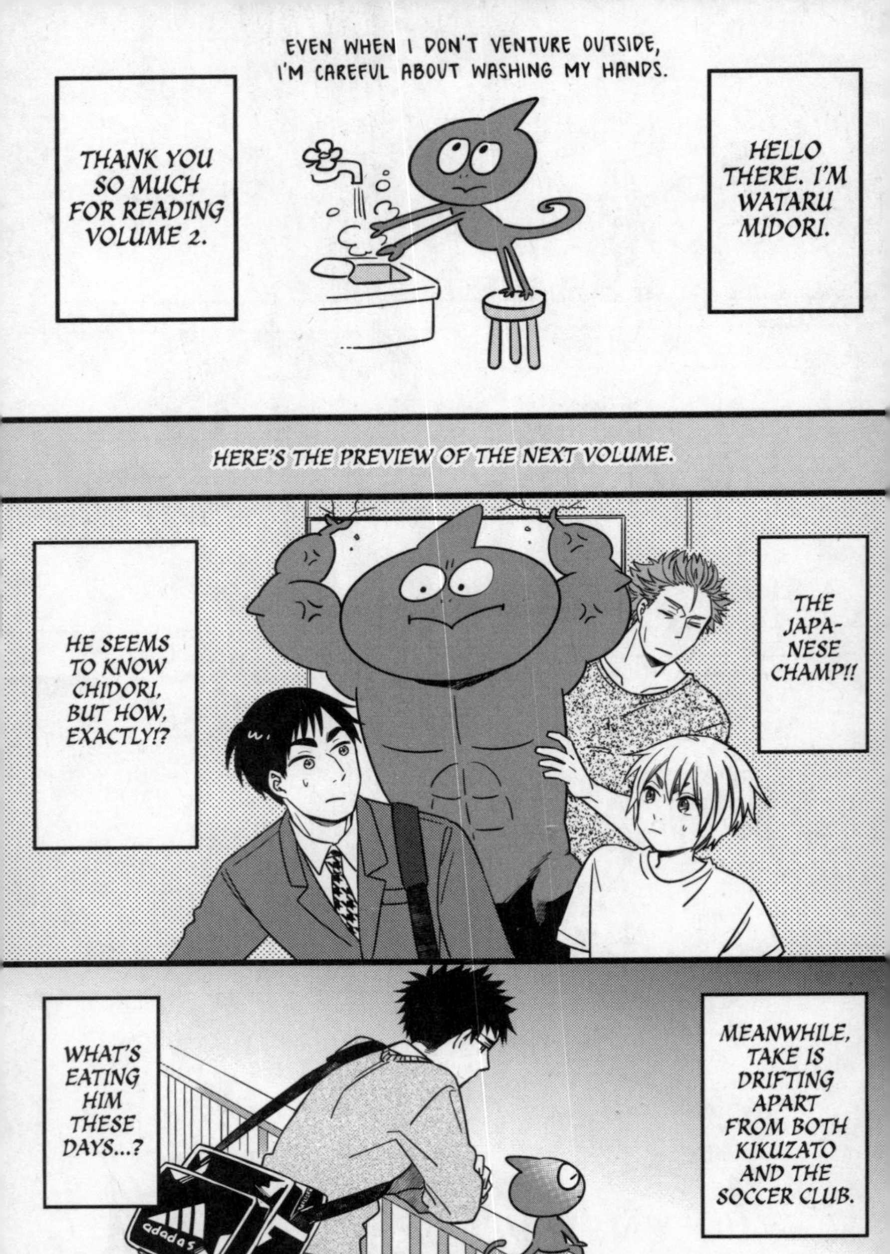
HELLO THERE. I'M WATARU MIDORI.
EVEN WHEN I DON'T VENTURE OUTSIDE, I'M CAREFUL ABOUT WASHING MY HANDS.
THANK YOU SO MUCH FOR READING VOLUME 2.
HERE'S THE PREVIEW OF THE NEXT VOLUME.
THE JAPA-NESE CHAMP!!
HE SEEMS TO KNOW CHIDORI, BUT HOW, EXACTLY!?
MEANWHILE, TAKE IS DRIFTING APART FROM BOTH KIKUZATO AND THE SOCCER CLUB.
WHAT'S EATING HIM THESE DAYS...?

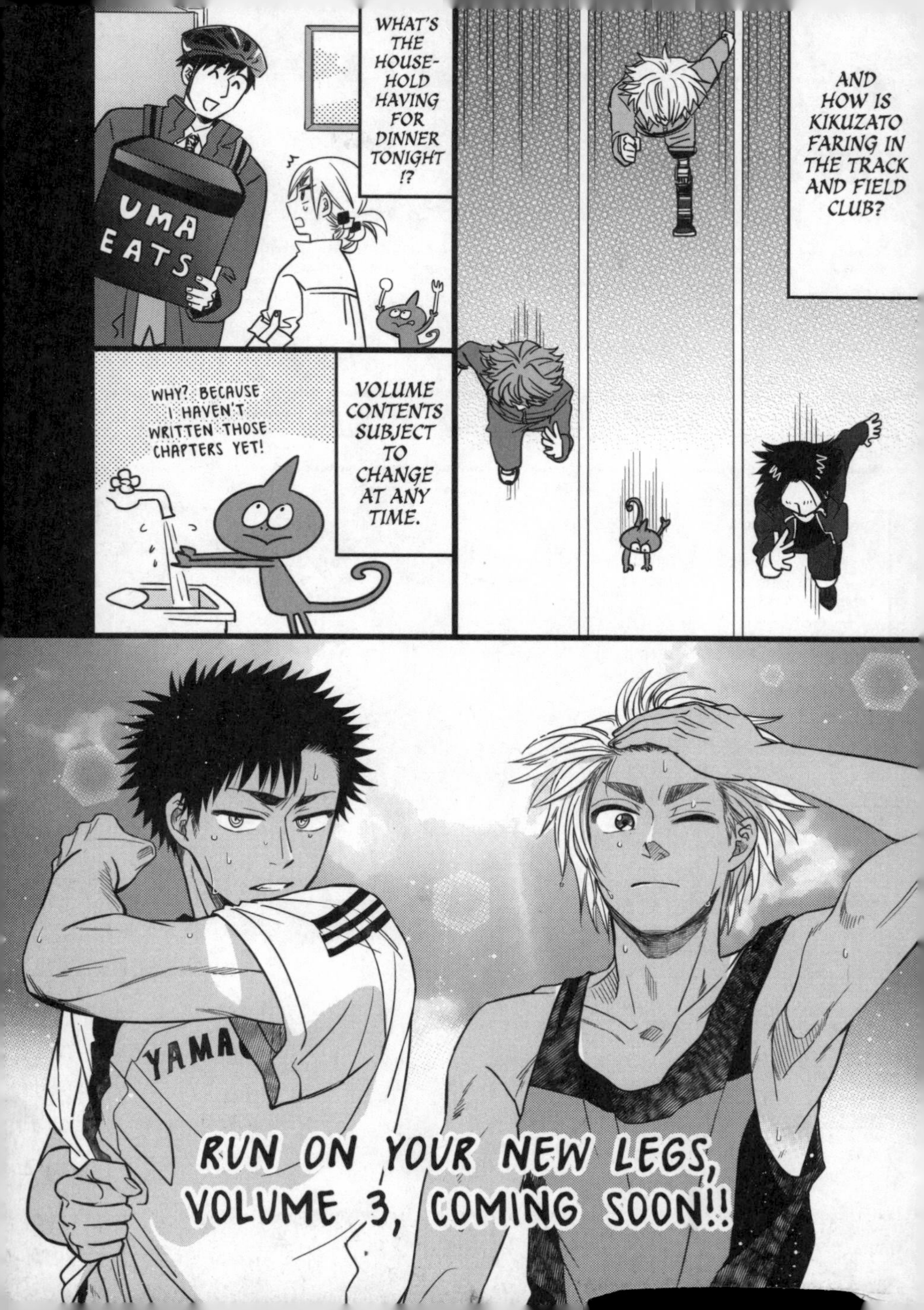
AND HOW IS KIKUZATO FARING IN THE TRACK AND FIELD CLUB?
WHAT'S THE HOUSE-HOLD HAVING FOR DINNER TONIGHT!?
UMA EATS
VOLUME CONTENTS SUBJECT TO CHANGE AT ANY TIME.
WHY? BECAUSE I HAVEN'T WRITTEN THOSE CHAPTERS YET!
YAMA
RUN ON YOUR NEW LEGS, VOLUME 3, COMING SOON!!

RUN ON YOUR NEW LEGS 2

WATARU MIDORI

TRANSLATION: Caleb Cook • **LETTERING:** Abigail Blackman

ATARASHII ASHI DE KAKENUKERO. Vol. 2
by Wataru MIDORI

Original Japanese edition published by SHOGAKUKAN.
English translation rights in the United States of America, Canada, the United Kingdom, Ireland, Australia and New Zealand arranged with SHOGAKUKAN through Tuttle-Mori Agency, Inc.

Original Cover Design: Yoko AKUTA

Yen Press
150 West 30th Street, 19th Floor
New York, NY 10001

Visit us at yenpress.com

facebook.com/yenpress
twitter.com/yenpress
yenpress.tumblr.com
instagram.com/yenpress

First Yen Press Edition: July 2022
Edited by Abigail Blackman & Yen Press Editorial: Carl Li
Designed by Yen Press Design: Liz Parlett, Wendy Chan

Yen Press is an imprint of Yen Press, LLC.
The Yen Press name and logo are trademarks of Yen Press, LLC.

The publisher is not responsible for websites (or their content) that are not owned by the publisher.

Library of Congress Control Number: 2021951359

ISBNs: 978-1-9753-3901-2 (paperback)
978-1-9753-4570-9 (ebook)

10 9 8 7 6 5 4 3 2 1

WOR

Printe [redacted]